The Resistance of Reference

The Resistance of Reference

Linguistics, Philosophy, and the Literary Text

ORA AVNI

The Johns Hopkins University Press
Baltimore and London

© 1990 The Johns Hopkins University Press

The Johns Hopkins University Press
701 West 40th Street, Baltimore, Maryland 21211
The Johns Hopkins Press Ltd., London

LIBRARY OF CONGRESS CATALOGING-IN-PUBLICATION DATA
Avni, Ora.
    The resistance of reference : linguistics, philosophy, and the literary text / Ora
Avni.
        p.   cm.
    Includes bibliographical references.
    ISBN 0–8018–3993–9(alk. paper)
    1. Literature—Philosophy.   2. Reference (Linguistics)   3. Reference (Philoso-
phy)   I. Title.
PN49.A94   1990
801—dc20   90–30585
                                                                    CIP

To Sheerly

If a cat is called a tiger it can easily be dismissed as a paper tiger; the question remains however why one was so scared in the first place. The same tactic works in reverse: calling the cat a mouse and then deriding it for its pretense to be mighty.

PAUL DE MAN

Contents

Preface   xi

Acknowledgments   xv

1   Introduction   1
     Knowledge   2
     Ignorance   3
     The Two Aims of Language   8
     Learning   11

2   Saussure   17
     Saussure's Influence   17
     The *Cours de linguistique générale*   18
     The Starting Point: Gödel, Ogden, and
     Richards, Culler   28
     Saussure's Theory of Language   40
     The Quarrel over the Arbitrariness of the Sign   55
     Value   60
     Saussure in Perspective   76

3   Frege   78
     The Difficulty of the Project   78
     "On Sense and Reference"   82
     Vorstellung   99

4   The First Person   113
     A Test Case for Language: *I*   113
     The First Person in Kafka's "Report to an Academy"   116
     Frege   122
     Russell   128
     Strawson   139
     Benveniste   146

Anscombe   154
"A Report to an Academy"   159

5 Speech Acts   175
Speech Acts and the First Person   175
Mérimée's "Venus of Ille"   178
Nerval's "King of Bicêtre"   202
Austin's Final Word on Performative versus Constative   226

6 The Semiotic Value: Dumas' *Three Musketeers*   230
Objects and Narratives   233
Law and Cuckoldry   239
On Third Parties: Marcel Mauss   248
Conclusion   256

Afterword   265

Appendix: "The Little Mouse in the Rag Basket"   269

Notes   273

Index   307

Preface

Over the last twenty years, literary theory has come to encompass so many schools, approaches, and definitions that the term has become clouded. In colleges and universities, survey courses in theory rival more traditional surveys of literature. Job descriptions invite applicants showing interest in theory. Scholars pronounce for or against theory. For better or for worse, theory has become part of the canon of the academic literary institution. And yet, oddly, when asked to define *theory*, we encounter difficulties. Is it opposed of *history?* Recent interest in theoretical perspectives on history and literature invalidates this hypothesis. Is it the antonym of *practice* or of *interpretation?* The theory of literature would then be antithetical to either its practice (whatever practice means) or the interpretation of literary texts—two perspectives I find highly troubling despite their essential naïveté. Is the history of theory itself theory? Is a survey course in theory a theoretical course? On the other hand, can a literature course requiring mostly close readings and interpretations be theoretical? The meeting of disciplines has exacerbated the general confusion about the status of theory. Today it includes psychoanalysis, linguistics, philosophy, history, art history, sociology, logic—and I have probably forgotten some. In fact, hailed by some, denigrated by others, it has become a blank screen onto which students of literature project their fears, anxieties, insecurities, hopes, ambitions, personal preferences, personal loyalties, political allegiances, etcetera.

Is this another book about theory? It clearly has a strong theoretical orientation, but then, after exposing numerous time-consuming theories, it seems to conclude against theories altogether—or at least against certain kinds of theories. Why, then, the long detour? If the bottom line is that theories miss the mark, why bother with them at all?

The apparent contradiction stems from the confusion that the word *theory* invites. Today, it is hard to determine whether theory is an approach, a method, a field, a discipline, or a genre. Mostly, it has come to designate two activities that I find largely antithetical. Theory has become part of the *doxa* that we, as teachers, see as our responsibility to communicate to our students. Books or courses on theory often consist of an account of neatly grouped schools of thought organized in the purest, albeit discreet, positivist historical perspective: each school is explained as a cogent, predictable development of or reaction to its predecessor (or the times); usually, the last in line is the good one, the improvement toward which linear progress has led our literary perfectibility. There is also a different practice of ardent believers with a missionary calling, genuinely convinced that they hold the key to a better understanding of literature, who try their best to save the soul of their lost students or readers and convert them to the truth. Let me hasten to add, if it is not already clear, that this book takes exception to these two conceptions of literary theory.

The way I see it, theory is not a subject matter, let alone a discipline. It is an attitude a reader adopts toward texts (including one's own), whether they are literary or other. It is a way of engaging a text, of entering into a dialogue with it. Rather than arguing for "theory" or "theorizing," this book advocates an active engagement with theoretical concerns, one in which the cognitive and speculative activity is inseparable from the most pragmatic involvement with literary and critical texts. It would be naïve to believe that such an engagement is free of predeterminations, but I like to think the truly theoretical mind capable of reflecting on these determinations and integrating them to some extent into its readings. The end result of the theoretical engagement with texts that I uphold is not necessarily itself a theory. More often than not, there will be loose ends (remainders as I call them in chapter 6, after Lacan and Derrida), elements whose heterogeneity cannot be resorbed into the prevailing patterns. Modernism and post modernism have already highlighted and valorized these elements. Therefore, my contribution does not hinge as much upon their discovery as upon their orchestration—an orchestration that grants them their fundamental heterogeneity yet allows the critic to reach beyond aporia and nihilism.

At the same time, the failure of strict theories underscored throughout this book should not be mistaken for a failure of the theoretician: it is built into language itself (not only into literature, as the romantics held, but into language in general). Both the need to generalize and the partial failure of the theories to which this need gives rise are constitutive of language; both the "system" (law, norm, rule, etc.) and its interferences (what Michel Serres calls *parasites*) are inscribed *in* language—thus rendering such theories at once inevitable or even indispensable, and inadequate.

Quarrels about the object and the function of literature have spread and died. On one point, however, most students of literature agree: the primary "stuff" of literature, its raw material, is first of all language. Even as they harness themselves to values, debates, and ideologies, rhetorical or narrative creations remain linguistic constructions: they consist of words and, except for the all too famous suspension of disbelief, are subject to the laws that normally govern language. As such, they cannot fail to enact the syntactical and rhetorical complexity of language as well as its irreducible reliance on the heterogeneity of signs, concepts, and objects (to name only the most obvious). But while some scholars animated by a laudable scientific spirit strive patiently to iron out this complexity and reduce their discourse to its deictic force—an effort I find necessary despite its essential naïveté—the literary text and the different kind of theory I advocate rejoice in playing the various forces against one another, thus actualizing the full range of language with a fanfare of so-called agrammaticalities. Throughout this book, what interested me is not the actual apparent agrammaticalities found in literature but the fact that we can communicate such agrammaticalities and that they make sense (perhaps an *other* sense): unlike pure noise, they are part of the moves *avowed by language,* and therefore they are, in fact, perfectly grammatical despite their apparent oddity (all this will, I hope, be clearer as we proceed). These are therefore not exceptions (besides, what is an exception if not the acknowledged preference of the rule to the facts, along with a certain haste or even complacency that prevents the theoretician from reevaluating the rule that fails the facts?), and the critic who brushes them aside under the pretext that these agrammaticalities are exceptions may well end up with a theory that stops short of accounting for the breadth of linguistic and literary phenomena and, perhaps, of its more telling aspects. This does not imply that a better theory consisting of more refined rules would succeed where the first failed; I am not advocating a search for the philosophers' stone of theories of language and literature. I am, however, advocating a theoretical thinking that is problem rather than solution oriented; that addresses, explores, and exploits precisely those same instances that seem to constitute an obstacle for the elaboration of an all-encompassing theory; that takes the resistance of its subject matter seriously—not as something to overcome but as something built into the relationship between that subject matter and the theoretical thinking that attempts to understand and explain it.

Acknowledgments

The Resistance of Reference was a long time in the writing and would have taken even longer without the assistance of a Christian Gauss Mellon Preceptorship and a summer travel grant from Princeton University, a National Endowment for the Humanities summer stipend, and a grant for the preparation of the manuscript from Yale University. I am grateful to them all.

The master plan for this book took shape during a graduate course I taught at Princeton. To the students who patiently endured my still unfocused thoughts and enthusiastically participated in the delineation of patterns of contradictions and tensions, many thanks. I also take this occasion to thank the countless friends and students on whom I have tried some of the ideas that found their way into this book. My gratitude also goes to the friends and colleagues who have commented on various parts of the manuscript: Frederick Tibbetts, Jay Atlas, Glenn Moss, Gerald Prince, and especially Thomas Pavel, who generously offered a detailed and rigorous critique of the chapter on Saussure.

I am also grateful to Mark Gross, Sheerly Avni, and Lauren Doyle-McCombs for proofreading the manuscript, and to Philippe Mounier, curator of the manuscript collections of the Bibliothèque Publique et Universitaire de Genève for his unconditional help throughout my research in the Saussure archives in Geneva. Finally, I wish to thank Jon Delogu for translating the citations from the Saussure archives, Lori Walters for translating the *fabliau* "De la sorisete des estopes," and John Rosenthal and Virginia Jackson for translating my essays on *The Three Musketeers* and "Le Roi de Bicêtre" from French to English.

Abridged versions of chapter 6 appeared in French in *Poétique* and *MLN*. Chapter 5 borrows from other essays in French published in *Poétique* and *MLN*. For permission to reprint them in revised or translated form, I am grateful to the editors.

The Resistance of Reference

1 Introduction

You don't make yourself a cotton cap out of a metonymy, you don't put on a comparison instead of a slipper; you can't use an antithesis as an umbrella: unfortunately you couldn't lay a few multicolored rhymes on your stomach by way of a waistcoat. I have a deep conviction that an ode is too light an apparel for the winter, and that one wouldn't be better dressed with a strophe, an antistrophe and epode than the cynic's wife who contented herself with her virtue alone for shift, and went about stark naked, so the story goes.

GAUTIER

Semiotics is the science of signs. What, then, is a sign? As we browse through books that elaborate theories of semiotics, we soon find out, to our distress, that they disagree vehemently on the definition of what makes a sign a sign. This divergence entails considerable difficulties for the bewildered scholar who sets out to compare the diverse semiotic theories. How can we compare them if they cannot agree on their object? Haven't we heard about apples and oranges? An orange by any other name is still an orange and cannot be examined alongside apples—or can it? In *The Chronicles of the Reign of Charles IX,* Mérimée (inspired by Rabelais) tells of soldiers sitting at a table in a country inn and deliberating whether they would go to hell for ordering chicken on Friday. As the temptation grows irresistible, they find a semiotic solution to appease their religious qualms. Upon spotting a priest nearby, they invite him to baptize their "godchildren": one is to be named Perch and the other Carp. Needless to say, the "children" awaiting baptism are the mouth-watering chickens previously spotted running around in the yard. Theoretically, we could argue that the soldiers' clever semiotics have saved them from hell. But then again, we could also ask, "what's in a name?" and argue the opposite. Our stand would depend on our conception of signs. Such a discussion would therefore bear not so much on the eternal life of the soldiers as on the relation between signs, conventions (or laws), and reference, that is, precisely the issues this book purports to address. Rather than staging this debate up front, however, I shall tell another story, in which signs and meaning are clearly put into question. This story will remain a major point of reference throughout my discussion of signs and language.

Knowledge

A salacious *fabliau,* "De la sorisete des estopes" ("The Little Mouse in the Rag Basket"), opens as follows: "Next I will tell you about a silly peasant who took a wife, and knew nothing of the pleasure that came with holding a woman in his arms, because he had never tried it." [1] These lines oppose *knowledge* and *experience:* since he has not experienced the pleasures of a woman's body, the young man *knows nothing.* Thus from the start, experience and knowledge go together—one holds a woman in one's arms: one knows; one does not hold a woman: one knows nothing. The emphasis on nothing (*rien, nul*) underscores the underlying contention that knowledge is exclusively empirical (one might wonder, for example, if the silly peasant could not have known at least something that he had not experienced, for example, by hearsay). The text seems to advocate a brute, stripped, sheer, unmediated experience as the essential component of knowledge ("knew nothing . . . *because* he had never tried it").[2]

The distinction experience/knowledge is both traditional and traditionally controversial. Our text imprints a new twist on centuries of controversy, however: for while it states for the benefit of the reader that what the simpleton does not know is "the pleasure that came with holding a woman in his arms," it deprives the peasant himself of such information. Consequently, the peasant does not know that he does not know. Now, if one does not know that one does not know, this implies that one thinks one knows. Furthermore, when called upon to act on this "knowledge," one is doomed not only to expose one's ignorance but to face the consequences of one's misguided action. As the story unfolds, the reader discovers that the peasant is somewhat aware of his shortcomings, but precisely because he can have no grasp of what he does not know, he does not realize its importance. The *fabliau* hinges upon the peasant's delusion. What is at stake in this *fabliau* is neither the incomplete sexual education of the silly peasant nor his conception of knowledge but rather his delusion, namely, the fact that he does not and cannot know that he does not know. (Had he known that something important was escaping his grasp, our simpleton might have sought information. He might even have insisted on one of the obligatory father-son talks before his wedding night.) In other words, something essential to the efficacy of the story as a story stands between the young man and his ignorance (rather than between him and knowledge, as one might have expected). His delusion undercuts the symmetry that the narrative voice establishes between knowledge and experience and shows them to be intricately and inseparably interwoven.

The reader is in a similar position. At first glance, the opening lines establish an apparent complicity between the reader and the narrative voice, implying that, unlike the peasant, *they* know that knowledge comes from experience only. They also know that since the lad is newly wed, he is on the threshold of experience and about to join them in knowledge. Unlike the typical "boy meets girl, boy gets girl" story, the *fabliau* relies not on factors extraneous to the original situation (jealous husbands or rivals, possessive fathers or brothers) but on the very terms that constitute the frame's apparent *données*. In other words, in order to constitute itself as a narrative, the *fabliau* cleverly exploits the opening lines, which ensure its reader's complicity, thereby implicating the facile acquiescence of its knowledgeable reader in the narrative process. Indeed, whether the reader realizes it at this point or not, in order for the story to take place in these circumstances, there has to be something that he or she does not know: that *he or she does not know that he or she does not know.* The *fabliau* enacts a fundamental law of narrative (and, by extension, of thought): displacement of ignorance goes hand in hand with displacement of knowledge. Thus the apparent complicity between the implied reader (the "narratee," not to be confused with the empirical reader) and the narrative voice soon vanishes: as the reader snickers complaisantly with the narrative voice at the expense of the peasant, he or she is in fact doubling him: the ignorance of the character and that of the reader follow the same pattern.

Ignorance

Alone with his young wife, "he took her in his arms and embraced her roughly for he did not know how to do otherwise, and flattened her out completely under him. She who had put up a good defense said: 'What do you want to do?' " The young man's amorous move is not unrelated to the consummation of his marriage. As she protests, the young bride does not object so much to what he does as to that which, in his ignorance, he does not do ("he did not know how to do otherwise"). How can she know what he *does not* do?—experience is again the obvious counterpart of ignorance: "But his wife already knew everything that men know how to do [*sevent faire*], because, to tell the truth, the priest did with her as he wished [*son boen en faisoit*] whenever he wished and as it pleased him." By subtracting her unsatisfactory present experience from what *she knows* that a man ought to know, the woman should soon find out what her husband does not know; but this arithmetic brings forth *her* knowledge. What has experience taught her? On this point the *fabliau* is clear and consistent: she knows "everything that men know how to *do*," and has learned that much ever since the priest "*did* with her as he wished." In fact, she knows what men do, not what they know.[3] Performance speaks of performance, not of knowledge. The narrative voice opposes her knowledge to his ignorance, following the same empirical criterion of excellence: he is *sot* (silly) because *rien ne sot* (he knows nothing). This raises delicate questions for the reader: is the reader in complicity with the narrative voice and the knowledgeable wife or on the side of the ignorant peasant, as I have previously suggested? Is the reader meant to espouse the pragmatic principles of the narrative voice? Again, who is the butt of the joke?

Clearly, empirical knowledge depends on some performance, or at least on the ability and the will to perform. To the woman's impatient "What do you want to do?" the husband replies in the best male tradition: I want and I shall . . . if I can: "I want," he replies, "to get up my prick. Afterwards I'll fuck you if ever I can and. . . ." At this point in our story, we may still attribute the lad's lack of self-confidence to his lack of experience and to the excitement of this memorable night, for, except for all his too normal doubts, his sexual education seems quite adequate. He obviously knows what to do, as well as when and where to do it. Even as his reply goes on "I'll fuck you if ever I can and *if I can find your cunt,*" this sexual education is still adequate: he was taught, that is, *told,* everything there is to *say* about his conjugal duties and privileges. He knows that his and her genitals hold opposite positions in a differential system and that the unknown *cunt* names a function in this system rather than a constant.

Let me clarify this last point. The young peasant clearly takes it for granted that both of them are in possession of the right attributes required for sexual performance. One may object that since he is familiar with his own anatomy, there must be at least one constant. Not so. In his mind, his anatomy is irrelevant—until the right moment comes: although clearly interested in sex, if he knows "nothing of the pleasure that came with holding a woman in his arms," it is "because *he had never tried it.*" Sex is not an unmediated pleasure, as the narrative voice and the woman suggested, but one of the functions that make up the social system to which he adheres. As is conventionally the case in medieval literature, "pleasure" (*deduit*) is mediated by this system. If the silly peasant is still inexperienced, it is not because he is shy, has not had the right opportunity, or does not appeal to women but because *he has never tried:* so far, he has lived his life in accordance with a system that defines *wedding night* as the moment at which a man holds a woman in his arms for the first time. In the system he espouses, premarital sex is not an option (conversely, his wife represents a principle of total subversion—moral, social, religious, and linguistic). The peasant's anatomy and sexual drive are not functional unless the circumstances call for functioning from within the system (in this case this translates into "on one's wedding night" rather than, say, "on a haystack").

That his social code of behavior is fundamentally structuralist is, I hope, evident. I shall therefore rephrase my comment: the peasant's sex education has been an initiation into the language of sexuality rather than into sexuality itself. Furthermore, it has been a Saussurean initiation into the language of sexuality. As such, it is perfectly adequate: while he does not know what *con* (cunt) *refers to,* he comprehends it as a differential function and, subsequently, is able to produce coherent sentences on the subject (such as his wedding night plans). We can oppose this view once more to the one expressed in the opening lines. There the understanding is that to know is to have experienced. Here it is that to know is to understand the relationship of one term with the others in the same system. The opposition is then not between knowledge and ignorance, as the onesided viewpoint of the narrative voice suggests, but between one mode of knowing and another, the former anchored in the extralinguistic reality (a woman's body) and the latter anchored in language only. The text's pun on the word *sot* (either "silly" or "knows") thus traverses the distance separating these views: Is the peasant silly or knowledgeable? Does he know more or less? The narrative voice takes the side of the nimble wife and mocks the husband's stupidity ("A more foolish fellow was never seen"), but its insistence on the word *sot* undermines the very difference it purports to establish between knowledge and stupidity.

Saussure's well-known comparison with a chess game will further illustrate the peasant's point: "A new comparison with the set of chessmen will bring out this point. Take a knight, for instance. . . . Suppose that the piece happens to be destroyed or lost during a game. Can it be replaced by an equivalent piece? Certainly. Not only another knight but even a figure shorn of any resemblance to a knight can be declared identical provided the same value is attributed to it." [4] As I discuss this comparison in my chapter on Saussure, I shall limit myself for now to the following analogy: just as "even a figure shorn of any resemblance to a knight can be declared identical provided the same value is attributed to it," any figure shorn of any resemblance to a woman's genitals should prove suitable for the wedding night game, provided the same value is attributed to it. That provision proves crucial to our lad: may he attribute any value to any object? Are all objects equally suitable? (Even in Saussure's example, will an elephant do as a replacement for the missing knight?) And if some objects are more suitable than others for certain values, what standards are we to apply to judge the degree of suitability?

The Saussurean peasant does not limit his structuralist skills to the word *con*. He can also name *foutre* (fuck) the activity compatible with the value *con* and use this word "properly" too—at least, properly from the point of view of language: the lines "I want to get up my prick. Afterwards I'll fuck you" may lack delicacy, but they are perfectly grammatical. Yet the lad's incongruous last condition "if I can find your cunt" exposes the limitations of his carefully constructed *semantic* system: "if I can find . . ."—where? Surely not in language but in the "real world," a world on which language as our Saussurean groom sees it has only partial bearing, and in which the teaching of his sex educators does not necessarily latch onto specific objects. The condition "if I can find your cunt" breaches the boundaries of an autonomous and self-sufficient system-language and aims at a non-linguistic world, which, as the *if* of the condition implies, may be at odds with language or individual intentions. What we have here is a clash between two forces: one vertical or deictic, from words to objects, and the other horizontal or semantic, from one word to the other within a given system.[5]

An example may help to clarify this point. I most probably would not know a sperm whale if I saw one; or, in other words, I have never seen a sperm whale and therefore could not recognize one (I would not take a sperm whale for a penguin, but I might easily mistake one for a dolphin—a mistake that could cost me my life). But my lack of experience has not impinged on my ability to read, discuss, or even teach *Moby Dick*, since the novel (that is, its language) constructs a complex system or network in which the white whale occupies a privileged position and a particular function. As they proceed in the novel, readers soon relinquish any visual or mental representation they may have of a whale (its signified), and substitute for the preprogrammed representation the newly constructed signified "Moby Dick" as defined by the context and in agreement with the positions and functions that the novel assigns to the signifier—in agreement with a new (or at least modified) semantic system. Thus, as long as I, the reader, remain just this—a reader who moves within the language of the text only—I shall be well served by Saussurean semantics: the concept of value will allow me to construct new systems of representation as I progress through the pages. However, I can also turn the tables and ponder a different question: if I were to face a sperm whale, would I rather arm myself with a harpoon or with *Moby Dick* (or whatever my interpretation would have offered as the antidote for the evil represented by the white whale)? At this point, most people would undoubtedly abandon the self-referential semantic system created by the novel and opt for the object, the harpoon. Richard III's famous "A horse! a horse! my kingdom for a horse!" illustrates the same conflict. The young peasant faces a similar crisis: his theoretical and purely linguistic knowledge cannot carry him through experience, through his encounter with the otherness of the female body. The lad's initiation to knowledge through language (his *Weltanschauung*) is polarized between words and things, education and performance, theory and practice, semantics and deixis. As long as he can keep them apart, he is safe: his deficiencies do not show, and he can function perfectly within the parameters that he has defined for himself. Similarly, as long as he uses heterogeneity as an alibi to exclude any consideration that may endanger the narrow base on which he has chosen to stand, he does not incur any threat.

The young peasant has ample company; his position is characteristic of all dogmatism: as long as we stand firmly within the boundaries we have delineated and block away any intrusion, we are relatively safe and remain in a state of happy solipsism. The blindness resulting from such entrenchment is responsible for numerous academic misunderstandings, not to mention the sad silence of scholars engaged in similar lines of research who blissfully choose to ignore one another. Yet burying one's head in the sand does little to protect one's tail, as our *fabliau* shows. The young peasant has reached the point where dichotomies are no longer operative: precisely because of the impermeability of his polarizations, the urgency of the excluded experience is bound to displace, at least temporarily, the prevailing semantic construct that attempts to preclude the deictic aspect of language.

The cunning wife is quick to exploit the *deictic* weakness of her husband: as long as she does not disrupt his *semantic* system, she can scramble reference as she pleases to suit her needs: " 'My cunt,' she is quick to answer, 'my cunt you won't find.'—'Where is it then? Don't hide it from me!'—'Sir, since you want to know, I'll tell you where it is, on my soul. It is hidden at the foot of my mother's bed where I left it this morning.'—'By Saint Martin,' says he, 'I'll go get it.'" And so he does. The lad's pursuit of his wife's genitals is, in fact, a pursuit of the locus in which theory and praxis, education and performance, language and phenomena, functions and objects, semantics and deixis might meet. And yet, unless he revises his linguistic *Weltanschauung,* his attempts lead him to a catch-22: how can he look for a specific object (let alone find "it"), if he does not know what this object is or what it looks like, if all he knows is the relation that this object, *once found,* entertains with others (his own body, for example)? Indeed, he would not know a *con* if he saw one, just as I would not know a sperm whale. For all he knows, the *con* may be almost anything (and indeed, his choice falls on a mouse), therefore almost anywhere (the mouse runs away). And the shrewd woman can send her frustrated husband on a wild goose chase to a neighboring town while, in his absence, she is free to entertain her priest friend.

The Two Aims of Language

This pleasant *fabliau* undoubtedly deals with morals: naïve and trusting husbands fooled and cuckolded by their worldly and fickle wives. Literary critics will probably suggest various interpretations casting light on social, marital, religious, and cultural aspects of French medieval life. While I shall dispute none of these interpretations, I contend, however, that any interpretation will have to reckon with the *fabliau*'s clever exploitation of language or, more precisely, of the risks of errors inherent in language.

Left to his "mute" instincts (or to his wife's), the young man would probably have had a more conventional wedding night. Inexperience usually ends when circumstances call for experiencing. The odd predicament of the groom stems not from his soon-to-end ignorance but, on the contrary, from an excess of knowledge; more specifically, an excess of *linguistic* knowledge: he knows *words* for which he does not know (that he does not know) the object, the *referent.* We could, for example, imagine a different situation: our lad could have experienced "the pleasures of a woman" in another context and not have realized that these pleasures corresponded to the words *con* and *foutre* (let's say in the context of "innocence": they did not know what they were doing). Experience alone cannot result in knowledge, as the opening lines of the story suggested. The most elementary conception of knowledge still requires the convergence of taxonomies with some form of objects (more exactly, with both these objects and their representation) and with a context. A glance at an illustrated textbook (*Gray's Anatomy*, for example) would have put an end to most of the groom's difficulties (this is still a far cry from experience). A child's first book is often a source of such knowledge: each page depicts clearly one object and names it in bold characters, to the delight of the proud parent whose child is learning to "speak" or "read" by repeating *apple, bee, car*, etcetera, all the way to *zebra*. The parent-teacher does indeed know that words aim at objects; they are verbal gestures toward these objects (to ensure that the child understands, the parent points at the picture as he or she reads the word). This gesture functions as a copula connecting the word with the object (this *is* that) and subsequently allows that word to replace the object in discourse. Once the copula is understood, the parent no longer needs to point, and the physical gesture is omitted or rather subsumed by the "verbal gesture" built into language (its deictic force). I shall call this aptitude of language to take aim at nonverbal objects *the deictic aim of language*.[6]

And an aptitude it is. We would misconceive the importance of the deictic aim of language if we were to limit it to a stage in the development or the acquisition of language. In my example, I made no claim as to the learning process: it is not because the parent has pointed a finger at an object that the child has learned its name but because words themselves aim at objects at all times. Well-meaning parents simply exploit this fact. Our anthropocentric habits mislead us into thinking that the parent's gesture connects the word and the object for the benefit of the child: in fact, the connecting copula is at work at all times, whether the parent enacts it by pointing or not. A child living in a speaking community would learn to speak without a storybook and without being "taught" by any other means. (How this child would learn may be a fascinating subject, but it is not one that I intend to broach.) Similarly, I am not suggesting that we evoke the beginning of time and develop a more or less mythical theory about the origin of language, as eighteenth-century philosophers were fond of doing. (Russell's theory of word-objects, which I shall examine, toys with such a temptation and hesitates between a *historical* and a *logical* account of the origin of language; see the section on Russell in chap. 4). The deictic aim of language that I am proposing here is inherent in language per se, at all times, and independent of the uses a speaking subject chooses to make of language.

Language is not content with merely aiming at objects. Even if I were to memorize all the words of a language, I would still not be able to speak that language. Another fundamental characteristic of language is that words combine horizontally to make statements and sentences;

to express ideas, judgments, descriptions, and so on, *about* objects. These ideas, judgments, and descriptions, are contained not in a single word but in the proposition as a whole. A proposition exceeds the sum of the deictic charges of its components. We say that the proposition expresses, conveys, produces, carries, communicates *meaning*. (The horizontality that I am suggesting here is not to be confused with Jakobson's syntactical metonymy. It subsumes both Jakobson's metonymy and his metaphor, both syntagm and paradigm. Rhetoric and metaphor, which Jakobson situates primarily on a vertical axis, belong to horizontal semantics, even with all the detours, twists, distortions, variations, and hesitations that it forces on the deictic aim of language.) The general semantic effectiveness of language depends on the ways in which words relate to the contexts they create and on the functions they hold in these contexts (how shall I know that *lion* is a metaphor, unless the context rules out the reference to an animal and suggests that *lion* in fact designates Achilles?). Rhetoric is one of the ways in which such interactions result in meaning; syntax is another. At the risk of repeating myself, I emphatically remind the reader that I am not dealing here with something that the speaking subject chooses to do with words, nor am I evoking a special use of language, but rather, I am describing the aptitude of language itself to combine units so as to create a meaning that does not amount merely to the sum of its constituents. Just as words aim vertically at objects, they likewise aim horizontally at other words. I shall call this function *the semantic aim of language*.

In theory the two pulls are clearly distinct. In their purest state they are also mutually exclusive. We must remember, however, that theories are but fictional constructs that we use to impose order on the world. In language, the deictic and the semantic aims coexist. It would be a realist mistake to look for a referent for either the semiotic or the semantic aim. Like most theoretical distinctions, mine offers a viewpoint on an object rather than the object itself. But even from this viewpoint we must realize that as language consists simultaneously of numerous and often contradictory similar pulls and forces, what we witness when we observe it is a series of vectors, from which we infer the underlying forces to which it is subject. In adopting the word *aim*, I am attempting to render the French *visée* and the German *Zielung*, so as to bring to the fore the threat of miss or misfire. Each force takes aim in vain: under the conflicting influences of other forces, it is likely to swerve and miss its intended mark.[7]

"De la sorisete des estopes" has successfully, albeit temporarily, disjoined the semantic and the deictic aims of language. The semantic aim of the young man's language has displaced and replaced the deictic aim. Language has become self-referential. What is a *con?*—That which one can *foutre.*—Well, what is *foutre?*—What a man can do with a *con.*— What, then, is a *con?* . . . So goes the merry-go-round of tautological semantics: in a system grounded in paraphrases and definitions, that is, in verbal equations, the *definiens* is doomed to be part of the definition.[8]

We can contrast the lad's predicament with a diametrically opposed situation. The young man might have pointed at his wife's genitals and asked for "this," thus relying on the deictic aim of language. We may even imagine that the wife, shocked or puzzled, asked "What, my *con?*" To which he might have answered by repeating imperiously, "This!" while still pointing at her body. This situation, however, would entail quite a different story, one that Russell or even Kant might have liked to tell.

Our young man, on the other hand, purports to enact the normative aspect of his definitions rather than to reach objects. His frame of reference is not his acquaintance with or desire for the world around him but his narrow structuralist view of language. Thus, upon being told that a basket of rags contains the wandering *con*, he, forever faithful to his system of definitions, proceeds to *foutre* the basket. When a mouse, disturbed by the commotion, jumps out of the basket and disappears in the grass, the young man despairs of ever recovering the lost *con*. Not once does he doubt that the mouse is the *con*, although it is evident that he has seen mice before and that he can situate them in his world—at least, with regard to cats: " 'I truly believe," he says, 'that our cat, God keep him, would eat it if he met it." His knowledge of cats and mice on the one hand, and of *foutre* and *con* on the other, belongs to two totally different spheres of his life: the former relates to the world of experience (he must have seen a cat chasing and eating a mouse) and the latter to the world of language. The two worlds are so separate in his mind that even the sight of the familiar mouse does not dent his faith in tautological semantics. And indeed, the "system" proves a grateful master: as long as he stays faithful to its exclusive semantic aim, the peasant is rewarded with blessings of coherent discourse and with the solipsistic knowledge that language alone can impart. Will he ever learn?

Learning

The ending of the *fabliau* leaves this question open. He surely learns something, but what exactly? As he returns to his wife empty-handed, the young man firmly believes that the pleasures of wedded life have eluded him forever. In bed with his young wife, he lies chastely on his back and "does not say more than a monk to whom conversation is forbidden, but rather just lies beside her." His language has failed him: although the circumstances are right, the peasant's faulty language has led him to a misrepresentation of his situation. The wife, who has other plans for him, is not about to give them up, however. When she finally understands his mistake, she undertakes to initiate him into the deictic aim of language by pointing at objects and exposing him to unmediated pleasure. It is clear however that she, herself, has not learned much from his misfortune: her faith in the priority of "doing" remains unchecked. She does set out to correct not his theoretical linguistic system but his performance. First she checks carefully what he intends to do ("If you were holding it now, what would you *do* with it. Tell me.") Upon receiving a satisfactory answer ("I would fuck it, by my faith"), she proceeds to instruct him. Note that the whole exchange hinges on the word *it* ("what would you do with *it*"), which each of them is free to identify with the referent of his or her choice.[9] She does not inform her husband that "it" is not the "it" he lost in the meadow. One might be tempted to explain this omission psychologically—for example, she does not want him to know of her trickery—but such an explanation is absurdly superfluous since, when no change occurs, as is the case, there is no need for explaining: the woman simply hangs onto her conception of knowing as doing. If he can fulfill his marital duties, he knows enough. Thus, as long as she gets him to *do* the proper thing, she can believe in good faith that he has her to thank for his new knowledge. Ultimately, her teaching remains consistent with her exclusively deictic vision of language. Like her husband, she separates language and performance. The result is highly ironic as her instruction only confirms him in his error: "She quickly replies to him: 'Sir, *it* is now there between my legs. . . . Caress *it* well with your hands. . . . Keep a good hold on *it* so that *it* doesn't escape from you.' " Even as he fondles "it" the husband learns nothing. His *Weltanschauung* remains split up between language and objects. Instead of finding the locus in which his theoretical structuralist understanding of language and her pragmatic experience of men might have met, he is surer than ever that "it" is detachable, likely to run about in the dew again, prey to misbehaving cats—in short, a typical mouse.[10] In other words, he is as *sot* as he was at the opening lines of the *fabliau*. Experience alone has not enlightened him.

We might wish to object that as long as he has both language and experience, he has made at least some progress, if only with regard to pleasure. The *fabliau* is quick to dispel this optimistic view. The young man will never experience the expected pleasure, even though he is factually already engaged in foreplay: "Then he begins to fondle it until he feels that it is wet: 'Alas! it is still soaked from the dew into which it fell!' the peasant says. 'Ah, ah! How angry you made me today! But you will never be yelled at by me for being wet. Go rest and sleep now, I don't want to tire you further. You are fatigued from running about.'" He who loses loses; but she who wins loses, too. Neither of them will eventually reach the pleasure they both wanted (at least, not with each other). His exclusively semantic and her essentially deictic visions of language do not meet, although all the circumstances seem otherwise appropriate. What is missing in this case is some cognitive mediation between the two visions. Language involves not only two aims but also the cognitive articulation between them, traditionally referred to as representation. Language loses its effectiveness unless words, objects, thoughts, bodies, intentions, representations come to interact, while maintaining their essential heterogeneity.

So who is the butt of the joke? Everyone, it would seem. Certainly the young man, who has not learned that "making sense" without asking this sense to bear on the world around it can be very frustrating. Mastering the art of circular arguments does little to ground these arguments and render them functional. Systems, like theories, can run endlessly in private grooves, condemned forever to tautologies. We should also mention the clever wife, who knows all about performance but omits to relate her experience to language. Ultimately, this oversight bars her from the experience she so cherishes. We would associate the narrative voice with the woman, were it not for the irony permeating its apparently naïve judgments. The role of the reader is a little more complex. The *fabliau* owes its effectiveness to a sequence of surprises: firstly, when the young man declares his intentions and doubts; secondly, when his wife sends him off to fetch her genitals; thirdly, when he mistakes the mouse for the object of his quest; and finally when he decides to let "it" sleep without further ado. The pleasure the readers derive from each of these moments is in direct proportion to the linguistic absurdity illustrated and to the readers' realization that the absurdities are not absurd in themselves but *become absurd when the different forces that act on language are called upon to function in isolation.*

This peculiar class of absurdities runs throughout our study like a leitmotif. Although the theories of language that we shall examine are incomparably richer and more subtle than the crude conceptions illustrated by our *fabliau,* they share with it some essential traits, just as a caricature shares unmistakable traits with its original. The great medievalist Joseph Bédier defined *fabliaux* as *contes pour rire*, tales intended only to make us laugh. And yet, although the entertaining (or even moralizing) aspect of "De la sorisete des estopes" is undeniable, this *fabliau* tells us little more than cultural (and sexist) platitudes or obscenities unless we read it as a radical denunciation and questioning of some of our most intuitive (and therefore most "theoretical") assumptions about language. "De la sorisete des estopes" plays the deictic and the semantic aims of language against each other, thus isolating and introducing most of the problems of reference that will be of continuous interest to us throughout this book.

It also highlights the limitations of knowledge—at least the limitations of a certain structure of knowledge. J.-F. Lyotard, with his usual acuity, suggests a distinction between the theoretical and the philosophical modes: what is at stake in the philosophical mode is the *discovery* of its own rules; the theoretical mode, on the other hand, just like the young *sot*, starts with the assumption that it already *knows* them.[11] Throughout this book, we shall explore the limitations of such "theoretical" knowledge. We shall therefore alternate between examining theories that generalize and conceptualize linguistic phenomena, exposing the presuppositions on which these theories rest (in Lyotard's philosophical spirit), and reading literary texts that illustrate similar presuppositions and forces. I shall not adopt Lyotard's terms, however, since they seem to privilege philosophy whereas, as we know (and as this book will readily show), "theories" abound in philosophy; instead, I shall use quotation marks around the kind of "theory" whose rigidity I shall criticize.

Chapters 2 and 3 establish the conceptual framework as a diptych occupied by the two masterminds of today's thinking about language, Saussure and Frege. Throughout the presentation of their thinking, I shall pay special attention to their hesitations and to the element of language they explicitly dismissed as unsuitable for their theoretical constructs. This two-fold construction also allows us to address the difference between the work done in European linguistics (mostly French and Swiss) and in Anglo-American philosophy: while the former concerns itself mostly with the semantic aim of language, the latter bases its theory of signs primarily on the deictic aim.[12]

Chapters 4 and 5 tackle special cases that have posed problems for theories of reference. Chapter 4 deals with the first person: it opposes the performance of the ape in Kafka's "Report to an Academy" to various structuralist and analytic theories of the first person, which, despite their obvious divergence from one another, nonetheless stumble on the same aspect of the literary text: the ways in which "A Report" owes its gripping irony to the tension between the story told by the ape (the predicates he assigns to his *I*) and the referent of that *I* (his body, behavior, reactions, etc.). In Chapter 5, I examine speech act theories, again contrasting these theories with two literary texts: Mérimée's "Venus of Ille," which opposes, on the one hand, the brute resistance of *things* to the quasi-magical grip of language over reality and, on the other, the resistance of literary contextuality to the theoretical circumscription of circumstances and conventions, and Nerval's "King of Bicêtre," which examines the relationship between legislation and jurisprudence and situates speech acts and the discourse of power in the context of the law. In this story, Spifame, the king of France's look-alike, begins his career as an attorney and, upon becoming a self-proclaimed legislator (which coincides with his delusion that he is Henry II, king of France), is committed to a mental institution, where he befriends the poet Vignet, whose delusion consists in claiming that the Pléiade poets have plagiarized his work.

Chapter 6 rehearses and summarizes the problems encountered in the previous four chapters and offers a way out of the impasse to which the theoretical diptych has led us, with a reading of an episode of Dumas's *Three Musketeers* in conjunction with Mauss' *Essay on the Gift* and Lacan's "Seminar on the 'Purloined Letter.'" In this chapter, I suggest adding what I call the semiotic (contextual) values of signs to the deictic and semantic aims delineated in this Introduction.[13]

The chapter on Saussure presented a special problem since most of what we today call Saussure's teaching is in fact a synthesis of his teaching, performed by his students and colleagues after his death. Despite their enthusiasm and dedication, their efforts were crowned with partial success only. *The Course in General Linguistics* often papers over Saussure's most insightful scruples with easy generalizations and assertive pedagogy. I have tried to recover Saussure's original hesitations and contradictions, not for the sake of pedantic authenticity but because they expose a sharp awareness of the unresolved aspects of his teaching and in fact anticipate most of the criticisms that structuralists, linguists, and analytical philosophers alike later addressed to the *Course*. Since the public, though well acquainted with the *Course* itself, generally ignores its sources, I quote extensively from the manuscripts and Engler's critical edition (he published the manuscripts side by side with the *Course*) to allow the readers some unmediated contact with Saussure's sharpest insights and scruples.

I also quote extensively from analytical philosophers, for similar reasons: since the average literary critic is not familiar with their style and theories, I hesitated to paraphrase, comment, or discuss them without first letting their voices be heard. Throughout these presentations I have done my best to write simply and avoid jargon without oversimplifying the teaching of these thinkers. For those readers already familiar with these theories, I have included more specialized discussions and references in the footnotes.

Finally, I have chosen to write mostly about thinkers who have enormously influenced the way we think about language today and for whom I have the highest respect and admiration. My objective was not so much to inform my readers about their theories, however (although I spend many pages doing just that), as to expose what these theories imply (what assumptions or suppositions they had to rely upon), or entail (what further consequences they command). My own discourse is therefore very much at the starting and finishing lines of the theories I discuss, in their margins rather than at their center. Discussions that have fascinated and stimulated linguists and philosophers are of little interest to me, while the points that I raise may seem to them secondary if not odd. Similarly, I may iron out distinctions crucial for philosophers and linguists while dwelling on others that the same philosophers and linguists may find barely relevant to the philosophical or literary inquiry (in chapter 3 on Frege and the section on Russell in chapter 4, for example, I focus largely on footnotes—a practice rarely found among philosophers; in the chapter on Saussure, I focus precisely on the hesitations of the master, which the editors found unworthy of integrating in the *Cours de linguistique générale*). This shift in pace and focus reflects my overall project: as I set out to examine extreme cases of what language can do, including—and especially—its ability to program and produce irregularities, I lingered on the very same aspects that "theoreticians" generally evoke reluctantly in passing only to dismiss them as cases of etiolation and nonserious language.

2 Saussure

*If everything were in continual flux, and nothing maintained itself
fixed for all time, there would no longer be any possibility of getting
to know anything about the world and everything would be plunged
into confusion.*

FREGE

Saussure's Influence

Saussure's name is associated with innovative concepts in the theories of signs, language, and linguistics. Structuralism, for example, originates in an adaptation of the basic tenets of Saussure's philosophy of language to other disciplines. Lévi-Strauss' "L'Analyse structurale en linguistique et en anthropologie," [1] which is generally regarded as the founding structuralist text, acknowledges its debt to Saussure. It suffices to leaf rapidly through the pages of the influential *Qu'est-ce que le structuralisme?* to realize the impact of Saussurean concepts like signifier/signified, value, system, linearity of discourse, *langue*, synchronic investigation, and so on.[2] It is interesting to note that as long as Saussure remained known to linguists only, his most innovative and productive insights were often overlooked: his fellow linguists, trained as linguists only—that is, in the historical comparative philology that prevailed at that time—did not always realize the full epistemological implications of his teaching; instead they adopted and discussed his more technical, purely linguistic insights and overlooked the more theoretical aspects of this thinking—his philosophy of language, as he called it while teaching his famous three courses. Only after his discovery by Lévi-Strauss and Merleau-Ponty[3] was Saussure's revolutionary emphasis on nonhistorical (synchronic) systems, the parts of which do not preexist the whole, fully understood. What was adopted by and integrated into other disciplines is not so much the content or message of his teaching (the linguistics proper) as the underlying epistemic principles on which he built his theory of linguistics, and the methodology he developed to suit these principles. Poststructuralism, an ill-defined intellectual movement inaugurated principally by Derrida and Foucault, still relies heavily on the same tenets. Even today, after Poststructuralism and Postmodernism, the framework of the most vigorous investigations remains unchanged: current approaches that rely on the interplay between culture (or literature) and social and historical contexts (Marxism, new historicism, feminism, black studies, etc.) nonetheless rest their views on the unquestioned premise of cultural constructs akin to *langue* and on the relativity of the ideological systems of thought and signs that they command.

Of particular interest to us is the influence of Saussurean concepts on literary theory and its impact on French literary modernity and postmodernity. Lévi-Strauss, Barthes, Lacan, Derrida, and Foucault, to name just a few of the most seminal figures of modernity, have all admitted their debt to Saussure. Deriving all semantics from a construct (*langue* for Saussure, and text, ideology, or language for literary critics) along with a professed disregard for any interaction this construct may have with other factors—of which reference to objects is the most obvious—can be traced directly to the influence of the *Cours de linguistique générale*. Combined with the French discovery of Russian Formalism, the adaptation of Saussure's methodological and epistemological principles to literature is responsible for Postmodernism's emphasis on the notions of text, intertextuality, literarity, formal and semantic constructs, closure, function, slippage of values, etcetera—in short, for the major concepts associated today with literary criticism.

Saussure's influence hinges upon his analysis of a few key concepts: *langue* (and the synchronic approach to linguistics it reflects), the dual nature of the sign, and value—all of which contribute to the flawed linguistic conceptions that ruined the peasant's wedding night. These concepts, along with some inevitable observations about the publication of the *Cours* by Bally and Sechehaye, will therefore constitute the organizing principle of this chapter.

The Cours de linguistique générale

The Difficulty of the Project

The impact of Saussure's teaching was such that, after his death, Bally and Sechehaye collected the notes his students had taken during his three courses on general linguistics (Geneva, 1906–7, 1908–9, and 1910–11) and attempted "a reconstruction, a synthesis, by using the third course as a starting point and by using all other materials at [their] disposal, including the personal notes of F. de Saussure, as supplementary sources."[4] This endeavor led to the publication of the *Cours de linguistique générale* (1916), which in turn stirred up an intellectual revolution.

The editors were faced with formidable difficulties: Saussure had not kept the (very partial) notes that he had used for his course. The material found in his drawers consisted for the most part of different drafts and versions of unfinished papers often written long before the three courses. To make matters worse, Saussure himself had raised two major objections to the publication of his courses.

First, the pedagogical concern inherent in a course had dictated certain simplifications and compromises incompatible with the scientific objectivity required for a publication. For example, since complexity was intrinsic to his subject matter, how could he simplify its presentation to his students without betraying it and defeating his teaching? On the other hand, how could he share his doubts and hesitations—however fruitful or revealing they might be—when these doubts and hesitations constituted the very stuff on which his students would be examined at the end of the school year?[5]

Second, Saussure considered his course more a tentative inquiry, a work in progress, than a coherent theory. Therefore, he judged it unpublishable in this early stage ("As for a book on this subject, one could not imagine it: it must, says M. de Saussure, give the *definitive* thought of its author" [interview with Riedlinger, 19 January 1909, *SM*, 30]).[6] It seems that he found it disheartening to bring just about everything to what he saw as completion: "(*I had asked him if he had written up his ideas on this subject.*)—'Yes, I have some notes buried in piles [of paper], and I wouldn't know how to find them again.' (*I had hinted that he ought to have something published on these subjects.*)—'It would be absurd to begin again the long research for the publication, when I have there [he gestures] piles and piles of unpublished work'" (interview with Gautier, ibid. Godel's emphasis).

Fortunately, Bally and Sechehaye, colleagues and admirers of Saussure, paid no heed to his scruples. With the help of Dégallier, who had attended the last two courses and taken detailed notes, they rounded up all the students' notes and proceeded to collate them in order to represent Saussure's teaching as faithfully as possible. At all times, they say, they did their best to respect the intention of the master, "even when his intention, not always apparent, had to be *surmised*" (*Course*, xv). Surmising the intentions of the master would have been very risky if the notes had not been so complete. Despite the editors' claim to the contrary,[7] these notes were remarkably coherent, and the variations from student to student rarely exceeded minimal changes in formulation.[8]

Very little was therefore left to surmise. The comparison of notes with the *Course* generally yields few differences, with the exception of one category that, incidentally, is not mentioned in the editors' Preface: when Saussure added restrictive clauses to an otherwise dogmatic assertion, or when he left his own question unanswered, they generally "cleaned it up" so as not to weaken his case (see examples below, pp. 60–72).

But the editors had to grapple with an insoluble problem, one that accounted for Saussure's acknowledged reluctance ever to write his course.

> What makes this subject difficult is that one can take it, like certain geometric theorems, from many sides: *everything is corollary* from everything else in static linguistics [*tout est corollaire l'un de l'autre* en linguistique *statique*]: whether one speaks of units, of differences, of oppositions, it comes back to the same [*cela revient au même*]. *Langue* is a tight system and the theory must be a system just as tight as *langue*. *There is the difficult point,* for it is nothing to present assertions and views one after the other about *langue; the whole thing is to coordinate them in a system.* (Interview with Riedlinger, 1909, *SM,* 29)

Hence the real problem was not, as the editors claimed in their Preface, the ever changing nature of Saussure's thinking and the "conflicting" views he expressed from one course to another. (Besides, at another point in the same Preface, they also recognized that the courses complemented rather than contradicted one another; see, for example, "To limit the book to a single course—and which one?—was to deprive the reader of the rich and varied content of the other two courses; by itself the third, the most definitive of the three courses, would not give a complete accounting of the theories of F. de Saussure" [*Course,* xiv]). Even so, if indeed Saussure had revised or renewed his theory from one course to another, to be consistent with their declared method Bally and Sechehaye should have reproduced and even stressed the increasing doubts, hesitations, and half-restrictions that abound in the last course and should have construed them as a telltale sign of the evolution of Saussure's thinking. They did not, however, but borrowed instead the most theoretical passages on *langue* from the second course—a practice that contradicts their professed method.

One thing is indisputable: if we consider only the actual content of each course, we find no major discoveries in the later courses. Except for a few taxonomic refinements, the first course already presented all of the major concepts of the later two. More importantly, the Introduction to the second course offers the most comprehensive and systematic account of Saussure's general linguistics, one in which the multiple elements are best coordinated into a wide-ranging "system." Saussure ended his Introduction in January 1909, at about the same time that he complained about the circular "difficulty of the subject" in his interview with Riedlinger. We may therefore safely assume that, despite its definitive tone, the Introduction had not satisfied his exigency to present the part and the whole simultaneously. On the contrary, we may also assume that it is *because* the second course was the most comprehensive, the most emphatically and dogmatically "theoretical" of the three, that Saussure came to realize the number of arbitrary choices he had been compelled to make in order to align his thoughts in the proper "theoretical" form. His discouraged comments to Riedlinger underscore the difference—or even the tension—between individual notations or observations and their coordination into a system ("it is nothing to present assertions and views one after another about *langue;* the whole thing is to coordinate them into a system"). They constitute a critique of the "theoretical" system that he elaborated for his students' sake In the second course, and they hint at the reasons behind the pedagogical changes he would introduce in the third course.

A brief comparison of the three courses is all we need to ascertain that the changes in focus and emphasis from one course to another do not reflect Saussure's so-called new or evolving perception or conception. His revisions do not affect so much the factual content of his teaching as its form, as the order of introduction of concepts. What changes is the narrative he uses to present to his students the logical relations that build a system out of a series of random notations and observations; in short, his pedagogical and rhetorical strategies.

The Pedagogical Concern

The First Course (1906–1907)

In the first course, Saussure adopted an inferring strategy: throughout most of the year, he accumulated numerous divergent linguistic phenomena and raised hosts of questions. His aim was clearly to frustrate his students and arouse their curiosity by confronting them with a considerable number of problems that comparative philology and neogrammar—the main linguistic trends of his time—could not solve. The partial solutions he offered to each new problem he raised implied, again and again, the existence of *langue* as an underlying system responsible for the otherwise unexplainable linguistic phenomena. At that time he was also toying with the idea that a more philosophical conception of *langue* might be suitable material for a different course, thus separating the pragmatics of linguistics from its philosophical overview (an idea he would try to realize in the second course but abandon in the third): "Linguistics: One can hesitate a lot as to the best procedure [*le meilleur plan*]. *It is more profitable to place certain general ideas at the end of the course rather than at the beginning.* This is why we do not want to define the nature of language [*la nature du langage*]. *This will in fact make up the object of a course:* one will have to notice that language is not an immediately classifiable object" (I R 1.47, E 317).[9] The first course (1907–6) abounded in details. In a typical neogrammarian vein, its major part dealt with diachronic linguistics: it attempted to track down and to comprehend various aspects and patterns of the evolution of languages. Forever consistent with his opposition to historical linguistics, however, Saussure also cleverly brought each and every discussion of morphological changes to a dead end. Only toward the end of the course did Saussure introduce a clearly stated solution providing a unifying pattern for the various irritating questions and partial answers he had furnished all along. While comparative philology explained each and every morphological derivation diachronically, the end of the first course suggested that a derivation not be taken in isolation: each instance is determined by the state of the general system in which it is taking place at any given time, or in short, by *langue*. Not surprisingly, however, before the grand solution of the end, each time Saussure sketched a partial or tentative answer to a specific linguistic phenomenon, he had to rely heavily on the still unpresented (yet ever implied) importance of *langue* for the study of linguistics as well as on the two-fold and unmotivated nature of the linguistic sign. This methodological difficulty gave his course a rocky pace and caused numerous repetitions. It was also probably frustrating for his students, who must have sensed that their teacher was holding back something crucial that would have dissipated their difficulties. And yet, from this line of questioning and the partial solutions with which he punctuated his course, it is clear that he himself was not discovering *langue* as he proceeded but rather waiting for the right moment to introduce it as a key concept. There can be no doubt that he already had a firm grasp on the findings and the conclusions to which his inquiry seemed to be leading him. In short, the first course is a fake "inquiry" into language, a heuristic play staged for the benefit of his students.

The Second Course (1908–1909)

In the second course (1908–9), Saussure reversed this strategy: "In order to assign a place to linguistics, one must not take *langue* from all its sides. It is evident that in this way many sciences (psychology, physiology, anthropology, ⟨grammar, philology⟩, etc.) will be able to claim *langue* as their object. This analytic route has never amounted to anything [cette voie analytique n'a donc jamais abouti à rien]: We will pursue a synthetic route" (II R 11, E 30). Abandoning the analytical method that he used in the first course, Saussure drew a broad synthesis for the second course—in fact, the broadest he was ever to sketch.

> It is now evident that before all else *langue is a system of signs* and that it is necessary to go back to the science of signs, which introduces us to what signs are made of, their laws, etc? This discipline does not exist within the known disciplines. This would be a *semiology*. . . .
>
> It is also evident that *langue* does not encompass every kind of system formed by signs. There must exist therefore a science of signs more vast than linguistics (system of maritime signs, systems of signs for the blind and deaf, and finally ⟨the most important⟩: writing itself!)
>
> But right off it must be said that *langue* will occupy the principal place of this science; it will be its master model [patron]. (II R 12, E 46–48, Riedlinger's emphasis)

This time, Saussure widens his scope of interest to a panoramic perspective: whereas the first course culminates in *langue,* the second opens onto a system larger than *langue,* of which linguistics is simultaneously a branch and a model (a *patron*). The umbrella term is *semiology,* the yet inexistent general science of signs indispensable for a full comprehension of the isolated facts of language.

This highly theoretical, dense, and even at times aphoristic Introduction took up about half of the year-long course. It is undoubtedly the clearest account we have today of the wide scope of Saussure's intellectual enterprise and the originality of his thinking. This is due not so much to the novelty of the material as to its strikingly coherent organization. The concepts themselves did not differ significantly from what he had presented two years before in the first course, but their compact organization and their forceful systematic presentation succeeded in creating a "theory," whereas the dispersion of the notations in the first attempt did not give the same impression of conceptual power and cogency. The only important change was the extension of the study of *langue* to a new science: semiology. Even this was hardly an innovation,

however, since Saussure had already alluded to this science as early as
1894: in his notes on Whitney, for example, he wrote that "the faculty
of speech" (*la faculté du langage*) and the faculty by which we perceive
"conventional relations" are one and the same (N. 10, p. 18, E 36, Saus-
sure's emphasis).[10] As early as thirteen years before the first course and
fifteen before the second, he was already convinced that there had to be
a connection between a theory of language and a general theory of
signs. The only possible innovation we may therefore attribute to the
period of the second course is the name he coined for the science he had
envisaged in 1894 and the emphasis and force with which he mentioned
the new discipline. Godel, who sees in the omission of semiology from
the first course a case of didactic restraint, comments, "In his first
course he did not dare speak, straightaway, about semiology" (*SM,*
133).

I am not convinced that this was a case of simply "daring." The
meticulously detailed inferring strategy of the first course did not lend
itself to the large vistas Saussure intended to open with semiology. By
the end of the first course he must have realized that his inferring peda-
gogy was not totally suitable for the project at hand: the system he had
in mind (even if we limit it to *langue*) exceeded by far the sum of the
linguistic puzzles he had presented to his students. It was larger than
anything that had been done before him in linguistics. In addition, his
pedagogical strategy consisted of well-chosen cases in diachronic lin-
guistics whose narrow specificity may have proven disproportionate to
the generality and complexity of *langue*. The "connect the dots"
method of the first course simply did not do justice to the scope of his
vision; enlarging this vision even more into semiology would have been
downright forced.

We may also think of the reception of the first course. Couldn't the
accumulation of details and questions have blurred the consistency of
the answers and their underlying principles? Didn't his baffled students
perhaps fail to see the forest for the trees? It would explain why, in the
second course, Saussure chose to reverse the order of presentation,
spelling out at length his theoretical principles and presenting his stu-
dents with a panoramic, conceptual introduction.

The second course avoided the mistakes of the first one, but it went
to the opposite extreme. Saussure's theoretical Introduction seems
harsh, dogmatic, and not always convincing (mostly for lack of ex-
amples or real demonstration). Considering the level of abstraction of
the Introduction, I doubt that this course made his students happier
than the first one did. While correcting *devoirs* and exams (which he did

often and very thoroughly), Saussure must have realized for the second time that his method had not done justice to his subject.

The Third Course (1910–1911)

In the third course, Saussure struck the golden mean. He borrowed the best of each from the previous courses: while the first part (from October to April) was mostly analytical (inferring) again and dealt with LES *langues* (languages) in the tradition of comparative linguistics, the second part (25 April to the end of June) returned to the panoramic synthesis, reiterating the importance of the distinction between *langue, langage,* and *parole,* the election of *langue* as a "platform" for linguistics, and the nature of the linguistic sign. It is in fact a return to the strategy of the first course, with two noticeable differences: 1) the first part of the third course replaced diachronic evolutions within one language with synchronic oppositions between languages, thus opening a larger picture and opposing one system to the other (rather than working within the same system); and 2) unlike the hurried synthesis he whipped up at the end of the first course, Saussure gave himself enough time to develop fully a larger theoretical perspective.

In the introduction to the third course, he explained this new strategy (note in particular the insistence on the linear presentation of the linguistic facts and on the pedagogical motivation of the chosen sequence): "Let us return to the outline of the course [*plan*]. Let us take up again this term: languages [*les langues*]. Linguistics has to study the social product, *langue*. But this social product manifests itself through a large diversity of languages. . . . One must first study languages, a diversity of languages. Through observation of these languages, one will extract that which is universal. He [the linguist] will then have before him a set of abstractions: this will be *langue* (*la langue*), where we will study that which is observable in the different languages" (III D 8, E 65).[11] In this quotation, Saussure's main objective is clearly pedagogical. In the best French academic tradition, he justifies his outline or order of presentation (*plan*) so as to make his students' task more manageable. The theory itself remains essentially identical to that of the earlier courses, while the problems with which he grapples concern the method, that is, the transition from the specific to the universal and vice versa. The new organization of the material was undoubtedly more successful than the previous ones (hence its definitive character in the eyes of the editors): it allowed him to illustrate and motivate the most difficult and crucial points of the second course.

I did not delve into the three courses for the sheer pleasure of displaying an erudite historical account of Saussure's pedagogical dilemma. For the *Cours de linguistique générale,* the stakes were high: if indeed in synchronic linguistics "everything is corollary, from everything else," any point of entry would and should lead the teacher and his students (or the editors and the readers) to the system as a whole as well as to the other points. Hence the "difficulty of the subject" deplored by Saussure: if each point implies the whole, and if the whole presupposes the points, then *the subject matter can no longer logically dictate the order of presentation;* logically, we are in a circle. *Only a rhetorical or pedagogical preoccupation can affect the sequence in which these points will be presented in the classroom.* Long before his three courses, in 1894 (in a draft for a book about general linguistics that he never wrote), Saussure recognized this circular aspect: "There is ⟨therefore⟩ a real ⟨necessary⟩ absence of any starting point [*point de départ*], and if some reader wants to follow attentively our thought from one end to the other of this volume he will recognize, we are convinced of it, that it was as it were impossible to follow a very rigorous order. We will permit ourselves to submit, up to three and four times, the same idea to the eyes of the reader, because *there exists really no starting point more valid than another upon which to ground the demonstration* (n. 9.1, p. 3, E 25). The lack of a starting point derived naturally from Saussure's distinction between diachronic and synchronic linguistics and his privileging of the latter over the former: once a linguist decides not to address the temporal aspect of language, the very idea of firstness clearly becomes irrelevant. If all the functions and the units in a given synchronic system are corollary, causal and temporal firstness vanishes. The starting point can no longer be either the state of affairs that preceded the one examined or some logical axiom. It becomes merely a heuristic device. This was a revolutionary concept in an age imbued with Darwinism, in which historical linguistics was the rule. It is with regard to this concept that Saussure is often associated with sociology and particularly with Durkheim. As we shall see, Frege, too, insisted on the irrelevance of a historical approach to epistemological problems (see pp. 94–95). Despite the marked differences between them, these thinkers were engaged in the same critique of the philosophy of knowledge that prevailed at the time, and of the scientific method of investigation it entailed. It is highly ironic that this essential point of Saussure's thinking has been so badly misunderstood by later critics who have found fault with his starting point see pp. 28–40).

The Editors

Faced with the change of organization from one course to another, Bally and Sechehaye came to the same impasse: the nature of their project required the existence of a starting point in order for them to ground their demonstration on some simple principle—in a typical Cartesian manner. We can even look at their problem from a simpler and more pragmatic viewpoint: they *had* to start somewhere. They realized that the point with which they chose to start would necessarily be arbitrary (since there is no real starting point) but would nonetheless acquire a logical priority over the rest in the eyes of the readers. Since the third course was more recent, more diverse in nature, and better constructed pedagogically than the first two, the editors resolved to use it as the basis for their reconstruction. The first course was used mostly for the chapters "Analogy," "Analogy and Evolution," and "Phonetic Changes," while numerous inserts from the second course complemented and expanded the third. It is important to stress that while they did indeed use the content of the third course as the basis of the *Cours,* they did not follow its sequence, its line of reasoning (the principle of organization is in fact closer to that of the second course—although it does not espouse it either).

This decision entails a series of editorial paradoxes. As his comments to Riedlinger toward the end of the second course indicate, Saussure's difficulty—and consequently his revisions—lay not in the actual content of any of the courses but in the organization of the content's parts into a system. It is in this respect that he had experimented the most and also expressed reservations about the results of such experiments. Unfortunately, because of the differences that resulted from these experiments, it is also in this respect that the editors were compelled to make the most editorial decisions. Since they had intended to base their collation on the third course, it would have been logical to adopt its outline as well as its content, all the more so since, pedagogically, it was the most satisfying of the three. They opted instead for a combination of the three courses. As a result, *the principle of organization of the Cours is not to be found in any of the courses given by Saussure:* in search of a "starting point" that would allow them to derive the other elements with maximum coherence, the editors wrote yet a fourth course, electing a fourth pedagogical strategy that Saussure himself had not tried.

The *Cours* opens rather traditionally with a brief glance (*coup d'oeil*) at the history of linguistics and moves on to a vague definition of its project (totaling nine pages). It then presents forcefully its foundation: *langue*. In choosing *langue* as the foundation stone of the theory, the editors relied on the second course, in which Saussure had expressed his preference for such a synthesis. They did not follow the outline of the second course either, however. This is one of the rare instances in which the editors knowingly and assertively "corrected" Saussure. (On other occasions, even when they had to write sections to fill in gaps, they made a laudable effort to respect the spirit if not the letter of Saussure's teaching.)

The editors were aware of the tentative aspect of the *Cours,* but they were also aware that to ensure the wide acceptance of Saussure's teaching, they had to make it hold together as coherently and cogently as the material allowed, even at the price of some editorial sanctions. Therefore, when they write, "We are aware of our responsibility to our critics. We are also aware of our responsibility to the author, who probably would not have authorized the publication of these pages" (*Course,* xvi), I suggest that we take them literally: their warning is not the conventional final bow of the editors to the "author," but the candid admission of crucial, albeit inevitable, editorial choices that risk opening the door to various textual distortions, repetitions, or omissions.

The Starting Point: Godel, Ogden and Richards, Culler

Godel

And criticized they were.[12] Three years after the publication of the *Cours,* P. Regard objected to the reconstruction of the editors and suggested that the publication of the students' actual notes might have been more useful.[13] More importantly, Godel, in his remarkable *Sources manuscrites du Cours de linguistique générale de F. de Saussure,* wonders about the logic of some sequences, finding in particular that setting forth *langue* in the introduction "brings forth the abstract character of the Saussurean theory of *langue,* a character that one could not deny, but which surprises one less if the problem of *langue* was put forward in light of this concrete and positive fact: the existence of different languages" (*SM,* 99).[14] In fact, from Godel's tactful scattered remarks, it seems that he would have preferred to maintain Saussure's organization of the material and to adopt the outline of either the second or the third course. He also mentions that the merging of the two courses upon which the editors settled impaired the logic and the coherence of each course and of the *Cours.*

In general, what I find most interesting in Godel's criticism is his alternative outline for what the *Cours* ought to have been: he suggests that the logical foundation of Saussure's thinking might well have been the question of "identities," since the delineation of identities entails a comprehensive view of both *langue* and the linguistic sign. Indeed, Saussure often wondered how one can determine linguistic entities (sound? morphemes? meaning? how much meaning?). Thus the question of identities would be the logical foundation for Godel's revised *Cours,* the starting point from which the rest of the theory is inferred: "Lacking the definitive law for the system [*A défaut de l'ordonnance définitive du système*], one can attempt to discern within it the starting point [*le point de départ*]" (*SM,* 136). Godel's search for a starting point is again in clear contradiction with Saussure's insistence on the circularity of the system ("there exists really no starting point more valid than another" [Nn. 56–57, E 25]). This suggestion is all the more surprising in light of the fact that earlier, Godel himself quotes in full Saussure's note about the lack of a proper starting point. I can only guess that the need for a proper epistemological "narrative" with a clear beginning, middle, and end is so imperious that even a linguist as objective, sharply critical, and attentive to details as Godel overlooked Saussure's warning and sought a beginning where he had been told there was none.

Ogden and Richards

Among Saussure's early analytic critics, the most influential were Ogden and Richards. In *The Meaning of Meaning,* Ogden and Richards strongly objected to Saussure's formulation of *langue* (more on *langue* pp. 42–45). And yet, in a historical perspective, their discussion about logical and ontological priorities in linguistics has proved unproductive despite its widespread acceptance: when one party sees white where the other sees black, there is little left for discussion and exchange; as a result, Anglo-American studies of language, by and large, simply overlooked Saussure.[15] Among nonlinguists, the readiness of the Anglo-American world to heed Ogden and Richards' verdict and dismiss the *Course* as an interesting work that went wrong is perplexing. Since the readers of *The Meaning of Meaning* accepted that verdict without much questioning, we may assume that they found the authors' argument convincing. What is strange is that there is no real argument, just a nasty case of libeling. How did the three pages about Saussure in *The Meaning of Meaning* establish Saussure's "error" beyond question? We shall not find an answer to our question in the tightness and relevance of the argument that is not there. The Anglo-American world rejected

Saussure not so much because Ogden and Richards proved that he was wrong but, on the contrary, because they did not have to prove it: they knew their readers would be receptive to their sketchy critique and pamphleteering style. In other words, they knew that these readers shared with them the underlying assumptions that triggered their own violent criticism. The treatment of the *Cours* in *The Meaning of Meaning* is not the idiosyncratic view of two individuals; it is *the prise de conscience* of a generalized, albeit dispersed, thought that subsequently assumed a paradigmatic value for most Anglo-American inquiries into language. Here lies the importance of Ogden and Richards' treatment of Saussure and, consequently, the necessity to expose the epistemological postulates on which it rests.

Following its brief, general, and vague remarks on the history and task of linguistics, the *Cours* strategically asks, "What is both the integral and concrete object of linguistics?" (*Course*, 7; this question more or less opened each of the three courses). In *The Meaning of Meaning*, Ogden and Richards object to this reasoning on the grounds that it begs the question: asking what the object is implies that the person who asks believes that such an object exists. According to them, Saussure "does not ask whether [linguistics] has one, he obeys blindly the primitive impulse to infer from a word some object for which it stands, and *sets out determined to find it*" (*MM*, 4).[16] The discussion then focuses on the term *object*. What is, or should be, an "object"? What is or should be the object of a science? What is or should be the *attitude* of the scientist toward the method of investigation that Lyotard called philosophical (p. 14) and Saussure practiced, that is, a method that purports to reflect upon its own presuppositions and to determine if and how these presuppositions dictate and delineate its scope, its method, or even its findings—as the *Course* clearly states, a method by which one of the first tasks of a science is "to delimit and to define itself (*Course*, 20)?

Ogden and Richards do not delve into these questions. Instead, they offer a decisive answer (this move is characteristic of "theoretical" thinking): "Saussure sets out determined to find *it*." With a brush of the pen, they attribute to Saussure ontological preoccupations and existential resolutions. Moreover, since their reformulation of Saussure implies that such an object does not exist (at least, not as Saussure "concocted" it), Ogden and Richards' Saussure is also shown to be trapped in circular metaphysics. It would seem that the authors of *The Meaning of Meaning* read only this one paragraph of the *Cours*—at least, they did not read the one that might have explained to them what Saussure meant when he used the term *object*. In the very next paragraph in the

Cours, they would have found that "other sciences work with objects that are given in advance and that can be considered from different viewpoints; but not linguistics. . . . Far from it being the object that antedates the point of view, it is the point of view that creates the object" (*Course,* 8).

As the manuscripts point out, this idea was very dear to Saussure. In the manuscripts, there are many notes regarding the question of point of view, such as the following ones:

> But all that we are aiming to establish is that it is false to admit within linguistics any fact as defined in itself [*un seul fait comme défini en soi*]. (N. 9.1, p. 3, E 25)

> But in no way do we cease to run back to a ⟨very positive⟩ operation of the imagination: the illusion of things that *would be naturally given* in language runs deep. (N. 9.1, p. 7, E 25, Saussure's emphasis)

> The third way of reasoning, for us the only admissible way: There is nothing, that is to say nothing that would be determined in advance outside of the point of view, but not even a point of view that would be more valid than the others [*mais pas même un point de vue qui soit plus indiqué que les autres*]. (N. 9.1, p 7, E 26)

> One does not ⟨ever⟩ have the right to consider one side of language as ⟨anterior and⟩ superior to others, and to make use of it as a starting point. One would have this right if there were one side which was given outside of the others, that is to say outside of every operation of abstraction and generalization on our part; but one need only reflect a moment to see that there is no such side which would be such a case. (N. 9.1, E 29)

> This is our *profession de foi* in linguistics. In other fields, one can speak of things from "*this or that point of view*" certain as one is to find firm ground in ⟨the object itself⟩. In linguistics we deny in principle that there be *things,* ⟨which continue to exist when one passes from one order of ideas to another⟩, and that one may permit oneself to consider the "things" in many orders as if they were ⟨given by themselves⟩. *The most general résumé:* Here is the most general sense of what we have been looking to establish: In linguistics we are forbidden ⟨even though we do not stop doing so⟩ to speak of "*a thing*" from different points of view, ⟨or of a thing in general⟩, because it is the point of view which MAKES the thing. . . . I do not hesitate to say that each time one introduces a distinction from a so-called "point of view" the true question is to know if we are facing the same "things," and if this is the case, it is by the most complete and the most unexpected of accidents. (III C 11, E 26, Constantin's emphasis)

I have quoted the Notes at length to give the reader an idea of Saussure's insistence on this delicate aspect of his inquiry.[17] Since Ogden and Richards did not have access to the manuscripts, it may seem unfair to criticize them. This is not the case. Although the *Cours* underplays this point's importance, Ogden and Richards could have found it immediately following the sentence they criticized about the object of linguistics, if they had not been so eager to discredit Saussure at the price of some imprecisions and oversights. We may therefore wonder how they derived the positivist stand they attribute to Saussure or the claim that Saussure "obeys the primitive impulse to infer from a word some object for which it stands, and sets out determined to find it" (*MM,* 4). In brief, even a superficial, albeit honest, examination of the *Cours'* section on the point of view should suffice to ascertain that their criticism of the object does not have a leg to stand on.

Upon reading Ogden and Richards' decisive verdict, one may also wonder how *they* knew so surely what does or does not exist and what does or does not constitute the acceptable object of a science. Excessive "knowledge" is dangerous knowledge, as our *fabliau* has shown, and the first to fall prey to ignorance is precisely the "knowledgeable" one. From their criticism of Saussure and from their theory of symbols and meaning, it is clear that their standards of acceptability lie in verification ("Unfortunately, this theory of signs, . . . was from the beginning cut off from any contact with *scientific methods of verification*" [*MM,* 6]). Science has taught us that to verify means to verify repeatedly. Thus verifying entails examining the same object repeatedly, submitting it to the same processes and reaching the same results with each examination. The object of such repeated operations would have to be an identifiable, limited, and permanent state of affairs—one that can be examined analytically (i.e., by means of statements of a general nature whose truth is accepted by definition). This same "scientific method of verification" would then require that the examination be logically and empirically carried to other manifestations of the properties examined, to similar identifiable, limited and permanent objects—with, once more, either the exact same results or minor differences for which the scientist would be able to account by virtue of the same analytically true statements (this view illustrates the eight epistemological postulates denounced by O. L. Reiser and Gaston Bachelard in their critique of the applications of Aristotelian logic to modern science[18]).

These standards dictate a specific and limited selection of "objects." In the realm of language, for example, Ogden and Richards' "scientific method of investigation" limits the object of actual utterances that can be examined repeatedly. Since such a mode of examining requires the object to be absolutely identical each time it is examined and since contexts tend to affect expressions, this object will necessarily be out of context at all times. The general rules inferred from these particular utterances can then be double-checked with a number of similar actual utterances, until these rules are extended and said to apply to all such utterances. Virtual utterances and fluctuations due to context (theoretical, historical, cultural, etc.) are therefore excluded from the scope of Ogden and Richards' "scientific method of investigation." [19] The criterion of verification they advocate hinges on a pragmatic approach, one that accepts for its object only incidental utterances, that is, utterances that came to be only because, by some accident, someone made them up. Saussure, on the other hand, did not ask what an utterance is or what it says but *by virtue of what* it comes into being: *by virtue of what* can human noises generally be recognized as meaningful utterances; by virtue of what can someone—say, Ogden or Richards—make a noise that is also a recognizable utterance? For him, an incidental utterance (*parole*) is not a case from which a general truth can be inferred. Instead, an utterance is made possible only because *langue* is precisely not contained in the examples: no utterance can reflect the complexity of *langue* because, being a part, no single utterance can exemplify the whole. *Langue* is the "system" that regulates the meaningful variations from one utterance to another. *Langue* is not so much the utterances themselves as the meaningful differences between them. It is a form, a formal construct in which there are neither objects nor sets of properties but significant differences only: as such, it cannot be submitted *in toto* to empirical verification. For Saussure, such a formal construct is not an "abstraction," as Ogden and Richards claimed—and as has been uncritically repeated—but the "integral and *concrete* object of linguistics."

In fact, Ogden and Richards do not criticize *langue* so much as the position it occupies in the general theory. They reacted to what they took for the epistemological and ontological anchorage of the subsequent theory. Had *langue* been presented as a concept inferred from actual utterances, as indeed Saussure chose to do in the first course, they might have reacted in a more civilized manner. We are clearly dealing again with a variant of the starting point issue. According to the method they defend, this point must be observable: a scientific procedure ought to have a proper beginning, a proper middle and a proper end. Science is therefore structured like a classical narrative (or the other way around, the priority being of no importance in this case). We are ob-

viously no longer discussing a theory of linguistics but the very condi-
tion of knowledge—which raises the stakes tenfold and explains the
virulence of Ogden and Richards' attack on Saussure.

By defining *langue* as a formal system and taking it for the "concrete
object" of linguistics, Saussure in fact skews the distinction between
form and substance (otherwise, how can a form be concrete?) His dis-
tinction between *langue* and *parole*, and especially his preference for the
former, challenges the very foundation of the analytical and pragmatic
perspective shared by Ogden and Richards and by the subsequent read-
ers who accepted their verdict so readily: indeed, a difference cannot be
described analytically (it would be a contradiction in terms, since an
analytic statement rests on the very same fixed truths whose relativity
the Saussurean concept of difference exposes); nor can a system of rela-
tions. Both escape the thrust of the pragmatics enterprise. From the
point of view of pedestrian empiricism, the theory must belong to the
realm of fantasy. Therefore, "such an elaborate construction of la lan-
gue might, no doubt, be arrived at by some Method of Intensive Dis-
traction analogous to that with which Dr. Whitehead's name is asso-
ciated, but *as a guiding principle for a young science it is fantastic.*
Moreover the same device of inventing verbal entities *outside the range
of possible investigation* proved fatal to the theory of signs which fol-
lowed" (*MM,* 5). Fatal? The theory of signs that followed has been one
of the most productive in modern thought, thank you.

It is hard to conceive that a work as serious, rich, and suggestive as
The Meaning of Meaning would resort to such unscholarly rudeness:
name-calling, dogmatic and aphoristic judgments, and obvious omis-
sions. If Saussure were indeed a fantastic, inventing, concocting, primi-
tive, blind, naïve and ignorant scientist (all these terms were used in the
two and a half pages that Ogden and Richards devoted to Saussure),
why would serious scientists such as the authors of *The Meaning of
Meaning* allow him to occupy the opening pages of their work, just
preceding their own by now famous diagram of the "symbol?" Why did
they pay such undeserved attention to a naïve, ignorant, fantastic
theory that "obeys blindly [a] primitive impulse"? Surely, among the
innumerable theories of language, they could have found a more wor-
thy foil. What's more, why is Saussure the only target of such violent
rhetoric? (No other theory cited in the opening pages of *The Meaning
of Meaning* occupies more than a few lines or elicits such violent epi-
thets—with the significant exception of Bréal, Saussure's teacher and a
proponent of value, who occupies one paragraph.) Since they did not
really discuss Saussure's theories, wouldn't it have been more economi-

cal, elegant, and courteous if Ogden and Richards had simply ignored him? The answer to these questions can only be that, despite their efforts to present Saussure as a mad scientist misled by continental metaphysics, the authors did, in fact, sense the challenge of Saussurean linguistics and did respond to it—however inarticulately.[20]

Culler

An interesting case of criticism of the *Course*'s organization is Jonathan Culler's book *Saussure*. About the editors, Culler writes that "in general they did an admirable job, but there is a strong case for saying that in three respects they were less successful than one might have wished: *their order of presentation is probably not that which Saussure would have chosen* and thus does not reflect the potential logical sequence of his argument; the notion of the arbitrary nature of the sign receives much less discussion than it does in the notes; and in discussing the second plane of language, the editors are much less scrupulous and consistent in their terminology than Saussure seems to have been. . . . I shall not hesitate to rectify the original editors' occasional lapses" (Culler 19).[21]

On one count, Culler is right: Saussure was extremely scrupulous in his choice of words. Paradoxically, however, his attention to the perfect wording resulted in considerable terminological fluctuations: the manuscripts show that he commented relentlessly on the terms he chose and deplored his inability to find just the right expressions for the distinctions he introduced. Consequently, he was forever forging new terms and criticizing the old ones (in this respect, Peirce is the only philosopher I find comparable to Saussure). Thus we can find strings of synonyms and periphrases in his students' notes (the same synonyms and periphrases recur from one student to the next, so that we cannot blame their carelessness for the inconsistencies). The task of the editors was then to adopt a consistent terminology so as to ensure coherence and continuity. With the exception of some rare mistakes, they did a remarkably conscientious work. Some inconsistencies, mostly Saussure's, still made their way into the *Cours;* others, for example *unmotivated* versus *arbitrary,* are due to the excessive respect of the editors for the master: they did not dare replace terms that Saussure was known to have used for many years, even when he had indicated his preference for new terms much later in his teaching (see p. 56). To make matters worse, Saussure himself often reverted to old terms even after coining new ones (as in the case of *signified* and *signifier*). We may disagree with some of the editors' choices, but we must concede that they are much more consistent than Saussure ever was: the few inconsistencies that transpired in the *Cours* are due specifically to the editors' excessive scruples and their respect for the master's teaching. (Even a quick look at Sechehaye's collation would suffice for one to notice the number of remarks written in the margins in which Sechehaye and Bally wonder about the exact meaning of a word, discuss the accuracy of a term, express their concern over a uniform terminology, and try to figure out how to "translate" Saussure's various terms into the taxonomy they had adopted for the sake of consistency (see pp. 61–62).

We can easily condense the two other objections into one: what Culler criticized in the *Cours'* order of presentation (his second point) is that the editors emphasized *langue* as the foundation of the theory, rather than emphasizing the arbitrary nature of the linguistic sign (his third point). Indeed, in his book on Saussure, Culler "rectifies" the editor's interpretation and reverses their order; he opens with a presentation of the linguistic sign from which he derives *langue* as a logical consequence: "But in fact, as Saussure's notes suggest and as the sequence of argument which we have adopted should have demonstrated, the distinction between *langue* and *parole* is a logical and necessary consequence of the arbitrary nature of the sign and the problem of identity in linguistics. . . . The isolation of *la langue* is not, as the published *Course* may suggest, an arbitrary point of departure but a consequence of the nature of signs themselves" (Culler 34).

It is unfortunate that to back up his argument Culler relies mostly on a vague "as Saussure's notes suggest" without presenting any further evidence, since my reading of Saussure's notes and of those of his students reveals no evidence to support this claim. On the contrary, in each of the courses, I found that a systematic attention to *langue* preceded any representation of the linguistic sign: the sequence is very clear in the second and third courses and is furthermore emphasized by the subdivisions of the chapters. In the first course the inductive strategy blurs the notion of logical priorities altogether, so that any affirmation about causal, historical, and ontological priorities can only be gratuitous. Even if we go as far back as the Notes (probably 1897–1910), before the three courses on general linguistics, Saussure rarely speaks of signs as an independent entity; instead, he usually writes *système de signes* rather than *signe*. This consistency suggests, even at that early stage, a strong dependency between the "sign" and the "system," whereby any attempt to attribute more ontological weight to one than to the other will, in fact, distort the presentation of his views. By the third course Saussure recommends explicitly "moreover, *not to begin with the word or the term* in order to deduce the system. This would be to believe that the terms have an absolute value in advance; on the contrary, it is from the system that one must begin, from the solidary whole [*du tout solidaire*]" (III D 269, E 256)—advice Culler clearly did not heed.

I cannot emphasize enough the importance Saussure attached to his deep conviction that "everything is corollary." From one course to another, he tried out different orders of presentation, different ways of breaking through the circle. The more he refined his perception and presentation of his philosophy of language, the harder his predicament appeared to him—precisely because he could find no starting point, no aspect of his theory that could serve as logical, epistemological, or ontological foundation for the whole. The circularity of his subject matter at times seems overwhelming. In the third course, one year before his death, for example, he notes that "for the moment, general linguistics appears to me like a system of geometry. One ends up with theorems that must be proven. Then one realizes that theorem 12 is, in another form, the same as theorem 33" (*SM*, 30). If each theorem turns out to be the same as another theorem, the geometrician in search of theorem 1 is walking a tightrope, since no theorem can claim priority without having to dispute this claim with its twin.

If, as I previously suggested, the editors of the *Cours* opted for a fourth course, Culler has elected to write a fifth course, in which the analysis of the linguistic sign serves as the ontological foundation for the theory as a whole. Served by Culler's masterly writing, this interpretation is clear and elegant. It does not reflect the poignancy of Saussure's struggle, however, and moreover, it underplays one of the most suggestive aspects of his philosophical reflection. Provided that "everything is corollary" and that there is no starting point, Culler's interpretation is neither more "right" nor more "wrong" than that of the editors.[22] The point remains that, among the many reasons Saussure may have had not to write the *Cours,* there is one he gave explicitly time and again that happens to invalidate Culler's arbitrary "rectification": his subject matter was such that he did not know where to start: "One does not ⟨ever⟩ have the right to consider one side of language as ⟨anterior and⟩ superior to others, and to make use of it as a starting point. One would have this right if there were one side which was given outside of the others, that is to say outside of every operation of abstraction and generalization on our part; but one need only reflect a moment to see that there is no such side which would be such a case" (N. 9.1, E 29). Therefore, imagining the order of presentation "which Saussure would have chosen," as Culler claims (the naïveté of the claim notwithstanding), is

a contradiction in terms. One can only regret that Culler deemed it nec-
essary to pin his preference for the nature of the linguistic sign on Saus-
sure and to motivate it by some intrinsic and logical necessity inherent
in Saussure's theory—which, as the manuscripts quoted above point
out, was not the case.

A different perspective may cast light on Culler's bias. After its "dis-
covery" by Jakobson in 1945, while the *Cours* enjoyed a notable success
among French and most European nonlinguists, English-speaking
scholars (again, especially nonlinguists) widely ignored it. Of the few
philosophers who read the *Cours*, most criticized it harshly. Jonathan
Culler addressed his book to the very same public that for half a century
had chosen to dismiss Saussure. Thus his project was in essence peda-
gogical and polemical: pedagogical because he wanted to explain Saus-
sure's theory to his readers and "insure that Saussure be considered not
only an important figure of the recent past but also, and perhaps mostly,
a major intellectual presence today" (Culler 12); polemical since he was
trying to refute the arguments of the first Anglo-American readers of
Saussure who were responsible for his neglect in Britain and America.
These considerations undoubtedly affected Culler's argument. For ex-
ample, most of his presentation of the linguistic sign is constructed *a
contrario:* it explains not what the Saussurean sign is but what it is not
(namely, a "taxonomy"). While this is perfectly true of Saussure's
theory, the rhetorical strategy may seem odd—unless we specify that
the label *taxonomy* is precisely Chomsky's main critique of Saussure's
linguistics.[23]

More importantly, Culler's emphasis on the nature of the linguistic
sign (rather than on *langue*) betrays a pragmatic addressee; it is as if he
had attempted to "translate" Saussure into American Pragmatism. For
example, in his attempt to clear Saussure's name, Culler stresses at
length that the editors—and not Saussure—are responsible for opening
the *Cours* with *langue:*

> Saussure's editors organized the *Course* so that it began with the distinc-
> tion between *langue* and *parole*. Saussure was thus portrayed as saying that
> language is a confused mass of heterogeneous facts and the only way to
> make sense of it is to *postulate* the existence of something called the lin-
> guistic system and to set aside everything else. *The distinction has thus
> seemed extremely arbitrary to many people: a postulate* which had to be
> accepted on faith if one were to proceed. But in fact, as Saussure's notes
> suggest and as the sequence of argument which we have adopted should
> have demonstrated, the distinction between *langue* and *parole* is a logical
> and necessary consequence of the arbitrary nature of the sign and the prob-

lem of identity in linguistics. . . . The attempt to study signs led us, inexorably, to take this as the proper object of linguistic investigation. The isolation of *la langue* is not, as the published *Course* may suggest, an arbitrary point of departure but a consequence of the nature of signs themselves. (Culler 34)

A correction is in order: the *Cours*—that is to say, the editors—never says that one ought to "postulate" *langue*. The idea of a postulate is in fact totally alien to Saussure's thinking and the *Cours* itself. From the Saussurean viewpoint (emphasizing that he had defined things and not words) the word *postulate* is scandalous. The *Course* is emphatically explicit on this matter: "Language (*langue*) is concrete, no less so than speaking (*parole*); and this is a help in our study of it" (*Course*, 15). The word *postulate,* which Culler uses twice to represent what "others" criticized in Saussure's emphasis on *langue,* echoes the harsh judgment that Ogden and Richards passed on Saussure. In Culler's sentence "The distinction has thus seemed extremely arbitrary to many people," I do not hesitate to read under "many people" Ogden and Richards and their followers. Culler's criticism of the *Cours* is perhaps a laudable and timely attempt to appease Saussure's pragmatic critics, but it is done at the expense of the editors and, more importantly, at the expense of some crucial, albeit difficult, aspects of Saussure's thinking.

On the surface, Culler's rearrangement of the *Cours* seems to counter Ogden and Richards' sentence and to redeem Saussure in the eyes of Anglo-American readers. When pushed to its outer limits, however, Culler's argument, paradoxically, confirms Ogden and Richards' criticism: just like them, he anchors the whole theory of language on the ontology and epistemology of signs (this choice irons out the richest and most productive of Saussure's "doubts and hesitations"). Worse yet, unlike, for example, Continental linguists—and indeed, unlike Saussure himself—Culler relegates *langue* to a tributary position, as the "effect" of the sign, thus factually repeating Ogden and Richards' gesture and conforming to their wishes.

In short, the pragmatic resolution that Culler imports into Saussurean circular linguistics bridges the gap between French and Anglo-American linguistics very effectively, but it does so at the expense of Saussure's originality. Even so, Culler's introduction to Saussurean linguistics remains valuable. Compounded with its clear presentation and its enthusiastic tone, his *Saussure* is an excellent introduction to Saussure. It behooves the reader to remember that the derivation of *langue* from the nature of the linguistic sign—essential though it may be to Culler's argument—reflects Culler's circumstantial background and polemics, not Saussure's philosophy of language: Culler's preference is yet another starting point dictated by pragmatic historical concerns; it is not inherent in the theory.

Saussure's Theory of Language

Today, Saussure's distinctions between diachrony and synchrony, signified and signifier, *parole, langue,* and *langage* seem at once indispensable and questionable. Their structural simplicity has allowed their integration into a variety of disciplines and thoughts, while their conceptual complexity has challenged three generations and puzzled scores of scholars.

Both simplicity and complexity derive from the nature of Saussure's probing into language, from the questions he addressed to language, rather than from the answers he offered. He did not so much describe how language works as wonder what, in language, guarantees that it *will* work. Hence his interest in *langue* rather than in *parole:* as our reading of the *fabliau* has shown, any agrammaticality occurring in discourse (of the kind we shall examine in chapters 4, 5, and 6) can and will be perceived as such only if some rule or system of rules precludes the utterance in accordance with these same rules. Saussure's elaboration of *langue* as a synchronic system grounded in a convention, his theory of the two-sided and arbitrary linguistic sign, value, and systems, along with his visionary insistence both on the need for semiology, a new "science of signs more vast than linguistics" and on the leading role *langue* would play in such a science, have been adopted extensively by other branches of the humanities and the social sciences (II R 12, E 46).

Since my discussion focuses largely on quarrels about the nature of signs, I shall begin with the relatively less controversial concepts (*langue, parole,* and *langage*). As I proceed, I shall add the controversies concerning the more delicate problems regarding the nature of signs, units, and entities.[24]

Parole, Langage, Langue

Parole is any actual individual utterance that conforms enough to the rules governing an idiolect so as to be understood by any person within this same linguistic community. Sheer noise and "private" languages are not acts of *parole.* Simple noise is not linguistic (the "bee doo bababada boo beep" noise made by Ella Fitzgerald, pleasant as it may be, is not language). Note that to become truly linguistic, human noise must conform to a large number (if not to all) the pertinent rules: thus

Jabberwocky is only an approximation of language. *Parole* can be written (the sentences of which this book is made up pertain to *parole*), spoken, or thought (I can think, "the sky is blue" without actually saying it out loud). *Parole* is thus not necessarily perceived by the senses, as it has often been claimed; rather, it is only what an individual produces when he or she appropriates *langue* for personal use, and it is therefore essentially individual, accidental, and circumstantial. In addition, since no single utterance or sentence can enact all the lexical and syntactical rules and possibilities of its idiolect, and since the number of possible utterances of a given language is for all purposes infinite, we cannot establish empirically a list of phrases that would exemplify all of the lexical and syntactical resources of an ideolect. Therefore *parole* is also, by definition, incomplete. To make matters worse, any time an individual utters a phrase, he or she chooses to say one thing, in one manner, to the exclusion of other things and other manners. These choices reflect and enact the will, intelligence, purpose, and competence of that individual. Such properties do include undeniably linguistic elements, but these elements are mixed with so many nonlinguistic factors that they are not easily observable—at least not as long as the declared object is language. Since properties such as intelligence, purpose, and competence are psychological (rather than linguistic), Saussure assigns them to the study of people, not to the study of language. This is not to say that he thought there could be no linguistics of *parole* (in fact, Saussure promised his students that he would teach an entire course on this one subject, the way he taught entire courses about *langue*). The purpose of the distinction between *parole* and *langue* is therefore not to exclude *parole* from the study of linguistics, as it has often been said, but to realize that the principles that govern the mechanisms of *parole* and *langue* are not identical and should not be confused.

The term *langage* (speech) that we find in the *Cours* is misleading. Saussures does not use it in his Notes: instead he uses almost consistently *the faculty of speech* (*la faculté du langage*). The word *langage* can occasionally be found in the students' notes, but these occurrences are rare: invariably, they appear in sentences in which Saussure is trying to explain the difference between *parole, langue,* and *faculté du langage* and in which the word *langage* is therefore clearly an abbreviation for *faculté du langage*. *Langage* is not so much, as the *Cours* may lead us to believe, a special category as a general term that precedes all distinctions, and that because "there is for each individual a faculty that we can call the faculty of artificial language. This faculty is given to us first by the bodily organs and next by the play that we can extract from them. *But this is only a faculty* and it would be materially impossible to exercise it without another thing which is given to the individual from the outside: *langue*" (III C 12, E 31, Constantin's emphasis). This precision is crucial: we are clearly speaking about a prelinguistic, mental, and psychological faculty found in people and not in language per se (prelinguistic because this faculty presides over the formation of all systems of signs, whether linguistic or other). As a purely mental faculty, *langage* is potential only. Unless this potential is realized, it is in fact nothing; but to be realized, it needs something that is not in the individual but outside, not private but collective; something that will be the "object" upon which the individual will direct and exercise this private faculty—in short, *langue*.

Langue is that which, from the outside, combines with *la faculté du langage* to produce *parole*. First, "*Langue* ⟨will be for us⟩ *the social product* whose existence permits the individual to exert the faculty of language" (III D 173, E 31, Dégallier's emphasis). This obvious social function aside, Saussure's real innovation is his realization that *langue* is not a particular combination whose end result is a finite set of words that combine with a specific idea but a "system of distinct signs corresponding to distinct ideas" (*Course,* 10). The key word in this definition is *system: langue* is the code that regulates the exchange of signs; at the same time, it is the principle of cohesion that holds this code together so that one element cannot be altered without affecting the balance of all the other elements in the same system. *Langue* is therefore contained neither in a particular utterance (*parole*) nor in the faculty that governs signs (*langage*). This system is not a metaphysical abstraction conveniently concocted for the sake of answering a poorly posed question, as Ogden and Richards claimed; on the contrary, since *parole* is subject to the individual's whims, and since *langage* is but a faculty, *langue* is the only real and dependable, purely linguistic element and, as such, the obvious choice for the "object at once integral and concrete of linguistics" (*Course,* 7).

In our daily experience we can sometimes isolate *langue* from *parole:* a man paralyzed after a stroke may not be able to speak or write. This man will have lost the use of *parole;* he will still be in full command of *langue,* however. He will be able to hear and understand another person, or to read any written material. The same can be said for the *faculté du langage:* we say of a man suffering from sever aphasia that his *faculté du langage* is impaired; yet his personal affliction will not affect the linguistic skills of his community or, more precisely, the *lan-*

gue of this community. This is because *langue* is found in the social body, while the faculty of speech is in the individual brain. (Saussure relies on Broca's experiments, which proved that the same lobe of our brain is responsible for both speech and writing—from which he derives the far-reaching conclusion that *la faculté du langage* is, in fact, the faculty that governs man's ability to handle conventional signs. See *Course*, 10–11).[25]

Saussure's preference for synchronic linguistics is inseparable from his perception of *langue* as a system. Unlike other sciences (he cites history and geology), depending on whether it is taken historically or at a given time independently of precedents, linguistics answers to different sets of laws. This, he says, is because linguistics, like economics, deals with value only and a history of values is a science distinct from the one attempting their delineation.[26] The distinction between synchrony and diachrony is therefore not a separate dichotomy but another way of defining and addressing the problems posed by *langue*. That a descriptive history of the various changes of *langue* through time can be traced is undeniable, but it should not weigh on the study of *langue* either teleologically or causally since the various values that constitute *langue* at a given moment are "caused" not by some historical factor but by the place they occupy in the system at that moment. Saussure did not dispute that the almost exclusively diachronic comparative philology practiced by his contemporaries was a valid project, but he saw it as a science closer to the history of linguistics than to linguistics itself. (In this respect his epistemological principles and methodological thrust are very comparable to Frege's, although, at the onset, the two were committed to dramatically opposed projects [see pp. 93–95]).

At the same time, we should beware of useless dogmatism. Since *langage, langue,* and *parole* depend on one another, their boundaries are hard to determine ("One must admit that parole and langue, social fact and individual fact, execution and fixed classification come to mix together more or less" [III D 184–85, E 286]). In order to define any of these categories, we must situate it in the context of the others, so that any "definition" turns into a string of definitions studded with cross references, of which the following is exemplary: "Therefore *langue* is a set of necessary conventions adopted by the social body to permit the use of the faculty of language by individuals ⟨definition⟩. *The faculty of langage* is a distinct fact of *langue,* but which cannot exercise itself without *langue.* By *parole* one designates the act of the individual giving reality to [*réalisant*] his faculty by means of the social convention which is *langue* ⟨definition⟩. In *parole*, there is an idea of a realization of what is permitted by *the social convention*" (II R 6, E 32, Riedlinger's emphasis).

The relation between *langue* and *parole* is similar to a particular move during a game. Each move is a function of the general system of rules. A false or incorrect move neither escapes nor invalidates the code. On the contrary, it is perceived as false or incorrect only insomuch as another, "proper" move could have taken its place in accordance with the code. The false move, though false, is still perceived as a move *within* the system. When playing chess, if I scratch my nose with a knight, I doubt that my partner will accuse me of cheating; my action will have no meaning, no relevance to the ongoing game, since I will have stepped out of the boundaries defined by the rules of this game. Scratching my nose is not a move. (Given another "game," however— say, an auction—my gesture *can* be taken as a move: if I raise my hand to scratch my nose, I may find myself the proud owner of a cracked vase.) If, on the other hand, I move my knight on the board as I please, my partner will complain vehemently, since this would be a move, however irregular, false, or dishonest. Translated to our linguistic corpus, scratching my nose is analogous to any noise I might make outside the boundaries of a recognizable language, while moving my knight on the board is comparable to *parole*—even if my utterance is ungrammatical or exhibits some kind of dysfunction. In a similar way, in "De la sorisete des estopes" the peasant's mistake is neither an irrelevant incident nor the result of some accidental misuse of language having no bearing on the "proper" uses (nor is it a case of ordinary language vs. literature or fiction). On the contrary, the element responsible for his nuptial misfire can be found in *langue* at the general, social, essential, and normative levels. This misfire is definitely a move. The *fabliau* owes its comic effect precisely to the fact that the peasant's confusion occurs *within* the language game in which we are engaged and in relation to that game's governing rules—independently of whether the immediate context is "literary" or "ordinary."

A literary work such as "De la sorisete des estopes" is pure *parole*. One could therefore hastily assume that the incongruous exchange between the young husband and his bride does not pertain to linguistics as defined by Saussure. Such a reading will then dismiss any individual work altogether as an object unworthy of the attention of a true linguist and will consider the questions of mistaken reference that the *fabliau* raises irrelevant for a theory of *langue*. Some (like Strawson or Wittgenstein) will even wish to carry this line of reasoning to an extreme by distinguishing within *parole* between an "utterance" and the "use of an utterance" and, favoring the latter, will thus acknowledge the pragmatic aspect of language only (see pp. 139–45). If a literary work is a case of *parole* only, and if *parole* is not the object of linguistics, then the *fabliau* will no longer function as a test or puzzle for a Saussurean conception of language: it will fall outside the boundaries of the theory.

This reductive understanding of *langue* (as well as many of the discussions about particular instances requiring the distinction between *langue* and *parole*) suffers from an essential flaw that I call the postulate of realism: the popular belief that objects invariably precede words independently of any viewpoint and that words, secondary with regard to these objects, only designate them. This is not to deny the existence of an extralinguistic reality (see my reading of "The Venus of Ille" in chap. 5); rather, both discrete objects and words result from the slicing of the epistemic and phenomenal pies. It is my belief that Saussure was expressing the same view when he suggested two amorphous masses, one real and the other linguistic, formally segmenting each other into discrete entities. Indeed, the interdependence of *langue* and *parole* is such that it would be futile to look for a referent for each that would not be contaminated by its counterpart. We should instead treat each term as a viewpoint on the mass of linguistic phenomena and, therefore, as a way of defining our own philosophical and critical stand regarding these phenomena. This was, I believe, Saussure's position: despite his explicit preference for *langue,* he rarely missed a chance to remind his students that "1° [there is] nothing in *langue* which has not entered it (directly or indirectly) through [a] received *parole* [*par parole reçue*]. Reciprocally, *parole* is possible thanks only to the elaboration of the product called *langue* [*l'élaboration du produit qui s'appelle la langue*], which furnishes the individual with the elements enabling him to make up *parole*" (III D 208, E 56, Dégallier's emphasis, trans. mine).

Saussure often stated that ultimately the distinction between the two collapses. This was also Godel's opinion ("One must not show oneself here to be more Saussurean than Saussure by considering *langue* and *parole* as entities" [*SM,* 159]). As is the case for other famous Saussurean dichotomies, *langue* and *parole* are two different viewpoints on an ongoing human social activity. The preference for one viewpoint over the other is a matter of pragmatic choice dictated by the methodological imperatives of science—and not by the subject matter. This is undoubtedly the reason why Saussure warns his students that even though the distinctions he has drawn do not translate properly from one language to another, they are still valid in that they apply to things and not to words.[27] Far from being a plea for realism, as it has been advanced, this warning is in fact a defense of scientific pragmatic measures since—we must never forget it—"it is the point of view that CREATES the object" (*c'est le point de vue qui FAIT la chose*—this sentence must have been written on the blackboard since the students' notebooks invariably capitalize the word *FAIT*). Had de Mauro—whose critical edition of the *Cours* is otherwise remarkable—remembered that *object* for Saussure is almost identical with *viewpoint*, he would not have been embarrassed by Saussure's careful distinction and would not have tried to play it down in his Notes to the *Cours* by calling it "professor's mirages or unsuccessful metaphors" (*Cours,* 423).

The absolute separation between *langue* and *parole* originates in the project of the editors of the *Cours:* since they intended to make known the theory of language of their admired colleague and teacher, they stressed the dogmatic aspect that is necessarily part of teaching, while overlooking the hestitations, reservations, and retractions that were likely to blur the theoretical distinctions. And yet *our* object is precisely the slippery area of hesitation in which distinctions are summoned to reflect on the principles to which they owe their existence. In our example the mistake of the naïve peasant exposes the mutual dependence of *langue* and *parole*. At the risk of repeating myself, I must stress that, from the viewpoint of a theory of language, what requires an explanation is not the specific agrammaticality of an utterance (*parole*) so much as the possibility for language (*langue*) to produce and communicate such agrammaticalities. At the same time, from the viewpoint of literary theory, what requires an explanation is the relationship between the aptitude of language to produce agrammaticalities and the readiness of the literary text to expose, exploit, and enact this aptitude. Thus "De la sorisete des estopes" is a platform from which to examine how *langue* can allow or even produce an utterance such as "if I can find your cunt," which is at once in agreement with the rules of the language game (the Saussurean system) and immediately perceived as agrammatical with regard to the referential function of linguistic signs (their deictic aim).

Signifier/Signified

The Saussurean sign is never a tangible, perceptible entity to which a meaning of some kind is added. Even though it can be seen and described from two viewpoints, each of these viewpoints (the signified and the signifier) is and remains a mental factor: the signified is a "concept" and the signifier a "sound-image" (*image acoustique*). The signifier is not the actual sound that the ear perceives but the imprint of this sound on the mind (*empreinte psychique*), the representation we hold of what this sound *ought* to be in order to signify. Thus slight, meaningless variations of pronunciation do not affect the Saussurean sign, for the actual sound is immediately converted into its mental, ideal representation, its sound-image.

Signifier and signified are inseparable. For Saussure, there can be no concept or thought independent of a sound-image, since "without language, thought is a vague unchartered nebula. There are no pre-existing ideas and nothing is distinct before the appearance of language" (*Course* 123); only the convergence of this amorphous prethought with some "phonic substance" can allow the delineation of actual ideas. The idea of interdependence between thought and language is hardly a novelty. With the emergence of phenomenology and its success in France, it gained renewed currency. With some delay, Saussure's conception was thus readily assimilated into a preexisting general philosophical framework (Merleau-Ponty, for example, embraced Saussure's philosophy of language enthusiastically). Soon certain elements underwent changes, however, mostly because of the influence of Russian Formalism and the work of the Prague Linguistics Circle (perhaps also because of some cloudiness in the *Cours* that encouraged "interpretation"). The signifier is a case in point. When stating that the signified did not precede the signifier and had no priority of any kind over it, Saussure never claimed nor implied that the opposite might be true, namely that the signifier might have priority over the signified (as it was said time and again, especially in the 1960s and 1970s). Saussure was very clear on this point: pure noise does not belong to language until it becomes meaningful and, subsequently, identifiable. Contrary to Barthes, Althusser, and Lacan, to name a few, a signifier that does not mean anything (that is not attached to a signified) does not exist; it is a contradiction in terms: a Saussurean signifier is perceived as such specifically and only because it corresponds to a meaning. Indeed, "Against the floating realm of thought, would sounds by themselves yield predetermined entities? No more so than ideas. Phonic substance is neither more fixed nor more rigid than thought; it is not a mold into which thought must of necessity fit but a plastic substance divided in turn into distinct parts to furnish the signifier needed by thought" (112). Only a shift in perspective can single out the signifier or the signified—not the fact that they may be detachable from each other. Saussure illustrates this important principle with the well-known model of a sheet of paper of which "thought is the front and sound the back; one cannot cut the front without cutting the back at the same time; likewise in language, one can neither divide sound from thought nor thought from sound; the division could be accomplished only by means of an abstraction, and the result would be either pure psychology or pure phonology" (*Course,* 113, modified trans.). I may choose to look at one side of a sheet of paper or the other, but I cannot say that one side exists without the other. Unless they combine with their corresponding concepts, the representations of sounds escape the grasp of linguistics.

In short, the much advertised (floating, etc.) signifier bears little resemblance to the signifier Saussure was describing when he examined the nature of the linguistic sign. Saussure's signifier differs from its homonymic avatar in two essential ways: 1) it is a representation, the mental imprint of a sensorial perception; and 2) it is inseparable from its signified, so that it carries a meaning at all times (although it *is not* this meaning; for further discussion of the signifier, see pp. 242–43).[28]

Difference and Opposition

The perception of the dual nature of the sign raises an obvious question: How do we know what noises are words and what noises are noise? How do we know that *broiling* is a word and *brillig* is not? Saussure's answer is that we do not perceive words as words but as differences between words. Thus we perceive *bet* as different from *but, bit, boot, bat,* etcetera and attach a meaning to that difference. *Bet* is significant only inasmuch as it is not *but, boot, bit, boat, bat,* or *let, set, wet,* etcetera. Difference for Saussure is a purely negative concept. It means: *not* the same, *not* identical ("*in language, there are only differences.* Even more important: a difference generally implies positive terms between which the difference is set up; but in language there are only differences *without positive terms*" [*Course,* 120, eds.' emphasis]). Saussure does not stop at difference, however, since *bet* may be different from *bat,* but it is also different from *chair, airplane, strawberry,* or any other conceivable meaningful utterance: everything is different from everything else, and truisms of this sort do little to deepen our understanding of language. Difference is of little interest unless we consider it with its counterpart, *opposition.* When we choose to oppose *bet* to *bat* rather than to any other absurdly unrelated utterance, we are undeniably guided by the perception of a difference, but we are also guided by the perception of a relation: *bet* and *bat* are alike in a way that does not apply to *bet* and *airplane.*[29] This double perception of likeness and difference is no longer a difference; it is what Saussure calls an *opposition*.[30] *Bet* and *airplane* are different, but *bat* and *bet* are opposed because they both belong to the same system b-?-t.

This last distinction leads us to the term *value* and its key position in Saussure's theory of language. Saussure did not care as much for either *difference* or *opposition* as he cared for *value*, which he presented as the third stage in the series of differential refinements leading from the simple *difference* to the more complex *value* via *opposition*. The much quoted aphorism "In language there are only differences" was only the first step in an argument that concluded in the second course with "There is only difference used as opposition and opposition gives value" (II R 75, E 274). The distinction among the notions difference/opposition/value is crucial to our understanding of Saussure's philosophy of linguistics and, by extension, to our understanding of language and communication (I shall take up the discussion of "value" pp. 60–75).

When the Saussurean peasant of our *fabliau* declares, "I want to get up my prick . . . Afterwards I'll fuck you if ever I can and if I can find your cunt," he shows clearly that he opposes *cunt* and *prick*. Indeed, they both belong to the system that we call sexuality. However, the opening line of the *fabliau* warns us that the peasant had no access to this system (this is why he is a *sot*). He does nonetheless have a "structural" understanding of systems, even though he does not happen to be acquainted with this particular one. Thus he understands that on their wedding night the bride and the groom are not simply different: they are opposed. In other words, while they differ from each other in important ways, they maintain a certain rapport that, according to the system, they should act upon on their wedding night. He also understands that their opposition is contained in the terms *prick* and *cunt* (the way the letters *e/a* will contain the opposition between *bet* and *bat*). Indeed—and here lies the irony—the mouse *is* different, that is, it does not fit in the system, just the way *airplane* does not fit in the series *but, bet, bat*, etcetera. But how is a simple peasant whose perception of language is limited to systems to know this? If he looks to Saussure for help, he will find to his dismay that nothing in the master's teaching indicates how one should sort out oppositions and differences. Saussure seems to assume that the intuitive speaker will *know* what things or words belong together; in other words, he assumes that homogeneity is intuitive and that one will not mix systems inadvertently. The *fabliau* presents a special case: our lad does not know; he is a *sot* because *rien ne sot.* He lacks the empirical (referential) knowledge on which Saussure's analysis implicitly relies despite its claims to the contrary, lacks the classifying sixth sense that would have informed him that mice do not belong to the paradigm of human sexuality. In *langue,* indeed, there are only differences and oppositions; and yet how can one distinguish between them unless one leaves the boundaries of language—or redefines them? (And as the peasant found out, this distinction is crucial.) In other words, how can we reconcile the deictic and semantic aims of language; how can we reconcile taxonomies and systems?

Taxonomies

Theories of signs similar to Saussure's have existed since the dawn of the reflection on language. Saussure's major contribution to the delineation and identification of signs is his refusal to subordinate the signifier to the signified. Other theories viewed language as a taxonomy in which signifieds were the faithful representation of preexisting objects or concepts, whereas the signifier could change either historically (etymological morphology) or geographically (the multiplicity of languages). This view is best conveyed by the principle underlying bilingual dictionaries: the signifier *boeuf* is believed to correspond to the signified *Ochs,* while the animal referred to is considered given, and the concept (the signified) representing it universally and intuitively known. Its theoretical naïveté notwithstanding, this sense of translation is often adequate, but it is unsound: even the simplest of concrete objects perceived with the senses may be hard to delineate and to name without further inquiries. For example, whereas French has the word *mouton,* English requires an additional viewpoint on the same animal: is it grazing in the pasture or hanging in the butcher shop? Is it *sheep* or *mutton*?[31] In his Notes, Saussure remarks:

> The problem of language does not occur to most minds except in the form of a nomenclature. In chapter 4 of *Genesis* we see Adam giving names . . . Three things are invariably missing from the given that a philosopher believes to be that of language. 1°. ⟨First this truth upon which we are not even insisting⟩, that the foundation of language is not made up of names. It is an accident when the linguistic sign happens to correspond to a definite object for the senses like a horse, fire, the sun, ⟨rather than to an idea like "the place"⟩. Whatever the importance of such a case, there is no ⟨obvious⟩ reason, just the reverse, to take it as the model of language. But there is there, implicitly, some tendency which we cannot mistake nor allow to get by as to what would be ⟨definitively⟩ language: namely, a nomenclature of objects. ⟨Of objects already given⟩ First the object, then the sign; therefore

(something we will always deny) an exterior base given to the sign and a figuring of language by this relation:

$$\text{objets} \quad \left\{ \begin{array}{l} * \underline{\hspace{2cm}} \text{a} \\ * \underline{\hspace{2cm}} \text{b} \\ * \underline{\hspace{2cm}} \text{c} \end{array} \right\} \quad \text{names}$$

while the true figure is a———b———c, outside of every knowledge of an affective relation such as *———a based on an object. If an object, wherever it is, could be the term upon which the sign is fixed, linguistics would cease instantly to be what it is from ⟨top⟩ to ⟨bottom⟩, . . .

Much more serious is the second mistake made generally by philosophers which is to represent the following:

2° Once an object is designated by a name, it is then and there a whole which is going to be transmitted, without conjuring up other phenomena! [*sans autres phénomènes à prévoir!*]. . . . What is characteristic are the innumerable cases where it is the alteration of the sign which changes the idea itself and where one sees all of a sudden that there was no difference at all, from moment to moment, between the sum of the distinct ideas [*la somme des idées distinguées*] and the sum of the collective signs. (N. 12, p. 19, E 147–48)[32]

Language, claims Saussure, does not name objects. This warning raises the familiar question of the relation and the hierarchy between perception and understanding: do the linguistic categories correspond to the objects that I perceive as autonomous, self-defined entities (the case of Adam naming animals), or, on the contrary, do these categories (the words of my language) dictate my perception of objects, the way the number of guests and their appetite would determine the number and size of wedges into which I might cut a pie, as Whorf or Malinowsky would have it?[33] This distinction between the subject and the object of language, simplified though it may be in the present rendition, lies nonetheless at the heart of all epistemological investigations and was particularly productive in Saussure's day (for example, Husserl, a contemporary of Saussure, devoted a major portion of his work to relating the two, while Frege, another contemporary, set out to distinguish between them radically—see chap. 3). Saussure addressed this query in a synchronic perspective only. In the true manner of the new philosophy of language informed by linguistics that he advocates, he limits his interest to the distribution of meaning within a given system, while explicitly dismissing as purely speculative the question of the origin of language dear to traditional philosophers:

The ideal act by which, at a given instant, names would be distributed to things, by which a contract would pass between ideas and signs, signifieds and signifiers, this act remains in the realm of ideas [*dans le domaine de l' idée*]. (III D 213, E 160)

If we eliminate all speculations about mythical beginnings, as well as all ways in which the subject (say, intentionality) or the object (reference) may play a part in the elaboration of a theory of language, what remains is the *langue* into which each individual is born. In his long development about naming, Saussure takes aim at two major historical foils. The first is reference: words do not name objects; the scheme *———a is inadequate to represent the workings of signs. The Cratylic discussion is neither right nor wrong: it is irrelevant. The second point is more delicate: not only do words not name objects, claims Saussure, but they do not name concepts either. As we remember, the original figure he used to represent the dual nature of the linguistic sign established a vertical relation between the signified and the signifier, pictured by a vertical arrow.

This model implied an intrinsic rapport between a concept and its signifier. Even though the two were inseparable, they were distinct. What is more, the vertical arrow suggested that the signifier was indeed something on the order of a name given to the concept. In his discussion of the biblical scene, however, Saussure brings in a different model, in which the elements do not interact vertically, as previously, but horizontally:

The immediate consequence of this new model is that words no longer name concepts either. They merely interact so as to divide up the sum of meaning among themselves (whether meaning can be summed up is a question Saussure never addressed). Hence Saussure's remark about the "serious fault of philosophers" who hold that once a sign is created, the designated idea (signified) remains unchanged, whereas, he says, it is always subject to change due to the effect that a possible variation of a second term may have upon the first. The true figuration of language would have to take into account the ways in which differences and oppositions distribute all the meaning available to a community into blocks (units) and the mutual dependence of these blocks on one another: a variation in the distribution of signifiers will affect the distribution of the concepts to which these signifiers relate. For example, Saussure claims that if *langue* had only two signs, the sum of meaning would be divided equally between them; if a third sign were added, it would proportionally reduce the allocation of meaning of the original two. The foremost characteristic of linguistic units is their relativity within the system—independent of any external "reality," be it objective or conceptual. In the Saussurean philosophy of linguistics, words refer neither to objects nor to concepts.

The obvious outcome of these two points is that linguistic units can forever shift around and that all attempts to provide them with an anchorage are "serious faults of philosophers." The semantic charge of each unit remains quasi-constant only by virtue of the overall cohesion of the system. The architectural model is that of a geodesic dome, rather than a post-and-beam building. The vertical deictic aim of language vanishes. *Con* would not name an object, or even a concept (both require vertical arrows); it would merely interact within its system in a horizontal manner, and since its system is *langue*, it would not have to relate to extralinguistic elements at all.

What, then, of the first schema representing the dual nature of the sign with a vertical arrow? One might think that upon finding a better formulation, Saussure simply changed his mind and adopted the second schema with horizontal lines only. This was not the case, however, as the two diagrams coexist throughout Saussure's Notes and teaching and indeed make their way into the *Cours*. More importantly, how can Saussure object so emphatically and repetitively to an approach to language that would entail taxonomies while maintaining his theory of the dual nature of the sign in which the arrow between the signifier and the signified is indeed vertical, thus implying that the combination resists contamination with other terms?

A comparison with traditional rhetoric may elucidate this last question. Today the distinction between denotation and connotation is widely accepted. In different contexts (cultural, historical, social, etc.) the same word may have different connotations. Its connotation is a function of the system (contexts) in which the word occurs: it operates horizontally. At the same time, despite the variety of systems and connotations, its denotation remains untouched—at least theoretically. The resistance of this denotation to contextuality implies the very same vertical relationship Saussure attributes to the first schema of the dual nature of the sign. Traditional rhetoric admits that part of the semantic charge of a term is subject to circumstances while another essential part resists all changes. Clearly something has to resist semantic permutations and contaminations if we are to agree on the meaning of linguistic units and communicate among ourselves. Saussure himself traces this resistance to "the immutability of the sign," which he attributes to the general cohesion of the system and the speaking mass. But if this is the case, his emphasis of "the true figuration a ↔ b ↔ c" no longer holds, since words will not be free to interact horizontally: their immutability will limit their horizontal interaction and thereby force on them the vertical relationship that Saussure suggests when presenting the dual nature of the sign. The relation illustrated by the vertical arrow (the distinction between the signified and the signifier and their combination as a sign) and the horizontal arrow (the way in which signs split all meaning among themselves) is one of diametrical opposition and mutual exclusivity. To make matters worse, Saussure himself is of little help since at different times he seems to favor the one or the other without attempting to circumscribe their respective frames of operation or influence.

The question cuts farther once we notice that in his lectures, Saussure consistently uses the examples of *arbor, apple,* and *equus,* simple nouns and indeed "definite objects for the senses." Even more disturbing is that these examples rely on the very same view of the translation of taxonomies that he himself denounces so vehemently:

> The word *Apfel* is just as capable as *pomme* for designating the known fruit. (II R 14, E 270)

> The idea of sister is not linked by any inner relationship to the succession of sounds *s-ö-r* which serves as its signifier in French; that it could be represented equally by just any other sequence is proved by differences among languages and by the very existence of different languages: the signified "ox" has as its signifier *b-ö-f* on one side of the border and *o-k-s* on the other. (*Course,* 67–68).

If the ideas of sister or ox are clear and universal, as the examples imply, then these ideas are the signifieds. This of course requires the signifieds to be permanent and only the signifiers to be variable. As a result, language *would* be a taxonomy whose function it would be to designate ideas, while these ideas themselves would be fixed representations of natural objects. There would be a "known fruit" that can in turn be designated by *Apfel, pomme, apple,* or any other sign. Linguistic mechanisms would then hinge on the same representation of objects by con-

cepts and concepts by language, elaborated by the Stoics that he so ve-
hemently rejects in his discussion of the linguistic value.

However disturbing these examples are when compared to Saus-
sure's opposition to taxonomies or, more precisely, when compared to
his claim that the value of a term is determined by the system as a whole
rather than by representation, we must emphasize that they are per-
fectly in line with his presentation of the dual and arbitrary (unmoti-
vated) nature of the sign. We could have overlooked or indulgently dis-
missed an infelicitous example given in the heat of a class discussion,
but this is not the case. The example is perfectly suited to the context: it
illustrates the two faces of the sign as well as the arbitrary manner in
which they combine in a given language to form a sign and hence to
signify. The rift is therefore not between the theory and the example but
between two different aspects of the theory itself, namely, the dual na-
ture of the sign and the value of a term as determined by the overall
system. The problem of iterability so dear to Derrida was a difficult one
for Saussure: if entities have to remain identical to themselves in order
to be recognized and to allow for communication by becoming the units
of language, what of the free play of values that is essential to *langue* as
a system?[34]

The "immutability" of the sign further complicates this problem: an
individual cannot change at will the system of differences and opposi-
tions that determines the two faces of the sign; nor can one change the
way in which the "slice of sound" is cut and made to signify. At any
given moment, entities are therefore predetermined. A *horse* is a horse,
fire is fire, *he placed* is "he placed." Each of these terms is an entity
whose function is to name some corresponding reality—difference or
not. In short, it would seem that, seen synchronically only, Saussure's
definition of the sign-entity relies in fact on a taxonomy despite his ve-
hement claims to the contrary. This unsettling aspect of Saussure's defi-
nition of the sign was so blatant that Godel and Benveniste, among the
most prominent Saussurean linguists, both noted the problem and tried
to come to Saussure's rescue.

The Quarrel over the Arbitrariness of the Sign

In 1939, Benveniste attempted to account for this inconsistency by
relating it to Saussure's view of the arbitrariness of the linguistic sign.
For Saussure, the link between the signified and the signifier is arbitrary:
nothing in the sound *chair* evokes the concept chair by some instrinsic

quality it carries. In other words, there is no reason for the signifier *chair* to correspond to the signified chair—hence the arbitrariness of the pairing up of the signifier and the signified (this should not be confused with the Cratylic discussion about the arbitrary relation between words and things). After having used the word *arbitrary,* Saussure suggested replacing it with the term *unmotivated,* that is, "for which no reason or cause is given." This would have explained the nature of the arbitrariness he had in mind. Had the editors followed his recommendation, they would probably have avoided the nitpicky and unproductive scholarly discussion about the arbitrariness of the sign that ensued. Speaking on the dual nature of the sign, Benveniste rightly comments:

> It is clear that the argument is falsified by an unconscious and surreptitious recourse to *a third term* which was not included in the initial definition. This third term is the thing itself, the reality. Even though Saussure said that the idea of "sister" is not connected to the signifier *s-ö-r,* he was not thinking any the less of the *reality* of the notion. When he spoke of the difference between *b-ö-f* and *o-k-s,* he was referring in spite of himself to the fact that these two terms apply to the same *reality.* Here, then, is the *thing,* expressly excluded at first from the definition of the sign, or creeping into it by a detour, and permanently installing a contradiction there. . . . There is thus a contradiction between the way in which Saussure defined the linguistic sign and the fundamental nature which he attributed to it.[35]

Benveniste's observation is correct: a third term *is* implied, which he calls the thing or reality, and we call the referent. He is equally right in underscoring that the very possibility of the existence of such a term is in contradiction with the fundamental nature Saussure attributes to the sign, namely that the semantic charge of the sign (its meaning) is not fixed but constantly derived from the play of all values in the system.

Benveniste finds Saussure's contradiction unacceptable and feels compelled to resolve it—at any price to the richness and complexity of the thinking that led to that contradiction. In order to correct Saussure's "error," Benveniste tightens the relation that unites the signified and signifier, thus making it practically impossible to distinguish between them and to isolate a signified such as the *idea* "sister," which presupposes the existence of a referent, sister. In Benveniste's version of the Saussurean sign, no longer are the signified and the signifier two viewpoints on the same object, as Saussure suggested; a viewpoint still permits the process of abstraction against which Saussure warned his students, and this abstraction in turn might enable us to conceive of a signified or a signifier independently of its counterpart. Benveniste therefore replaces the image of the sheet of paper (that can be observed from either one of its sides) with a new term: the *consubstantiality of the signifier and the signified*—hence establishing a necessary rather than arbitrary relation between them. He reserves the term *arbitrary* for the relation between signs and referents, that is, in the Cratylic tradition, the relation between the order of words and the order of things. Now, if the signified and the signifier are consubstantial, we can no longer evoke the signified alone (let alone the referent); consequently we can discard the ghost of reference that threatened for a while to fix the play of values. With this correction Benveniste hopes to rid *langue* of Saussure's uneasy distinction between the two faces of the sign and of the possible intrusion of nonlinguistic elements into the study of linguistics.

It is worth emphasizing that not once does Benveniste wonder what brought Saussure to contradict himself. Nor does he reexamine the part of the theory that he wishes to retain, so as to check whether the contradiction might not fulfill some function after all. His "solution" follows the law of the excluded middle: an object cannot have properties A and not-A at the same time. One of them has to go. In this case, Benveniste keeps the one with which he identifies (the free play of values) and, with the help of additional distinctions and historical considerations, reduces the not-A to A. Note that I am criticizing not so much his "solution" (the notion of consubstantiality of the signified and the signifier) as the attitude and ideological bias that brought him to adopt it rather than reexamining both A and not-A and weighing the ways in which they may complement each other or enter into any other relationship.

Unfortunately, except for a quarrel that has generated over a hundred articles, the results of his correction prove meager: the discussion tends to emphasize one answer at the expense of another, instead of examining what is at stake in Saussure's embarrassing contradiction. Most of the contributors to the discussion merely took sides with the champion of their choice, so that the string of essays reads like a ballot. With few exceptions the most common practice of the participants in the quarrel about the arbitrary nature of the sign seems to rely on searching the *Cours* for evidence that would support the author's stand while overlooking the evidence that would invalidate it. Since we are dealing with a contradiction in the *Cours*, the task was relatively simple: each party gathered ample material. I found the reading of this string of papers repetitious and tedious.

Benveniste attributed the confusion to the times: Saussure was, after all, a product of his time and was imbued with "the historical and relativist thought of the end of the nineteenth century," according to which "the infinite diversity of attitudes and judgements leads to the consideration that apparently nothing is necessary" (Benveniste, 44). Therefore, writes Benveniste, Saussure was not equipped to distinguish between *necessary* and *arbitrary*—which in turn caused some regrettable inconsistencies in the theory. I do not find this historical alibi very convincing: the contradiction in the *Cours* goes much deeper than a quarrel over terms; even if the term *arbitrary* had been systematically replaced with *necessary*, the contradiction would have remained. As I said earlier, it had to do not with an unfortunate choice of words but with two conflicting theories that Saussure presented simultaneously and held until his death, despite his awareness of their conflict.

Like Benveniste, Godel underlines the difficulty. He notes that "if the two elements of the sign cannot be separated except by an abstraction, what does one say to the concept *'boeuf'* compared to the signifiers *Ochs* and *boeuf*, if not that this results from a double abstraction: the one which separates the signifieds 'boeuf' and 'Ochs' for their respective signifiers, and the one which identifies them with a *concept given in itself, outside of all langue [hors de toute langue]*" (SM, 196). In stressing the negative effects of the "double abstraction," Godel remains faithful to Saussure's teaching: if indeed one abstraction is bad, two must be twice as bad. How could Saussure have been guilty of the very same bad practice against which he warned his students? Moreover, the consequence of this bad practice is not a vague extrapolation but something that Saussure himself stated very clearly (the idea of sister or ox) and that, as Godel is quick to point out, is "a concept given in itself, outside of all langue," that opposes and even neutralizes the play of values characteristic of *langue*.

Against his better judgment, Godel then tries to defend Saussure: the master could not have "meant" something in such striking contradiction with the rest of his teaching. Ergo, it must have been a conscious and perhaps unfortunate simplification of the relation between the nature of the sign and its value, which the master had presented in the heat of a class for the benefit of his bewildered students "out of pedagogical concern" (*par souci pédagogique*, SM, 195); therefore, "this reference to preexisting concepts, no doubt legitimate for the signs of other systems (signals, maritime flags, coats of arms), can only be *a ruse of the presentation [un artifice de démonstration]* when it comes to *langue*" (196). The argument is hardly convincing: in order to "simplify" his teaching, would a pedagogue as scrupulous as Saussure actually modify his presentation of one sticky point so as to contradict and undermine the very foundation of the theory so dear to his heart? Can a pedagogical concern lead to a contradiction? Aren't contradictions even more confusing for students? Can a strategy that modifies the most essential point of the theory still be considered a mere ruse? Can such a radical deviation from the general principle be reduced to *un artifice de démonstration*—especially when it comes to bear on every subsequent aspect of Saussure's philosophy of linguistics? These points did not escape Godel's probing eye: his only argument in favor of his hypothesis is that the consequences of the contradiction in Saussure's teaching would be so far-reaching and so damning for the theory that an explanation *must* be found to exonerate Saussure ("If this hypothesis was to be discarded, one would have to admit a hesitation on his part about the importance [*portée*] of the fundamental principle of linguistics, perhaps [*sinon*] a contradiction" [195–96]). Even so, acccording to Godel's explanation, the division of the sign into a signifier and a signified was then, at best, an unfortunate pedagogical simplification that resulted essentially—ipso facto—in contradicting the general theory.

I do not think that this was the case. There is indeed a "hesitation" in Saussure's thinking, as Godel noted (it probably contributed to his reluctance to write the *Cours* himself). I see little value in attempting to lessen the hesitation or mitigate the tension by attributing hypothetical motivations to Saussure himself. The contradiction lies not in the theory but in its object (in language itself): Saussure could neither resolve it nor abandon one of its alternatives. Instead, he was pulled in different directions by the irreconcilable demands built into language itself. Driven first to one extreme, then to the other, he was in the thrall of the very same opposites his methodological discourse had set out to master. Even in the relatively simple and dogmatic Introduction of the second course, he acknowledges the difficulty that an object, itself riddled with contradictions, presents for the discourse of science: "*General linguistics*. Linguistics is not simple in its principle ⟨in its method,⟩ because *langue* is not. At first sight, it seems quite the contrary: *langue* appears within reach. . . . This is an illusion. *Langue* offers the most disturbing contrasts to those who wish to grasp it from one side or another" (II R 1, E 244). Linguistics may well present "disturbing contrasts," but in doing so, it only reflects the disturbing contrasts found in language. If Saussure's theory did not acknowledge them, it would shamefully simplify its object. The difficulty encountered by Benveniste and Godel, but mostly by Saussure, accounts for one of the most troubling of these contrasts: the need for some anchorage that would secure meaning and communication (but would result in a taxonomy) in a system in which only oppositions are said to be meaningful.

To define the problem better and, mostly, to evaluate better the degree of Saussure's awareness of the difficulty—rather than impute it to his naïveté (Ogden and Richards), to the editors (Culler), to the times (Benveniste), or to the pedagogical imperative (Godel)—we must delve into the chapter on value, which is conceptually inseparable from the elaboration of *langue*.

Value

The chapter on value is the most difficult in the *Cours*. The concept is undoubtedly complex, but this fact alone cannot account for the difficulty of the chapter or the reader's perplexity. This original impediment is compounded by editorial choices: while the rest of the *Cours* relies mostly on the third course, the chapter on value elects the second course as its primary source. This shift entails methodological changes. Of all of Saussure's pedagogical experiments, the second course is the clearest and most comprehensive; but it is also the most aphoristic, assertive, and dogmatic—hence its relative simplicity. The editors' choice seems therefore irreproachable: faced with a variety of texts with differing degrees of clarity and explicitness, they chose the clearest and most comprehensive for their platform. Since they were aiming for a "reconstruction" of the "definitive form" (*Course*, xv) of Saussure's thinking, they also incorporated into their text scattered material collected from the Notes and the third course and inserted these fragments at the appropriate points of Saussure's second course. But here precisely is the catch: the pieces of the puzzle do not fit to form a clear picture.

A glance at the history of *value* in Saussure's teaching may help us to understand why this chapter presents such difficulties. Unlike other key concepts of his teaching, the term was not coined by Saussure for the courses—he had used it from the beginning of his writing and teaching days. Nor did he ever declare that he was conferring upon it a new meaning (Hans Aarslef, for example, traces the term back to Taine and Bréal[36]). Be that as it may, from the beginning *value* was the key term in the elaboration of Saussure's thinking (unlike the role it plays in the theories of Taine and Bréal); as such it was continuously retested, revised, and refined.

The editors did not find the clearest version of "value" in the second course by chance. Around 1908 or 1909, Saussure thought that he had found the proper place for value in the theory and that he could finally give it a definitive form; at no other time in his teaching did he present the concept so assertively and clearly—albeit dogmatically. Of course we can also speculate that since he chose to sketch a *comprehensive* theory, he simplified the most recalcitrant aspects, out of pedagogical concern. This was, we remember, one of the choices he had to make as a teacher, one that he found paralyzing ("At each step I found myself stopped by these scruples" [above, n. 5]). However we choose to interpret his scruples, one point is clear: never before or after 1908 did Saussure offer such an unproblematic picture of value.

A comparison will bring forth the nature of the difficulty encountered by the editors. When speaking about the dual nature of the linguistic sign (concept/sound image), Saussure was describing what was, in his mind, a well-delineated "object." He knew exactly what he wanted to say. Already in his days at the Ecole des Hautes Etudes (1881–91), he affirmed the dual and purely conceptual nature of the sign (it was, in a nutshell, the theory he presented some twenty-five years later in the courses); for him the linguistic sign was a clear "thing" (see above, n. 27) that he had to present to his students using the very inadequate lexicon of comparative linguistics. Throughout his career he grappled for the right expressions, all the while deploring the lack of such expressions in French, until he coined his own on 11 May 1911, two years before his death. Thus the task of the editors was relatively simple: once they decided to adopt *signifier* and *signified*, they substituted the new terms for Saussure's previous lexical experiments. In the margin of Sechehaye's collation, we can find their explicit resolution: "We shall make everywhere the proposed substitution: signified for 'concept' and signifier for 'acoustic-image'" (Collation, 299, E 152). The case of *value* is exactly the opposite. Unlike that of *signifier* and *signified*, the inauguration of *value* cannot be pinpointed to a particular moment: Saussure never said "and now, let's call this phenomenon *value*". He had a word, whether from Taine, Bréal, or someone else; however, the "thing" for which this word stood kept evolving in his mind. The result is that throughout his career, the exact meaning of *value* changed; there were occurrences where *value* encompassed all the categories of meaning and others where Saussure tried painstakingly to distinguish between related terms such as *valeur, significativité, signification, sens,* etcetera—terms that he wound up discarding. More importantly, the relation between "value" and the rest of Saussure's philosophy of language and linguistics kept shifting. This fact made the montage work of the editors delicate: for fear of reproducing inconsistencies in the *Cours*, they had to interpret Saussure. So they interpreted.

See, for example, Sechehaye's jubilant remark in the collation's margin, when he unraveled the mysteries of Saussure's quasi-synonymous experimental terms: "I believe I have interpreted well this puzzle: *signification* and *sens* are synonyms and *that which surrounds* [*ce qui entoure*] must mean the occasion, the context, and not the relations which establish the value as one might believe." To which Bally replies, still in the margin: "In fact, de Saussure never defined signification." (The sentence that gave them such a hard time was: "From the system, we arrive at the idea of value, not of sense [*sens*]. System leads to term. Then one will see that signification is determined by that which surrounds" [Collation, 447, E 261]). On yet other occasions, they refrained from interpreting and inserted into the *Cours* the numerous sections on value from the early Notes. Since these Notes were not as sharp and focused as their counterpart in the second course, however, their insertion into the *Cours* has a disorienting effect on the reader.

To make matters worse, the third course proves the most innovative in particular with respect to value: the euphoric optimism of the second course gave way to self-criticism and perplexity. Of particular interest to us are the numerous occasions on which Saussure expressed his awareness of the conceptual difficulty underlined later by Benveniste and Godel. While we can detect traces of most of these remarks in the *Cours*, they are so understated that they carry very little weight—especially when compared to the self-confident and assertive tone of the rest of the chapter.

Because the editors of the *Course* weeded out the sentences in which Saussure's hesitations and detractions blurred his point, I shall proceed in three steps: first, in order to clear the ground, I shall present the relatively simple and unequivocal aspects of value that emerge from a reading of the Notes and the first two courses; next, I shall present Saussure's doubts and quasi retractions and situate them in the context of the quarrels that followed. Finally, I shall underscore their importance both for a theory of language and for my own interest in language and literary criticism.

On "value" and "system"

"Value" and "system" are inseparable in Saussure's thinking. There can be no system whose terms would not carry value, and vice versa: there can be no value unless it is part of a system ("Every value implies a system of value" [N. 23.6, p. 5, E 177]). As we have seen before in Saussure's criticism of the biblical scene in which Adam names the animals, the formation of meaning cannot be a name per object, as in

Naming does not take place between objects and words following the pattern *(object)→a(word); rather, it boils down to the "effect" that results from the "opposition" between the terms, as reflected by Saussure's cherished pattern (word)a↔(word)b↔(word)c, while the objects (*) are implacably excluded from this dynamic. Moreover, adds Saussure, taking up linguistics' side in its controversy with philosophy, "if an object, wherever it be, could be the term upon which the sign is fixed, linguistics would cease instantly to be what it is from ⟨top⟩ to ⟨bottom⟩" (N. 12, p. 19, E 148). Thus we cannot speak of two distinct objects, one called sheep and the other mutton; only the juxtaposition of the two and their coexistence in the same system will guarantee their semantic difference, that is, the *value* of each. Saussure lists other examples: "By the same token the synonyms *to fear, to dread* [*craindre, redouter*] exist only the one next to the other; '*to fear*' will take on all the contents of '*to dread*' in the event that *to dread* does not exist. This would also be the case for '*dog, wolf*' even though one considers them to be isolated signs" (II R 18, E 261). Adam would be naming not dogs and wolves but the difference between dogs and wolves. We can view this process as Boolean logic: the two animals fit the same description (let's call it D) except for some difference (or in Saussure's term, an opposition). Thus if a dog is D, a wolf would be: "D but not domesticated." By subtracting the latter from the former we get the opposition from which the value of each is derived.

Carried to its outer limit, this principle could hypothetically yield a language in which there would be only two terms (but not a language with one term): "Reciprocally, if in some impossible way one had chosen in the beginning only two signs, all the meanings [*significations*] would be divided up between these two signs. One would designate one half of the objects and the other, the other half" (III D 213, E 160). Again, we may picture language as the proverbial pie: the pie is the totality of all possible meaning; to cut it would result at least in two parts—although the number of portions is theoretically infinite. The number of portions would determine the size of each portion—and vice versa. The system—the pie—remains *one*. If one person "pigs out," there will be less for the rest, and a redistribution will be in order. In other words, the size of the pie—its oneness—imposes certain limitations: ten persons cannot each have a quarter of the pie, even if, as a good hostess, I would like to satisfy all of my guests. This principle limits the arbitrariness or even the "immotivation" of each portion-sign. "Every language [*toute langue*] forms a corpus and a system. . . . It is from this perspective that it is not entirely arbitrary and that we must acknowledge a relative causality. The contract between signs and ideas is more complicated, and we ought not to consider it like this: ȯ ȯ ȯ but like this: o——o——o" (III C 316, E 163, trans. mine).

This conception is already apparent as early as 1878, in the *Mémoire sur le système primitif des voyelles dans les langues indo-européennes,* which Saussure published at the age of twenty-one. The work was an overnight success in the philological community. In it, Saussure inferred the existence of a yet unknown vowel in Sanskrit. The details of the demonstration are of little importance for the present reading of the *Cours*; what matters is the method that led the young scholar to his spectacular discovery. He did not "find" the missing vowel by scanning archives, nor did he present any tangible proof to buttress his thesis. Instead, he started off from the hypothesis of Sanskrit as a highly regulated system in which certain relationships among sounds could be observed. Then, insisting on patterns of differences in the formal functions attributed to these sounds (rather than on their actual sonant substance), he traced an "opposition" for which the system of vowels known at that time could not account; hence he inferred the existence of an intermediate phoneme that shared some properties with vowels and others with consonants. His discovery did not consist so much in adding a sound to Sanskrit (he never ascribed his find a sound value) as in demonstrating the existence of a function (or "move") for which there was no known value, like an algebraic x. It is as if he were witnessing a game of chess in which the king were invisible, and then he had to infer its existence by observing the board before and after each move of the invisible king. The missing vowel and the invisible king can enter into a quasi-infinite number of actual combinations (moves) with the other elements of the game during one session, and yet this interaction is highly codified and limited. We shall say, then, that in some respects each move is arbitrary (the invisible king can make any number of moves on the chessboard, depending on the player's talent, logic, knowledge of the game, mood, etc. in the same way a phoneme can combine endlessly with other configurations—all of which are arbitrary with regard to the game being played); but at the same time, it cannot make just any move or combine phonemes in just any manner, since the relationship it entertains with the other terms of the given system precludes some moves. The consistency of the interdependence of the system and the terms (or *langue* and sign) in Saussure's thinking is, as I stressed in the section on the critiques of the *Cours*, remarkable. In the courses, Saussure surely refined his theory; but mostly he problematized it.

A more elaborate comparison with the game of chess will further illustrate the basic tenets of the system. Each piece on the board has a certain value determined by its relation to the other pieces. We call them pawns, knights, kings, and queens. The names are obviously borrowed from a certain social and political order. In Britain, for example, there are knights, kings, and queens. The names of the pieces do not refer to the existing social order, however: their power (their value) holds only in and for the game. It would be semiotically absurd to rename the pieces congressman, senator, and president in the United States. What does matter is that each of them can move in ways that give it more or less power within the rules of the game. Whether the balance of power is knight/king/queen or congressman/senator/president is irrelevant—hence the absurdity of my proposed democratic improvement. This is, I believe, the meaning of Saussure's refusal of the pattern ○ ○ ○ and his preference for ○↔○↔○. Value (the ability to perform within the system) is determined not by some outside object (congressman or knight) but by the relations between the terms of the system.

Notice that the value of a unit taken in isolation is also unmotivated: a knight could just as well have had a Z-shaped move. Nothing intrinsic dictates the value of each piece. *The system is always there;* without it the value of a piece would be reduced to that of the material of which it is made. We then reach one more paradox: it is because there is a system that there are values that, viewed from outside this system, seem arbitrary. But it is also because there is a system that this arbitrariness is limited: I cannot arbitrarily change the value of the pieces; I cannot say, "Kings are more fun; let's have only kings." Nor can I "knight" my pawns to raise their value in recognition of their past services. The internal cohesion of the system and its acceptance by a collective body guarantee both the mutability and the immutability of signs and values, their absolute arbitrariness as well as their relative motivation *(une raison relative).* (This paradox is nonetheless absolutely essential: it is for not having understood it that Carroll's Humpty Dumpty is irremediably shattered.)

In summary, my exercise in single-mindedness on the chessboard illustrates the priority of the system over the terms ("not to begin with the word or the term in order to deduce the system. This would be to believe that the terms have an absolute value in advance; on the contrary, it is from the system that one must begin, from the solidary whole" [III D 269, E 256]). At the same time it reminds us that the very priority of the system constitutes *une raison relative*, limiting the arbitrariness of signs and even the free play of value.

Now, let's imagine that in the middle of a heated game, one of my pawns rolls under the couch. Since moving the heavy couch could prove quite an endeavor, I instead place a quarter on the board: my quarter will not *be* a pawn; it will not look like a pawn; and still, it will have the value of a pawn, so that the game can go on without any further hindrances. Then although in one sense my quarter is not a pawn, in another, it is. Instead of a quarter, however, I might have found in my pocket a nugget of gold. Would I claim that, since gold is so much more precious than either a wooden pawn or a quarter, my nugget should be promoted to the status of king? The argument would be absurd again: whatever the value of gold may be on Wall Street (a different system), on my board a nugget is and will remain a pawn. Ultimately, a gold nugget, a quarter, or a piece of wood do not have any intrinsic value: as they move from one system to another (from Wall Street to a chessboard), they acquire different values. Thus in Proust, *faire catleya* becomes synonymous with "to make love," although nothing in the word *catleya* invites a priori erotic connotation: for a gardener or a botanist, catleya is but a flower. *Faire catleya* owes its erotic value to the referential circumstances in which it entered the play of meaning the first time (for a sharp contrast, see Frege's example of Bucephalus, p. 99).

This relativist position is not entirely satisfactory. What scientific claim can a science make for itself, if the units on which it bears are not recognizable from one occurrence to another? Can linguistics be a science without fixed recognizable units? Are we not setting ourselves up for a game of croquet with Alice and the Queen of Hearts? In other words, can Saussurean linguistics account for the confusion between a woman's genitals and a mouse? Saussure was indeed the first to raise this question: "Viewed in its ⟨internal aspect, in its very object⟩ *langue* is then striking, ⟨for there is its prime characteristic⟩ as not presenting concrete units ⟨first of all⟩, and *without us being able to give up the idea that there be some,* and that it is their play which makes langue. ⟨Here is the first point: *a character that turns into a problem*⟩" (II R 35, E 242). Is there or is there not a "concrete unit"? Does "the idea that there are some" imply that this idea is right or wrong? If the idea is "wrong" and there are no predetermined concrete linguistic units, there should be no *"problem."* If, on the other hand, a character turns into a problem, this must result from a contradiction in the theory. A comparison with the editors' version of this segment will illustrate their malaise when faced with an ambiguous statement of the master. They write, "Language then has the strange, striking characteristic of not having entities that are perceptible at the outset and yet of not permitting us to doubt that they exist and that their functioning constitutes it. Doubtless we have here a trait that distinguishes language from all other semiological institutions" (*Course*, 107). Their version is fairly faithful to the original except in one respect: what was a "problem" in the source becomes in the *Course* "a trait [*un trait unique*] that distinguishes language from all other semiological institutions." Whereas the final statement is generally in line with Saussure's thinking, the *problem* with which he was grappling is ironed out in the wording of the *Course*. The editors did not go so far as to remove the contradiction—they only removed Saussure's awareness of the inconsistency, trying to integrate it in the homogeneous "theory" by sheer fiat. Unfortunately, their effort to remove the *problem* wound up dulling the sharpness of Saussure's insights and exposing him to undeserved criticism.

And a problem it is: if there are recognizable units, the peasant will soon discover his error and consummate his marriage; if there are not, he will go through life cherishing mice. To my knowledge, Saussure did not offer a definitive solution, that is, one that satisfied him (see: "As for a book on this subject, one could not imagine it: it must, says Mr. de Saussure, give the *definitive* thought of its author" [interview with Riedlinger, 19 January 1909, *SM*, 30]); instead, he tried to reformulate the problem itself. I believe it is to avoid this troublesome question that he eventually suggested the replacement of the words *word* or even *unit* by *term*, taken in its accepted mathematical sense: "from the moment we say term instead of word the idea of system is evoked . . . The latter divides itself [*Ce dernier se décompose*] among certain terms which are not so easy to distinguish as they might seem" (II R 35, E 242).[37] Whereas we expect a sign or a word to be an autonomous entity, we know that a term enjoys a certain relativity, say a relativity attributable to its function in a system: different values represented by different signs can occupy the same position. In an algebraic equation, for example, we can use any letter of the alphabet to represent a value; we can even tamper with the value itself as long as we change all the other values accordingly, so that their relations remain constant within the equation. Thus if $x = 2y$, as long as the actual values remain proportional, they can be 2 and 4, 100 and 200, 7 and 14, and so on.

Despite this improvement, after replacing *unit* with *term* and evoking the idea of a system, the question remains intact; we still cannot quite give up the idea that there must be, within the evoked system, some permanent units for us to examine; and it remains the more troublesome when we recall the taxonomic implications of Saussure's presentation of the dual nature of the sign, signifier/signified. If we could abandon the idea that there are units of some kind, what, then, of the dual nature of the sign? of the sign itself? What, then, of the signified in particular? What of Benveniste's criticism of Saussure and of the long discussion that followed his "correction"? What of the peasant's predilection for mice?

There is no easy answer. Although he was well aware of the problem ("a character that turns into a problem"), at no point did Saussure indicate that he was willing to abandon either his theory of the dual nature of the sign or his theory of value. We must then try to understand why he chose to maintain at the very heart of his theory a contradiction that he found problematic. More importantly still, we must try to understand how the theory of the dual nature of the sign and the theory of value relate when brought to bear simultaneously upon language.

Saussure on the Relation between Signified and Value

The *Course* could lead the reader to think, with Benveniste, that Saussure was not aware of the difficulty—or at least not aware to the point of discomfort. As the manuscripts show, such a view would be downright wrong. In the third course, after his dissatisfaction following the theoretical euphoria of the second course, Saussure consistently views value against the backdrop of the signified. More often than not, he also deplores his inability to distinguish properly between the two and states his awareness of possible contradictions between them, all the while emphatically maintaining that the distribution of meaning into discrete terms results only from the play of values. Not once does he indicate that one of the two theories may be dropped.

A quick comparison between the second and the third courses will illustrate Saussure's growing awareness of this difficulty. In the second course, he proposes clear distinctions: "Value, this is not signification. Value is given by other givens; ⟨it is given, in addition to signification,⟩ by the relation between a whole and a certain idea, by the reciprocal situation of the pieces [*pièces*] in *langue*" (II R 52, E 257–58). I take *signification* here to mean "signified" (let's not forget that Saussure would not coin the word *signified* until two years later). Here then, value is *added* to the signified ("in addition to signification"). The two are definitely distinct. First, there is an unproblematic sign consisting of a signified and a signifier; only then comes a "certain idea" whose reciprocal situation with the whole modifies the original semantic charge of the signified ("idea" is not clear; is it a "term" to which a context is added? an utterance? *parole?*). Pragmatically speaking, this original signified would then be a theoretical substratum, while at any time a subject uses language to express a "certain idea," we shall have to reckon with value. In short, not only do I see very little difference between this presentation and the more traditional distinction between denotation and connotation, but I also find it strongly tinted with realism.

Two years later, in the third course, Saussure presents a very different picture in which "a word does not exist without a signified as well as a signifier. But the signified is only the sum [*résumé*] of the linguistic value which supposes the play of the terms between themselves [*supposant le jeu des termes entre eux*], in each system of *langue*" (II D 284, E 264).[38] Now, this passage says that the signified is only the sum of value; this time, then, the signified is denied a distinct existence. In fact, in this passage, I see no difference between signified and value: to all intents and purposes, they are synonymous. The signified is no longer a substratum: on the contrary, it is the end result. It does not precede the play of values; it sums it up. In light of this new twist, what remains of the distinction between *value* and *signified* emphasized in the second course? Is *signified* another word for many values generically connected so as to form a "sum" (a sort of bundle of values)? As we can see, the second passage is much more aware of complexities and liabilities. And yet it must be noted that even as he factually reduces signified to value, Saussure holds on to the theory of the dual nature of the sign ("a word does not exist without a signified and a signifier")—all the while undermining it by stressing the priority of the play of values over the rigidity of the signified. We might have questioned the logic and tenability of such a position if Saussure had not already done so himself: "Value is surely an element of sense [*sens*]. But it is important not to take the sense first, other than as a value. [It is] *very difficult to see how the sense remains dependent and still distinct from the value*" (III D 270, E 258, trans. mine). Value here is but one component of sense. Is the signified another? Risking an answer to this question may prove delicate since the word *signified* is not featured in this sentence, and its exact extension may be a case of skewed semantics rather than of cloudy thinking: even after he had already coined the terms *signified* and *signifier*, Saussure continued to use other synonyms of which *sens* is the most frequent, so that it would be risky to determine whether *sens* here is synonymous with *signified* or is a generic semantic category, subsuming both signified and value. What is clear is that whether *sens* is synonymous with *signified* or not, it makes up the whole of which value is a part. One way or another, then, Saussure takes back with one hand what he gives with the other: even as he states that value is a component of sense, he hurries to add that sense is nothing but value. Now, clearly, the part cannot equal the whole, and this simple arithmetic could not have escaped the attention of a thinker as rigorous as Saussure.

Once more, Saussure anticipates our comments: he underlines the difficulty and analyzes its components with a much more critical eye than his critics have ever done. In a key development that, like most of the instances in which he expressed his sense of confusion and frustration, was not reproduced in the *Cours*, he muses:

> And here is the *cave* (Bacon) containing a trap: it is that ⟨the⟩ signification appears to us as the counterpart of the sound image and equally as the counterpart of the terms coexisting in *langue*. We have just seen that *langue* presents a system where all the terms can be considered as linked

> The value of a word will result only from the coexistence of different terms; value is the counterpart of the coexisting terms. *How does this get confused [comment cela se confond-il] with that which is the counterpart of the sound image?* Other figure, series of boxes [*cases*].

		signified	
		sound image	

> The relation on the inside of a box and between boxes is very difficult to distinguish [*Le rapport à l'intérieur d'une case et entre les cases est très difficile à distinguer*]. (III D 271, E 258–59)

> Signification as the counterpart of the image and signification as the counterpart of the coexisting terms gets confused [*se confondent*]. (Constantin's rendition of the same sentence, III C 392, E 25–59)

Saussure starts out with a very reassuring statement: signification is the counterpart of both the sound-image (signifier) and the coexistent terms in *langue* (value). This would lead us to believe that the two are distinct but compatible, just as the *Cours* implies. Yet no sooner has he appeased our qualms than he raises a disturbing question: speaking of value, he wonders *comment cela se confond-il avec ce qui est la contrepartie de l'image auditive* (how does it get confused with the signified)? If the two are as distinct as the opening of the paragraph suggests, one can hardly see Saussure's problem. At this point, instead of answering his question, Saussure backtracks and draws an alternate diagram. To illustrate graphically the difference between signified and value, he puts them both on the same diagram (his second diagram). This is the only diagram on which he puts the two together; even so, when the two figure on the same diagram, the arrows disappear altogether, because, as he readily admits, he no longer knows how meanings are derived—he no longer knows if meaning is derived vertically ⊂⊃↑or horizontally ↔o↔o↔o. (It is highly ironic that in the *Cours*, the editors combined all the diagrams and ended up with one that solves the problem graphically—not conceptually—but that Saussure himself never drew. Their diagram appears as

[*Course,* 115] and maintains the horizontal arrows, which Saussure had eliminated.) Saussure's second diagram works: the two appear graphically distinct. Now is he satisfied? Clearly not, since he reaches the conclusion that despite the apparent ease of distinction in the diagram, the two concepts are in fact very much alike (Dégallier writes *"difficile à distinguer"* [hard to distinguish] and Constantin writes that they *"se confondent"* [get confused]). The closer he is to ironing out the difficulty with rhetoric and gadgets (diagrams), the more emphatically he warns his students against the "trap" he is laying for them.

At the end of this thorny discussion, Saussure concludes that "from the system, we arrive at the idea of value, not of sense [*sens*]. System leads to term. Then one will see that signification is determined by that which surrounds it" (III D 275, E 260). This last quotation implies that the vertical arrow between the signifier and the signified is no longer functional. Such an important deviation from the original theory did not escape the attention of the editors, who then "corrected" Saussure, reaffirming the need for the verbal equivalent of a vertical arrow by adding one more sentence nowhere to be found in the sources—against all logic and against their sources: "Being part of the system, [a word] is endowed not only with signification but also and especially with a value, and this is something quite different" (*Course,* 115). Of course, the readers of the *Cours* are then left in the dark as to how these two modes of production of meaning work together, and how "this is something quite different" (different from what, exactly?).

These examples show the acuity of Saussure's perception of the problem that I am painstakingly raising in this book, namely, the incompatibility between the exigency for a fixed meaning of words, essential to communication, and the contamination of meaning due to the interaction of each unit with others around it (be it *langue*, as in Saussure's case, or the semantic aim and the semiotic values that I propose). It should be stressed again that not once does Saussure give us cause to believe that he even considered dropping one of the two theories so as not to weaken the other or the theory as a whole. Clearly, the signified would have been a good candidate since it was the one sore element in an otherwise very cogent theory. Indeed, such were Godel's and Benveniste's positions in the quarrel over the arbitrariness of the sign. The editors, on the other hand, opted for a compromise: they did not drop either of the conflicting theories, but they did eliminate the explicit indications underscoring the problem, as if this could ensure that no one would notice the contradiction.

To better understand why Saussure held on stubbornly to his perception of the dual nature of the linguistic sign and the importance of the signified, I remind the reader of Frege's warning quoted in the epigraph of this chapter. Saussure must have realized that unless we maintain some fixed units, we may lose our grip on knowledge and wallow in confusion. He must also have known that his elaboration of the concept of value denied the possibility of such fixed units. If value is the result of endless differences and oppositions within a system, we may easily imagine subgroups who share special views and interests (subsystems) and whose system of differences and oppositions would be slightly different from the rest of their *langue*-speaking community. De Mauro, for example, goes as far as imagining that since each individual is a subgroup of sorts, we could wind up with private languages.

> A variation, however minimal, of the lexical background [*du patrimoine lexical*] between two individuals (and one senses that these variations are generally not small but very great . . .), ought to make one conclude, and does make one conclude if one wants to remain loyal to Saussurean premises, that two individuals are always speaking different languages because, leaving aside the exceptional case of perfect and total coincidence between two personal linguistic backgrounds, even the words which appear externally alike by phonetic resemblance or seemingly obvious similarity of denotation are in reality words with different signifieds, because inserted in different networks of relations.[39]

Despite the obvious absurdity of this prognosis, it is perfectly logical if and only if we eliminate the semantic anchorage provided by the signified, and if we quantify differences so that even the slightest difference becomes a radical otherness—something Saussure would never have agreed to and would have easily refuted by evoking the immutability of the sign: some variations may be possible from one subgroup to another, but the cohesion of the system is such that these variations remain minimal and cannot result in private languages; they may result only in insignificant differences. A case in point is Saussure's example of the letter *T*, which can be written in a number of ways, depending on personal handwriting, and still remain a *T* as long as it is distinct from the other letters of the alphabet—not an *L*, not a *P*, not an *H*, or any other letter.

So, for Saussure, the signified stays. He then faces two choices: either he leaves a blatant contradiction at the heart of the theory (which he does part of the time), or he eliminates the contradiction by resorbing one concept (consistently the "signified") into the other ("value"), in which case he falls prey to Frege's prediction. In other words, either he accepts a new model for sexual behavior—and I doubt that mice will ever do—or he calls the peasant on his error, urges him not to use terms not anchored in reality, and finds a way to integrate into the theory the warning given to the peasant—which would mean radically reversing the theory. Needless to add, he did neither.

Bally

Bally, one of the most creative and philosophical of Saussure's followers (and one of the editors of the *Cours*), took note of this aspect of the problem and proposed a distinction between *signification* and *valeur*,[40] according to which the former would be the minimal denotation of a term, almost indexical in its specificity (his example is "the tree that I see from my window")—which is not without posing yet a different set of problems. Bally suggests that *signification* stands for a factual and sensorial representation *(représentation actuelle, sensorielle)* and I take it to be equal, in extension, to the simplified Saussurean signified. Conversely, *value* refers to a "virtual concept," that is, the maximal virtual semantic field that a subgroup can associate with a term, within a given language (in this manner, Bally contains the free play of values so as to secure the minimum general agreement among speakers necessary for communication): "The word tree is not thought in exactly the same way by a botanist, a logger, a carpenter, or a painter; for a veterinarian the steer and the sheep are first of all castrated animals; most people ignore this 'detail' or hardly think of it. Finally—a borderline case because it comes from *parole*—one of the elements of the associative field can, in a given circumstance, dominate at the expense of all the others:

a traveler moving painfully along a road drenched with sun will think of a tree uniquely for its shade." The result of this distinction is in fact very similar to the familiar pair denotation versus connotation. It is also of particular interest to us, since it closely parallels Frege's analysis of *Vorstellung* (see the section on *Vorstellung* in chap. 3), a category that he sets out to exclude from any serious theory of language. The snag in this otherwise elegant theory is that it is still subject to contradictions— at least theoretically: if value can be purely subjective, and if it can dominate at the expense of all the other semantic fields, as is the case in the example of the tired pilgrim, then we could end up—at least theoretically—with private languages, one language per person. What would then become of communication?

Furthermore, Bally's refinement leaves the theory more vulnerable than ever to abuses. In Saussure, the immutability of the sign protected it from semantic changes from one person to another and hence protected the theory from the threat of private languages. Since a tree entertains many semantic rapports with other terms in *langue* (it is alive but not an animal, a plant but not grass or a flower, a big bushy thing but not a shrub or a bush, etc.) it is unthinkable that its ability to provide shade would ever overstrike these other differences and oppositions. Bally's example is not to be confused with the case of the young peasant. The difference between the silly peasant and Bally's pilgrim is precisely that the peasant did not change any of the relationships that *con* entertains with other terms in language; neither did he privilege one over all the others: *con* remains opposed to *vit* in the system of sexuality while at the same time relating to the activity *foutre*. Even the word *animal (bête),* which the peasant uses to refer to the mouse, is a known euphemism for a woman's genitals, so that in some respects, it maintains exactly the same relationship with the system (see: "I'll fuck it anyway, to know if *what is said about it* is true or not, *that in cunt is a sweet and pleasant animal*"). The difference between the peasant and Bally's pilgrim is that the latter assumes that reference is intuitive. Even as he evokes only one of the aspects of a tree (its shade), the pilgrim clearly knows what a tree looks like and would probably not take the shadow of, say, a kite, for the shade of a tree. This assumption, shared indeed by Saussure, is precisely what the *fabliau* puts into question and what our study sets out to explore.

Bally's distinction could have been very useful if he had restricted it to *langue*. Not only did he shift to *parole*, however, but he took the case of an individual outside any social context: the man is alone and not engaged in communication (in the *fabliau*, as long as the peasant is alone, he can err to his heart's content: only when he enters the realm of communication, i.e., shifts from private and idiosyncratic use of language to the presuppositions encapsulated in *langue* and acted out by *parole*, do things go awry). As Bally half-recognized, the example was simply not appropriate ("a borderline case because it comes from *parole*"). Indeed, this is a case of a refinement that might have worked, if it had not been for a faulty example; at the same time, the faulty example illustrates perfectly the extent to which Bally's refinement was vulnerable to abuses. In shifting unexpectedly from collective *langue* to private *parole*, Bally lost the protection and relative anchorage of the immutability of the sign and fell prey to an idiosyncratic sense of value.

Two parenthetical details are worth noting at this point: first, it is highly ironic that Bally would develop and defend Saussure's theory of signification since, in Sechehaye's collation of the third course, there is a note in Bally's handwriting complaining that "in fact, de Saussure never defined *signification*" (Collation, 447, E 261). Whose theory is he then presenting in his article? Surely not Saussure's, since by his own admission he does not know what it was. Second, I doubt that Bally grasped the full implication of Benveniste's criticism. In 1940, the year in which he published this essay redefining *value* so as to thwart further critiques, he published a short note in collaboration with Albert Sechehaye (the second editor of the *Cours*) and Henri Frei (one of the many contributors to the string of essays on the quarrel inaugurated by Benveniste). After a series of picky arguments, the authors conclude, "In truth we do not see on what basis the doctrine of the arbitrariness of the sign was criticized [*nous n'arrivons pas à voir en quoi la doctrine de l'arbitraire du signe a été entamée*]: one attacks it openly, but when one gets right to it, one concedes in passing everything which constitutes it." [41] This statement is strange. As we saw, the doctrine of the arbitrary conjunction between signifier and signified was radically criticized (*entamée*) by structuralist linguists such as Godel and Benveniste, who saw value as the founding block of the theory. Before them, it was radically *entamé* by Saussure himself: "value" cannot ground and constitute the entire semantics of signs if the signified remains the way Saussure defined it. The two are strictly antithetical, so that one cannot concede both, as the authors of this article contend. Saussure certainly saw this point, and it is surprising that Bally and Sechehaye, the editors of the *Cours* responsible for the skillful removal of most traces of his doubts (hence they must have been aware of them), refused to admit to the difficulty. That Bally did not fully "see" this point ("we do not see on what basis . . .") may also explain his unorthodox conception of value in the first article: there was indeed something he failed to see—an oversight that is manifest in the two essays he wrote that year. The truth of the matter is that the point of the quarrel was not *"the* doctrine": Saussure never elaborated *a* "doctrine." Even the *Cours* did not. At most it advanced two doctrines: if the doctrine of the arbitrary nature of the sign is not *entamée,* then the doctrine of *langue* and value must be. Conceding one of them must entail dismissing the other and, in the process, radically impoverishing Saussure's teaching. I find Bally, Sechehaye, and Frei's essay an enigma.

Saussure in Perspective

Saussure's influence has spread far beyond the limits of linguistics. If his teaching was so readily adapted to anthropology, history, philosophy, psychoanalysis, and other fields, it is because it offered a method, a way of asking questions and organizing both knowledge and the enquiry into knowledge. The aspects of his thinking that have influenced our modernity the most are, first, the revolutionary adoption of *langue,* that is, of a system in which everything is corollary and which therefore ought to be considered only synchronically, for the object of a science; second, the analysis of the dual nature of the sign (and the ways in which it purported to eliminate reference and limit the arbitrariness of the sign to the relation signified/signifier); and third, the emphasis on value as the product of the respective pressures exercised on the mass of meaning by the units of the system. I have therefore organized my reading of Saussure along these three lines.

Two aspects of the method, which have given rise to critiques and quarrels that reach beyond limited linguistics, have especially retained our attention: the first is that in language everything is corollary from everything else, so that there is no proper ontological or epistemological starting point; and the second is that Saussure knowingly presented conflicting theories to his students, mostly because he could neither reconcile nor discard either of them.

Clearly, what made history is not the manuscripts, which I quote at length, but the *Cours* itself, however "faulty" it might have been (I prefer the term *unfeasible*). As it is, the *Cours* has already made its mark on the way we think and write today. It is one of the monuments of modernism. My project was therefore not to establish what Saussure *really* thought, taught, or wrote. I have no more attempted to "correct" the *Cours* than I would the Homeric corpus if I had stumbled upon its manuscripts and had been able to attribute them to a dozen people living at different times. If we were to write a different reconstruction of Saussure's teaching today, it would be just that, a *different* reconstruction: it would not nullify Bally and Sechehaye's reconstruction. My interest in the manuscripts stems from a concern other than the legitimate respect for and insistence on the accuracy of a particular report. It comes from having realized to my surprise that Saussure was in fact one of the most acute and probing critics of the *Cours*—anachronism notwithstanding. The manuscripts indicate a vision and comprehension of both the details and the scope of the problems that the *Cours* raised or created—unmatched by Saussure's harshest critics. My effort was therefore not so much to rehabilitate Saussure in the eyes of contemporary readers as to present yet another critique of the *Cours*, one that I find more suggestive, provocative, and poignant than anything I have read on the subject.

3   Frege

*Il n'y pas du tout d'expression simple pour les choses à distinguer
primairement en linguistique. Il ne peut pas y en avoir. L'expression
simple sera algébrique ou ne sera pas.*

SAUSSURE

The Difficulty of the Project

It seems paradoxical to evoke Frege in a study about language and
literature. Although he had had minimal training in philosophy as a
student, he was first and foremost a mathematician by training and vo-
cation. During his lifetime he was a rather obscure, frustrated professor
at the University of Jena whose writings attracted little attention, even
though he exchanged letters with Husserl, whose first work, *Philoso-
phie der Arithmetik,* he criticized in a sharp review of the book in 1894,
and was admired, mostly privately, by Russell and Wittgenstein.

Today, however, Frege is regarded as the founder of modern logic
and of the analytic philosophy of language. It is largely accepted among
philosophers that his major contribution to mathematics is one of
method as much as content: he introduced logic and mathematics to
each other, while advocating the importance of logic as the methodo-
logical foundation of mathematical thinking. Until then, logic had been
regarded as part of philosophy, not of mathematics. Frege's involvement
with logic was thus innovative not only for mathematics but also for
philosophy: he showed philosophers new uses for an old tool. Today, if
in some branches of philosophy (in particular in analytic philosophy)
logic has come to replace epistemology as the foundation of any query,
it is due largely to the new vistas that Frege's work has opened on the
subject.[1]

Of particular interest to us is Frege's ferocious antipsychologism. He
saw in the distinction between subject (or the subjective) and object (or
the objective) a *sine qua non* for any attempt to account for science,
philosophy, or language. The subjective is, so to speak, in the head of
the speaking subject: as such, it is not verifiable and perhaps not even
communicable. Rather than to a precise science like mathematics or

philosophy, this subjective belonged to psychology (for which Frege had little respect).[2] He dreamed of a radical formal separation between the object examined, the act of examining, the intention of the examiner, the means used in the examination, and those used to convey and communicate the results of such examinations. Only the objective entered the field of his intended investigation, while elements presenting any threat to the neatness of his distinctions were vigorously ruled out of the scope of his theoretical endeavor.

Among such elements the most salient was undoubtedly language: his own as well that of other mathematicians. Frege wanted to secure two related conditions: 1) that scientific language be as precise and unambiguous as a mathematical formula; and 2) that scientific thought be communicated among scholars, without leaving room for ambiguities or misunderstanding. He held that one's responsibility as a philosopher was not only to think properly but also to ensure that one's thought was perfectly accessible to others, so that no element extraneous to that thought would alloy with it as it is transmitted to other philosophers. We can therefore understand why it was so important that the meaning not be in the head of a person: another person would then not have access to it or at least would never be sure that the meaning in his or her head was indeed the very same meaning that was in the first person's head. How would they know for sure that they were speaking about the same things or agreeing about the same thoughts? Unless we secure meanings, all scientific disagreements may very well be quarrels over words. Scientific communication and inquiries into truth require that we weed out all subjective contributions to meanings (and the ambiguities they cause), so as to end up with "pure thought," that is to say, objective thought, which could be communicated unadulterated. Language should then be the most discreet and inconspicuous of media and its effects limited to its use as a vehicle for pure thoughts.

That this sounded like a Christmas wish list did not escape Frege's attention: natural languages clearly fell short of this goal. His logic was then irreproachable: since natural languages were inappropriate, he would create a different kind of language, free from the ambiguities that plagued natural languages. The title of his first major work sums up the thrust of his intellectual enterprise: *Begriffsschrift; A Formula Language, Modelled upon That of Arithmetic, for Pure Thought.* This "formula language" of absolute logical precision (*Begriffsschrift*) would remedy the shortcomings of natural languages. So now Frege had a marvelous tool that, he thought, would eliminate misunderstandings and ensure proper communication among scholars. He was confident that as soon as they fully understood his language, scholars would bow to its inescapable logic and gladly adopt it—which would open a new era for science. A last step separated him from his goal, however: he had to bring his new language to the attention of other scholars, to present, explain, and teach it so that all scholars could use it. And yet, in what language was he to present his "formula language, modelled upon that of arithmetic, for pure thought"? The only means of communication available to him was natural language—the very same natural language in which he saw the source of all scientific evils and to which he did not want to entrust his thought to begin with; the same natural language that he was discrediting and that he had set out to bypass by means of his formula language. The catch is obvious: to communicate his formula language properly, he had to raise natural language to a level of precision as close as possible to that of a formula language, so as to present with it the formula language intended to supersede it. Frege then found himself compelled to rescue natural language, to "purify" it, in order to be able to use it against itself.

Ironically, then, Frege's need for precision undercuts his original project: if indeed natural language can achieve the degree of clarity and precision necessary to present and communicate the formula language without imprecisions or ambiguity, then the said formula language will become superfluous; if, on the other hand, natural language does not lead itself to unambiguous expression, then this very expression (muddled, ambiguous, equivocal, etc.) risks betraying the formula language that it purports to present to readers. The logician would then need to perfect this mode of expression by means of another mode of expression; in short, this logician would be caught in a web of infinite regress.

Perhaps more importantly, driven by a keen desire to communicate his thoughts in a way that they could not be misunderstood or misconstrued, Frege began to wonder about the precision of his own expression. Realizing that the imprecision of the natural language he was using set a limit to the precision of his own expression, he turned his attention to the logical precision of natural language (or lack thereof), hoping to remedy its shortcomings; only then could he communicate his thought without risking ambiguities and misreadings ("If our language were logically more perfect, we would perhaps have no further need of logic, or we might read it off from the language. But we are far from being in such a position. Work in logic just is, to a large extent, a struggle against the logical defects of language, and yet language remains for us an indispensable tool.")[3] Thus, paradoxically, Frege's desire to avoid ambiguity and to find a new formal language as sharp as a mathematical formula caused him to dwell on the old natural language and, consequently, to deal precisely with that which he had set out to eliminate.[4] In a telling footnote, Frege wistfully acknowledges this paradox.

> I am not in the happy position here of a mineralogist who shows his hearers a mountain crystal. I cannot put a thought in the hands of my readers with the request that they should minutely examine it from all sides. I have to content myself with presenting the reader with a thought, in itself immaterial, dressed in sensible linguistic form. The metaphorical aspect of language presents difficulties. The sensible always breaks in and makes expression metaphorical and so improper. So a battle with language takes place and I am compelled to occupy myself with language although it is not my proper concern here.[5]

Frege's problem underscores our earlier distinction between the deictic and semantic aims of language. If, unlike a mineralogist, the philosopher cannot *show* her or his object, it is not only because the realm of things and words are radically distinct; nor is it simply the result of the imperfect mimetic properties of language. Rather, the philosopher's inability to show the object attests to the intrinsic existence of something that interferes with the deictic aim of language, "something" that we assign to the semantic aim and the semiotic values (see chapter 6). The conflict is essentially Kantian in that it opposes the truth of "showing" to the errors of "telling." Frege's move was typical of Lyotard's "theoretical" mode: as natural language was, *ipso facto*, becoming the object of his inquiry, he adopted a metalanguage, that is to say, scientific categories bearing on this object. He believed that these categories would function like compartments into which he could sort out the elements of natural language, tidy up its mess, and, only then, entrust his thoughts to it.

His inquiry eventually led to the distinction between sense (*Sinn*) and reference (*Bedeutung*), a distinction that has had unprecedented repercussions for analytical philosophy and has come to constitute the most fundamental tenet of the Anglo-American school of the philosophy of language. In this respect his most important essays are "Über Sinn und Bedeutung," ("On Sense and Reference") (1892) and "Der Gedanke. Eine Logische Untersuchung" ("The Thought: A Logical Inquiry") (1918). I shall therefore focus primarily on these essays and refer to other writings only inasmuch as they complement them.[6] As I noted in the introduction, my purpose is not so much to introduce the reader to Fregean logic and philosophy of language as to explore his theory's realm of application. More importantly, I intend to highlight the limits of this realm of application; underscore the reasons, standards, and criteria used to demarcate it and its "outside" (namely, *Vorstellung*); explore the implications of these reasons, standards, and criteria for the theory of language they entail; and, finally, examine the relationship between the theory's realm of application and its outside. I must also admit from the outset that my own inquiry is hardly disinterested since this outside to which the theory refuses linguistic and logical legitimacy includes literature and rhetoric—two projects to which as a student of literature I am deeply committed.

When daily parlance already has a close equivalent for a more precise philosophical or logical expression, I shall, at the risk of ignoring some logical distinctions, avoid the jargon of logic except when using specific Fregean terms. Since this book is intended primarily for scholars engaged in literary studies and therefore unaware of the discussions to which these specific terms refer, the subtleties of logic might create unnecessary difficulties. At the same time, I shall do my best to ensure that my use of daily language does not alter the spirit of the theories presented.

"On Sense and Reference"

As Frege's concern with language stemmed from a need to establish perfect equivalences between the objective world, his thoughts, and their expression, he opened his essay on the nature of linguistic signs with a question about the nature of the relation most apt to express equivalences: equality. The question proved embarrassing since language relies on equivalences between two orders that are essentially incompatible: the order of things and the order of language. Furthermore, can we even say that equality is a relation? It would follow that we should be able to say that identity is a relation, too (Frege does not distinguish between identity and equality: since his viewpoint is logicomathematical, he takes "$a = b$" to mean "a is identical with b" or "a equals b").[7] And yet, we intuitively perceive the relations that an object has to itself and to no other thing as something unique that cannot be adequately compared to other relations that objects may have with one another. Or again, perhaps, when I say that one thing is identical to another (as in his example, "Venus is the morning star"), I may be speaking not about these things themselves but about their names, thus establishing a relation between signs and not between objects. This in itself would be quite a satisfactory theory, were it not that this view of language entails that any cognitive statement bears on language only and not at all on the world that it claims to investigate and describe. Any time one of my utterances aimed at some objective reality, it would hit not that reality but some words representing it; these words, in turn, relate to still more words, to the effect that the objects will never stand in any relation at all to the words that are supposed to represent *them*.

This perspective may seem quite acceptable or even desirable to the student of literature, but it does little for the scientific spirit purporting to describe facts rather than words. More importantly still, if we hold— as Frege still did in 1879—that equality is a relation between names of objects only and not between the objects themselves,[8] would we not necessarily imply that the very words we were using to render such a relation are not themselves above such relations (at least not a priori), that they could be part of the very same set of relations (in our case, equality) that they are supposed to describe? (Such sets of relations would be comparable to Saussure's *langue;* however, it is clear from Frege's perception of *Sinn* and *Bedeutung* that he would have found *langue* as a system grounded in value totally unacceptable.) Our own so-called scientific discourse would then run two major risks: first, it could ultimately bring about a tautological discourse skidding dizzily into infinite regress (the young man's definition of *con* and *foutre* illustrates this risk [p. 11]); second, it could itself enter into a relation of equality with its object, thus mirroring the problems rather than solving them. Such a discourse would inhibit the possibility of knowledge, which, since Kant, depends on analytic truths free of linguistic ties. The philosopher would run the risk of speaking like the lad in the *fabliau,* who utters perfectly grammatical sentences while he himself is unaware that he does not know what he is talking about. Knowledge would then escape language and communication and would be confined either to endless verbal analogies bearing on words rather than reality or to mystical epiphanies that stand beyond the realm of words and therefore cannot be communicated without relying on some act of faith.

For science, this question is indeed pressing. It affects the foundation, and even the very possibility, of knowledge; at least it does so if by *knowledge* we mean precisely something outside language or psychology, something that language ought to describe but leave unchanged. If language exceeds this modest analytical function and, instead of obligingly serving in the quest for truth, starts reflecting upon itself, then it risks pulling the rug out from under the philosopher's feet. This perspective is particularly frustrating in that it can be dealt with, in turn, only by means of language, that is, with the indispensable help of the suspect. Socrates and Descartes may have had their demons, but these demons were very tame in comparison to Frege's: no longer an outsider like those of his predecessors, Frege's fiend lurks in the very language that purports to exorcise it, thus threatening to skew any effort to free the pursuit of truth from its malice.

What, then, of equality? Intuitively, we perceive an important difference between $a = a$ and $a = b$. While the former is a tautology (and is, in Kantian terms, analytic), the latter has a cognitive value: it tells us something that we may otherwise not have known about a and b; in other words, it informs us, imparts to us some knowledge. Thus in arithmetic, $5 = 5$ is useless while $2 + 3 = 5$ informs us that 2 and 3 are capable of being combined cumulatively and that this operation would yield 5; it also informs us that 5 can be split into 2 and 3. Similarly, the sentence "Venus is Venus" is a totally useless tautology: if the second *Venus* is supposed to be the predicate of the first, it does not predicate anything that the first does not already contain. But the sentence "Venus is the morning star" (one of Frege's favorite examples) imparts some information about Venus. Moreover, it then allows me to string other propositions into my equation: for instance, I can add to the last sentence "Venus is the evening star" and then, in a third step, construe that "the morning star is the evening star" (if $a = b$ and $b = c$, then $a = c$). Following this series of equations, I would have learned something that I might otherwise not have known about Venus, the morning star, and the evening star, and about their relationship to one another.

What exactly did I learn? Or, to go back to our initial question, did I indeed learn something about the object(s) Venus, morning star, and evening star—as science would wish it—or again about its names only (*Venus, morning star, evening star*)? To answer this question, Frege introduces the ground-breaking distinction between "object," "sense," and "reference."

Object (Gegenstand)

What is an "object"?[9] It is an expression that can function as the subject of a sentence (as opposed to its predicate); *grosso modo,* it is therefore what we *could* speak about (not what we *are speaking* about). Some objects are obvious: *tree* is an object; so is *person* or even *a single part of a person.* Expressions referring to concrete things that we perceive with our senses are thus evident objects. There are, however, abstract objects as well: words such as *malice, beauty, effort,* etcetera are not the names of concrete things; we cannot perceive malice, beauty, or effort with our senses, and, therefore, we cannot delineate them in the same manner as tree or person. And yet we can speak *about* them.

Now, clearly, this definition is subject to dire indeterminacies. For example, the peasant was "speaking about" a *con*. Can we say that the *con* was an object? Was it an object *for him?* Frege would probably answer at this point that the young man is of little importance as long as there is an object *con* about which the peasant could speak, even though he himself did not know what it was. (This clearly would do little to explain the lad's mishaps.) Therefore, while still wishing for the ideal simplicity of the model pertaining to concrete objects, Frege has recourse to a *formal* distinction: an object is that which can function as the reference (*Bedeutung*) for that part of a sentence that we would have traditionally called a subject. A *concept,* the object's counterpart, on the other hand, is exclusively predicative. In Frege's example "This rose is red," *this rose* is the grammatical subject for which *is red* is a predicate; as such, *this rose* is, in Frege's terms, an object. *Is red,* on the other hand, is a predicate; therefore it is a Fregean concept. We can avoid a possible taxonomic confusion if we remember that, for Frege, *object* is opposed not to *subject* but to *concept.* Thus the dichotomies are *subject/predicate* for traditional grammar, and *object/concept* for Frege.

It is noteworthy that a Fregean object rests on a formal distinction and does not refer merely to a thing, an existential entity. If the object were simply a distinct thing, it would stand outside the boundaries of Frege's investigation into language and would not pertain to the inquiry of logic, linguistics, or semiotics. A rock, a hand, a sculpture, the roots of a chestnut tree are man-proof, language-proof, "in excess" (*de trop*), as notes an anguished Roquentin in Sartre's *Nausea.* Inasmuch as its delineation is contingent on a virtual linguistic context, the Fregean object is therefore a function of language: it can be identified only within the framework of discourse (or, at least, of possible discourse). At the same time, however, this same object is not a linguistic entity either: it lies outside the boundaries of language; it is not my utterance but that which my utterance would be about if indeed I uttered one. Thus the Fregean object invites a double perspective: while it escapes the grasp of language, its formal delineation and definition nonetheless presuppose and require a linguistic backdrop; in a word, the object bridges the gap between the linguistic and the nonlinguistic worlds.[10]

Reference (*Bedeutung*)

A hair-thin line separates "object" and "reference." A reference is what we previously termed an object, *once this object is designated by a sign:* "The reference of a proper name is the object itself (*der Gegen-stand selbst*) which we designated by its means" ("On Sense," 60). This formulation harps on old questions. For once, it illustrates the problem of identity with which Frege opened his essay, thus underlining the in-escapable bind of "definitions": how are we to read *is* in Frege's sen-tence "The reference of a proper name *is* the object itself. . . ."? In other words, is this statement cut after *a* = *a* (analytic identity), or *a* = *b* (in which both expressions designate the same thing)? If we opt for *a* = *a,* we will be accusing Frege of a useless tautology, if not an absurdity (if object and reference are simply identical, there is no need for hair-splitting distinctions that dissolve into identity). We must therefore read the last segment of the definition, "which we designate by its means," as a proviso: only if and when we actually choose to designate an object by means of a proper name—only then does this object become a ref-erence. A reference is therefore the object previously noted, to which something is added: the reality of an utterance. From the viewpoint of language, one is virtual (although it has an actual existence outside lan-guage) and the other is actual: a thing we *can* speak about is an object, but a thing we *do* speak about is a reference. The object, previously a fence-sitter between the orders of words and of things, is thus decisively sucked into the linguistic space. A reference is akin to a point of view on the phenomenon, or more precisely, it is essentially the speaker's point of view on the selected object, the speaker's intention ("in order to justify mention of the reference of a sign it is enough, at first, to point out *our intention* in speaking or thinking" [61–62]).[11] Reference (*Be-deutung*) is neither the thing nor the object itself but the *intended* object.

By splitting meaning into two subcategories (*Sinn* and *Bedeutung*), Frege avoids the trap into which his initial treatment of equality-identity seemed to lead him. In one way, identity is between words only, but in another, it is between references. "Venus is Venus" is neither a relation of equality nor one of identity. It is a tautology. For there to be any relation whatsoever, the words on both sides of the copula must be different: thus "Venus is the morning star" fulfills the condition of equality. Despite their obvious difference, the expressions *Venus* and *morning star* are identical because the reference of both expressions is one and the same, totally unaffected by the choice of either one of the expressions; and since truth is contingent on reference only, it remains unaffected by the proliferation of senses.

This distinction constituted a radical innovation and a turning point in the study of language and truth: henceforth, philosophers engaged in the study of language could claim that their object was not simply the narrow field of language but the perennial and highly regarded philosophical investigation into the nature of truth. To Pilate's question "What is truth?" Frege's successors could answer that truth is a certain use of language, one in which *Bedeutung* functions properly, that is, in the predictable way determined by the rules of logic. Anything else became metaphysics.

It must be noted that in Frege's writings the word *Bedeutung* designates indifferently the bearer of the name and the activity of relating names and bearers: it is at once a thing and a relation.[12] This doubling is undoubtedly responsible for our occasional difficulty in distinguishing adequately between object and reference—at least in those cases when the term *reference* is used to designate the bearer of the name rather than the semiotic relation between that bearer and its name. Even in Frege's own writings we can find instances where, despite his usual meticulous taxonomic precision, he uses *object* as a synonym, for *reference*, and that without harming his argument. In "On Sense and Reference," for example, he juxtaposes them in a way that could lead us to believe them interchangeable: "to the sign there corresponds a definite sense and to that in turn a definite reference, while to a given reference (an object) there does not belong only a *single sign*" ("On Sense," 58).[13] In brief, words (or at least those defined as "a sign for an object" or, in Frege's terms, "proper names" ["On Concept," 47, n. 1]) are supposed to *designate* objects—in which case these objects become references.[14]

Frege notes a possible difficulty: exceptionally, an expression may lack a reference; such is the case with "the celestial body most distant from the earth" or "the least rapidly convergent series" ("On Sense," 58). King Arthur would be another example and with him the panoply of fictional characters. This seemingly harmless exception invites a host of questions and puzzles. For example, since, according to Frege, truth pertains only to reference, such expressions escape the truth criterion. And indeed, this is Frege's position with regard to another fictional character, Odysseus.

> The sentence "Odysseus was set ashore at Ithaca while sound asleep" obviously has a sense. But since it is doubtful whether the name "Odysseus," occurring therein, has reference, it is also doubtful whether the whole sentence has one. Yet it is certain, nevertheless, that anyone who seriously took the sentence to be true or false would ascribe to the name "Odysseus" a reference, not merely a sense; for it is of the reference of the name that the predicate is affirmed or denied. . . . We are therefore justified in not being satisfied with the sense of a sentence, and in inquiring also as to its

reference. But now why do we want every proper name to have not only a sense, but also a reference? . . . Because, and to the extent that we are concerned with its truth value. . . . It is the striving for truth that drives us always to advance from the sense to the reference.

We are therefore driven into accepting the *truth value* of a sentence as constituting its reference. By the truth value of a sentence I understand the circumstance that it is true or false. ("On Sense," 62–63, Frege's emphasis)

Truth is contingent on the reference only and not on the sense, and therefore, claims Frege, the truth criterion is not applicable to "Odysseus was set ashore at Ithaca while sound asleep." And yet how shall we account for our bored acquiescence with "King Arthur was a perfect knight" on the one hand, and our resistance to "King Arthur was a coward" (or "Odysseus was set ashore in America while sound asleep") on the other? Any intuitive reader, any child would indignantly rise to the defense of the defamed king and protest, "*No, this is not true! He was a knightly knight, a hero—as brave as they come!*" Indeed, there is no object by the name King Arthur and therefore no reference (*Bedeutung*). Still, we know that even though King Arthur is but a fictional character, somehow "King Arthur was a perfect knight" is more "true" than "King Arthur was a coward." Are there then different levels of truth, or even different kinds? Frege's answer to both questions would be vehemently negative.[15] And yet, as long as we retain his categories, if we want to account for our intuitive perception of the difference in truth value between the two statements about King Arthur—Frege's denial notwithstanding[16]—we will have no choice but to say one of two things:

1. "King Arthur" has a sense (*Sinn*) but no reference (*Bedeutung*); it follows that any perception of truth value will have to rely on that sense and not, as Frege would have it, on a reference—or even on some third aspect of the word still to be defined.

Or:

2. "King Arthur" does indeed have a sense, but it also has a reference. What it lacks is an object, a bearer for the name King Arthur, an actual man by this name who performed such exploits.

Needless to say, both assertions would be equally unacceptable on Frege's terms: the former because, according to him, truth value has no hold over sense; and the latter because a reference *has* to latch onto an object—without an object, there can be no reference.[17]

It seems to me that the difficulty lies in the distinction between ob-
ject and reference. Odysseus and King Arthur invite us to wonder what
is really missing: a reference—or an object? Strictly speaking, the term
reference should be reserved for instances such as those that enact the
ability of language to "designate"; but to be exact, how can language
designate something that is not there, that does not even exist? Al-
though Frege addressed the problem, his remarks on expressions that
lack reference are far from conclusive. It is clear, however, that within
the terms of his philosophy, any existential proposition should logically
bear on the object or even on the "thing" (which Frege does not dis-
cuss), but never on the reference. As reference pertains to the order of
language, or more specifically, to the capacity of the order of language
to "intend" the order of things (in "The Thought," Frege uses *hinzielen,*
"to take aim at objects" [296]), it cannot be the subject of an existential
proposition. Frege shows further inconsistency in stating that "in order
to justify mention of the reference of a sign it is enough, at first, to point
out our intention in speaking or thinking. (We must then add the reser-
vation: *provided such reference exists*)" ("On Sense," 61–62). Since *ref-
erence* implies primarily the speaker's viewpoint on the object ("our in-
tention in speaking or thinking"), the existence of a proper Fregean
object must precede the reference to it. In Frege's philosophy, (unlike
Saussure's), it would be totally aberrant to think that the point of view
creates the object; there can be no viewpoint on something that does
not already exist. The question of existence mentioned in Frege's reser-
vation is therefore irrelevant to reference as he previously defined it. To
be consistent with his own terms, Frege should have written: "provided
such *object* exists." What is missing in his examples of expressions void
of reference is not a reference as he would have it but an appropriate
object that would *become a reference if and when designated by these
expressions.*

This imprecision is largely responsible for further confusions: Dum-
mett, for example, seems to hesitate. On the one hand, he recognizes the
dependence of object and reference on language (see above, n. 10); on
the other, at other times, he does not acknowledge that a reference (or
more precisely, that part of reference which came to be recognized as
"the referent") is not simply an extralinguistic "thing." Not only does
he confuse reference and object (as did Frege), but he also sometimes
confuses the two with the actual designated thing. Hence the following
reasoning: What shall we do with reference? Nothing. Since reference
bears on objects (read: things), it does not pertain to meaning but to

other functions of language. "Reference is not an ingredient of meaning" (Dummett 84), therefore, theories of meaning (and Dummett takes Frege to hold just such a theory—which, given Frege's primary interest in mathematics and logic rather than language, I find questionable) need not concern themselves with it. Only sense is relevant to meaning.[18] But whereas Frege proceeds from sense to reference (the direction is irreversible: "it is the striving for truth that drives us always from the sense to the reference" ["On Sense," 63]) Dummett stops at sense. For Dummett, reference and sense do not belong in the same theoretical inquiry. Clearly, this radical distinction is possible only if *Bedeutung*— at least in its sense as "the bearer of the name"—is taken as an extra-linguistic entity.

I take this position to be in contradiction to Frege's analysis. I much prefer it when Dummett acknowledges that "*the objects which serve as referents cannot be recognized quite independently of language:* it is only because we employ a language for the understanding of which we need to grasp various criteria of identity . . . that we learn to slice the world up conceptually, into discrete objects" (Dummett 406–7). That this creates problems and inconsistencies for a strict "theory" is obvious, but to fancy that these problems can be resolved simply by discarding reference only negates something essential to the original theory and should not be proposed in Frege's name.

Furthermore, if we eliminate reference from the theory of meaning, we must also eliminate truth, which Frege pins explicitly and emphatically on reference. As dismissing truth is not an acceptable philosophical move, in Dummett's account truth slips back and forth between reference and sense, ending up mostly with sense. Thus Dummett can write contradictory statements, as in "The *sense* of an expression is, to repeat, that part of its meaning which is relevant to the determination of the truth-value of sentences in which the expression occurs" (Dummett 89), on the one hand, and on the other, "In Frege's view, it is precisely via the *reference* of the words in a sentence that its truth-value is determined" (93). In the first statement truth hinges upon sense and in the second upon reference. I must add that I find only the second in agreement with Frege (see "But now why do we want every proper name to have not only a sense, but also a reference? . . . Because, and to the extent that we are concerned with its truth value. . . . It is the striving for truth that drives us always to advance from the sense to the reference. We are therefore driven into accepting the *truth value* of a sentence as constituting its reference" ["On Sense," 63]).

Once more, we are dealing with a variant of the difficulties raised by the problem of heterogeneity. The orders of language and of things are clearly distinct. And yet we know that one of the functions of language is precisely to bridge the chasm between the two. The question—and this is the question I am raising throughout this book—is, how. In this case, the difficulty is compounded since, even as he eliminates the discordant element, Dummett must admit that *Bedeutung* "for Frege, is a notion required in the theory of meaning—in the general account of how language functions" (Dummett 84), and that it "has a vital role to play in the general theory of meaning" (93). Thus we end up with an odd, if not absurd, situation: the notion of reference is, by Dummett's admission, "vital" and "required" for a theory of meaning but, conveniently, is also not an ingredient of meaning and, as such, need not be questioned.

The fact is that Frege's theory rests, if precariously, on sense *and* on reference, on language *and* on its relationship to a nonlinguistic reality, on concepts *and* on the transition from concepts to existential phenomena: admittedly, accounting for apples and oranges may be delicate, but eliminating one for the other's benefit only distorts and impoverishes the general picture.

To avoid muddling the issue, we ought to examine the difficulty posed by reference against the backdrop of Frege's fierce opposition to "psychologism." If we define reference as a function of the speaker's intentions and volitions—as Frege implied at one point (see p. 86), it will no longer pertain solely to logic (and therefore will escape the grip of logical formulae): it will fall into the domain of the disciplines that deal with mental processes (primarily psychology). We cannot leave reference exclusively in the grip of psychology, however, since it most certainly belongs to language too: it is at once the link between the orders of things, words, and subjectivity; and it is also the basis for truth-value. It follows that logic may have to share in formulating the laws of language with the much denigrated psychology, as indeed was the case in the early writings of Husserl that Frege opposed so vehemently.[19] But then, the imprecision that Frege unflinchingly associates with psychology could drive a logical wedge in this formulation, so that his whole project of purifying language by following a mathematical model may fall apart.

In this perspective, I find it revealing that in "The Thought," written in 1918, that is to say, twenty-six years after "On Sense and Reference," Frege uses solely and consistently the term *object*. *Reference* is never used to designate the object; nor does it designate that to which the word may refer. In fact, throughout this essay, Frege does not once use the word *Bedeutung:* instead, he uses *object* exclusively (e.g., "For in both cases I have a statement that lacks an object" ["The Thought," 289]). It is not surprising that in "The Thought," where he grapples explicitly with psychology and idealism, he chose to avoid *reference* altogether: by bridging, and therefore muddling, the boundaries between language and the objective world, *reference* is exactly as we have seen, the term that risks opening the door to psychology or even idealism.

Today, we can only speculate about the extent to which Frege's avoidance of *reference* in "The Thought" testifies to his awareness of these consequences. Are we to deduce that he realized the difficulty I emphasized? Could he have decided to do away with *reference* and to reserve *object* for the referent? Did he find the psychological overtone of *reference* unacceptable? Or again, did he choose to condense the two into one concept (this last hypothesis is less likely)?[20] In the final analysis the case of the missing *reference* in the late essay only emphasizes the difficulty that I have already underscored: a theory purporting to show *how* language works (a fortiori, a theory that then sets out to ensure that words always designate the same objects and express the same senses) must grapple with incompatible elements such as words, concepts, things, and intentions—elements that simply do not add up. *Object* and *reference* were meant to bridge the gap, but as Zeno would show, such remedies are tentative at best. Frege's task was further complicated by the fact that his *Bedeutung* and *Gegenstand* were not always distinct; this was in turn compounded by his lack of attention to the distinction between the intended object and intending an object.[21]

Frege stood partly corrected by Ogden and Richards, who, in *The Meaning of Meaning,* called the bearer of a name the *referent,* and the mental process, the thought or intention to designate, the *reference.*[22] This correction is now largely accepted. I shall retain these terms, albeit with a word of caution. Let us call the bearer of the name a referent. At the same time, let us rid our terminology of the psychological and behaviorist inspiration that animates *The Meaning of Meaning:* my personal volitions have very little to do with the activity that I call reference. My words "refer" independently of my personal volitions and independently of my state of mind at that moment (if, at the table, I accidentally ask you to pass the pepper rather than the salt, pepper is what I shall get: although I neither want nor intend pepper, *my words* refer to an object, which in turn will spoil my soup). Referring is something that language, not the speaking subject, does. The speaking subject can only intend to refer. This is not to deny that speaking subjects are entitled to their volitions or that their intentions are, to some extent, constitutive of the final effect that their words may have; these factors do not enter into reference proper, however (I shall take them up later in the discussion of force and semiotic value in chapters 5 and 6).

Sense (*Sinn*)

To this somewhat problematic discussion of *reference* Frege adds a definition of *sense*: "It is natural, now, to think of there being connected with a sign (name, combination of words, letters), besides that to which the sign refers, which may be called the reference of the sign, also what I should like to call the *sense* of the sign, wherein the mode of presentation is contained. . . . The reference of 'evening star' would be the same as that of 'morning star,' but not the sense" ("On Sense," 57). *Sense* is probably the term that proved the hardest to define. We may say that it is the minimal semantic charge that *all* the speakers of a given language recognize as being carried by an expression. "Sense" is cognitive: it is the information that a name imparts to a speaker of the language about its referent. It was Frege's firm belief that all our linguistic expressions correspond to objective, if abstract, entities, and that the unadulterated apprehension of such abstract entities constitute the foundation of knowledge. A sense is not something we make up: it is unquestionably given (Frege's example of something that is objective is the equator or the axis of the earth). Thus an expression may vary, but its sense can no more be altered than can the axis of the earth itself. This is undoubtedly the most essential characteristic of *Sinn*, the one from which Frege's logic derives (it is also the aspect of Frege's theory of language that has contributed the most to earn him the name realist). Among the speakers of a language, the sense of an expression is akin to an epistemological a priori: it is not subject to one's understanding, beliefs, awareness, etcetera; nor is it subject to contingencies and accidents. "Sense" is where epistemology meets ontology.

Frege and Saussure

In one respect, Frege and Saussure agree on the immutability of signs (or at least on the immutability of the conceptual component of signs). If language is to be shared, we cannot simply change it at will. Frege's reasons for advocating this principle are very different from Saussure's, however: while Saussure believes that the most minute change of one element of language causes a chain reaction encompassing all of the others (hence the immutability *and* the mutability of signs), Frege insists on the independence of each individual sense and sees in this independence the condition for the immutability of signs and, in fact, for communication. We should therefore limit our comparison of Frege's theory to what Saussure's analysis of the linguistic sign might have been, had it not been tempered: 1) by Saussure's insistence on *langue* as a convention; and 2) by its play of values and its dependence on the global system. In this sense, Frege's *Sinn* is comparable to Saussure's signified (even so, we must add that the comparison is short-lived since the tension between signified and value in Saussure's thought displaces the fixity of the signified, thus preventing us from pursuing farther the analogy between the two thinkers[23]).

There is a second point of comparison between Saussure and Frege: both refuse to mix diachrony and synchrony and opt for a decidedly synchronic approach to language. See, for example, Saussure:

> Language [*langue*] is a system of pure values which are determined by nothing except the momentary arrangement of its terms. (*Course*, 80)

> Here it is evident that the synchronic viewpoint predominates, for it is the true and only reality to the community of speakers. The same is true of the linguist: if he takes the diachronic perspective, he no longer observes language [*langue*] but rather a series of events that modify it. People often affirm that nothing is more important than understanding the genesis of a particular state; this is true in a certain sense: the forces that have shaped the state illuminate its true nature, and knowing them protects us against certain illusions; but this only goes to prove clearly that diachronic linguistics is not an end in itself. What is said of journalism applies to diachrony: it leads everywhere if one departs from it. (90)[24]

And Frege:

> The historical approach, with its aim of detecting how things begin and of arriving from these origins at a knowledge of their nature, is certainly perfectly legitimate; but it has also its limitations. If everything were in continual flux, and nothing maintained itself fixed for all time, there would no longer be any possibility of getting to know anything about the world and everything would be plunged into confusion. (*Foundations*, vii[e])

> It is as though everyone who wished to know about America were to try to put himself back in the position of Columbus, at the time when he caught the first dubious glimpse of his supposed India. Of course, a comparison like this proves nothing; but it should, I hope, make my point clear. (viii[e])

A closer look at Frege's argument for synchrony and immutability will reveal that this line of reasoning is, to say the least, peculiar: some things escape continuous flux, he claims, but not by dint of some intrinsic property that would warrant their immutability (like Saussure's argument), but because, *otherwise*, we might be led to conclusions that he deems unacceptable. In Frege's version, the case for the immutability of some elements (of which *Sinn* is the most important) in fact begs the question: sense is unchangeable because the theory as a whole requires it to be unchangeable (and not because this conclusion is drawn from the argument itself through deductive reasoning). *Otherwise*, the theory may suffer. Even as he makes explicit what it is that hangs upon the discussion of flux and historicity, Frege confirms my reservations: we are in fact speaking not about language but about knowledge: "there would no longer be any possibility of getting *to know* anything about the world and everything would be plunged into confusion."

If indeed sense is the component that will identify reference, will lead us to pick the correct reference for a word, and if reference, in turn, enables us to establish the truth-value of the proposition in which the name is found, it is clearly essential for Frege that sense be unchangeable; *otherwise*, this proposition may be true at one time and false at another ("We must remind ourselves, it seems, that a proposition no more ceases to be true when I cease to think of it than the sun ceases to exist when I shut my eyes." [*Foundations*, vi^c]). How shall we then secure knowledge? Only if we anchor *reference* (and consequently truth-value) in an objective and cognitive *sense* can we account for a world that can be made into the object of science—at least if we share Frege's understanding of "object" and "science." But we have to remember that this is a requisite of the theory and not an observation about the nature of language, as Frege would have us believe.

There is one more sense in which Frege's inquiry parallels Saussure's: both thinkers were concerned not only with their particular ideas on their respective subjects but also (and firstly) with the delineation of their respective disciplines and the justification of their methods. They adopted very different paths, however: while Saussure's question leads to the elaboration of *langue*—that is to say, of a *system* in which relations prevail over objects or individual entities (hence the shift from "entity" or even "word" to "term," and the emphasis on value)—Frege shifts with unchangeable objects and proceeds to construct a theory in which, between these objects (the atomistic constituents of reality) and mankind, there is a set of immutable cognitive entities (senses) subject to one's apprehension. Upon such apprehension, one is led to reference, truth, and knowledge.

On the Objectivity of Sense

We are now in a position to understand better why it is so essential for Frege's distinctions that sense be objective. To the extent that the sense of an expression remains the same independently of the variety of speakers who may utter or even think that expression, this sense is not contingent on the capricious speaking subject. Sense is not *in* the consciousness of this or that particular speaker; nor is it affected by the volitions of a speaker. If communication is to succeed (and this was Frege's goal), then *Sinn* has to be *outside* that consciousness, forever identifiable as such, forever available to any speaking subject. It has to be some sort of object. Note that *objective* is not to be confused with *actual* or *real,* nor can it stand independent of reason (but, for Frege, reason itself is objective). In the *Foundations,* Frege writes: "I distinguish what I call objective from what is handleable or spatial or actual. The axis of the earth is objective, so is the centre of mass of the solar system, but I should not call them actual in the way the earth itself is so. We often speak of the equator as an *imaginary* line, but it would be wrong to call it an *imaginary* line in the dyslogic sense; it is not a creature of thought, the product of a psychological process, but is only recognized or apprehended by thought" (*Foundations,* 35ᵉ; translator's emphasis).²⁵ Thus objectivity, immutability, and universality are interdependent: each guarantees the other, and together they secure knowledge and truth.

This was Frege's answer to Skeptics and Idealists who questioned semantic categories (and consequently knowledge itself): simply stated, they claimed that our knowledge of the world is mediated by our imperfect perception and/or by the mental representations that we have of this world; therefore, we can know only our perception in representations of these objects, not the objects themselves (in Germany, the most notable Idealists were Fichte, Schelling, and Hegel; the British Idealists may also have been present in Frege's mind). By presenting sense as an objective entity, independent of percepts or representation, Frege hoped to escape the radical subjectivity and psychologism that had plagued some Idealists and to establish objective grounds for a new epistemology and perhaps even a new ontology.²⁶ Today the fear of the legacy of Idealism is underscored by Rorty: "One can imagine serious-minded philosophers on both sides of the Channel murmuring about 'idealism.' There is a deep terror among Kantian philosophers of a certain job-related health hazard: the philosopher, after overstrenuous inquiry into our relation to the world, may lose his nerve, his reason, and the world simultaneously. He does this by withdrawing into a dream world of ideas, of representation—even, God help us, of texts." ²⁷

Frege's *Sinn* mediates between the crude material object and pure consciousness: we cannot *show* one another our thoughts, therefore we resort to signs. Communicating a thought consists in expressing it for another person to apprehend. The apprehended sense will continue to exist in the world even after one has apprehended it (*fassen*); similarly, once apprehended, sense cannot be colored or contaminated by other subjective factors with which it may come in contact. The reasoning behind this exigency is familiar: if sense were at any given time exclusively in one person's consciousness, then others would not have direct access to it. They would be able only to guess the speaker's intended sense without any guarantee that their understanding corresponds to what this first person has in mind. This situation would entail the end of knowledge (at least of the objective knowledge Frege was advocating).

In a long and interesting footnote, Frege comments on this problem.

> Nowadays people seem inclined to exaggerate the scope of the statement that different linguistic expressions are never completely equivalent, that a word can never be exactly translated into another language. One might perhaps go even further and say that the same word is never taken in quite the same way even by men who share a language. I will not enquire as to the measure of truth in these statements; I would only emphasize that *nevertheless different expressions quite often have something in common, which I call the sense, or in the special case of sentences, the thought.* In other words, we must not fail to recognize that the same sense, the same thought, may be variously expressed; thus the difference does not here concern the sense but only the apprehension [*Auffassung*], shading and colouring [*Beleuchtung, Färbung*] of the thought, and is irrelevant for logic. It is possible for one sentence to give no more and no less information than another; and for all the multiplicity of languages, *mankind has a common stock of thoughts.* If all transformations of the expression were forbidden on the plea that this would alter the content as well, *logic would simply be crippled;* for the task of logic can hardly be performed without trying to recognize the thought in its manifold guises. Moreover, *all definitions would then have to be rejected as false.* ("On Concept," 46)

Frege was right: what hangs on this discussion—and indeed on my reading of the analytical texts—is the well-being and the validity of logic, and, by extension, of any theoretical discourse about language and literature: "If all transformations of the expression were forbidden on the plea that this would alter the content as well, *logic would simply be crippled. . . .* Moreover, *all definitions would then have to be rejected as false.*" Subjectivity or relativity can and will jeopardize language's usefulness as a vehicle for thought. Unless we can safeguard the stability and objectivity of semantic contents, we may have to revise knowledge as our Western tradition has come to define it. What is at stake here is not language per se but knowledge.[28] Whether Frege was a Realist or a Platonic Idealist is therefore best left to historians of philosophy. What matters for our inquiry is that it was a choice he made almost by default. His line of reasoning is as follows: science must go on, mathematics must go on; *therefore* logic will have to fend off all fiends (as we shall see, in particular, *Vorstellung*). *Otherwise,* knowledge will be lost. What I find interesting here is not so much the position (it is not very original) as the backward strategy: sense is objective and immutable not because it can be proved that such is the case but because *otherwise* . . . etcetera. Frege's whole philosophy of language is built as a dike against the flow of indeterminacy that threatens knowledge.[29]

This dike is grounded on one notion: "a common stock of thoughts" separates humanity from intellectual chaos (thought is to sentence as sense is to expression, so that in an argument they are for the most part interchangeable). In order to secure the all-important objectivity of thought and sense, Frege objects to the expression *to have a thought.* For lack of a better word, he suggests the verb *to apprehend:* "We do not have a thought as we have, say, a sense-impression, but we also do not see a thought as we see, say, a star. So it is advisable to choose a special expression and the word 'apprehend' [*fassen*] offers itself for the purpose. . . . In thinking, we *do not produce* [*erzeugen wir nicht*] thoughts but we *apprehend* [*wir fassen*] them" ("The Thought," 295).[30] Defined in this manner, the sense of an expression is immune to the objections Idealists might raise and allows the transition to reference and truth, and consequently to science and knowledge.[31]

An obvious difficulty arises: given that sense is crucial (it is the first step in reasoning), how are we to quantify and divide meaning (for lack of a better word), so as to circumscribe the minimal objective component that falls under Frege's definition of *Sinn* and is subject to apprehension? Obviously, an expression may evoke, in addition to this minimal universal element, a larger semantic field in a person's mind. Can we procure an epistemological divider between *Sinn* (and, by extension, *Gedanke*) and that which "exceeds" it? Can we identify this excess in a way that would not be empirically and pragmatically quantitative (contain more or less meaning, according to the circumstances in each case)? More importantly, even if we could delineate the part that pertains to *Sinn,* what are we to do with the excess?[32] To address these questions Frege introduces a third term, *Vorstellung,* to which he assigns all additional semantic charges.

Vorstellung

Frege notes that "a painter, a horseman and a zoologist will probably connect different ideas [*Vorstellungen*] with the name 'Bucephalus.' This constitutes an essential distinction between the idea [*Vorstellung*] and the sign's sense" ("On Sense," 59–60). When a horse is but a horse, we may speak of the sense of *horse*. However Bucephalus is not just a horse: it is at once more, and less, than a horse (in Saussurean terms, we would say that its value exceeds that of *horse*). It immediately evokes different mental representations for different people, according to their attitudes toward the various contexts that have brought *Bucephalus* to their attention (legend, art, history, literature, etc.), or even depending on their degree of familiarity with the contexts in which *Bucephalus* may occur. We can even imagine a person who knows perfectly what a horse is, but who, ignorant in matters of mythology, has no clue as to the identity of Bucephalus. One might therefore question Frege's example and argue that *Bucephalus* is not any horse, but a particular one, so that the name has a limited extension and a unique reference. Such an argument would not be totally relevant given the context of Frege's discussion; it raises just enough questions to cloud the issue, however, such that, for reasons of economy, I shall not attempt to defend the example. If we leave out for the present Frege's unfortunate example, we may still examine his proposition, as the distinction that it purports to illustrate extends easily to all names, whether they are grammatically proper or common (in *Posthumous Writings,* Frege himself repeats the whole argument, this time using *horse* instead of *Bucephalus* [139]). For instance, the word *water*—itself unquestionably a common noun—evokes a different association in a nursery, a pub, and a desert, for a man after strenuous exercise and another who has just eaten a copious meal. Bally's example of a tired pilgrim longing for the shade of a tree suggests the same distinction: to all intents and purposes, Bally's signification parallels Frege's *Sinn;* and his value, Frege's *Vorstellung* (see pp. 73–76). It is equally obvious that our mental representation of objects differs widely from one subgroup to another (in the case of Bucephalus, say, horsemen, painters, zoologists, or dogfood companies), and in any given subgroups, from one person to another—or even from one moment to another in a person's life: after Tchekhov's young character ate too many cherries, the "idea" that he had of the word *cherry* differed radically from the one he may have had before his binge.[33] This is not the aspect of *Vorstellung* that Frege stresses the most, however. What characterizes *Vorstellung* is that any such association is personal and circumstantial. Frege is quite emphatic on this point.

> The idea [*Vorstellung*] is subjective: one man's idea is not that of another. ("On Sense," 59)

> The same sense is not always connected, even in the same man, with the same idea. (59)

> in the case of an idea one must, strictly speaking, add to whom it belongs and at what time. (60)

> Another man's idea is, *ex-vi termini*, another idea. (*Foundations*, 37ᵉ)

This perception raises numerous problems that we have already broached in our treatment of *Sinn:* since I have access to the content of my consciousness, but only to mine, how can I tell what is in another person's consciousness? How can I tell for sure that my idea and that other person's idea of the meaning of a word are one and the same? I cannot ask him or her to confirm my idea since, precisely, it is *my* idea. The other person would experience difficulties analogous to mine: he or she will have some access to his or her consciousness, but then none to mine. Indeed, our languages could then "differ," thus fulfilling the worst Idealist nightmare. Such was, for example, De Mauro's criticism of the importance Saussure placed on value (see pp. 72–73). The risk and the stakes are evident: are we locked into individual inner worlds filled with "ideas"—to each his own—with no means to bridge the chasm from one world to other? If such is the case, what of communication? More importantly, what of mathematics, knowledge, science? If we acknowledge the existence of ideas and concede to them the degree of individuality and of subjectivity described by Frege, then our choice is clear: either we give up on language (*qua* communication) and science, or we find another way for language to relate to the world—a way that will bypass the dangers posed by ideas.

This preoccupation resonates throughout Frege's writings with an anguished persistence. In 1884, at the beginning of his career, he wrote in *The Foundations of Arithmetic:*

> If the number two were an idea, then it would have straight away to be private to me only. Another man's idea is, *ex-vi termini*, another idea. We should then have it might be many millions of twos on our hands. We should have to speak of my two and your two, of one two and all twos. If we accept latent or unconscious ideas, we should have unconscious twos among them, which would then return subsequently to consciousness. As

new generations of children grew up, new generations of twos would continually be being born, and in the course of millennia these might evolve, for all we could tell, to such a pitch that two of them would make five. (37ᵉ)

Thirty-four years later, in "The Thought" (1918), he repeated the very same argument, thus proving that his foil had not changed in these years and that the distinctions that he had painstakingly elaborated remained, at best, negative.

> If the thought I express in the Pythagorean theorem can be recognized by others just as much as by me then it does not belong to my consciousness, I am not its bearer; yet, I can, nevertheless, recognize it to be true. However, if it is not the same thought at all which is taken to be the content of the Pythagorean theorem by me and by another person, one should not really say "the Pythagorean theorem," but "my Pythagorean theorem," "his Pythagorean theorem" and these would be different. ("The Thought," 289)

If two and two are forever to make four, and if the Pythagorean theorem is to be of further use, then we must agree on the value of *two* and the *Pythagorean theorem* unequivocally, totally independently of human shortcomings, misgivings and errors, and, indeed, totally independently of language. In other words, the number *two* and the *Pythagorean theorem* must have some immaterial yet objective reality: hence the distinction between *Sinn* and *Vorstellung*. Whereas *Sinn* is that precise minimal and unchangeable semantic charge that Frege calls objective, *Vorstellung* escapes delineation: it is all the mental and pictorial aspects of an individual's relation to the world that escape a strictly logical formulation; in other words, it is everything else.

> Even an unphilosophical person soon finds it necessary to recognize an inner world distinct from the outer world, a world of sense-impression [*eine Welt der Sinneseindrücke*], of creation of his imagination [*der Schöpfungen seiner Einbildungskraft*], of sensations [*der Empfindungen*], of feelings and moods [*der Gefühle und Stimmungen*], a world of inclinations, wishes and decisions [*eine Welt der Neigungen, Wünsche und Entschlüsse*]. For brevity I want to collect all these, with the exception of decisions, under the word "idea" [*Vorstellung*]. ("The Thought," 287)

What then is *Vorstellung?*—a world of sense-impressions, of creations of the imagination, of sensations, of feelings and moods, a world of inclinations, wishes, and decisions—in brief, a ragbag of mental and psychological activities that the scientific mind may not be totally able to sort out. Surprisingly, despite the endless diversity and subjectivity of ideas, despite their proclaimed irrelevance to a theory of meaning, Frege does not seem to experience difficulties in elaborating a set of exact criteria meant to identify them; our sense of bewilderment is heightened when we recall that, at the same time, he was at a loss to define *Sinn* with comparable rigor—although *Sinn,* and not *Vorstellung,* was the logical foundation of his theory of signs (this imbalance alone should alert us to the resistance of the subject matter to his "theoretical" project). As we remember, Frege's usually sharp and assertive language became surprisingly vague as he tried to assemble his key terms into one definitive formula: "The reference [*Bedeutung*] of a proper name is the object itself [*der Gegenstand selbst*] which we designate by its means. The idea [*Vorstellung*], which we have in that case is wholly subjective; in between lies the sense [*dazwischen liegt der Sinn*], which is indeed no longer subjective like the idea, but is yet not the object itself" ("On Sense," 60). Our landmarks for a definition of *sense* would then be "the object itself" and the "idea"; at this point, Frege considers them to be easily, if not intuitively, grasped, while the ever evasive sense floats as something (!?), somewhere (!?) "in between" (*dazwischen*). As readers in pursuit of sense (the real space of the theory) try to navigate between the "objects" and the "idea," however, they soon realize that these landmarks are of little help since they are in fact excluded from Frege's theory of meaning, outside the boundaries of his investigation rather than within them. Should the baffled navigators let the apparent safety of "objects" or "ideas" seduce them and attempt to land on either one, shipwreck is their inevitable lot—at least as far as the pursuit of meaning is concerned. If they manage to avoid both Charybdis and Scylla, however, and to stay within the straits of the theory constructed, then, for lack of a proper map, they may still risk missing the "sense" that is said to lie somewhere in between (*dazwischen liegt der Sinn*). In their search for the evasive "sense," these readers are likely, at best, to go indefinitely around in circles.

To Frege's credit, we must point out that he was probably as unsatisfied as my hypothetical navigators with this definition of *Sinn* as an "in-between." In the next sentence he suddenly cuts short his string of definitions and, adopting a different rhetorical strategy, proceeds to illustrate his point: "The following analogy [*Gleichnis*] will perhaps clarify [*verdeutlichen*] these relationships" ("On Sense, " 60). In other words, when transmission of the sense of his own discourse fails (the transmission of his thought)—or at least partially fails (why?)—he resorts to an example and, in the best Platonic tradition, elects to convey his point by means of an imaginary construct: a story about two characters who look at the moon through a telescope and who do and do not see the same thing through the lenses (the moon is analogous to *Bedeutung,* the sight seen through the telescope's lens to *Sinn,* and the individual retinal image of each viewer to *Vorstellung*). The example is indeed very well chosen, and it does clarify the point. My intention is therefore not to question or even examine the specificity of the example but to address its rhetorical mode as an analogy [*Gleichnis*]. The little story about the two viewers and their telescope is just that: a story. And yet Frege expects a much disclaimed fiction to succeed where his highly precise philosophical discourse has failed. This is all the more odd since he is clearly trying to communicate a thought, like two and two or the Pythagorean theorem. To be consistent, he should find that the most adequate language to communicate such a precise scientific thought is the kind of language he advocates: a natural language as close as possible to a formula-language, that would leave no room for ambiguities. How can an analogy, that is to say, something pertaining to *Vorstellung* rather than to *Sinn,* "make plain" or "clarify" (*verdeutlichen*) the obscure locus that his logic allocates to sense? How can *Vorstellung* be made to carry the weight of the stickiest yet most essential point of Frege's essay? Obviously, unlike typical analytic discourse, Frege's little story neither describes nor defines the word *sense.* Its rhetorical "mode of presentation" is therefore such that it stands in contradiction to the very thought it expresses: communication between the writer and the reader no longer implies an active writer-logician conveying a distinct and well-defined objective thought to his alert but purely receptive reader. Contrary to his claim regarding the objectivity of sense and thought, Frege is not asking his reader to "apprehend" a thought containing the definition of *Sinn* (the definition of sense is not contained *in* the analogy: rather, it is in the space connecting this story with the analytic discourse previously held). By resorting to an analogy he is in fact requiring the active participation of the reader: no longer passive, the reader is invited to contribute to the process, to *draw* the analogy that will enable her or him to perceive the *other* thought (tenor) hidden in that story (vehicle)—in order to reach a sense that has proved difficult to express despite its claim to universality.

Within Frege's definitional framework this process is highly problematic. It emphasizes that the thought containing the definition or description of sense has not achieved the minimum clarity needed to make sense (it needs "clarifying"). And yet, claims Frege, it *is* there, just the way the Pythagorean theorem is there, whether I understand it or not. Supposedly, Frege's language has only to point the reader in the right direction for the reader to "apprehend" it. This is clearly not the case, however, as Frege resorts to an analogy after having already explained his distinction four times (why four times?). How can a sense as objective as the sense of *Sinn* prove so hard to present "objectively"? How can a distinction as essential as that between *Sinn, Bedeutung,* and *Vorstellung* be better served by a figure of rhetoric than by an indicative sentence containing a clear thought, subject to easy "apprehension" by all? I shall propose that in practice, sense is not, as Frege would have us believe, a neat, objective entity at hand; rather, it is inextricably entwined with its parasite, *Vorstellung.* Were we able to isolate senses, we could use them to communicate scientific thoughts, so that logic would triumph without the help of a formula-language. But this is clearly not the case. By resorting to an analogy to convey the sense of *sense,* Frege implicitly invalidates the distinction he is eager to make: whereas he claims that *Sinn* and *Vorstellung* are radically and objectively different, his failure to communicate this difference by means of literal and objective discourse (that is, without the help of *Vorstellung*) illustrates in fact their interdependence and underscores the precariousness of a "theory" of language that, like his, relies heavily on the exclusion of *Vorstellung.*

The confusion underlying this problem is heightened when we realize the frequency of such turns in Frege's writings and the degree to which he was aware of his inability to do without the forbidden "ideas" [*Vorstellungen*], "tone," "coloring and shading" [*Färbungen und Beleuchtungen*], "fragrance" [*Duft*], "mood" [*Stimmung*], "illumination" [*Beleuchtung*], and so on. His woeful remarks, usually in footnotes, highlight this difficulty.

> The expression "apprehend" [*fassen*] is as metaphorical [*bildlich*] as "content of consciousness" [*Bewusstseinsinhalt*]. The nature of language does not permit anything else. ("The Thought," 295, n. 6)

> I admit that there is a quite peculiar obstacle in the way of an understanding with my reader. By a kind of necessity of language, my expressions, taken literally, sometimes miss [*verfehlt*] my thought; I mention an object, when what I intend is a concept [*ein Gegenstand genannt wird, wo ein Begriff gemeint ist*].
> I fully realize that in such cases I was relying upon a reader who would be ready to meet me half-way—who does not begrudge a pinch of salt. ("On Concept," 54)

> The metaphorical aspect of language [*die Bildlichkeit der Sprache*] presents difficulties. The sensible always breaks in and makes expression metaphorical [*bildlich*] and so improper [*uneigentlich*]. So a battle with language takes place and I am compelled to occupy myself with language although it

is not my proper concern here. I hope I have succeeded in making clear to my readers what I want to call a thought. ("The Thought," 287, n. 4)

We are all the more intrigued in that Frege does not seem to experience the same difficulties when he comes to defining ideas. Since ideas are subjective, that is, in a person's head, are they not, therefore, inaccessible? Are they not supposed to escape the realm of language and precise communication? Above all, why should anyone bother to identify, define, and exemplify that which falls outside the theory? And still, the delineation of the annoying and eventually excluded term is poignantly telling and well worth a closer look.

Frege offers four criteria according to which we can identify (and eliminate) ideas.

1. Ideas are not objects of sensorial perception: "Ideas cannot be seen or touched, cannot be smelled, nor tasted, nor heard."
2. Unlike *Sinn,* which can only be apprehended, "ideas are had," that is, are had by one individual at a time, with the result that they cannot be shared, or verified, by many,
3. Since an idea is had, it requires a person who would have it, a person whose ideas it is: therefore, "ideas need a bearer."
4. From the two previous points, it follows that an idea cannot circulate from one person to the other. All verbal renditions of an idea purporting to communicate that idea to another person would be at best tentative: "every idea has only one bearer." ("The Thought," 288–89)

For fear of being dragged into a thicket of bad arguments, I shall not discuss the validity of these criteria: after all, Frege did not intend to examine ideas. In setting up these criteria, his purpose was not so much to define an object as to determine the proper timing for a gesture of exclusion: an object that meets these criteria is not to be considered part of his theory of signs and meaning.[34] Having stated these requirements, Frege was free to dismiss all troublesome "ideas" and pursue what he considered a more appropriate line of inquiry, in which two and two would forever make four without fear of interference: "In what follows there will be no further discussion of ideas and experiences; they have been mentioned here *only* to ensure that the ideas aroused in the hearer by a word *shall not be confused* with its sense or reference" ("On Sense," 61).

The underlying argument leading to this exclusion is, to say the least, peculiar: *Vorstellung* is individual and subjective; *therefore,* it is

said to evade a scientific theory of meaning. Now, let us imagine a some-
what perverse or, shall we say, literary mind; could such a person not
find fault with this discreet syllogism (That which is not objective is not
part of a theory of language; *Vorstellung* is not objective; therefore *Vor-
stellung* is not part of a theory of language)? There is a further source
of confusion in that the first premise of this syllogism stealthily begs the
question. Indeed, would it be any less true to reverse the causal relation
and propose that something escapes systematization and logic and
therefore has to be conveniently relegated to the individual's inaccessi-
ble head? Couldn't we rather say with Wittgenstein that "we interpret
the enigma created by our misunderstanding as the enigma of an incom-
prehensible process"?[35] Wouldn't our literary misgivings be exacer-
bated when Frege, while striving rather awkwardly to avoid any pos-
sible confusion or contamination between sense/reference, on the one
hand, and ideas, on the other, holds the latter responsible for art, in
general, and poetry in particular?

> We can recognize three levels of difference between words, expressions, or
> whole sentences. The difference may concern at most the ideas, or the sense
> but not the reference, or finally the reference as well. With respect to the
> first level, it is to be noted that, on account of the uncertain connexion of
> ideas with words, a difference may hold for one person, which another
> does not find. *The difference between a translation and an original text
> should properly not overstep the first level.* To the possible differences here
> belong also *the colouring and shading which poetic eloquence seeks to give
> to the sense.* Such colouring and shading are not objective, and must be
> evoked by each hearer or reader according to the hints of the poet or the
> speaker. ("On Sense," 61)

And again in "The Thought":

> An indicative sentence often contains, as well as a thought and the asser-
> tion, a third component over which the assertion does not extend. This is
> often said to act on the feelings, the mood of the hearer or to arouse his
> imagination. Words like "alas" and "thank God" belong here. . . . *Such
> constituents of sentences are more noticeably prominent in poetry, but are
> seldom wholly absent from prose.* Therefore all constituents of sentences to
> which the assertive force does not reach *do not belong to scientific exposi-
> tion* but they are sometimes hard to avoid, even for one who sees the dan-
> ger connected with them. . . . On the other hand, the constituents of lan-
> guage, to which I want to call attention here, make the translation of
> poetry very difficult, even make a complete translation almost impossible,
> for *it is in precisely that in which poetic value largely consists that lan-
> guages differ most.* . . . What is called mood, fragrance, illumination in a

poem, what is portrayed by cadence and rhythm, *does not belong to the thought*. ("The Thought," 284–85)

Ideas, as unpredictable as the strokes left by a monkey's tail on a canvas, could affect or even blur the crisp precision of sense and the metalinguistic terminology sought by Frege, followed by analytical philosophers or linguists. There are hybrid creatures, however. Though subjective and personal—and therefore excluded—ideas strangely imply some general traits, quasi-objective, and subject to communication since "without some affinity in human ideas [*eine Verwandtschaft des menschlichen Vorstellens*], art would certainly be impossible" ("On Sense," 61). The rug of objectivity and universality has just been pulled out from under our baffled reader's feet. Are ideas no longer personal, individual, subjective? What exactly does the word *affinity* mean here? This affinity in human ideas without which there could be no art—is it not something "common" to all? Can some aspects of ideas be generalized? What, then, of the distinction between *Vorstellung* and *Sinn* (or *Gedanke*)? In what ways is "affinity in human *ideas*" different from "a common store of *thoughts* which is transmitted from one generation to another," previously evoked to justify and illustrate "sense"?[36] What, then, is the difference between *affinity*, which Frege uses to express the ways ideas are shared, and *common*, upon which hinges his preference for sense? Can ideas be redeemed? And what will become of translation, art, and poetry, contingent *then* on the singularity of ideas, *now* on "some affinities," on some possibility of generalizing? Will the logician call back translation, art, and poetry from exile? No, continues Frege, "but it can never be exactly determined how far the intentions of the poet are realized" (61). Back to the metaleptic syllogism: that which I cannot determine "exactly" is to be excluded from my "exact" theory. End of discussion. (I am leaving out the intentional fallacy, which is irrelevant to our argument.)

On the Translation of Vorstellung

In the context of our discussion of Frege's distinctions, the translation of his terminology is revealing. While *Sinn* and *Bedeutung* were translated into English without much difficulty (some hesitation between "reference" and "denotation" for *Bedeutung*), *Vorstellung* proved much more thorny. "Idea" is not the most obvious translation, all the more so because English does not have a related verb for *vorstellen*. Thus, while Frege purposely crowds together the noun and the verb to create a powerful effect, the English translation resorts to two totally different words, *idea* and *to picture* (see, for example, "If two persons picture the same thing, each still has his own idea" for "Wenn zwei sich dasselbe vorstellen, so hat jeder doch seine eigene Vorstellung" ["On Sense," 60]). Austin, who translated *The Foundations of Arithmetic,* felt the need to warn his readers: "*Vorstellungen.* I have translated this word consistently by "idea," and cognate words by 'imagine,' 'imagination,' etc. For Frege, it is a psychological term" (*Foundations,* V^{e}, translator's note). Furthermore, by pulling *Vorstellung* toward "idea," the English translation condemns itself to inconsistencies: when Frege, as is often the case, uses the word with a strong visual overtone, the English translation abandons "idea" for "image," thus losing the cross-referential power of Frege's writing (see for example "images and feelings" for *Vorstellungen und Gefühlte* ["On Sense," 63]). By contrast, the French translation takes *représentation* for *Vorstellung* and *représenter* for *vorstellen,* thus preserving the family resemblance between the two words and the consistency of Frege's terminology. It then uses *image* for *Bild* (while English alternates between "image" and "representation"), and *idée* for *Idee.*[37] We should also note that *représentation* evokes the visual quality of *Vorstellung,* emphasized by Frege, whereas "ideas" implies a conceptual framework only.

Austin's Translator's Preface to the second edition of *The Foundations of Arithmetic* explains and defends his choice of "idea":[38]

> The translation originally chosen for Frege's principal terms remains unchanged, except that *Begriffswort* has now become "concept-word" instead of "general term" and *wirklich* "actual" instead of "existent." Critics of some others of these translations have perhaps not sufficiently realized that Frege's inherited philosophical vocabulary (at least as he was using it at this period) is a dated one. It is that which was Englished by his contemporaries the "British Idealists": and they certainly used, for example, "idea" for *Vorstellung* and "proposition" for *Satz,* though not unnaturally they attached to those words meanings different from (and doubtless less clear than) those fashionable half a century later. Frege's thought cannot be reproduced accurately, nor can his terms be translated consistently, unless we are prepared to accept, even in him, something short of complete (or contemporary) sophistication. (*Foundations,* Translator's Preface to 2d ed.)

"Idea" was apparently selected because, taken historically, it referred to Frege's quarrel with the Idealists and directed the reader's attention to that ever present foil in Frege's writing. Furthermore, since, from Leibnitz on, *idea* was translated into German as *Vorstellung,* it seemed only logical to revert to the original *idea.* Since one of Frege's primary intentions was indeed to separate logic and psychology,[39] and since the Idealists were, in their own way, advocating the opposite, one may then assume that his debate with them was of such primary importance that it justified his using a common terminology. I shall not debate the historical importance of Frege's disagreement with Idealism;[40] I shall question instead whether this concern justifies adopting a less-than-perfect translation, which results in taxonomic inconsistencies. The readers could be informed of contemporary circumstantial debates in footnotes, prefaces, introductions, and so forth. Had the translation been more satisfactory, philosophers would not have felt the need to adopt other terms (*tone* for Dummett, *colouring* for Baker and Hacker) to replace *idea*.

On the Exclusion of Vorstellung

Be the translation as it may, the fact remains that with the exclusion of *Vorstellung* a substantial component of linguistic competence is missing from the purported scope of the theory. Frege's theory of language is then not a "theory of language" as much as a theory of a particular and rather restricted *use* of language, namely, the language of science, in which the only factor accepted in attaining a general meaning is its assertorial force (today, we would say, following Austin, constative). Even so, Frege still recognized that although some constituents of language associated with *Vorstellung did not belong* to his scientific endeavor, they were "sometimes hard to avoid, even for one who sees the danger connected with them." One would be all the more inclined to think so inasmuch as Frege had already laid his cards upon the table in his *Begriffsschrift:* he was not elaborating a grammar; nor was he investigating the nature of our capacity to produce and understand an indefinite number of utterances (as did Chomsky). He had set out not to describe natural language but to purify it, to wrench the constituents that might interfere with the ability of natural language to rival a logical or mathematical formula.[41] His purposes were very different from those shared by most modern analytical philosophers or linguists. To speak of Frege's "theory of meaning" is simply wrong, since he did not elaborate a theory of meaning in the modern sense; rather, he set out to isolate and formulate the components of language that were the most appropriate for the scientific communication of "thoughts."

And yet, despite Frege's explicit awareness of the limited scope of application of his project, his theory was adopted with enthusiasm by Anglo-American philosophers as a general theory of language: spurning his words of caution about the pervasiveness of *Vorstellung,* these same philosophers have construed Frege's project as a theory of meaning while generalizing his views and extending them to include all aspects of language, with the exception of "minor," "parasitic" utterances—literature, for one.

They paid a high price for this generalization: the forbidden term was simply ignored (or mentioned in a short paragraph stating that *Vorstellung* did not belong in a theory of language). Thus, while squads of philosophers in Britain and the United States battled over reference and, by extension, truth-value, most of them marginalized the three pages dealing with ideas and, consequently, with poetry and art. Once more, poetry was excluded from the Republic of serious thinkers.

Among the few exceptions to that practice of general exclusion, I shall mention two, Dummett, and Baker and Hacker, which I find particularly significant. Dummett, in his monumental *Frege: Philosophy of Language,* shifts Frege's propositions around. First he eliminates reference from Frege's theory of meaning: reference "is not an ingredient of meaning at all" (Dummett 84). Then he dwells at length on two components that Frege excluded: force and tone. It is interesting that his opening chapter, "Sense and Tone," deals almost exclusively with *Vorstellung*.[42] The insistence on the relationship between sense and tone stresses the weakness of Frege's distinction and the need to justify the exclusion of tone (like Frege, however, Dummett cannot explain sense independently of *Vorstellung*). It is also revealing that Dummett is hard put to delineate tone analytically (indeed, tone is best shown in action, i.e., rhetorically). Eventually, in contradiction to Frege and to his own first chapter, he ends up suggesting that a theory of meaning would have to take into account not only sense but also tone and force (416). However, the substantial implications of this suggestion are partly neutralized by a third point: Dummett suggests that we distinguish between the theory and the practice of language. The real "object-language," that is to say, the "imperfect" language we encounter in our linguistic practice (the one making up the woof and warp of puzzles, rhetoric, and literature, and in which force and tone prevail) would be superseded "*in thought*" (i.e., in theory only and by abstraction), by a metalanguage (by *metalanguage,* Dummett means an ideal theoretical construct). Philosophy would adopt this metalanguage for its sole object and would finally be able to solve any problem "in theory," if not in practice (105–9). Indeed, adopting a perfect (and, by Dummett's own admission, inexistent) language for the object of philosophy is tantamount to realizing Frege's dream by eliminating a priori all puzzles and stubborn difficulties. Dummett's metalanguage comes dangerously close to metaphysics: dangerously, not because metaphysics in itself is to be avoided but because Dummett claims that his theory, bearing on an inexistent object, is a theory of meaning. All in all, if we have to extend the theory's object to Dummett's metalanguage—an ideal theoretical construct to which no reality corresponds—in order to generalize and strengthen Frege's philosophy of language, then the theory is perhaps best left to the limited scope of application that Frege assigned to it.

Baker and Hacker in their lucid *Frege: Logical Excavations* underline the weakness of Frege's attack on Idealism (see esp. Baker and Hacker 33–62). The arguments are too numerous, varied, scattered, and complex to be presented in our framework. Their conclusion is that Frege's distinction between sense and ideas consists of philosophical truisms and platitudes and that his attempted refutation of ideas, tone, and coloring was, at best, reductive, simplistic, and altogether poorly conducted. They end their critique with the harsh but accurate estimate that his argument against *Vorstellung* "collapsed in the face of more sophisticated forms, e.g., Carnap's methodological solipsism" (49). In the same vein, they are very clear and explicit on the question of *Vorstellung* (for which they use the term *colouring*): "Yet if there is to be a global Fregean account of language, the boundary lines between sense and colouring must be redrawn, and the different types of linguistic phenomena wrongly lumped together must be carefully distinguished" (337). Theirs is then a two-step program. First we must distinguish between the "different types of linguistic phenomena wrongly lumped together" under *Vorstellung;* this will allow us to address the various wrongs that Baker and Hacker underscored in Frege's treatment of ideas. Then we shall find out that some linguistic phenomena wrongly lumped under "colouring" can in fact be recovered under sense and subsequently integrated into a "global Fregean account of language"; (this account, we may add, would no longer be Fregean, since, wrongly or not, Frege had specifically elected to lump them together under *Vorstellung* and not under *Sinn*). The fact remains that despite their formidable criticism of Frege (and theirs is the harshest immanent critique of his theory of language) they do not recommend the *inclusion* of "colouring"—whatever the new boundary lines may be—in a global Fregean account of language. Nor do they address either the special traits of language best manifest in literature or literature as a whole. As their scattered mentions of literature take place mostly within the broader context of "reference-failure," their stand remains strictly logicophilosophical. Unfortunately, they do not advance any criteria to help sort out Frege's muddle: their introduction makes it clear that they see themselves strictly as historians of philosophy and that they do not intend to go beyond a critical presentation of Frege. As historians they attempt to disentangle Frege's own thought from its subsequent integration into later philosophers' writings (Dummett is their favorite target). Thus they depart from the line usually adopted by philosophers, who see in Frege the fountainhead of their own work and tend to attribute to him their own concerns and interests. Their critique is unique in that their historical perspective results in a disruptive conception of the history of philosophy, one that relentlessly reminds their fellow philosophers that Frege, whose philosophical training consisted of a limited acquaintance with anthologies of philosophy, was *not* a philosopher: he was mostly a mathematician, who happened to hold that mathematics' deepest structure is in fact logical and who therefore worked on logic—only to stumble onto the many points of contact between logic and natural language.

In conclusion, Frege's contribution to theories of language hinges mainly on his distinction between sense and reference. Ideas were evoked *a contrario* to illustrate what sense is not and to refute the claims made by psychologists and subjectivist logicians. And yet *Vorstellung*, summoned only in order to avoid confusion and to illuminate the boundaries of this taxonomy, has cast long shadows on his theory. The exorcist's endeavor has met with partial success only: he has indeed conjured up the devil but has failed to cast it away. I must repeat that, to his credit, Frege was well aware of the seriousness of the problem posed by *Vorstellung* to his purely logical account of language: his solution was to strip away the disturbing element and construct a theory suitable for and applicable to the communication of scientific thought *only*. His successors adopted a different attitude, however: like him, they diagnosed *Vorstellung* as an irregularity, a nonserious use of language, unworthy of the theoretician's attention. Then they proceeded to execute, in Frege's name, something that he clearly never intended to do, namely, the construction of a comprehensive theory of meaning grounded in his purely logical distinctions—again, without *Vorstellung*.[43] In the process, literature, which he intended to exclude from mathematical logic only, was expelled from the philosophy of language.

4 The First Person

If I had before me a fly and an elephant, having never seen more than one of such magnitude of either kind; and if the fly were to endeavor to persuade me that he was larger than the elephant, I might by possibility be placed in a difficulty. The apparently little creature might use such arguments about the effect of distance, and might appeal to such laws of sight and hearing as I, if unlearned in those things, might be unable to wholly reject. But if there were a thousand flies, all buzzing, to appearance, about the great creature; and, to a fly declaring, each one for himself, that he was bigger than the quadruped; and all giving different and frequently contradictory reasons; and each one despising and opposing the reasons of the others—I should feel quite at my ease. I should certainly say, "My little friends, the case of each one of you is destroyed by the rest."

AUGUSTUS DE MORGAN

A Test Case for Language: *I*

A disgruntled student once asked me, "Why are you teaching a course on the first person?" During the ensuing discussion, I came to realize that what he meant was not just why "the first person," but why "the first person" rather than "autobiography" or "first-person narrative." In other words, a course named "The First Person in Philosophy and Fiction" seemed to him either too broad or too narrow, technical, and perhaps pedantic. I have since mused upon the question, or rather upon the range of presuppositions it brought out. Roughly sketched, these presuppositions follow two paths. If I isolate the first person from its context, how can I treat it literarily? Doesn't literature consist of strings of words producing certain effects (cognitive, rhetorical, perlocutionary, etc.)? Shall I spend a whole semester tracking a single word from text to text? On the other hand, if I treat the first person in its context, how can I not specify what this context is (autobiography, fiction, dialogue, soliloquy, narrative, memoirs, diaries, etc.)? It is clear that the context largely determines the rules of the game, thus greatly shaping our understanding of the role and function that befall the first person, or even dictating the referential, epistemological, and ontological values that we can attach to each of its uses. A study of the first person would then seem to oscillate between two alternatives, both equally unacceptable to the student of literature: either an exercise in futility or a blind and stubborn refusal to acknowledge the effects of contextuality and literary conventions. Not a very nice perspective indeed, and I can sympathize with my student's annoyance.

There is another perspective, however, which would not distinguish between ordinary and literary language, thereby avoiding the snare of questions that surfaced in my discussion with the student. Whatever else literature may be, it is undeniably a practice of language also (there is no literary text without such a practice). We tend to forget the lesson of Mr. Jourdain, who is astonished yet delighted at his discovery that he speaks prose even as he asks his maid for his slippers. Indeed, the same words, the same sentence, may appear on the marketplace and in a novel. (This fact alone should remind us that the various contexts in which the same expression may appear are themselves to a great extent conventionally and ideologically construed—more on this subject in my next chapter). Whether one uses *I* in a work of fiction, a grocery store, or an election speech, there must be something recognizable from one occurrence of *I* to the other.

Simply put, saying "I" is tantamount to stepping forward and calling attention to one's self as the source, origin, and control of discourse. This is a unique moment when the object and the subject of an utterance coincide—at least rhetorically. It should then epitomize the transparency of expression, the perfect linguistic moment. And yet, whether *I* is used to "mean" or to "refer," it presents an odd particularity: every time it is used, its reference slips to someone else, while its semantic charge is not only totally different but also too complex and private to be fully communicated. Let me clarify this last point. When I say "I," no listener of mine will have the sense of myself that I have; there is therefore something essential to *I* that I cannot communicate. At the same time, *I* must evoke some kind of sense, otherwise no one would understand me. If this is the case, however, it is a strange kind of sense, since we cannot say that the sense of *I* is "that which is common to all I's," the way we can say by abstraction that, despite their differences, there is something that all tables share: it would be hard to delineate something that we might wish to call I-ness. It would seem, then, that *I* cannot be a name (in the philosophical sense); therefore, it follows that it cannot be a subject (but we know that this is not the case); and yet it is not a predicate or a description, either. Thus *I* is a very troubling puzzle for most theories of language, and in some way a test for their ability to be, as most claim, total and comprehensive. (It is interesting that even Frege, who did not set out to account for just any occurrence of language but for only those that could be part of scientific language, eventually examined *I*. Similarly, Russell, who claims that scientific language can and should dispense with indexical expressions, nonetheless takes the time to formulate views meant to include indexical expression in his general theory.)

And still, one cannot discard the intuition that *I* seems one of the easiest words to understand, almost irreducible in its simplicity. Intuitively, if not linguistically or philosophically, we tend to see *I* as some kind of reflexive gesture, accomplished by verbal means, while at the same time bearing on all linguistic expressions: any utterance seems to presuppose some speaking subject, voice, persona, or instance, which, in turn, can best manifest itself by saying "I." *I* is, in fact, the ultimate presupposition. When Descartes, in search of a method, chose to systematize and generalize doubt, he arrived at an irreducible element, his famous *cogito:* an "I" that is by definition engaged in knowing (thinking) that it is an "I." Hence *sum.* Hence also the elaboration of a system founded on the irreducibility of the subject, eventually leading to a systematic recovery of the universe and its creator.

Now, it is this odd conflation of the contradictory aspects of *I*, at once exceptional and paradigmatic, that makes it so valuable for a theory of language. I shall therefore examine *I* not so much for some intrinsic quality that it, and it alone, has (although I shall dwell on attempts to extract such qualities), as for the qualities it shares with all parts of language, insofar as it is a part of language—albeit one that does not hide inconspicuously behind its content, pointing instead to itself *as language.* My interest in *I* in the present chapter reflects an economical concern. My contention is that *I* does not differ essentially from other words (at least not from a theoretical viewpoint). Whatever we take the relation of the part to the whole to be (the isolated word to the whole of language), *I* is and does *more of the same:* no other term does so much, so fast, to point to the various mechanisms at work in language and exemplify them, as well as to the various presuppositions underlying theories of language. Whether theories are based, like Frege's, on vertical reference or, like Saussure's, on horizontal semantics, *I* consistently compels them to address precisely the axis that each sets out to disregard, thus exposing at once the strengths and the limitations that strict "theoretical" predeterminations command. Our examination of *I* will therefore alternate between intuitive and counterintuitive affirmations, truisms and highly controversial views, general rules and idiosyncratic situations—in short, between so-called normal and aberrant practices. In choosing literary texts, I am not affirming the specificity and singularity of literary language as much as shunning the creation of simple contexts fabricated by the theoretician to demonstrate a point: a story is a relatively larger and complex context not created to suit an occasion, and consequently its language cannot be limited by the necessarily biased pedagogical or explanatory purpose of the philosopher or the linguist.

The First Person in Kafka's "Report to an Academy"

"A Report to an Academy" is written in the first person. That this choice was carefully premeditated and experimented with there can be no doubt. We have three fragments of drafts of "A Report"; Kafka discarded them all. We may ask why. We may wonder with what exactly Kafka was experimenting as he wrote and rewrote his story. These questions bear on the differences between the final published version and the fragments. One needs but a quick comparison to notice that the three fragments present the same obvious difference from the published text: whereas in the final version the story is told entirely by the ape itself, in the fragments a narrator relates his encounters first with the performing ape's impresario and then with the ape itself; in the shortest fragment, he writes to the ape, after having read its "report." In a nutshell, then, the major change consists in the expulsion of the human narrator.

The two major fragments clearly experiment with the dialogue form.[1] The first fragment is told completely from the point of view of a wide-eyed narrator, in the past tense, and with one section in direct discourse (marked by quotation marks). Incidentally, the interlocutor in this fragment is not the ape itself but its trainer (the ape plays no part at all). Kafka seems to have intended to tell the story of the trainer, and not that of the ape, but to have eventually eliminated the speaking human trainer (and not only the human narrator) as unfit for the effect for which he was striving. In this regard, it is worth pointing out that in this early draft the trainer, though human, behaved in an odd manner: although "almost timid," he greeted his visitor with the undiscriminating eagerness of a pet: "Hardly had he caught sight of me . . . when he . . . jumped up, shook me by both hands, urged me to sit down, wiped his spoon on the tablecloth, and amiably offered it to me so that I might finish his omelet. He would not accept my grateful refusal, and promptly tried to feed me. I had some trouble calming him down and warding him off, as well as his spoon and plate." [2] There is therefore no doubt that, from the outset, a certain ambiguity regarding the nature of the speaker was essential to Kafka's project; however, while the final version pins this ambiguity on the ape—and, more specifically, on his use of language—the first fragment seems to attribute it to some odd behaviorist contamination between man and ape. (I find this fragment rather forced and not very effective.)

The second fragment consists of a dialogue between the narrator and the ape itself. Kafka was evidently not committed to conventional literary dialogue, however: in a conventional dialogue we assume that there are at least two speakers, that they alternate, and that we know who is saying what to whom. Kafka was striving for a different effect, one that, unlike the conventional dialogue I have just described, would blur the clear distinctions between speakers: when alternating between sentences uttered by the narrator and by the ape, Kafka did not use quotation marks to indicate the speaker. As a result of this omission, the use of *I* shifts from one person to the other without warning and in a rather disconcerting manner—until the ape starts telling its story (this section constitutes the longest and last paragraph of the fragment). Only this last section was retained in the published version, albeit considerably expanded. Eventually, as we read "A Report to an Academy" today, the story itself coincides with the report. It would seem that Kafka discovered his subject while writing this section; only then did he proceed to elaborate on the ape's speech to the exclusion of the other forms he had attempted to use (and since this is one of the few stories that he submitted for publication, we may presume that he was reasonably satisfied with the final effect). The "discovery" that led to the publication of the story is then not the biography of the ape (which remains consistent throughout the three versions), but the circumstances in which this biography is delivered and conveyed to the reader, namely, *the autobiographical speech of an ape*. A reading of "A Report" that fails to account for the special effects achieved by the curious *I* of the ape, will fail to address the story proper. [3]

I shall therefore not attempt to offer yet another neatly packed interpretation of yet another neatly packed story. Nor shall I wonder what the ape "stands for" (does it have to stand for anything but its own function and effect in the fictional world created by "A Report"? Does it have to exceed its linguistic existence in the story, *as an ape?*) "A Report" is not a parable begging for its "other" interpretative reading (in fact, I would argue that parables do not beg either). Even if and when such interpretations seem possible, they wind up telling yet an-

other story, one that runs at times parallel to the story at hand but has
little grip on it. Commenting on Kafka's animal stories, Benjamin no-
tices with his usual acuity that "they are not parables, and yet they do
not want to be taken at their face value; they lend themselves to quota-
tions and can be told for purposes of clarification. But do we have the
doctrine which Kafka's parables interpret and which Kafka's postures
and the gestures of his animals clarify? It does not exist; all we can say
is that here and there we have an allusion to it." [4] Indeed, reading a
literary text as an allegory does little more than substitute one text (the
critic's interpretation) for another. Readings that have tried to present
the ape as an allegory (or at least a metaphor) have mostly exposed their
naïve referential presuppositions: apes do not speak; ergo the speaking
ape in "A Report" is not really an ape; it must stand for something
(someone) else blessed with language. Or again, in the words of Leo
Hamalian, "Too often Kafka was judged by critics bent on subordinat-
ing the events and mood of his work to their own preoccupation, from
metaphysics to Marxist dialectics. Though the nonliterary approaches
may yield certain valid insights . . . on the whole they have damaged
Kafka's reputation and have made his work the happy hunting-ground
of the eccentric, the bizarre or the overly ingenious mind. The answer,
of course, is that criticism which begins with special premises ends up
ignoring the artist's intention and, at its worst, the work itself." [5] In "A
Report" the first person is not an interpretative extrapolation like meta-
physics or Marxist dialectics; *it is textual,* as is the shift from the bright-
eyed narrator of the fragments to the ape.[6] I shall not ask what the *I* of
the ape (or the ape itself) "means," but how it works.

Other notations of Kafka testify to his awareness of the textual
power of *I* and further compel us to delve into a text that uses the first
person so effectively. For instance, in "Wedding Preparation in the
Country," Kafka writes: "*One* works so feverishly at the office that
afternoon that *one* is too tired even to enjoy *one*'s holiday properly. But
even all that work does not give *one* a claim to be treated lovingly by
every*one;* on the contrary, *one* is alone, a total stranger and only an
object of curiosity. *And as long as you say 'one' instead of 'I,' there's
nothing in it and one can easily tell the story;* but as soon as you admit
to yourself that it is you yourself, you feel as though *transfixed* and
horrified".[7] Now, why should *I* be so horrifying? Why is it easier to tell
"one's" story than "I's"? The question is all the more urgent since in his
journal, Kafka notes with a tinge of surprise, albeit with marked plea-
sure, that he entered into literature as soon as he was able to substitute
he for *I*.[8] Why, then, does the ape tell *its* story so readily? (Is *it* horri-

fied?) What does this readiness tell us about its story or his "I"? (In fact, as we shall find out, it does not tell its story, or at least, not the whole story.)

It would be easy enough to claim that apes do not speak and that therefore the story is irrelevant to reality as we know it; that as we are dealing with fiction, we are engaged in a different language game, with different rules; that since we are required to suspend disbelief, there is nothing wrong or even peculiar in the ape's use of a human *I*; that the story is not really about an ape, and that his *I* is therefore of little importance; that *I* is a formal marker only and consequently not essential to the meaning of the story; in short, that either this use of *I* presents no particular interest within the literary convention, or it is so aberrant with regard to the normal use of language that it is out of place in a serious critical inquiry. Either way, the result would be the same—it would eliminate the ape's *I* from the scope of worthy investigation. This dismissal would merely displace the problem I raise here: the question is definitely not whether or not an ape can speak. My focus of interest is not the ape—nor is it "apeness." "A Report" is not a fantasy story. Its main prong is not that an ape can speak but that *this ape seriously claims not to be an ape and that something in language as we understand it intuitively allows for the communication of such an absurdity* (in Aristotelian terms, I would question the relation between meaning and the law of the excluded middle). I am even willing to concede that this feature of language may not be the theme of the story (or may not be the theme intended by Kafka), but I do maintain that it is the essential ingredient without which there would have been neither theme, nor story, nor moral or allegorical interpretation. In short, there is no passing from the literary text to its critical paraphrase without first establishing what constitutes its formal specificity.

The ape's claim brings us back to Frege's question of identity: I may not know that the morning star is Venus, but how can I not know who or what I, the one who possesses such knowledge, am? Our questions are then as follows: if, in an utterance containing *I*, the subject and object of this utterance do indeed coincide, how can there still be room for error, ambiguity, and irony? What is it in the very structure and mechanism of language that *allows* for such misuse of a term? Can anyone change the rules of language at will, or is there something inherent in language (*in* language, and not in this or that particular use or misuse) that allows for rule changes or even for aberrations such as the one illustrated by "A Report"? Above all, how do comprehensive "theories" account for such phenomena?

The story is very emphatic about its own status. It is a report and a report only, proclaims the ape in both the opening and closing sentences:

> Honored Members of the Academy!
> You have done me the honor of inviting me to give your Academy an account of the life I formerly led as an ape. (*Stories,* 50)

> I am only imparting knowledge, I am only making a report. To you, honored Members of the Academy, I have only made a report. (59)

It all seems simple and familiar enough: a learned academy has invited a lecturer to read a paper, the way academies, colloquia, conventions, and other institutions do—a simple public lecture meant to enlighten the listeners. The text we read is the paper itself, with its polite opening addressed to the hosts and its modest ending—one can hardly think of any circumstantial context as straightforward, regulated, and harmless. And still, as we read the "paper," we come to realize that the situation may not be as simple as it appears at first sight. For example, we learn that our speaker is a performer. Now, this alone should alert us to possible difficulties: what is the logical status of the paper in these circumstances? Is it still a "serious" speech, or is it a "nonserious" performance (serious philosophers have traditionally found stage performances unworthy of their attention)? Was the performer invited to speak or to perform?[9] As we remember, the answer to these questions will determine our ability to examine the truth-value of the ape's paper and consequently the spirit in which it should be read (still within the suspension of disbelief). As we keep reading "A Report," we also learn that our speaker stirs up considerable interest in the press (and in learned academies), in which he is a subject of controversy. We may of course wonder why. We may ask how the media perceive him; above all, we may ask how he himself interprets the interest he arouses in others. Furthermore, we cannot but notice that he is not just any performer: his show takes place in a circus, where trainers habitually present well-trained animals who can perform "tricks," that is to say, who exhibit patterns of behavior unusual for their species. Am I pressing the point? The story leaves little room for suspense: the obvious answer to my questions is that the interest that the ape provokes is not linked intrinsically to his actions or to the content of his speech—though the interest of a report on the life he formerly led as an ape is undeniable—but to the fact that he is and remains an ape, however "human" he claims to have become. In short, the speaker is a freak (all the more for taking itself so "seriously")—and it is as a freak that he has been invited to perform for the academy. The speech is then not so much informative, constative (a report), as it is performative. In this context irony prevails. As the ape mentions his "former life as an ape" or the five years that have elapsed "since [he] was an ape," as he refers to itself as an "erstwhile ape," his fuzzy body and erratic behavior subvert the truth-value of his speech, to the delight of academies and readers.[10]

Inviting the ape and assigning him a task (a topic for its paper) are acts of authority, with which the honored members of the academy state their power and superiority over the performing freak. The academy is dictating the rules of the game. Oh, but revenge is sweet! The ape's acceptance of the invitation turns the tables on the honored members of the academy: they are no longer in control. The space of "A Report" is occupied entirely by the voice of the ape, leaving the academy speechless (powerless), subjected to *his* discourse. Furthermore, their request, their initial wish, and the program they have established for their guest's lecture will be brutally thwarted: if they intended to take advantage of the special skills of their "subject" in order to explore an otherwise inaccessible domain (the life of apes)—that is, if in any way they took seriously the transformation of their subject—then their disappointment is certain. The ape has decided otherwise: instead of the entertaining experiment that they planned, they will passively endure a report that they did *not* invite, by a lecturer who is abusing the power that they bestowed upon him: "I regret that I cannot comply with your request to the extent you desire" (*Stories,* 250), says the ape as he nonetheless proceeds to speak about everything *except* that for which they invited him. Now, how was an animal, an ape, to perform such a feat and, single-handed, subdue an honorable academy? *He* was not.

I did it. Truisms will point out that he who says "I" is a speaker. He is at the center of the linguistic event that is taking place, both as the origin of discourse and as its apparent referent; in a position of power where *I* alone assumes all the functions of discourse, including the narrative and the referential functions—the *telling* of a story *about* himself. Whereas the academy asked for a story about an ape-self, the speech that they endure is one about how-not-to-be-an-ape-self. The disparity between the two lies, on the one hand, in the relationship of *I* to "self"—in which *self* can mean, among other things, either "self-image" (self-representation and consciousness) or "self-body" (fuzzy, furry, scratching, jumping up and down, etc.)—and, on the other hand, in difficulty in perceiving at the same time the present (the speaker in the process of delivering a speech to an academy) and the past ("the life I formerly led as an ape"); a difficulty, that is, in interweaving a temporal sequence of *I*'s in which each one will be at once distinct (so as to function linguistically as the subject of a verb in a specific expression), yet the same (so as to ensure continuity of reference throughout a string of expressions). These difficulties do not originate in this particular academy. Others have debated them as well. In fact, indexical expressions, and *I* in particular, have been the source of hair-splitting controversies among philosophers, ranging from the claim that *I* is a purely referential term to the claim that it is bereft of any referential power or function. Once more, the thrust of this discussion among analytical philosophers was determined by Frege's pioneering inquiry.

Frege

In *The Thought,* after underlining the need for "certain accompanying conditions of utterance" (namely, the time and place in which the utterance occurs) in order for us to communicate and understand properly the thoughts conveyed by expressions containing indexicals (*here, now, I, yesterday,* etc.), Frege concludes:

> In all such cases the mere wording, as it is given in writing, *is not the complete expression of the thought,* but the knowledge of *certain accompanying conditions of utterance,* which are used as means of expressing the thought, are needed for its correct apprehension. The pointing of fingers, hand movements, glances may belong here too. The same utterance containing the word "I" will express different thoughts in the mouths of different men, of which some may be true, others false.
>
> The occurrence of the word 'I' in a sentence gives rise to some questions.[11]

While *I* is an indexical (it requires "the knowledge of certain accompanying conditions of utterance"), it also differs from other indexicals in that it "gives rise to some questions." To make his point on the logical status and truth-value of a thought containing *I,* Frege tells us a little story: Dr. Gustav Lauben has been wounded. Now, what happens to the thought "I have been wounded," expressed by Dr. Lauben, when various people who do or do not know him and who do or do not know his name hear this sentence, first when Dr. Lauben himself says, "I have been wounded," then when a third party reports the incident in the third person (or using the name Dr. Lauben)? What happens if the third party takes somebody else to be Dr. Lauben? Is it still the same thought (comparing "I have been wounded" in Dr. Lauben's mouth and "Dr. Lauben has been wounded" in the mouth of the person who mistakes someone else for Dr. Lauben)? In one sense, it is evidently the same thought with the same truth-value (the expressions have the same sense and the same reference), but in another, when said by the person who is wrong about the identity of Dr. Lauben, this thought is false. Can the same thought then be true for one person and false for another? If a thought is objective, and if this objectivity guarantees that two and two will forever make four, then this last alternative is unthinkable; *otherwise,* science may have to proceed with true and false Pythagorean theorems.

Frege's answer is therefore very cautious: in an expression containing indexicals, sense and reference are not as distinct as they are in other expressions. In such cases (and in such cases only), securing the reference *is* related to apprehending the sense. Thus, for example, in a case of mistaken identity, two different persons can think, "Dr. Lauben has been wounded," while one of them attributes the wound to someone who is not Dr. Lauben; in such a case, we can have two thoughts for one expression—the thought of the person who is right and that of the person who is wrong—with the odd result, from a Fregean viewpoint, that the same utterance can be true in some circumstances and false in others.

This analysis is markedly different from the one that Frege advanced earlier, in which, once a thought is proven true, it remains true forever, unaffected by circumstances. Indeed, this account of "I" invites thoughts such as "my twos" and "your twos" that he feared earlier. I find no solution for this contradiction in Frege's writings, but I find it worth underlining that when he had to grapple with a word that implied *simultaneously* the representation of subjectivity (the "self," consciousness, memory, etc.), the very same discourse in which this representation appears, and the act of enunciation itself, Frege had to surrender his realism, at least momentarily, to some form of relativism (in this sense *I* represents a test for his theory, and it is for this reason that we are focusing on the problem it raises).

Of course, Frege's example relies on the assumption that Dr. Lauben has truly been wounded: thus someone, at least, will speak the truth. What if in fact Dr. Lauben has not been wounded but still claims that he has (let us say, in order to receive a Purple Heart)? Let us simplify the example and assume that we do not have a case of mistaken identity and that the thought "I have been wounded" expressed by Dr. Lauben will be correctly understood by a number of interlocutors and third parties. However, while Dr. Lauben himself knows that he is lying (and that, therefore, his thought is false), others do not. What, then, of *their* thoughts? Are they false or true? Since, according to Frege, truth is not a correspondence between expressions and reality (that would make truth into a relation, while it should be absolute [see "The Thought," 280–81]), we cannot simply say that, as Dr. Lauben has not really been wounded, their thoughts are false. Paradoxically, to be consistent with Frege's analysis, we shall have to assume that as their thoughts are identical with the one expressed (falsely) by Dr. Lauben's, they must be true. The same absolute thought, bearing on the same reference and carried by the same expression, will again be true in one case (the dupes) and false in the other (the liar). (This is the paradox built into the judiciary: if their testimony was given in good faith, witnesses cannot be accused of perjury—even if these testimonies are later proven false.)

We may even wish to add a new twist to Frege's little story: what of the truth-value of the same thought if Dr. Lauben, still wishing for a Purple Heart, suffers from amnesia and does not remember that he has indeed been wounded, so that while he thinks that he is lying, he is in fact telling the truth? (One can quote here the case of Oedipus, who, until the final recognition, is wrong in almost everything he says about himself.)

This last question brings us closer to "A Report." The ape suffers from amnesia, or so he claims; he does not remember his life before his capture by the hunters. Let us play along and concede his good faith when he claims no longer to be an ape: I doubt that anyone will think that, since he does not remember his life as an ape, he must not be an ape. He may not be lying, but he is clearly wrong: his furry body and apish behavior deny the core of his message. Even his rhetoric (his choice of smiles and examples) draws on experiences incongruous in a human academy, all the while calling attention to his ape body and frame of reference.[12] Furthermore, his listeners (and indeed the readers) know that there is something odd in his use of *I*, something that defies the clear true/false criterion proposed by analytic philosophy; yet, this "something" is precisely the most essential component of the story: it is clear that, had the story been told in the third person, we would have lost the effect of this something. We would have had a different story, one that, as the fragments illustrate, Kafka did not elect to write. In the published version, something in the (wrong) use of *I* allows for the series of displacements to which "A Report" owes its remarkable effect, some feat that *I* performs—not as a fluke but because it is in its inherent power to perform such feats and secure such effects. Indeed, Frege had not read "A Report," yet he was aware of the particularities of *I*. In one of his most insightful sentences he distinguishes between two aspects of *I*.

> Now everyone is presented to himself in a particular and primitive way, in which he is presented to no-one else. So when Dr. Lauben thinks that he has been wounded, he will probably take as a basis this primitive way in which he is presented to himself. And only Dr. Lauben himself can grasp [*fassen*] thoughts determined in this way. But now he may want to communicate with others. He cannot communicate a thought which he alone can grasp [*den nur er allein fassen kann*]. Therefore, if he now says "I have been wounded," he must use the "I" in a sense [*in einem Sinn*] which can be grasped [*fassbar*] by others, *perhaps in the sense of "he who is speaking to you at this moment,"* by doing which he makes the associated conditions of this utterance serve for the expression of his thought. ("The Thought," 287)

The distinction drawn here is by now familiar: it cuts once more between subjective and objective; and, as we well know, that which is subjective—in the speaker's head, known to this speaker alone and therefore exempt from communication—is not part of the theory. In this sense, *I* pertains to *Vorstellung;* it is an "idea" (this view of "I" as an idea would be developed later by Anscombe; see the section on Anscombe below): "A certain idea in my consciousness may be associated with the idea of the word "I." But then it is an idea among other ideas and I am its bearer as I am the bearer of other ideas. I have an idea of myself but I am not identical with this idea. What is a content of my consciousness, my idea, should be sharply distinguished from what is an object of my thought" ("The Thought," 33; throughout this passage, Frege uses *Vorstellung* for idea).

It is therefore not surprising that the discussion of *I* is framed by the grey areas of Frege's theory: it follows a discussion of "force," in which once more theater and poetry are summoned and repudiated, and immediately precedes Frege's four criteria for identifying ideas. The context leaves no doubt: sandwiched between two factors for which the "theory" had no use, *I* is one of these linguistic elements that Frege never intended to treat thoroughly but found himself compelled to examine in order to justify their exclusion.[13]

"I" must have another aspect as well: we know empirically that unlike *Vorstellung*, "I" can be communicated; we use *I* all the time. As Bar-Hillel pointed out humorously, even the strictest philosopher, the most opposed to subjectivism and psychologism, would not be able to do without indexical expression.[14] Frege acknowledges this aspect: "If he now says 'I have been wounded,' he must use the 'I' in a sense which can be grasped by others, *perhaps in the sense of 'he who is speaking to you at this moment. . .'* " The crucial point about the second aspect of *I* is that it can be *grasped* by others. But the translation is faulty; three times in this passage, Frege uses *fassen,* which is translated in other key moments by *apprehend,* while here, for a reason that escapes me, the translator chooses *grasp.* As we remember from our reading of *Sinn* and *Vorstellung,* Frege emphatically stressed that one "apprehends" a thought or a sense and that the word *fassen* has to be taken technically. Note that I am not objecting so much to the use of *grasp* rather than *apprehend* to translate *fassen* as to the inconsistency of the translation: it interferes with the coherence of Frege's argument. When Frege uses *fassen* in the passage about apprehending a thought, comments on his choice of *fassen,* and expresses misgivings about its inadequacy (see chap. 3, N. 30), and a few pages later uses *fassen* again to denote the aspect of I that both the speaker and the listener can access, a connection between the two passages is in order and the translation should not lessen the reader's ability to make just this connection. As it stands, if we acknowledge that the verb, and therefore the activity, is the same in the two arguments, then the distinction that Frege discerns in the two aspects of *I* parallels the one he stressed between *Sinn* or *Gedanke,* on the one hand, and *Vorstellung,* on the other (see "On Sense and Reference" in chap. 3). Even his attitude toward and reaction to this distinction remain unchanged: the part that pertains to idea is, as usual, acknowledged but excluded from the theory for fear of subjectivism, while the part that pertains to sense remains independent of any consciousness and can be "apprehended" by just about anyone. The latter characteristic guarantees that, analytically, an expression containing *I* will conform to other expressions, so that the criterion of truth-value will apply to it, notwithstanding its obvious subjective aspect.

In the final analysis, what is, for Frege, the sense of *I?* Here lies one of his most remarkable (and neglected) insights: while signs normally "express" their sense and "designate" their reference[15] *I* neither expresses one's self nor designates it. Whatever the sense expressed by *I* is, *it has nothing to do with the self,* and thus avoids the trap of subjectivism and psychologism. Here Frege goes beyond the simplistic opposition realism versus psychologism: unlike other linguistic signs, *I* is not a function of either a material or a conceptual reality but *of discourse.* *I* does not mean "myself" or any subjective perception and consciousness I may have of myself; it is a purely formal marker of the discursive origin of a given utterance: "*he who speaks to you at this moment.*" In an odd and unique way, *I* refers to discourse itself and to the circumstances of this discourse ("to you" and "at this moment") in a quasi-Benvenistic manner, and not to references and objects intended by language, as Frege devised in his important three articles on the subject.[16] In addition, this definition implies that "the associated conditions of this utterance" are constitutive of the thought expressed. (The most important of these is the positing of an interlocutor—"you." *I* would then also be a formal indicator of dialogue (I/you), in which the transmitting end is called *I* and the receiving *you*). This, again, is a unique moment in Frege's thinking, since his theory does not normally allow for "associated conditions" and "circumstances." Indeed, as circumstances change with each utterance of the expression, should its sense, reference, or truth-value change? What, then, of the Pythagorean theorem, and of two and two? It is clear that a component alien to the rest of the theory, one that could invalidate the very foundation of the theory, has surreptitiously sneaked into Frege's pen.[17]

Let us not forget that Frege stumbled upon indexical expressions on his way to something else. His remarks on indexicals are made in passing only, as somewhat annoying examples of cases in which the thought proper does not exhaust the content of an expression (ironically, it is precisely as such that they are of greater value to the reader of literature than his more elaborated logical formulations). The brief notations about *I* were clearly not intended as a bona fide theory of the first person. We cannot guess whether or not Frege was aware of the structuralist overtones of his hesitant treatment of the first person—although the cautious "perhaps" introducing his tentative definition of *I* as "he who speaks to you at this moment" suggests some awareness of the incongruity of his definition within the framework of the general theory. (I shall take up this lead and its structuralist implications later, in the section on Benveniste and in chapter 6). I did not bring up Frege so much to offer a theory as to indicate a direction that he suggested, one that was later taken by others and made into "theories" of the first person. As in the case of *Vorstellung,* Frege was aware of the difficulties that a purely logical treatment of *I* would encounter (and, for a while, he bent his rigid realism). We may say that in his examination he mapped the traps as well as the route for a theory of the first person. Unfortunately, only the route was retained while the traps were all but overlooked and too often fallen into. Frege's succinct treatment of *I* can be read as an anticipated critique of later theories.

Russell

Unlike Frege, Russell does not attempt to see signs, language, and truth as objective entities. And yet the overall logical projects of the two philosophers are similar: they were both engaged in the pursuit of truth, but they went about it in very different ways. Frege set out to isolate the objective facts needed for a rigorous science (mathematics). Realizing that proper formulation and communication of his findings would depend on an unequivocal language in which he could express his thoughts with absolute precision, he then deviated from his original course and set out to isolate and regulate an objective language. This difficulty was exacerbated by his strange assimilation of "individual" with idiosyncratic, and "subjective" with incommunicable. His mistrust of psychology led him to profess a total lack of interest in the imponderable consciousness of the subject and to focus relentlessly on the object. In order for two and two to make four and the Pythagorean theorem to endure, Frege sacrificed the human subject. Russell, on the other hand, tries to reinstate man, as a subject, in language and truth, albeit without sacrificing the Pythagorean theorem. Inasmuch as Russell includes the working of the brain in his theoretical formulation, his views attest to an unabashed psychologism: the speaker's consciousness, his perception, and the ways in which he translates percepts into knowledge all become objects of Russell's inquiry, with the result that elements and categories that Frege excluded find their way into Russell's formulations.[18]

Interestingly, the reasons for Russell's inclusion of a modified psychologism are exactly the same reasons that determined Frege to wage war on psychologism and idealism. Among them, the prevalent one was the philosopher's inability to reach an unmediated truth: Frege blames language, and Russell, the human mind. As we remember from the previous chapter, Frege often wistfully deplored the imprecision of language and apologized to his readers for his inability to find clear expressions devoid of metaphorical overtones and convey his ideas more clearly. Russell presents a similar apology.

> Our discussions, hitherto, have been concerned very largely with Man, *but Man on his own account is not the true subject-matter of philosophy*. What concerns philosophy is the universe as a whole; Man demands consideration *solely as the instrument by means of which we acquire knowledge of the universe*. And that is why it is human beings as capable of knowledge that have concerned us mainly in past chapters, rather than as centers of will or of emotion. We are not in the mood proper to philosophy so long as

we are interested in the world only as it affects human beings; the philo-
sophic spirit demands an interest in the world for its own sake. But since
we apprehend the world through our own senses, and think about it with
our own intellect, the picture that we acquire is inevitably coloured by the
personal medium through which it comes to us. Consequently *we have to
study this medium, namely ourselves,* in order to find out, if we can, what
elements in our picture of the world are contributed by us, and what
elements we may accept as representative of outside facts. (*Outline,*
247)

Russell's philosophy is then markedly anthropocentric: even in his most
logical and analytical writings, a considerable part of his effort goes to
relating the outside world to human perception and consciousness. His
project is particularly evident when he deals simultaneously with lan-
guage, consciousness, and percepts, as in the case of indexicals and,
more specifically, of *I*.

A brief excursion into Russell's general theory of language will help
clarify the crucial role indexical expressions play in his larger episte-
mology. He distinguishes between different levels of language, of which
the most elementary is the "object-language," consisting of "object-
words," whose meaning is learned by repeated confrontation with the
objects or instances that they designate. (The next level would be, for
instance, one in which the words *true* and *false* would appear, so that in
the second level we can tell whether an object-word applied to an object
in the first level is true or false of that object; the third level of language
would then be the one in which the definition of *true* and *false* would be
given, etc.[19]) Throughout the minor variations of the definition of
object-words, Russell insists emphatically on their prime characteristic:
their foremost function is *ostentive*. To fulfill this function "object-
words" must be acquired *in the presence* of the designated objects. In
the terminology that I suggested earlier, we can say that Russell's object-
language is a language in which the deictic aim prevails, while the se-
mantic aim is quasi-null (cf. Russell: "At the lowest level of speech, the
distinction between sentences and single words does not exist. At this
level, single words are used to designate the *sensible presence* of what
they designate" [*Inquiry,* 30]).

(It is interesting that Russell's atomic view of language is diametri-
cally opposed to theories of the concept, in which one has to leave out
the object-language in order to acquire and practice language. To take
up Rousseau's example, oak A and oak B can both be oaks only if I
disregard my immediate percept of the specific oak that I am looking at
and retain only the characteristics common to oaks A, B, C, etcetera.

The result of this theory is that I never see an oak, but rather an oak to which the characteristics of the specific precept are added; therefore the word *oak* refers to *nothing in the world,* but to a concept that I have created by abstraction.[20])

In the perspective presented by Russell, *this* soon proves the most primary and elementary word, since it is a master-word, apt to replace any object-word: instead of calling an object by its name, I can always say "this." Furthermore, even if I use the name of an object, this primitive use of an object-word remains in fact egocentric (*egocentric* is Russell's term for indexical), that is to say, will in some manner imply the word *this:* for a dog to cause me to say, "Dog!" it must be present to *my* senses, be a "this dog" rather than just any dog; only at a later stage of my verbal development shall I learn that *dog* may designate *in absentia,* at which time I shall differentiate between presence and absence by means of *this* or *that* (see "every object-word, in its primitive use, *has an implicit egocentricity,* which the subsequent development of speech renders explicit" [*Inquiry,* 158]).

Having established the ostensive nature of object-words and their ever possible reduction to *this,* Russell derives *I* from *this:* " 'I' means 'the biography to which this belongs' " (*Inquiry,* 141). Although Russell's atomism generally remains in the Cartesian tradition, it would seem that in this case it reverses Descartes' argument. Descartes, having doubted all exterior objects as well as the perception he might have of these objects, chose the *I* implicit in his *cogito* as the foundation on which to rebuild the world.[21] Russell, on the other hand, eliminates systematic skepticism and pragmatically bases his theory on the very same percepts that Descartes doubted. The question then is: can he maintain the derivation of the subject from the outside world throughout all the stages of his argument, thus bypassing the *cogito?* In other words, can he ground his epistemology and ontology in a no-nonsense primary form of phenomenology?

The force of Russell's analysis lies in its intuitive simplicity. But the elegance of a "simple" proof can be misleading: *this* does indeed function as a master-word, as a verbal substitute for a tireless finger pointing at objects—but what of the "finger" itself? Is it detached from the subject or is it, on the contrary, the physical extension of a consciousness in the process of communicating to other consciousnesses its relationship to the world at a given time and in a given place? We may attribute the first option (the detached finger) to Frege, but, to be consistent with Russell's project, we must associate the second with him. In other words, within Russell's perspective, although he claims that *this* is a paradigmatic proper name, there is still a significant difference between *this* and just any name, in that the word *this* implies my physical presence, here and now—otherwise, how can I designate the object to which *this* refers?[22] Whereas *dog* can refer to the dog that Johnny (not I) saw last year (now now) while visiting his friends in Antarctica (not here), there can be no *this* (say, "this dog") without an "I" for whom the designated object is a "this." The use of *this* clearly presupposes the presence of an "I," so that, in a peculiar way, *this* subsumes *I*.

The same can be said of any indexical expression: "here" is where *I* am,[23] "now" is the time contemporaneous with *my* utterance, and so on.[24] (Of course, the same can also be said of all object-words, since they imply presence, that is, a subject for whom these objects are present). I am therefore prepared to accept Russell's definition that an indexical expression "depends upon the relation of the user of a word to the object with which the word is concerned" (*Inquiry*, 138), but then, I can no longer accept either the choice of *this*, rather than *I*, as the foundation stone of the theory or Russell's casual suggestion that the whole argument could be made to rest on I-now without requiring further adjustments. I shall therefore correct my earlier assessment: despite his claim to the contrary, Russell remains within the strict boundaries of Descartes's *cogito*. His conception of language and knowledge remains anthropocentric: it rests not only on the outside world (nor does it rest on the ostensive gesture itself) but also and simultaneously on the subject (*I*) performing that gesture and relating to the world. (Need I emphasize that the very term he chose for this class of words is not *index*ical but *ego*centric?) The definition of *I* as "the biography to which this belongs" is then circular: *I* is defined in terms of *this*, but *this* already includes *I*. The *definiens* thus figures surreptitiously in both parts of the definition.

Why, then, choose *this* over *I* for the most fundamental word? Russell does not justify his choice, although he expresses his awareness of the tautological relationship between *I* and *this* (all the while awkwardly maintaining the priority of *this* over *I*). See for example: " 'This' is a name which we give to the object to which we are attending, but we cannot define 'this' as 'the object to which I now attend,' because 'I' and 'now' involve 'this' " (*Inquiry*, 135–36).[25] The fact is that in Russell's theorization *I* and *this* are inextricably linked: we are then condemned to a circular definition in which indexical expressions such as "those of which the denotation is relative to the speaker" (134), posit simultaneously the human subject and the outside world. This double foundation entails the subordination of language to both the subject's intentionality and the preexisting world, as well as its reduction to a shuttle between the two (see chap. 5 for a critique of intentionality).[26]

It is worth noting that, despite the tautological aspects of his definition, and despite his numerous claims that *I-now* could replace *this* as the paradigmatic word, not once did Russell hesitate between *I-now* and *this*. Once and for all, without motivating his choice, he opted for *this*. Given the circular aspect of our discussion, I am prepared to concede that *this* serves the theoretical purpose; there is, however, one more distinction to be made between the two words, which may account for Russell's choice: at least in English, *this* is by definition compresent with the time of the utterance. We say, "*This is* an ape" (or "This is not an ape") and "*That was* an ape." (Of course, we could point at some creature and say, "*This was* [in the sense of "used to be"] an ape," but, then, what is it now? This indeed is the problem raised by "A Report.") In fact, such is the case for all indexical expressions: they are compresent with the time of the utterance and would change if a time factor were introduced into the sentence: *now* would become *then, here there, today yesterday,* and so forth. However, we do not have the same temporal distinction for *I;* we have to use the same expression in the present and the past. Whether the meaning of my sentence is compresent with the time of the utterance or not, the word itself remains the same: we say, "*This* is sad" and "*That* was said, but "*I* am sad" and "*I* was sad." While *this* becomes *that, I* subsists throughout the change of time and tense. In our story the ape says, "*I* was an ape" and "*I* am not an ape," thus apparently defying the law of the excluded middle—at least if we believe that, as is normally the case, once an ape, always an ape. Once more, *I* proves simultaneously the paradigm and the exception—which could explain why Russell steered away from it. The stumbling block is time, or, more precisely, our perception that from the viewpoint of nonverbal referents, *I* is different from *this,* in that it implies consciousness and transcends time, space, and presence.

In *An Outline,* Russell states that "[a]s a matter of fact, 'I' seems to be only a string of events, each of which separately is more certain than the whole" (*Outline,* 251). *An Outline* was published some thirteen years before Russell elaborated his theory of "egocentric particular" in *Inquiry,* so we cannot hold him too strictly to earlier formulations. And yet his basic analysis of the question remained the same. The "whole," that is to say, "I" proper, the ego, is at best questionable, while each particular event in the "string of events" that composes this problematic "I" seems irreducible, just as "I-now" is irreducible in *Inquiry.* The problem is one of continuity: how can we add up these events to compose a "string"? How can we bypass the principle of presence required for object-words and establish *relations* among theoretically infinite events ("I-now," "I-a-minute-ago," "I-two minutes-ago," "I-three minutes ago," etc.)?[27] When I say "I," I am not only designating myself as a referent for my expression; I am not even perceiving myself as a pure "I-now," as if I had just been born fully grown from Jupiter's head. Instead, by saying "I," I am also stating something else. I am saying, for example, that my acquaintance with the referent of *I* extends beyond the ostentive gesture. I may be saying that my perception of the referent of *I* is related in a certain manner to my perception of space; or again, that of all words, *I* regulates my discursive space (my discourse, its syntax, coherence, meaning, etc.). Now, when we speak *about* expressions and mention *relations* between them, we are no longer simply pointing at objects—that is, we are no longer using the most primitive language, the object-language. We are at the next level of language, one where we can speak *about* the first primitive language. *I* should then belong to that next level—even though it is also a typical egocentric particular and as such ought to belong to the first level. To add insult to injury, we are not free to resolve the problem by boldly "moving" *I* from the first to the second level, since, as we saw earlier, it is surreptitiously present in *this,* which definitely belongs to the first level only.

The embarrassing logical conclusion to which the analysis of *I* leads us is that the most typical, the most paradigmatic object-word, an egocentric particular, belongs in fact to the next level of language and not to the object-language. This, of course, would be an inadmissible contradiction in terms; it would also undermine the distinction between levels of language, on which Russell builds his epistemology; finally, it would threaten to invalidate his logical atomism. Russell is clearly aware of the problem, although he never formulates it in these terms. "All egocentric words can be defined in terms of 'this.' . . . Perhaps if we gave a name to 'I-now,' as opposed to 'I-then,' this name could replace 'this' " (*Inquiry,* 134). The solution is remarkably ingenius. In order to preserve the *hic* and *nunc* essential to indexicals, we divide up *I* into its usable and its unusable components: *I-now* will then behave like a perfectly normal indexical expression, while *I-then,* subsuming all the troublesome elements of *I,* will be discarded. The strategy of exclusion is by now familiar enough to readers, and I shall not insist on its implications. Nor shall I insist on the obvious Zeno-like aspect of delineating what *now* means and when *now* becomes *then* (one may assume, for example, that every moment to which we refer as "now" can in turn be subdivided into a "then" and a "now"). I will, however, address a different problem, one that "A Report to an Academy" exploits: the relationship between memory and consciousness, or between memory and the constitution of the subject *as a subject of language.*

Having established the priority of *I-now* over *I-then,* Russell can discard continuity. Time is all but eliminated: the subject of language lives in an absolute present. While he grants the present an unquestioned ontological status, Russell relegates other temporal instances to a secondary (delayed) position, one that he calls causal: " 'Present' and 'past,' are primarily psychological terms, in the sense of involving *different causal relations* between the speaker and that of which he speaks; their other uses are all definable in terms of this primary use" (*Inquiry,* 141). Consciousness proceeds at a staccato pace: each moment is nicely labeled and stored away "in the brain" until one chooses to recall it, at which point the information recalled is altered to fit the time of recalling. How and by whom (or what) is this alteration performed? Russell's explanation is simple and elegant: the brain can delay its reactions to outside stimuli. The stimuli may be identical, but, if I respond to a stimulus right away, I say, "This is" or "I-now," whereas if my brain defers its reaction, creating a time gap between the stimulus and the response, I say, "That was" or "I-then." This process is purely mechanical: Russell compares the ability of the brain to process information to that of a machine (today, we would say a computer): he imagines a central unit, processing information. The computer can either process information immediately or delay the output. When there is no delay, the phrasing of the input and that of the output are identical: "This is a dog." When the reaction (output) is deferred, however, although the input remains "This is a dog," the machine is programmed to process it differently so that the output is "This *was* a dog." Or again, translating his explanation into neurological terms: "A verbal reaction to a stimulus may be immediate or delayed. When it is immediate, the afferent current runs into the brain and continues along an efferent nerve until it affects the appropriate muscles and produces a sentence beginning 'this is.' When it is delayed, the afferent impulse goes into some kind of reservoir, and only produces an efferent impulse in response to some new stimulus. The efferent impulse, in this case, is not exactly what it was in the previous case, and produces a slightly different sentence, namely one beginning 'that was' " (139).

The difference between utterances in the present and in the past tenses is purely economical: a "minimal causal chain" is one that goes from the stimulus to the brain without delay and triggers an immediate verbal response; it is *"the shortest possible chain* from a stimulus outside the brain to a verbal response" (*Inquiry*, 139); it entails the use of the present tense and exemplifies how *I-now* would be used, if we had such a word. "Thus the difference between a sentence beginning 'this is' and one beginning 'that was' lies not in their meaning, but in their *causation*" (140). Shall we then examine "causation"? No, says Russell. Causation is circumstantial. It bears neither on language nor on epistemology, therefore it need not be treated in the context of either one. Oddly—and this is a recurring oddity—this long and detailed analysis winds up eliminating its very foundation from the scope of its inquiry.

And still, one may ask, how can I retrieve a past perception unless I know that it is stored away and waiting to be recalled? What is the difference between recalling that I have an urgent appointment and recalling my last trip to Mars?[28] How do I know that I have in storage something that reads like "dentist at 2:00 P.M.," and nothing like "my last visit to Mars"? The argument is obviously circular: if I know that a certain recollection is stored in memory, this is logically and epistemologically tantamount to saying that I "remember" it, in which case I no longer need to "recall" it; here Russell is well served by behaviorist psychology (especially John B. Watson, whom he discusses often); he specifies that this information is stored *away*, that is to say, that I cannot recall it at will. Instead, if something related to the first experience happens in the present, it will represent an added stimulus, to which I shall respond by involuntarily recalling the first stimulus. Recalling then involves a stimulus in the past for the first occurrence and a second stimulus, in the present, that mobilizes the stored memory and brings it to bear on my present.[29] It brings to mind, on the one hand, Proust's "involuntary memory" as illustrated by the *madeleine* in *Remembrance of Things Past* and, on the other, Pavlov's dogs salivating at the sound of the bell.

Russell sums up this discussion with the word 'I,' since it applies to something which persists throughout a certain period of time, *is to be derived from 'I-now,'* as that series of events which is related to 'I-now' by certain *causal relations*. The phrase to be considered is 'I am,' which may be replaced by 'I-now is,' where the 'is' may be regarded as *timeless*" (*Inquiry*, 141). As we have seen before, since these causal relations pertain exclusively to psychology, only I-now is of interest to the philosopher. I-now accompanied by its timeless *is*, renders any discussion of time irrelevant. Paradoxically, the end result of the discussion of time with regard to *I* is that time does not really belong in a discussion of *I*.[30]

What, then, of "A Report to an Academy" in this context? Our ape would undoubtedly be delighted to subscribe to Russell's view: he has lost his memory, or so he says, of his former life as an ape. Without having to eliminate a cumbersome past, he is ipso facto a sheer "I-now," a clean slate on which various stimuli can cause appropriate verbal reactions without ever raising the question of identity. I shall quote the extraordinary passage dealing with time and memory *in toto*.

> I regret that I cannot comply with your request to the extent you desire. It is now nearly five years since I was an ape, a short space of time, perhaps, according to the calendar, but an infinitely long time to gallop through at full speed, as I have done, more or less accompanied by excellent mentors, good advice, applause, and orchestral music, and yet essentially alone, since all my escorters, to keep the image, kept well off the course. I could never have achieved what I have done had I been stubbornly set on clinging to my origins, to the remembrances of my youth. In fact, to give up being stubborn was the supreme commandment I laid upon myself; free ape as I was, I submitted myself to that yoke. In revenge, however, my memory of the past has closed the door against me more and more. I could have returned at first, had human beings allowed it, through an archway as wide as the span of heaven over the earth, but as I spurred myself on in my forced career, the opening narrowed and shrank behind me; I felt more comfortable in the world of men and fitted it better; the strong wind that blew after me out of my past began to slacken; today it is only a gentle puff of air that plays around my heels, and the opening in the distance, through which it comes and through which I once came myself, has grown so small that, even if my strength and my will power sufficed to get me back to it, I should have to scrape the very skin from my body to crawl through. To put it plainly, much as I like expressing myself in images, to put it plainly: your life as apes, gentleman, insofar as something of that kind lies behind you, cannot be further removed from you than mine is from me. Yet everyone on earth feels a tickling at the heels; the small chimpanzee and the great Achilles alike. (*Stories,* 250)

Let us consider in what ways the ape's rendition of the relationship between his past and his present may be compatible with Russell's view. An utterance (in our case a report) is, according to Russell, a "verbal response" to an "outside stimulus." In "A Report," we have indeed a stimulus (the invitation to deliver a speech) and a verbal response (the speech itself), which, incidentally, turns out not to be the one that the stimulus was supposed to have caused. How can we explain this important discrepancy? We may wish to see in the academy's invitation what Russell calls an "additional stimulus, causing the stored effect of the previous stimulus to be released and to produce a delayed verbal response" (*Inquiry,* 139), but, then, what shall we do with the ape's strange case of amnesia? The ape does indeed have his own explanation: the first verbal response ("the life I formerly led as an ape") is so well stored away, behind a tightly closed door, that the secondary stimulus is unable to trigger the expected delayed response ("an *account*" of that life). What matters here is that the ape eventually amounts to a pure "I-now"—indeed his dearest wish (the span of *now* can be a tricky matter: independently of the more general implications of this problem, we can posit that in our story *now* means "not ape." The distinction between "I-now" and "I-then" will therefore coincide with the one between "I-ape" and "I-not-ape"). Russell's theory thus validates the claim that the ape's past has no grip on his present and that he has no recollection of anything that might undermine his claim to humanity. We can go one step farther and add that Russell's theory serves the ape's purpose also in that it explains his odd amnesia: there is nothing in common between his I-now and his I-then, nothing in common between his two lives. It would then follow that nothing that happens to him in his new life can serve as the appropriate additional stimulus and cause the expected delayed "account of the life [he] formerly led as an ape."

This last point demands a closer analysis. When examining how one comes to write an autobiography, Russell advances the following causal sequence: "We start from some prominent incident that we remember easily and gradually associations lead us to things that we had not thought of for a long time. The prominent incident itself has remained prominent, usually *because it has many associative links with the present*. It is obvious that we are not always remembering everything that we can remember, and that *what causes us to remember a given occurrence at a given moment is some association with something in the present*" (*Inquiry*, 193).[31] This argument deals with what Russell calls the additional stimulus. Twice in this passage Russell stresses that to cause a recollection of past memories, the incident in the present (the additional stimulus) must present "associative links" with the incident being recalled. Proust's *madeleine* is once more the perfect example: when accidentally eating a *madeleine,* the taste and the texture of the little pastry remind Marcel of something in his past; that something turns out eventually to be the same pastry he used to dip in his tea at his aunt Léonie's when he was a child. In Russell's terms, we can say that "gradually associations lead [Marcel] to things that he had not thought of for a long time," or again, in Proust's words, "all the flowers in our garden and in M. Swann's park, and the water-lilies on the Vivonne and the good folks of the village and their little dwellings and the parish church and the whole of Combray and of its surroundings, taking their proper shapes and growing solid, *sprang into being, town and gardens alike, from my cup of tea."* [32]

There is no *madeleine* in the ape's life, however (or, at least, so he claims; as we proceed in our reading of "A Report," we shall strongly disagree with this claim); there is nothing at all in his new life likely to remind him of his past: how convenient! In Russell's terms, the ape's past and his present are so radically different that no stimulus can be found in the present that would be associated enough with the past to determine a delayed response. How can this be? "I could never have achieved what I have done," explains the ape, "had I been stubbornly set on clinging to my origins, to the remembrance of my youth. In fact, to give up being stubborn was the supreme commandment I laid upon myself" (*Stories*, 250). A good Russellian, the ape understands that the success of his enterprise requires the eradication of his I-then. To reach this realization, it suffices to follow the law of the excluded middle: since he cannot at once be and not be an ape, and since he finds himself, because of circumstances beyond his control, in a human environment in which apes are locked up in cages, he decides not to be an ape. However, willing oneself to be a man does not a man make. His past threatens to cling to his present and contaminate it (not once does he deny that he *used to be* an ape). He then establishes a dual program of himself: 1) he will live as a man in the present; and 2) he will obliterate his previous life. Or again, in Russell's terms: 1) he will ground his I-now in human behavior, so that this I-now will be an I-human event; and 2) he will store away, very far away and behind closed doors, his I-then. In case we wonder how an ape can repress his past beyond recall, apes *and* academies will gladly explain to us that, since an ape and a *homo sapiens* lead different lives, we can rest assured that nothing in the ape's present "human" life will present an "associative link" with his animal past, so that no additional recall stimulus will ever bridge this irreversible gap. The ape is quite clear on this point: "to put it plainly: your life as apes, gentlemen, insofar as something of that kind lies behind you, cannot be farther removed from you than mine is from me" (250). Surprisingly, this reasoning is coherent and even cogent despite its circularity. If Russell's presentation of what makes a biography is correct, the ape has then succeeded in having no biography—or at least no ape-part in his biography. Now, since a no-ape biography is exactly what the ape wants to achieve, Russell's theorization of his wish cannot fail to delight him.

In summary, Russell's theory of the first person is perfectly adequate to explain the "I" of the ape—or is it? Let me rephrase that. Russell's theory undoubtedly fits the ape's claim, but does it fit the story? Does it account for the irony of the story *as a story*? I shall leave this question open until we examine other theories of the first person, and I will retain for the present only the ape's joy upon finding such strong support in a theory as elegant and convincing as Russell's.

Strawson

By introducing a sharp distinction between "meaning" and "use," Strawson avoids the psychological quicksand toward which consciousness and memory carried Russell. In his "On Referring," in which he argues the case of "unique reference" against Frege and Russell, he differentiates between "an expression," "the utterance of an expression," and "the use of an expression."[33] An *expression* is any meaningful segment of speech. Thus "The present king of France is bald," one of Russell's most renowned puzzles, is an expression: independently of the linguistic or historical context in which it appears, it has a sense or meaning, immediately grasped by anyone who speaks English. This is only a beginning, however, since under normal circumstances, contexts are inevitable. For example, let us imagine that a person, in the reign of, say, Louis XIV, utters this expression; let us imagine a second person, in the reign of Louis XV, uttering the same words. The expression will be identical in both cases: it will mean "The king of France is bald," independently of the date, the place, and the identity of either the speaker or the king of France himself; it is therefore an expression. And yet it will have been uttered twice: we shall therefore speak of the first and the second utterances of the expression. The expression itself is then an abstraction, while, in reality, we have only various *utterances* of expressions. Indeed, we would be hard put to imagine an expression that has not been uttered at some time (utterances can be spoken or written expressions; I can even speak of mental utterances, i.e., utterances that I formulate to and for myself without actually saying them out loud).

From a pragmatic viewpoint, our task is still not complete, however, since normally a person does not blurt out expressions for no reason but utters them because he or she wants to communicate something, that is to say, to express a thought *about* some object for the benefit of another person (of course that person can be walking down a street and reading aloud, absentmindedly, some graffiti—but this is hardly the most common situation). Strawson then carries the distinction one step farther: one does not just utter an expression but also, and at the same time, *uses* it to convey a thought about a particular person, event, object, or the like (see Strawson "you *use* the expression to *mention* or *refer* to a particular person in the course of using the sentence to talk about him" ["On Referring," 8, Strawson's emphasis]). Therefore, not only can we not encounter a pure expression, but—still pragmatically speaking—we cannot encounter a pure utterance of an expression either, unless that expression is used by someone (we should note the truism on which this analysis rests, namely, that for every utterance, there must be an "utterer," a person who utters it and who uses the expression for some extrinsic reason—a reason related to drives or motives of that person rather than to language proper). It follows from this distinction that, while semantically (and abstractly) we can speak of or analyze expressions, pragmatically, an expression is nonetheless by definition incomplete: therefore, claims Strawson, instead of losing ourselves in the vagaries of expressions, we should discuss specific and well-delineated "utterances" and their "uses." A philosopher engaged exclusively in the abstract and quasi-scholastic pursuit of expressions would run the risk of drawing false conclusions; in short, more often than not, such a philosopher would simply be wrong (such was, in Strawson's view, the case of Russell, who did not specify how and by whom "The king of France is bald" is used, or for what purpose).

Strawson's distinctions entail important consequences for the philosophy of language, logic, and even ethics. The most important concerns truth. According to Strawson, truth pertains to use only. For example, he would ask himself whether the expression "The king of France is bald" is true or not only if someone (including himself) had used it to say something about the king of France. Two different men uttering this sentence in the reign of Louis XIV make the same use of the sentence (therefore both would or would not say the truth about the king of France), while if one person used it to say something about Louis XIV and another about Louis XV, each would use the sentence differently: their utterances could differ with regard to truth. Thus, when these are two kings, if one of them is indeed bald, we shall say that in one case the sentence expressed a true proposition and in the other, a false one (see Strawson: "Generally, and against Russell, I shall say this. Meaning [in at least one important sense] is a function of the sentence or expression; mentioning and referring and truth and falsity are functions of the use of the sentence or expression" ["On Referring," 9]).

But what if France is not a monarchy? If, today, someone whispered in my ear, "The king of France is bald," would this situation be comparable to the two previous examples?[34] Strawson's solution to this puzzle is that such a use of the sentence would be *neither* true nor false; in other words, I shall not be able to answer—as I would, had I been alive in the reign of either Louis XIV or XV—"You are right; he is," or "You are wrong; he is not."[35] Instead, Strawson suggests that one might say to that person something like: " 'I'm afraid you must be under a misapprehension. France is not a monarchy. There is no king of France' " ("On Referring," 12). Therefore, since France is not currently ruled by a king, whose scalp we might wish to discuss, we ought not even to consider whether the sentence is false or true. Even if my interlocutor believes France to be a monarchy, his belief is wrong, but the actual sentence "The king of France is bald" can be neither true nor false: it would be a "spurious use of the sentence" (13).

The same holds for the expression *I*. With *I*, as with all expressions, Strawson distinguishes between meaning, utterance, and use. Now, the apparently innocuous truism we noticed underlying the general distinction between expression, utterance, and use becomes a formidable weapon: since there must be *someone* who utters and uses an expression, and since only a "person" qualifies as such a "someone" (on "the concept of a person," see later, pp. 142–45), it follows that this distinction presupposes the existence of a subject, as well as the unquestionable part this subject plays in the illocutionary process—and, by extension, in the pragmatic analysis of any utterance (see: "it makes no sense to say of the expression 'I' that it refers to a particular person. This is the sort of thing that can be said only of a particular use of the expression to *mention* or *refer* to a particular person in the course of using the sentence to talk about him" ["On Referring," 8]).

This line of reasoning does wonders for the problems raised by *I*. As with "The king of France is bald," the words *true* and *false* do not apply to the expression itself (*I*) but only to its use. In the case of *I*, this use is limited to referring to oneself. But then, how can it ever be false? Indeed, there is a level at which it would be absurd to think that I might *use I* to refer to anything (or anyone) but myself. Whether I utter a subjective (unverifiable) sentence such as "I am cold" or an objective and observable one such as "I am a human being," *I* will refer to me (see: "the first personal pronoun refers to whoever uses it"[36]). Even if, like Dr. Lauben, I am wrong in thinking or proclaiming that I have been wounded, the proposition "I have been wounded" still establishes beyond any doubt the identity of the so-called wounded person—if only later to face the charge that I am a liar and that lying is no way to earn that Purple Heart.[37] In other words, the sentence (or, in Frege's terms, the thought) may be false, but the word *I* has not failed to refer to myself. Seen from this perspective, *I* is then an exceptional word: it is immune to reference-failure and, hence, to falsity. More curiously still, there can be no "spurious use" of the expression *I*: it will always refer to "myself" (although there can be a spurious use of a sentence containing *I*). In a nutshell, for Strawson, *I* is in a uniquely privileged position: "*it is guaranteed against lack of reference, and it is guaranteed against mistaken or incorrect reference* (i.e., against lack of coincidence between the intended reference and the reference conventionally carried, in the circumstances, by the expression used)" (*Phil. Subjects*, 266).

This is all very well, but if, as we follow Strawson's argument, we have a nagging feeling that we are somehow begging the question, we should take heed. The ape did: he cleverly used a similar circular arrangement to win a point.

The ape uses the first person. As we saw at the beginning of this chapter, such use is essential to Kafka's perception of "A Report to an Academy." What does it achieve? Among other things, the use of the first person guarantees its user "against mistaken or incorrect reference." As the ape emphasizes time and again, there is nothing odd in his condition, nothing odd in his appearance before the learned academy, nothing odd in his rejection of his erstwhile ape-condition—all of which Strawson's theory will readily grant him. Why? Because he is a user of *I*. And yet who can use *I*? Strawson's answer is, again, unequivocal: a "person." Then, since he uses *I,* the ape must be a person. To simplify matters, let us imagine a sentence that does not exist in the text (although it represents the thrust of the ape's speech): "I am no longer an ape."[38] The syntax of English and German requires that, before the ape even utters the predicate "no longer an ape," he utter the expression "I am." But then the very fact that he is uttering *I* categorizes him as a person, rendering the following predicate redundant and superfluous. He *must* be a person (and as we know, this is precisely what he sets out to explain to the academy). It seems that whether he boasts Russell's or Strawson's sanction, the ape triumphs over academies and readers!

Let us be careful, however. Have we shown that Strawson's presentation of the first person begs the question? I think not—at least, not entirely. To do Strawson justice, we ought to retrace our steps: since a person must utter an expression, thereby establishing a reference for *I,* we find ourselves compelled to look into the concept of a person. In

Individuals, Strawson devotes a chapter to "Persons." I shall skip over the details of Strawson's discussions with other philosophers (these discussions set out to show what a person is not) and briefly summarize his argument. He reminds us that, pragmatically speaking, predicates that can be ascribed to persons are of two kinds: "corporeal," and "states of consciousness." [39] Now, the major disagreement among philosophers lies in the importance they attribute to each of these sets of predicates (Descartes's *cogito,* for example, Strawson's prime target, emphasizes states of consciousness at the expense of corporeal attributes). Strawson goes the traditional philosophers one better by catching the concept of a person before it splits: "What we have to acknowledge, in order to free ourselves from these difficulties, is *the primitiveness of the concept of a person.* What I mean by the concept of a person is the concept of a type of entity such that *both* predicates ascribing states of consciousness *and* predicates ascribing corporeal characteristics, a physical situation &c. are equally applicable to a single individual of that single type" (*Individuals,* 97–98). Descartes's "mistake" was that he privileged states of consciousness over corporeal predicates since "a necessary condition of states of consciousness being ascribed at all is that they should be ascribed *to the very same things as certain corporeal characteristics,* a certain situation &c. That is to say, states of consciousness could not be ascribed at all, unless they were ascribed to persons, in the sense I have claimed for this word" (97–98). Thinking is a state of consciousness. Alone, however, it is not enough to sanction a person (I think, *therefore* . . .): it must be assigned to something, and that something must be of a kind able to accept other predicates as well, this time corporeal. Thus Descartes's *cogito* must err, since the "primitive" person doing the thinking should be such that we can ascribe to her or him the very same "material predicates" that Descartes sets out to question. It is therefore not enough to say that I am thinking; I must also be able to ascertain that I have other predicates as well, of a corporeal nature: for example, I am breathing; I am a biped; I have certain physical properties (which, incidentally, preclude a coat of fur); I am capable of certain physical activities (standing erect, running, etc.). Above all, I have to be able to speak in order to utter the *I* that will consecrate me as a person. [40]

I shall not enter the debate over "a person." My concern is not the person that Strawson's definition presupposes but language, and in this particular case, the expression *I.* I am therefore willing to concede that a subject to which I can ascribe these two sets of predicates (corporeal and states of consciousness) is a person. If, however, this definition plays as important a part as Strawson claims in the perceptions that *I* is immune from reference-failure, then there is room to drive a logical wedge in the theory—at least inasmuch as it purports to be a theory of language.

"A Report to an Academy" is just such a wedge. It is evidently a fact of language, whose only reality is its linguistic character. As such, it cannot escape the rules and definitions that apply to language. Any theory of linguistic semantics should then be cogently applicable to the story and to the ways in which it "makes sense." And yet, when examined in conjunction with "A Report," certain aspects of Strawson's theory bring about different and contradictory results. If, for example, I confine myself to the limited theory of *I* found in *On Referring* and in parts of the *Reply*, then the triumphant ape is a person. If I pursue my enquiry, however, stubbornly seeking to determine exactly what a person is, I shall naturally turn to *Individuals*, in which Strawson devotes a whole chapter to this question. But then, to my dismay, I shall find out that the once triumphant ape is now in dire trouble: his corporeal predicates are simply not those of a person. Whatever changes he claims to have undergone since he entered into the "human community," not once does he boast a human appearance; on the contrary, as he ascertains his new identity, he nonetheless relentlessly evokes his well-groomed fur, his strong teeth, and his inordinate agility. His insistence on his "well-groomed fur" and his ape body leaves us two choices: either he is wrong in using *I* and, therefore, not a person (but by the sheer authority of the story, he cannot be wrong: if he is using *I*, then he must be able to use *I*), or Strawson is wrong in insisting on the importance of corporeal predicates for the definition of a person. But then, if the ape is not a person, how can he be an utterer? "Person" and "utterer" are inextricably linked in Strawson's theory and, logically and analytically, if he is not a person, the ape cannot and should not speak. And yet, the story might retort, he *does;* furthermore, not only does he speak but his ability to do so is precisely the gist of the story.

Underlying this paradox is the millenary tradition of *logos* as the dividing line between man and beast, as the purveyor of truth and knowledge—which is exactly the point of both Strawson and the ape. Whereas Strawson says, "At the risk of being wearisome, I must repeat the point that the immunity of 'I' from reference-failure (of either kind) in the thought, or speech of *any human user of it*, whatever his condition, is guaranteed by the role of the expression in the ordinary practice, *well established among human beings*, of reference to themselves and each other" (*Phil. Subjects*, 267); the ape echoes, "I . . . called a brief and unmistakable 'Hallo!' breaking into human speech and with this outburst broke into the human community" (*Stories*, 257).

Let me rehearse the impasse to which a reading of "A Report" in conjunction with Strawson's theory of the first person has led us. Whether we follow the theory of the first person or that of the concept of a person, we find ourselves unable to *read* our story: according to the theory of the first person, the ape *is* a person—in which case we lose the irony of the story, and our reading misses the mark. Similarly, according to the theory of the concept of a person, the story—consisting entirely of the speech of the ape—is impossible: since an ape is not a person and therefore cannot speak, there can be no story. "A Report to an Academy" is then a mistake, an aberration, some monumental logical typo, unworthy of the attention of serious philosophers and equally unworthy of figuring among the semantic "facts" purportedly accounted for by their theories of language.

And yet the fact is that the story communicates a "sense"; furthermore, it is through its logical and referential aberration that it communicates it. In no way does this aberration communicate a sense by eliminating reference, however. On the contrary, the effectiveness of the story depends on reference. This is therefore not a simple case of the suspension of disbelief, in which we purposely do not read referentially. The problem of reference is at the heart of our story, not as a simplistic mimetic representation of reality but as the enactment of the structural resistance of reference to its assimilation into a normative (Strawson's, for one) or an intentional discourse (the ape's). Most evidently, in saying "I," the ape refers to himself, and the readers know who "I" is. At the same time, precisely because he is successful in establishing the identity of "I," precisely because language is defenseless against such an obvious abuse, the ape creates a highly ironical context for *all the predicates* of this "I," namely, the very criteria that Strawson uses to justify *I* and encapsulate it into a neat, if circular, theory of the concept of a person (and the story can be read as a string of such predicates). Now, everything that *is* done *can be* done. The ape's "abuse" is therefore part of the possible uses of *I,* and a theory based on *use* should be able to account for all possible uses, however skewed they may be. Saying that the ape's first person is or is not a properly referring expression, or that it does or does not fail to refer to an appropriate object, does not even begin to scrape the surface of the story. The story is undeniably not "about" theories of the first person and reference, but, whatever we take it to be about, it achieves its effect by using *I* in a way *at once improper and highly effective.* To make this point even plainer and at the risk of repeating myself: had Kafka put the story in the mouth of a character who fits Strawson's definition of a person, we would have had a totally different story—as the discarded fragments show so eloquently.

There must therefore be a way in which language produces meaning *differently,* through an improper use that skews reference, without eliminating or bypassing it—and a theory of reference should be able to account for this use as well—"improper" as it may be.

It seems to me that the logical difficulty lies not with Strawson's theory of the first person but with that of a "person," or more precisely, with the dependence of the former on the latter. And yet, how can we wrench the "person" out of "the first person"? Moreover, if we could curtail the extension of the theory and eliminate the "person," how would we still account for reference on the grounds delineated by Strawson? How would such a revision affect the case of the ape? A short detour into structuralist linguistics will allow us to explore this avenue.

Benveniste

Generally speaking, linguists hold a perspective on problems of language that precludes many of the questions philosophers might address. This attitude entails a mixed blessing: on the one hand, it brings language proper into focus, thus eliminating considerations that might be extraneous to it (such as Strawson's "concept of a person," or Russell's behaviorist model for memory, without which I-now cannot subsume I-then); on the other hand, however, for lack of a well-formulated, larger conceptual framework, it risks missing the essential place that language and speech occupy in our lives and losing sight of the relevance (or lack thereof) of peculiarities of any given idiom.

In France, Emile Benveniste leads a new trend of linguists who address the general questions that commonly interest philosophers, while maintaining that many such questions can be solved formally and linguistically. This particular viewpoint enables him to put into question apparently irreducible concepts, as he advocates a theory of language capable of accounting conceptually rather than pragmatically for all linguistic manifestations (including the shifting of reference of indexicals).

About indexical expressions, Benveniste notes that "the reference to the 'speaker' implicit in this whole group of expressions has been treated too lightly and as being *self-evident.* We rob this reference of its inherent meaning if we do not see the feature by which it is distinguished from other linguistic signs. Yet it is a fact both original and fundamental that these 'pronominal' forms do not refer to 'reality' or to 'objective' positions in space or time but to the utterance, unique each time, that contains them, and thus they reflect their own use" (*Problems*, 219).[41] What or whom, then, is Benveniste criticizing for robbing "the reference to the speaker" of its inherent meaning? Explicitly designated as culprits are those who hold that indexical expressions pose no problem for reference, either because these expressions' immunity to reference-failure is "self-evident" or because they hold it a "self-evident" truth that reference is irrelevant to the study of language and linguistics.[42] Benveniste is probably addressing, first, some of his most radical structuralist or Saussurean colleagues, and then some Anglo-American philosophical theories of indexicals (he was familiar with some analytical philosophers). All quibbles aside, what remains is the claim that indexicals "do not refer to reality . . . but to the utterance, unique each time, that contains them." This proposition is crucial to Benveniste's argument: it sets him apart from the philosophers we have seen so far and in fact, from the primary tenets of the philosophy of language.

Overall, Benveniste proceeds in a Cartesian manner: if, because of the multiplicity of possible bearers of *I*, we cannot pin down a fixed referent in "reality," we ought to systematize doubt and look elsewhere—until our eye meets with an element of indisputable certitude. Since *I* pertains to language and exists only in discourse (or in Strawson's terms, in utterances), Benveniste infers that discourse must be the irreducible reality to which *I* refers. Furthermore, still in the Cartesian vein, once he secures the primitive relationship between the speaking subject and this subject's discourse, he can deduce from this first relationship all the other relationships between language and reality. The details of this argument require some explanation.

From the outset, Benveniste's solution swings a sword on our Gordian knot: "What then is the reality to which *I* or *you* refers? It is solely the 'reality of discourse,' and this is a strange thing. *I* cannot be defined except in terms of 'locution,' *not in terms of objects as nominal signs*" (*Problems*, 218). *I* is not a word for which we must provide either a referent or a meaning, that is, a nonlocutionary correlative. It is contained and confined within the "reality of discourse" and the act of locution. Therefore, there is no need to ask who is saying "I," what *I* designates, whether the entity *I* designates is a human being or not, as we previously have; such a line of questioning would lead us away from both the situation of discourse and the particular instance containing *I*. All this, because the "form of *I* has no linguistic existence except in the act of speaking in which it is uttered. There is thus a combined double instance in this process: the instance of *I* as referent and the instance of discourse containing *I* as the referee" (218). What acts as referent or referee is not the subject ("human being," "person," or other) but the instance (Benveniste defines "instances of discourse" as "the discrete and always unique acts by which the language is actualized in speech by a speaker" [217]). It is a nodal construct, subsuming all deictic and semantic functions and assuming an absolute authority over any kind of objective reality. For Benveniste, then, *I* is a purely linguistic phenomenon.

If *I* presupposes the utterance of a locution of some sort, however, it also presupposes a second person, equally contained in the "reality of discourse," to whom this locution is addressed. This function befalls *you*. In verbal communication, a person (*I*) addresses another person (*you*), who, in turn, may utter locutions containing the word *I*, thus *becoming* an "I"—all the while remaining exclusively a linguistic function devoid of any grounding in "reality." This view explains why for Benveniste *he, she,* and *it* are not third persons, but "non-persons." They are not inscribed in the situation that we call discourse in the same manner: when I say "she," I normally *refer* to a person who is not here, who is elsewhere. *She* has a referential existential object, one that is not limited to discourse. In Strawson's terms, since *she* refers to an object to which we can ascribe the same state of consciousness and corporeal predicates as we do to *I*, "she" is a person. In Benveniste's terms, specifically because we can ascribe such predicates to *she* (while we need not ascribe them to *I*), "she" is a nonperson. The main difference between Strawson and Benveniste is that Benveniste has, as we hoped he would, wrenched the person out of the first person, thus constructing what should be an unassailable theory.

Note that even as he mentions reference, Benveniste remains in fact within language: he speaks of referring not to an extralinguistic entity but to the very act by which *langue* is actualized as *parole*. Benveniste's notion of reference is then contained within language. (Although he does not use Saussure's terminology, Benveniste endorses Saussure's distinction between *langue* and *parole;* see: "Habit easily makes us unaware of this profound difference between *language as a system of signs* and *language assumed into use by the individual*" [*Problems,* 220].) Both Benveniste and Strawson deny the possibility of error or reference-failure of *I*. The analogy ends here, however, since what they intend by *reference* is radically different: for Strawson, the referee of *I* is the actual, physical person uttering "I," whereas it is a formal construct (an instance) for Benveniste. Thus, while Strawson eventually resorts to the "concept of a person" to delineate the extension of the referee of *I* (and sometimes vice versa), Benveniste can elect to remain within the formal boundaries of language. It is in this sense that I have found Frege closer to Benveniste than to his fellow philosophers, as he eventually suggested that "I" might well be simply "he who speaks to you at this moment" (see pp. 126–27), a definition very close to Benveniste's instance of discourse. Whereas Frege introduced his definition with a cautious "perhaps," however, Benveniste erected his as the cornerstone of his theory.

We can cite another case of possible confusion due to the different semantic values that philosophers and linguists attribute to certain key expressions. Benveniste is particularly vulnerable to criticism when he writes that " 'I' signifies 'the *person* who is uttering the present instance of discourse containing 'I' " (*Problems,* 218). Indeed, the word *person* sounds a familiar tone. Should we delve into the "concept of a person" as we did with Strawson? I think not; as with *referee*, the word *person* does not mean the same thing in the contexts of structuralist linguistics and analytic philosophy. Strawson's realist bias compels him to treat the person referentially (asking whether animals or multibodied organisms fit the definition), thus moving away from language. No such turn occurs in Benveniste's writing. His framework is language and language only ("locution," "instances of discourse," etc.) and thus imposes firm limits on the extension of the term *person*. For him a person is a speaker. The value of *person* is coextensive with its locutionary function. *Person* accepts no other predicates or assignation (be it corporeal predicates or states of consciousness). It is much closer to "person" in the grammatical sense (first, second, third person) than to its ontological or phenomenological sense. In Benveniste's writings the "person" is reduced to the "speaker *as* speaker" ("This sign is thus linked to the exercise of language and announces *the speaker as speaker*" [220]). It is a bogus term that does not interfere with his linguistic reduction. In this respect, one need neither ask oneself what a person is nor ascribe any kind of realistic predicates to it. A "person" is borne and defined by language, and more specifically, by the instance of discourse containing *I*. It needs no other grounding than this *I* ("The use [of *I*] has as a condition the situation of discourse and no other" [220]). Dr. Johnson's refutation of Berkeley, for example, has no hold on Benveniste's *I*: he could kick an object to ensure its objectivity and reality, but could he kick an *I*? Whatever *I* is, no kickable object corresponds to it in reality. Discourse is the only context in which one might encounter an *I*. Therefore, even as we read that *I* is "the *individual* who utters the present instance of discourse containing the linguistic *I*" (218), we should beware: the individual may come in any shape or color; his corporeal qualities and his states of consciousness are irrelevant. Benveniste's individual (like his person) is defined only by the fact that he "*utters* the present instance of discourse containing the linguistic instance *I*." To avoid a possible confusion between Strawson and Benveniste, suffice it to say that, although they use the same terms, the objects they describe are radically different.

To elucidate what hangs upon the choice between these two positions, we must remember that we are not discussing the analysis of a single, capricious, and puzzling word. We are taking the word *I* as a touchstone for theories: since *I* is the locus where locution, consciousness, subjectivity, and reference crowd each other the most, we are using it to bring the premises of a variety of theories to the foreground—at the risk of a crash. What, then, is at stake in our discussion is not so much the merit of any one of the theories of the first person that we are discussing as the ways in which philosophy, linguistics, and literature treat or exploit to their advantage the heterogeneity of discourse, objects, consciousness, and the subject. So far, the theories we have encountered have been caught in a web of infinite regress and tautological moves, forever needing to escape from the troubling object of their examination (*I*) by examining instead other concepts, or relying on some variant of the *cogito*. Can Benveniste's linguistic reduction avoid this fate? Will his relentless formalist determination and his Saussurean heritage allow him to confine himself to language?

As we read through Benveniste's analysis, we cannot help but notice inconsistencies and unexplained leaps. For example, when arguing that the reference of *I* is foolproof, he writes that "'I' designates the one who is speaking: in saying 'I,' I cannot not be speaking of *myself*" (*Problems*, 197). Now, this is strange. Does *I* refer to "myself" or to the instance of discourse, as Benveniste emphatically states on other occasions? Is this odd confusion only an occasional slip? Is it a case of inadequate expression? Or perhaps it is a sign that Benveniste's sword has missed the Gordian knot, has not cut through the thick of problems that have plagued other theories? (See Kafka: "There is an excellent idiom: to fight one's way through the thick of things; that is what I have done, I have fought through the thick of things" [*Stories*, 258]). Can *I* refer to "myself," thus bypassing the formal "instance" that has helped us out of the problems raised by the theories of analytic philosophers? Could Benveniste's theory have displaced or rephrased the problems posed by Russell's and Strawson's theories without defusing them? To take Strawson's example, if I say, "I am bleeding," what does *I* designate: "myself" or the act of speaking in which *I* occurs? Indeed, it would be absurd to claim that my act of speaking or my utterance is bleeding, but, on the other hand, if we explain *I* in terms of "self" (*myself*), we shall be hard pressed to analyze the concept of self, the way Strawson analyzed that of a person, that is, once more to move *away* from the examination of language. The two solutions are equally unsatisfactory. A transition enabling the instance of discourse to become a speaker is clearly needed if the sentence is to pertain to an entity capable of bleeding. Until such a transition is found, Descarte's *cogito,* for example, will read "I think [or perhaps even " 'I' thinks"], *therefore language is.*" Confining ourselves to a purely formal conception of language has its reward: it allows the "theoretician" to string theoretical propositions; and yet, unless we find a way to bridge the gap between language and subjects, these propositions risk leading us to bleeding instances of discourse. This is, as we remember, the predicament of the young peasant in the *fabliau:* his structuralist conception of language held up until he tested it against reality.

The instance of discourse is not Benveniste's last word. Rather, the role of *I* is "to provide the instrument of a conversion that one could call the conversion of language into discourse" (*Problems,* 220). Since there is no discourse without a speaker (Benveniste says *"individual* discourse"), this conversion may well be the missing link we needed, or at least *a* link explaining how individual reference to discrete speakers (rather than to instances) can be established and how intersubjectivity ensues. According to Benveniste, because the first person refers to the instance of discourse that contains it, it also "establishes the basis for *individual discourse,* in which each speaker takes over all the resources of language for his own behalf. . . . When the individual appropriates it, language is turned into instances of discourse, characterized by this system of internal references *of which I is the key,* and defining the individual by the particular linguistic construction he makes use of when *he announces himself as the speaker*" (220). When an individual becomes a speaker, he lays the foundation for intersubjectivity and communication. This conversion takes place as the individual "takes over all the resources of language" by uttering "I," thus creating a space of internal references of which *I* is the key (*here, now,* and all other index-ical expressions that establish the typology of discourse). Now, it is this process that Benveniste means when he speaks of "subjectivity."

> The "subjectivity" we are discussing here is the capacity of the speaker to posit himself as "subject." It is defined not by the feeling which everyone experiences of being himself (this feeling, to the degree that it can be taken note of, is only a reflection) *but as the psychic unit that transcends the to-tality of the actual experience it assembles and that makes the permanence of the consciousness.* Now we hold that "subjectivity," whether it is placed in phenomenology or in psychology, as some may wish, is only the emer-gence in the being of a fundamental property of language. *"Ego" is he who says "Ego."* That is where we see the foundation of "subjectivity," which is determined by the linguistic status of "person." (*Problems,* 224, Benven-iste's emphasis on *says*)

Benveniste is clearly addressing the question that has haunted pre-vious theoretical attempts: unlike the analytic theories, his analysis of the first person, while remaining essentially formal and linguistic, even-tually comes to bear on the "totality of the actual experience" and the "permanence of consciousness." This last analysis would solve the thorny problem of heterogeneity that so far has been the stumbling block of philosophers, if it were not for leaving open the question of *how* "I" performs the feat of "appropriation" of "all the resources of language for his own behalf"; how this process dubs the "speaker" a "subject"—and thereby founds reality and extralinguistic reference. Unless this question is answered, Benveniste's attempt to wriggle out of this bind may well end up further tightening the knot.

Benveniste's answer rests on the privileged status of *I* with regard to reference: in language, there is "an ensemble of 'empty' signs that are nonreferential with respect to 'reality.' These signs are always available and become 'full' as soon as a speaker introduces them into each in-stance of his discourse. *Since they lack material reference, they cannot be misused; since they do not assert anything, they are not subject to the condition of truth and escape all denial*" (*Problems,* 219). Neither assertion, nor misuse, nor denial. The only test is the exercise of lan-guage: once a speaker appropriates language (how? the question of the transition from "use" to "appropriation" remains unanswered), the empty signs *become* full. Even so, they lack material reference, do not assert anything, and escape all denial, claims Benveniste. What, then, of discourse's system of *internal references* of which *I* is the key, as he also claims? How can *I* found subjectivity and intersubjectivity if it does not assert anything and escapes denial? How can appropriation suffice to create a world, a subject, and the place of this subject in that world, as if by fiat (whose fiat is it anyway, the speaking individual's or the theoretician's?), without either asserting or denying anything? Furthermore, having wrenched the subject from the first person and reference from language as a system of signs, how does the locutionary act reintroduce them to establish communication and intersubjectivity? All Benveniste tells us is that it does ("Ego is he who *says* 'Ego.' That is where we see the foundation of 'subjectivity,' which is determined by the linguistic status of 'person'" [224]). And yet, how Benveniste gets from A to B, where A is a formal system in which a sentence containing *I* refers to a locutionary instance only (no consciousness, no extralinguistic entity), and B is a subject, that is, a *"psychic* unit that *transcends* the totality of the actual experience it assembles and that makes the *permanence of the consciousness"* remains a mystery. We certainly *want* to arrive at point B, but I see nothing in Benveniste's exposé that tells me just how he gets there, except, perhaps, wishful thinking. Stating authoritatively that A leads to B does not suffice to make it happen. Benveniste could have stated just as authoritatively that two and two make five. His argument (or lack thereof) undoubtedly shows his awareness that a formal system cannot remain purely formal while purporting to reconcile the consciousness one has of oneself as transcending the pure instance of one's discourse with the *hic* and *nunc* of such a discourse and its reference, but it falls short of showing how such a system accounts for these contradictory demands without compromising its formal premises.

The transition from formal language to consciousness and the integration of the two into one all-encompassing theory are once more affirmed but not demonstrated. This explains why, once more, a theory provides at the same time a vote of confidence and an alibi for the speaking non-ape. His sheer presence as a speaker in the academy allows him to "appropriate all the resources of language" by means of the authority bestowed upon him by this very language (and not by the members of the academy, as it first seemed). No longer a mere ape, he is a "depository of language." As such, he may refuse to obey his hosts' wish and may even impose on them his unrequested speech. As he speaks, the empty sign becomes full and organizes a world of referentiality of which he is the sole anchor. With each instance of his discourse, with each appropriation of language, the ape affirms his own ontological argument, thus creating the world in the image of his speech: a world in which, as his speech claims, he is no longer an ape.

The ape's enthusiasm in espousing Benveniste's theory would rival only his enthusiasm when faced with Russell's and Strawson's theories. Better yet, this time he need not worry about his ape-memory or his corporeal predicates: Benveniste has taught him that "the exercise of language" eliminates these cumbersome concerns. In short, in Benveniste's words, the ape's speech is not "subject to the condition of truth and escape[s] all denial": it creates truth rather than submits itself to a preexisting truth. Where one supreme being claims, "I am who I am," another echoes " 'Ego' is he who says 'Ego.' " With this claim, Benveniste and the ape convert language into ontology. "A Report to an Academy" would then be a story about an absolute power grounding his own ontology in a discursive fiat, a rewriting of Creation. On a lower scale of power, we would also have the story of a mutation, some sort of science fiction, as, for example, Marthe Robert claims (see above, n. 6), and not a story in which irony prevails. In this new story we would learn that, with absolute and stubborn determination, mutations are possible, although there is a small price to pay: a partial loss of memory—altogether, a rather fair trade-off. I could elaborate on this new story, but I trust that the reader sees that this new, optimistic version of the self-made man has hardly any points of contact with "A Report to an Academy." Once more, a very complete theory has missed the rhetoricity of "A Report," its very literariness.

Anscombe

In her discussion of the first person, our last philosopher, G. E. Anscombe, discards altogether the question of reference: "Getting hold of the wrong object *is* excluded, and that makes us think that getting hold of the right object is guaranteed. But the reason is that there is no getting hold of an object at all." [43] This statement concludes the first two-thirds of her essay, the part in which she deploys a wealth of ingenuity to refute the most prominent theories of the first person. We shall not follow her throughout the maze of philosophical theories and their pitfalls, or her series of arguments and refutations. Suffice it to indicate here her general strategy: for each theory that she intends to criticize, she makes up a counterexample to demonstrate the uncertainty that one will get hold of the right referent for *I*. The above quotation is the pivotal move by which she concludes her series of refutations and introduces the tenets of her own theory of the first person. If "there is no getting hold of an object at all," then the question of the *reference* of *I* becomes irrelevant, and Anscombe can now declare that "this is the solution: 'I' is neither a name nor another kind of expression whose logical role is to make reference, *at all*" (60, Anscombe's emphasis).

This move away from reference is probably her foremost contribution to the analytic theories of the first person since, until then, the question was regularly envisaged as Descartes and Frege had posed it, that is to say, from an epistemological and ontological viewpoint, which translated into concerns of reference and truth in the analytic discourse.

Anscombe's own theory hinges on *ideas*. This solution places her at the opposite end of the spectrum from Strawson and Russell—albeit, as we shall see, without taking her to Benveniste's position. Her argument rests on the fact that if, in the proposition "I am not G. E. Anscombe," "I" is indeed G. E. Anscombe (let's say she is the one saying, "I am not G. E. Anscombe"), we should be able to substitute "G. E. Anscombe" for "I" in the way we can usually substitute a proper name for the pronoun representing it. Instead of "I am not G. E. Anscombe," we would then obtain "G. E. Anscombe is not G. E. Anscombe." But, as Anscombe rightly points out, "the sense of the lie 'I am not E. A.' is hardly retained in 'E. A. is not E. A.' " She then infers that the pronoun and its antecedent are not semantically identical, and therefore not necessarily interchangeable, as traditional grammar and analytic approaches have led us to believe. This example prompts her to uncover another string of propositions somehow implied in "I am E. A.":

> "I am E. A." is after all not an identity proposition. It is connected with an identity proposition, namely, "This thinker is E. A." but there is also the proposition "I am this thing here."
>
> · · ·
>
> "I am this thing here" is, then, a real proposition but not a proposition of identity. It means: this thing here is the thing, the person . . . of whose action this idea of action is an idea, of whose movements these ideas of movement are ideas, of whose posture this idea of posture is the idea. (Anscombe 60–61)

I is then to be understood as a proposition about a certain thing-person who has ideas of action, movements, posture. We must emphasize that Anscombe's *I* does not, like Strawson's, latch on to the speaker herself, but to the *idea* that the speaker has of the activities in which she is engaged. Indeed, she could be wrong, but as long as she has such an idea, her use of *I* and of I-thoughts is correct and justified.

Thus, unlike Strawson or Russell, Anscombe holds that the truth-value criterion is not contemporaneous with the use of *I*: instead, it activates *later* processes of verification, and these, independently of the actual (correct) use of *I* (see " 'this body is my body' then means 'My

idea that I am standing up is verified by this body, if it is standing up.'
And so on. But observation does not show which body is the one. Noth-
ing shows me that" [Anscombe 60]). Seen in this perspective, verifica-
tion is not inherently built into a theory of the first person. Nor is it
empirical. Someone is standing—well? How can I be certain that this
someone and "I" are the same person? Our only way to ensure such a
coincidence, says Anscombe, is by means of introducing a third term
(*idea*) that will provide the grounds on which the first two can meet (I
may not know that $a = b$, but if I know that $a = c$ and $b = c$, then I
can infer that $a = b$, upon which I can also go and verify if that is the
case; c will be the term added, the ideas, whose mediation I need in
order to grasp the identity between a and b [my use of I-thoughts and
reality]). To speak more plainly, if I have the idea that I am this thing
here, and this thing here "is standing" (check for yourself), then I must
be "this thing standing here." Furthermore, if "this thing here" is E. A.,
and if it so happens that I have just reached the reassuring conclusion
that I am *it*, then, indeed, I must be E. A. One may object that this is a
rather convoluted way to find out one's own identity. Perhaps so, but
Anscombe claims that identity is not what we are discussing, even
though, as she readily concedes, her discussion of *I* may entail a second
and secondary discussion about identity. What, then, is the point of her
discussion of *I*? Its primary merit lies in its attempt to bridge the gap
between language and consciousness, without getting into an ontologi-
cal argument of sorts.[44]

Some questions remain open, however. For example, it is clear that
Anscombe does not explain *I* in terms either of sense (*Sinn*) or of refer-
ence (*Bedeutung*). We may wonder how a good Fregean, who calls upon
Frege's distinction between *Sinn* and *Bedeutung* several times in the
course of her essay, accounts for something as essential and evidently
problematic as *I* outside sense and reference? There is indeed a third
term for Frege, *Vorstellung*, translated as "idea." Nothing in Ans-
combe's essay indicates that she is borrowing Frege's *Vorstellung*, how-
ever. Worse yet, if she did, she would be in direct contradiction with
Frege's attempt to account for *I* with sense only. As we remember, he
was at pains to eliminate the overtones that *Vorstellung* might cast on *I*
and to bring forth the ways in which *I* pertains to sense, and not to ideas
or force (see the section on Frege in this chapter). The question then is
this: Is Anscombe discreetly engaged in a dialogue with Frege in this
essay (in the way she is in its first part with, to name only those we have
encountered, Descartes, Russell, and Strawson)? Is she rehabilitating
Vorstellung? Is she reintroducing it into theories of language and truth?

And if, at her instigation, *Vorstellung* finds a legitimate place in analytic theories of language, what of poetry, translation, and rhetoric? Can we read an implied apology of arts in her treatment of the first person? Is she pointing out a direction that the philosophy of language might take, a direction that will encompass the rhetoricity of language and its sense-scrambling effects? I must admit that, as much as I would like to answer these questions affirmatively, and as much as I would like to find in Anscombe a champion of literature, I am unable to oblige. For fear of imputing to Anscombe intentions for which I find no other evidence in her writings, I shall content myself with underlining the choices and suggesting what is at stake for those who, like myself, would want to reconcile the philosophy of language with literature. I see two alternatives: either Anscombe means something other than *Vorstellung* when she says "idea," or she means Frege's *Vorstellung* but disagrees with his analysis; in either case, her discretion vis-à-vis Frege introduces a taxing confusion.[45]

Even if we suspend all comparisons with Frege, we shall not find relief from gnawing scruples: an idea is to be *had*, says Anscombe. By whom? By me. Then "I" have an idea; but what is/am "I"? Well, I am this thing here that has the idea, etcetera. We are obviously spinning once more in a tautological circle, with the *definiens* running across the definition. Anscombe would probably rewrite the *cogito* as follows: "I am this thing that has the idea that I am having ideas, therefore I am." This would unabashedly beg the question since this updated *cogito* sets out to demonstrate the truth of the very same proposition with which it opens. Moreover, displacing the ontological emphasis from "being" to "having" will cast no light on the "I" that either "is" or "has." Despite all Anscombe's disclaimers, saying "I have the idea that I am this thing here" along with "This thing here is the thing, the person, of whose action this idea of action is an idea, of whose movements these ideas of movements are ideas . . ." does not secure a way out of the subject/object dichotomy: as Frege insisted, "having" an idea ultimately requires a bearer. This very same bearer who will in turn become the subject of the proposition of identity that inevitably follows, is *already* implied in her "I am this thing here that has the idea . . . ," and thus her theory blatantly begs the question.

Kafka's most accommodating ape would not disclaim Anscombe's solution. The way out (*Ausweg*) he so eagerly seeks can be seen as an escape from now-identity propositions. He states emphatically that he *was* an ape. Not once, however, does he say what or who *he is*. Indeed, an identity proposition would fall like an axe on his speech. Pointing at his fuzzy apish body, he can say neither "I am not an ape" nor "I am a man." And yet, his whole speech aims to establish and communicate something comparable to an identity, however difficult it may be to render it lexically. Anscombe's theory offers him a convenient way out of this impasse: identity will come all by itself at a later stage. In the meantime he is content to develop and communicate ideas: that he is spitting in the sailors' faces; that he is smoking a pipe—even though he may mistakenly press his thumb into the bowl of the pipe; that he drinks schnapps or wine, sits on a rocking chair, gazes through the window, receives visitors "with propriety"—in short, a quintessential human being. Like Anscombe, he carefully chooses I-thoughts "relating to action, postures, movements and intentions . . . which are directly verifiable or falsifiable. . . . Anyone, including myself, can look and see whether that person is standing" (Anscombe 63). Above all, he has the idea that he is communicating I-thoughts in a report to an academy (this, too, can be verified by his listeners). Anscombe's account fits him like a glove.

The ape has one more reason to rejoice. Anscombe's way out of identity propositions presents yet another advantage by bypassing the thorny problem of an "I" rooted in the present and presence of deixis (like Russell's), while strangely subsuming temporality and becoming a consciousness (how this is achieved again remains a mystery): "The I-thoughts now that have this connection with E. A. are I-thoughts that had that connection twenty years ago. No problem of the continuity or reidentification of the *I* can arise. There is E. A. who, like other humans, has such thoughts as these"; and to the delight of the ape, she adds, "and who probably learned to have them through learning to say what she had done, was doing, etc.—*an amazing feat of imitation*" (Anscombe 63)—echoed by the ape, "*It was so easy to imitate these people. I learned to spit the very first day*" (*Stories*, 255). An amazing feat of imitation indeed.[46]

The list of philosophers and theories of the first person could be much longer. I am not trying to give a comprehensive inventory of theories of the first person. Among such various theories, I have chosen only those that, while acutely aware of the difficulties inherent in the first person, have nonetheless claimed to solve them.[47] My aim is not so much to criticize them as to let the ape praise them. In other words, the balance sheet indicates that they are all "right" from the ape's viewpoint. From the story's viewpoint, however, they all miss the mark.

Let me stress that I am not alluding to the well-established fact that a literary text can give rise to a variety of interpretations with one interpretation countering another. Polysemy is not at stake here: we are not discussing the pure semantics of either the story or the first person. Nor is my point that contradictory and incompatible theories can equally strengthen the claim of the ape—though this can in itself raise some eyebrows. What theories *do* and how such doings undermine or undercut one another are undoubtedly interesting questions, but it does not constitute the thrust of our discussion. The point is *what theories do not do*. Divergent as they may be, tightly formulated, comprehensive theories are strangely similar in what they do not do: without exception, they do not account for the ways in which the story exploits the rhetoricity that looms in language. Yet this rhetoricity is the single most essential factor of "A Report to an Academy"; the story would not be the same without it. None of the theories surveyed so far can account for the disavowal of the ape, his uncanny relationship with mirrors (Peter the performing ape and the little female—see pp. 165–67), his constant contradictions, and so on. What I find odd, and what I want to bring to the foreground, is therefore not so much what theories can do for the ape, although this in itself is considerable, but what they fail to do for the story. Theories take the ape's discourse literally and invite us with unflinching seriousness to do the same—which of course is the ape's dearest wish. The story wreaks havoc with this wish, however, and in so doing it wreaks havoc with the totalizing thrust of theories.

"A Report to an Academy"

> *Literary theory may now well have become a legitimate concern of philosophy but it cannot be assimilated to it, either factually or theoretically. It contains a necessary pragmatic moment that certainly weakens it as theory but that adds a subversive element of unpredictability and makes it something of a wild card in the serious game of the theoretical disciplines.*
>
> PAUL DE MAN

The reflexivity of the I-speech of the ape simultaneously presents and displaces the *knowledge* sought by academies ("I am only imparting *knowledge*, I am only making a *report*" [*Stories*, 259]). The reporter, even if he believes in a zero-degree of knowledge unimpaired by human limitations, must still struggle with his expression so as to communicate absolute knowledge without allowing human factors (in Frege's case, for example, *Vorstellung*) to creep into his expression and contaminate it with human imperfections. This is indeed the ape's predicament. Undeniably as he recounts and reports how, upon having been caught and put in an unbearable cage, he found a way out (*Ausweg*) of ape-ness, his report bears a clear constative value. He is, as he claims, imparting knowledge. And yet, it is imperative to distinguish between his life and his story: he may not have chosen his life (he was captured, wounded, imprisoned, etc.), but he *is* choosing the expression that converts his life into a story. A story is a narrative in which an author necessarily makes editorial choices as to the subject matter: at the most elementary level, the author decides which of the events of the life she or he intends to tell is worth noting, telling, and, of course, editing. Furthermore, the wording, interruptions, digressions, and even the very sequential construction of the story all belong to its rhetoricity and exceed its denotative, constative value. As he reels off his narrative, the ape undoubtedly communicates a denotative content, but this content by no means exhausts the *force* of the speech. There are therefore at least two ways of examining a story. One can take it at face value and read its denotative content or message. Such a reading does not necessarily imply either a lack of sophistication or literal-mindedness: for example, one could read "A Report" as a testimony of the birth of consciousness, while bearing in mind the literary and philosophical precedents of such an awakening into speech and humanity (Condillac's statue, for one) and thus wind up with a highly conceptualized interpretation. Or one can examine the loose ends (strange imagery, ambiguities, various outbursts, or snatches of other stories that interfere with the main train of thought without ever constituting subplots).[48] Neither approach alone can do justice to the text. They are linked to and dependent on each other: together they yield a reading that is neither the sum nor the substratum of the two. Two rocks sitting peacefully and autonomously side by side are but two rocks. But hit them against each other and you have a spark, after which, as the story of humankind attests, rocks, humankind, and the world will never be the same. Such a spark is the closest analogy I can find to what I call the rhetoricity of the story (this rhetoricity should not be confused, as is often the case, with the second approach used in isolation).

Self-Consciousness and Irony

To a large extent, the irony of the story stems from the ape's lack of self-consciousness: there he is, an obvious freak, performing in a circus side by side with trained animals; widely acclaimed by a public delighted with his antics; invited for a private showing for the sole benefit of the honored academy, the way our comedians are invited to perform, say, at the White House. There he is because he is an ape.[49] Would a man calling himself a man command the same attention? The attention bestowed on the ape stems from the difference that others perceive between his claims and his body, between his discourse and the referentiality of the "I" to which it pertains. He, however, is the only one who does not perceive this important difference, who thinks that his speech is genuine, that is to say, is anchored in reality and corresponds to the state of affairs ("I am only making a *report.*"). The rhetorical effect of his speech depends on the incompatibility between the consciousness that his public has of him (at the circus or in the academy) and the one he has of himself; in short, this rhetorical effect depends on the ape's lack of *self*-consciousness or, at least his lack of consciousness of his body and of his past. More importantly, it depends on the ways in which this body and this past counter the referentiality of the ape's claim that he has found "the way of humanity."

We should not fail in this respect to notice that twice in the story he is given access to the Socratic knowledge that comes from self-consciousness: twice, he glances at his reflection in a mirror—and twice, he flinches and rejects his reflection with a vehement disavowal.

The first occurrence is spread over two digressions, two violent outbursts associated with the original violence that eventually became his ticket to the "way of humanity." He is calmly relating to the academy the story of his capture: while he was still in his native land, the Gold Coast, a hunting expedition sent out by the firm of Hagenbeck shot him twice and caged him. As soon as he mentions the hunting expedition, the ape interrupts his sentence for apparently no reason, in order to inform us that he holds no grudge against his captors: "A hunting expedition sent out by the firm of Hagenbeck—by the way, *I have drunk* many a bottle of good red wine since then with the leader of that expedition—had taken its position in the bushes by the shore when *I came down for a drink* at evening among a troop of apes" (*Stories*, 251). The interruption of the account with the evocation of the good times he spent with his hunters results in a scrambling of the opposition man/beast. Instead, it secures the ape's cherished opposition between now and then: then he was drinking among a troop of apes; now he drinks with the leader of the expedition. Contrary to his expectations, however, his strange magnanimity calls attention to the oddity of his situation. The inserted comments about his present social life therefore mark the place of a repression: whether a repression of anger and resentment toward the hunters who have reduced him to captivity, or a repression of the very part of his story that the academy had commissioned. It is a scar on the narrative fabric, foreshadowing and mirroring the scars on his body that he is about to describe to the academy.[50]

The mention of these two scars occasions two other noteworthy digressions: the first in conjunction with his name and the second with his odd habit of taking off his pants in public. In both digressions the rhetoric is particularly violent, in fact so shockingly violent that one cannot help but suspect that it reflects the original violence of the hunting, shooting, and wounding that the ape has repressed—thus creating a second rhetorical trace that reproduces and mirrors in discourse the traces (scars) left on his body by the shots. This momentary acerbity is all the more noticeable since the ape meets all the other odd turns of his life with unfailing serenity. Even as the sailors slap him or singe his fur, he professes an imperturbable magnanimity. Reading his speech, we tend to forget that his is a story of entrapment, enslavement, domination, and exploitation, in which the speaker and the victim are one. The digressions broached by the scars constitute the only exception to this rule of accelerated adjustment and contentment. The wounds assume all the violence to which the victim is entitled and act as autonomous and vociferous mouths, clamoring a discourse that clashes with the professed resignation of the well-adapted ape, while all the time bearing witness to wrongdoing and violence.

Had the wound and the ape told the same story, had we not had one discourse of violence and another of contentment, had the ape "known" that he would forever remain an ape and that this was precisely the reason why he stirred up so much interest on stages and in academies, then we could have spoken of his self-consciousness (i.e., "the consciousness that such and such holds of himself" [See Anscombe, 51]). To make this point clearer I shall borrow from Anscombe an example with which she explains the special kind of self-consciousness implied by the use of the first person. She imagines a community in which each individual wears an A on the wrist, and a letter from B to Z on the back. When referring to another person, one will read the letter printed on that person's back (B to Z). One is also trained to respond to these utterances the way we respond when someone calls our name. Since one cannot see one's own back, one cannot know what letter is there. When referring to oneself, one will therefore read the letter in sight, that is, the one written on the wrist, with the result that all individuals will use the letter A when referring to themselves but a variety of other letters when referring to the other individuals in that community. Now, asks Anscombe, shall we compare A-

users with *I*-users? No, she answers, for *A*-users read the names on their wrist. They lack the self-consciousness essential to the *I*-user, who knows when to use *I* without having to read it every time she needs to refer to herself. She imagines, for instance, an *A*-user catching sight of someone else's wrist and mistakenly using that *A* to refer to herself, thus getting hold of the wrong reference for her *A*-utterance; the same misfortune is not conceivable with *I*-users. And Anscombe concludes this little experiment: "Thus for each person there is one person of whom he has characteristically limited and also characteristically privileged views: *except in mirrors he never sees the whole person, and can only get rather special views of what he does see.* Some of these are specially good, others specially bad" (49).

In a word, then, Anscombe pins the difference between *A*-users and *I*-users on the lack of either a mirror or self-consciousness. I must admit that, while I understand how *A*-users lack self-consciousness, I fail to comprehend why the self-consciousness that she attributes to *I*-users guarantees that they will not get hold of the wrong object. In other words, if, as she claims, an *I*-user has an idea of herself that can be verified by another person, we can imagine a situation in which that other person would disagree with the *I*-user, thus proving the self-consciousness of the speaker not simply false but false in one sense and true in another. The ape would be such an example. He obviously lacks self-consciousness in Anscombe's sense, and yet, in a different manner, he does have a *certain* consciousness of himself—whence the effectiveness of his speech. He is an *I*-user because he clearly has *some* self-consciousness, but he is an odd *I*-user because "himself" (in "the consciousness that such and such holds of himself") clearly misses the mark. Consciousness, self-consciousness, and knowledge do not necessarily coincide.

"In the Penal Colony"

That this last remark was central to Kafka's thought is underscored by a comparison with "In the Penal Colony," written three years before "A Report" (I find it significant that the two stories were among the very few published by Kafka himself). An apparatus executes unsuspecting criminals by dint of etching their crimes in their flesh. The victim executed in this manner has been informed neither of his crime nor of his sentence. In fact, he has not the faintest inkling of the significance of the scene in which he is about to play such an important part. "There would be no point in telling him. He'll learn it on his body," [51] explains his judge-executioner, since "*Enlightenment comes to the most dull-*

witted. It begins around the eyes. From there it radiates. . . . Nothing more happens than that the man begins to understand the inscription, he purses his mouth as if he were listening. You have seen how difficult it is to decipher the script with one's eyes; *but our man deciphers it with his wounds. . . .* Then the judgement has been fulfilled, and we, the soldier and I, bury him" (*Stories,* 150). The judgment does not consist simply in a punishment for a crime but in inscribing on the criminal's body the rule that he has violated and having him read it "with his wounds" (he cannot see the writing) as he dies slowly. We could even consider the machine to be "educational" inasmuch as it brings knowledge and enlightenment to the most dull-witted. Obtaining this knowledge, (which is a form of self-knowledge, as the criminal is informed of *his* crime and *his* verdict at the very same time that this verdict is enacted on *his* body and causes *his* death), is an epiphany of sorts, after which there is no return to dull wits. In the eye of the envious officer, death is but a small price to pay for such an absolute and intimate self-knowledge. What the officer-judge-executioner forgets, however, is that by the time "enlightenment" comes, the prisoner is mute with pain and cannot bear witness ("The first six hours the condemned man stays alive almost as before, he suffers only pain. After two hours the felt gag is taken away, for he has no longer strength to scream" [149]). We have to take the executioner's word for the victim's "enlightenment." Ultimately, the consciousness gained from the inscription befalls *the one who sees it* (but who of course knew the inscription all along), not the one who "reads" it. In fact, despite the officer's claims to the contrary, we have no evidence that the victim ever reads the inscription, that consciousness and self-consciousness ever meet; subject and object, discourse (the officer's) and knowledge (the criminal's) may well not coincide as he would like to believe. The wound-inscription does not testify so much to the "enlightenment" as to the possibility that such an enlightenment may be illusionary.

Indeed, when at last the frustrated devoted executioner decides to inflict upon himself the same radiant enlightenment, the machine refuses to write: "The Harrow was not writing, it was only jabbing, and the Bed was not turning the body over but only bringing it up quivering against the needles. . . . This was no exquisite torture such as the officer desired, this was plain murder" (*Stories,* 165). Once a subject who "knows" is committed to the truth-inscribing apparatus (unlike the other victims, the officer already knows the message he wishes the machine to inscribe on his body), a slippage occurs that jams the apparatus and scrambles the inscription, so that *his* truth no longer coincides with the inscription's. If "plain murder" is what happens when the victim does not read his crime with his wound, we must suspect that the machine is plainly a murderous apparatus, since nothing in the story—except of course, the officer's empty claim—indicates that any victim, whether still screaming or already exhausted, ever read his wound. Knowledge and self-knowledge, consciousness and self-consciousness, language and knowledge do not meet in "In the Penal Colony" (just as they do not meet in "A Report"). As in Babel, the subject's hubristic hope to achieve an all-encompassing consciousness brings about the dispersion and destruction of all sense, while men babbling in an infinite number of languages scatter on the face of the earth, and machines jab haphazardly instead of inscribing ultimate truths and bringing about enlightenment.

Had it worked, had the officer's flesh read the inscription that he himself had dictated to the apparatus, then Kafka might have been advocating that real, true self-consciousness—an exquisite torture—is possible; then he might have suggested that there is a way for "I" to be a "good" *I*-user, and that theories, like well-oiled machines, can enlighten us with the rules and truths they so surely convey to our deepest consciousness. The apparatus's inscription would have functioned like an ultimate mirror, from which there is no turning away—at no matter what price. But it did not. The officer's death is as absurd as the ape's life; his torn body and the ape's scars attest to the violence of the purported encounter that never took place.

The First Wound

The ape was hit twice, "once in the cheek; a slight wound; but it left a large, naked red scar which earned me the name of Red Peter, a horrible name, utterly inappropriate, which only some ape could have thought of as if the only difference between me and the performing ape Peter, who croaked [*krepierten*] not so long ago and had some small local reputation, were the red mark on my cheek. This by the way" (*Stories*, 251, modified trans.). Now, why is this name so horrible, so inappropriate? "Peter," whether red, blue, or whatever, is in itself a proper name, as arbitrarily assigned as any other; therefore it should not give rise to such strong feelings. Does the ape not like the color red? Would he have preferred a different color? In other words, does he object to *red* or to *Peter*? Would the name John have triggered a similar outburst? Surely not, at least not as long as the first ape's name remained Peter. Our ape's indignation hinges not upon the singular indexical value of the proper name but upon the fact that *Peter* has become a common name used generically, synonymous with *ape*. He does not rebel against the name itself but against the process of abstraction by which this name was reached, namely, the perception of similarities and the oversight of dissimilarities, "as if the difference between me and the performing ape Peter . . . were the red mark on my cheek." His virulence implies that the scar is not the only difference between them: Peter *is* an animal "who *croaked* not so long ago," claims the ape (the German *krepierten* normally used of animals, is more expressive and violent than the English *croaked*). Our speaker then claims that, unlike Peter, *he* is not an ape. The distinction we are called upon to make between Peter and our speaker is akin to the one between ape and not-ape. (Note that it is impossible to evoke "speech" as a marker to distinguish between the two apes, since nowhere does our ape claim that the performing Peter could not speak; for all we know, Peter may also have given reports to learned academies).

The inability to perceive the difference between ape and not-ape (*Peter* and *Red Peter*) turns one into an ape—at least according to our speaker ("a horrible name, totally inappropriate, which only some ape could have thought of"). This last detail calls our attention to the speaker's own inability to perceive differences: the difference between himself and the human academy, as well as the difference between his furry body and the human referent he claims for his speech. But then, by his own admission, his failure to perceive these essential differences, labels him an *ape*. The story's logic leaves him no escape, no "way out" (despite his claim to the contrary). Whether he scratches his fur (*Stories*, 253), takes off his pants (251), imitates human beings (255, 257), or calls others names (251), the result is the same: he remains an ape (or at least he remains *also* an ape), all the more so for trying to fend off those who call him on it.

The Female Ape

A similar incident occurs at the end of his speech: "When I come home late at night from banquets, from scientific receptions, from social gatherings, there sits waiting for me a half-trained [*halbdressierte*] little chimpanzee and I take comfort from her as apes do [*Affenart*]" (*Stories*, 259). We might point out in passing the expression "as apes do" (*Affenart*) and wonder why, being an "erstwhile ape" and having adopted all human customs (clothing, spitting in sailors' faces, smoking a pipe, drinking wine, receiving visitors with propriety, etc.), he still takes comfort from her "as apes do." (I am not suggesting that he should have had a human mate waiting for him, only that the expression "as apes do," in itself hardly indispensable in this sentence, underscores the ambiguity and the oddity of his situation.)

This is not the most interesting element in this section, however. Once more, instead of focusing on what he does, I find it more enlightening to examine what he does not do: in this instance, he does not look at the little female. Twice he repeats that he cannot bear to see her: "By day I cannot bear to see her; for she has the insane look of the bewildered half-broken animal in her eyes [*sie hat nämlich den Irrsinn des verwirrten dressierten Tieres im Blick*]; no one else sees it but I do, and I cannot bear it" (*Stories*, 259). No one else sees it. Among men and apes alike, he is the only one who finds her gaze intolerable, the only one who cannot bear the sight of her. He is therefore compelled to take comfort from her by night, in the dark. One may wonder what is a gaze (*Blick*) that no one can see. In other words, the question at hand is whether *her gaze* is intolerable or whether *he* is unable to tolerate something (let us call it "her gaze") relevant to him alone, which has neither bearing nor even existence for anybody else. I shall be more specific: what he cannot bear is not just her gaze but "the insane look of the bewildered half-broken animal in her eye." Again, we must ask: if the look is "in *her* eyes," why is he the only one to perceive it and to be so intensely affected? What is this thing that he alone perceives, that he and he alone calls "the insane look of the bewildered half-broken animal"? The answer is inescapable: she is his mirror image. What he cannot bear is not the ways in which she is different from him, as he would have us believe, but, on the contrary, the ways in which she is like him, the ways in which in her eyes his sees his own insane look; the ways in which she reminds him that he himself *is* this bewildered animal, forever half- (and only half-) broken.

The two apes, Peter and the female chimpanzee, elicit the same response. In both cases our speaker refuses to face up to something that he shares with them, the very thing that he has to repress to enter into "the way of humanity" and, paradoxically, the very thing without which he cannot enter into "the way of humanity": an appropriate reference for his discourse; more precisely an appropriate reference for the founding "I" upon which all representations, including the one he holds of himself, hinge.

"A Hunger Artist"

We can compare this treatment of reference to the one we find in "A Hunger Artist." The whole life of the artist, his identity for others, and whatever conception he has of himself come from his art (one is reminded of Kafka's diaries and letters, in which his anguished sense of himself echo his equally anguished dedication to his art).[52] His artistry consists in fasting. Dead creatures, however, can no longer fast. To be able to fast, the artist has to break his fast every once in a while to sustain the very same body it denies: in other words, to exercise his art he needs the support of the very same referent (his body and its needs) that his art purports to negate. His art could not be without the resistance of this referent. In this sense, the hunger artist's relationship to fasting is comparable to the relationship of the ape's "I" to his identity: both deny something about themselves, something without which they would neither be nor be able to deny anything. In "A Hunger Artist," as long as the fasting artist brings in a large audience, the impresario is careful to break his fast, so that he will live to fast more and bring in still larger audiences. When the public's taste changes and his act falls out of favor, however, the neglected artist is left to practice his art without restraint. Eventually he dedicates himself totally to his art, negates his body altogether, and dies fasting.

The ape is in a similar situation. His performance consists of speaking rather than fasting, but his speech denies his apish body just as much as (if differently than) the artist's fasting denies his. If, like the hunger artist, he were put in the nightmarish position of an artist without an audience, if academies and variety stages were to become bored with him, if he were no longer to have a chance to practice his art and were obliged to go through the rest of his life without an interlocutor, what would become of the ape? Would he still know so intimately and surely that he was an "erstwhile ape"? If, as he claims, speaking was his way out of the cage, and if a way out is all he ever wanted, what would he do if nobody asked him to speak anymore? On the other hand, if he, like the hunger artist, had succeeded in his struggle with reference and won the battle against his apish body, if he had become a man, it would undoubtedly have put an end to his popularity: few people have the patience to listen to a man explaining why he is a man. A certain conception of art (or language, or comprehensive theories) may well wish to negate the world of objects and bodies and to reign alone (thus keeping company with Kant's naïve bird that thinks it would soar to unlimited heights were it not for the stubborn resistance of the air). But there comes a time when the existential weight of "things" (or bodies) and the raw material of each art form or discipline (language itself in literature and, as Frege noted, in philosophy) will thwart its simplistic albeit essential wishful thinking and expose the extent to which these objects, bodies, and raw materials are the very foundation without which art (or language, or comprehensive theories) would not exist.

And yet, the ape does have a way out: denial and disavowal. When he does not have to see an ape (himself or another one), he can ignore his own fuzzy, flea-ridden, leaping, and scratching body and believe that his newly acquired skills will indeed pave his way to the "human community." Above all, he can say "I" and, oblivious to the incongruity of his "well-groomed fur" and to the impropriety of his gesture, can even take off his pants when visitors greet him: he has been taught by all the theories that "I" could not fail. And a good student he is, "I engaged teachers for myself, established them in five communicating rooms, and took lessons from them all at once by dint of leaping from one room to another" (*Stories,* 256). As he leaps from one room, teacher, and theory to another, his agility is indeed dazzling. His little mate or his colleague Peter may interfere with this euphoric leaping, however. Luckily for him, he has another option. He can cheat: he can remain in the dark, taking comfort from a body or an "I" in the dark, and using either one without having to face up to its incongruous reality: without having to account for well-groomed furs that risk undermining all theories and alibis. Or can he?

The Second Wound

"The second shot hit me below the hip. It was a severe wound, it is the cause of my limping a little to this day" (*Stories,* 251). "Below the hip" can be quite severe indeed, the more so when we read that should he take his trousers down, we would find—nothing: "I can take my trousers down before anyone if I like; *you would find nothing* but a well-groomed fur and the scar made [*man wird dort nichts finden als einen wohlgepflegten Pelz und die Narbe*]—let me be particular in the choice of a word for this particular purpose, to avoid misunderstanding—the scar made by a wanton shot. Everything is open and aboveboard [*Alles liegt offen zutage*], *there is nothing to conceal* [*nichts ist zu verbergen*]; when the plain truth is in question, great minds discard the niceties of refinement" (252). The emphasis on this odd "nothing" when one would surely expect something is striking. And yet, we are warned: if he shies from naming the parts normally found under trousers, it is not for the sake of decorum: "when the plain truth is in question, great minds discard the niceties of refinement." Then, when "everything is open and aboveboard," when "there is nothing to conceal," we have to accept that there is "nothing but a scar" under his trousers and that this scar stands *in lieu* of a missing member. This loss explains the displaced violence he displays in his diatribe against skeptical reporters.

> I read an article recently by one of the ten thousand windbags who vent themselves concerning me in the newspapers, saying: my ape nature is not yet quite under control, the proof being that when visitors come to see me, I have a predilection for taking down my trousers to show them where the shot went in. The hand which wrote that should have its fingers shot away one by one. . . . But if the writer of the article were to take down his trousers before a visitor, that would be quite another story [*allerdings ein anderes Ansehen*], and I will let it stand to his credit that he does not do it. In return, let him leave me alone with his delicacy! (*Stories,* 252)

The rhetorical violence of the ape's speech ("the ten thousand windbags who vent themselves. . . . The hand which wrote that should have its fingers shot away one by one") and the scar on his body bear witness to an untold story of difference and identity. (At this point, we may evoke the dichotomies relished by critics of "A Report": nature/culture, animal/man, violence/reason, ethnic identity/assimilation.[53]) Above all, it bears witness to the violence of any enterprise that endeavors to negate temporality and resistances and force them indiscriminately into a homogeneous discourse.

The way out (*Ausweg*) that the ape found is a case in point: "as far as Hagenbeck was concerned, the place for apes was in front of a locker—well then, I had to stop being an ape. A fine clear train of thought" (*Stories,* 253). Indeed, a fine clear train of thought, in fact the very same train of thought that the West has followed since Aristotle. We cannot miss the syllogism with which the ape explains his situation: all apes are in front of a locker; I am an ape; therefore I am in front of a locker. Now, our ape reverses the logic of this syllogism: all apes are in front of a locker; I am not an ape; therefore I am not in front of a locker.[54] It suffices to make true the second premise *I am not an ape,* and the happy conclusion will follow. That the ape would have recourse to a syllogism comes as no surprise, since it is a logical figure of inclusion and homogeneity, well suited to his determination to cancel out the differences that separate him from the human community. The difference between the ape's story and that of a third party (let us say the reporter who outraged him so by denying the validity of the second premise of his updated parasyllogism) parallels the difference we would find between them if, following the ape's invitation, the reporter also took off his pants: a mutilated referent testifies to the violence that coverups (trousers, speeches, and dogmas) impose on the irreducibility of difference.[55] Unfolding his narrative while performing for the academy is for the triumphant "I" the way to entrench itself in what the ape calls "an unassailable position"—indeed, the very same position that "theories" claim to occupy ("Yet I could not risk putting into words even such insignificant information as I am going to give you if I were not quite sure of myself and if my position on all the great variety stages of the civilized world had not become quite unassailable" [251]). And yet, parading in front of academies is a form of self-exposure: as the *I* of the performing ape steps forth, the story sneaks up on it and catches it *with its pants down.* "Well," a jubilant reader may say, "we have finally reached the naked truth; we are about to find out all we ever wanted to know about *I.*" "You will find nothing," retorts the ape, "but a well-groomed fur and the scar." The naked truth is but a scar attesting to the absence of the conclusive truth that would coherently bind together bodies, consciousness, and language.

Of Apes and Academies

It would be naïve to suspect Kafka of having a bone to pick with apes, or to imagine that "A Report to an Academy" owes its gripping irony to the idiosyncratic performance of a fictional misfit. The narrative does not spin the story of an ape who uses *I*, but the story of an *I* that can be used by an ape. Above all, it spins the story of language as it lies defenseless in the face of such abusive practices. From the point of view of language, the fact that beasts do not normally use *I* is purely accidental: there is nothing in *I* to prevent them from doing so. For millennia, empirical experience has taught us that language distinguishes man from beast. And yet, comments "A Report," structurally, language is a great equalizer: "The strong wind that blew after me out of my past began to slacken; today it is only a gentle puff of air that plays around my heels. . . . To put it plainly, much as I like to express myself in images, to put it plainly, your life as apes, gentlemen, insofar as something of that kind lies behind you, cannot be farther removed from you than mine is from me" (*Stories,* 250). Let us be careful. Language is an equalizer not because it brings all its users into the human community, as the ape, well trained in our Western intellectual tradition, rehearses ("With an effort which up till now has never been repeated I managed to reach the cultural level of an average European. In itself that might be nothing to speak of, but it is something insofar as it has helped me out of my cage and opened a special way out for me, the way of humanity" [258]); it is an equalizer because nothing in its own structure stands against its use by any creature or entity we may think up, because it may be used equally by a human being, an animal, or an inanimate object: it is up to the human being, animal, or inanimate object to appropriate and use language—if *they* can and wish to do so.

Furthermore, inasmuch as it reminds apes and academies of their common past, the ape's speech abruptly abolishes the distance between *homo sapiens* and primates. The story does not comment so much about the mean/beast dichotomy (and its multiple analogies) as about language—as it is used by man, beast or whatever. Indeed, "to put it plainly," the report that the honored members of the academy expected about the life their speaker formerly led as an ape is their own repressed past, their own uncanny I-then brought forth under the cover of otherness provided by the discontinuity of memory. In the face of time, apes and academies are alike: their I-then/I-now mirrors their I-ape/I-not-ape. A blessed eclipse of memory sanctions the ontological and epistemological grounding of their I-now by blocking the way to their I-then. Both then have equally repressed and sacrificed their I-then. Both have entered into humankind through the gate of forgetfulness and repression. Both have lost consciousness following the violence done to their ape-nature. Both have paid the price: they are equally wounded, equally mutilated, equally scarred (let us evoke the fragments once more: unlike the abandoned drafts in which a series of interlocutors addressed the ape, in the final "Report" the interlocutors are speechless in a scenario that assigns all powers to speech; this denial of speech makes them less than human and less than potent since, given the terms set up by the story, the two go hand in hand. This feature is also essential to the remarkable efficacy of the story). This loss is the price the speaking subject pays for grounding subjectivity in language.

As apes and academies match wits, mirroring effects thwart their efforts; an analogy takes place surreptitiously: the ape:the academy::Peter and the female:the ape (the ape is to the academy what the little female and Peter are to the ape). Just as the honored members of the academy invite him not as kindred but as other, he treats the ape Peter and his female friend not as kindred but as others; just as the ape chooses to see only the differences that separate him from reflections (his mate and his colleague), so do the honorable members of the academy: like the ape, they discard the resemblances that might threaten the position they wish to occupy in the hierarchy of evolution and discourse. They are metaphors for each other. In this sense they are interchangeable: audiences enjoy his performance, when, as a freak, he imitates people (isn't this what apes are supposed to do anyway?), but he, too, enjoys theirs, when circus acrobats imitate apes swinging on trees. Ultimately, the ape and the academy belong to the same community: the community of those condemned to choose between omniscient consciousness and language, between total remembering and the principles of selection and abstraction at work in speaking.

The ape stresses yet another trait shared by primates and academies: "the strong wind that blew after me out of my past began to slacken; today it is only a gentle puff of air that plays around my heels. . . . Yet everyone on earth feels a tickling at the heels; the small chimpanzee and the great Achilles alike" (*Stories*, 250). At the heels of erstwhile apes and warriors breathes a memory. The only chink in the present's armor (be it the present of discourse or of consciousness) is the point at which it is subject to the otherness of the past. (In a similar way, in "In the Penal Colony," the apparatus falls apart when the past represented by the officer who knows the inscription *before* it is inscribed attempts to meet with the absolute present of the victim who is supposed to learn the message *as* it is inscribed, in a euphoric coincidence of knowledge, consciousness, and experience.) The Achilles' heel of all users of *I*, as well as that of all learned subjects in search of total knowledge (academies and theoreticians) is the point at which the resistance of bodies and fragmentation of memories threaten the illusion of integrity of the discursive present. (But Achilles is also the "swift-footed." In a remarkable intuition the *Iliad* has focused both his weakness and his strength on the same spot, a gesture we have traced in the projects of the ape, the officer of "In the Penal Colony," the hunger artist, and even Kant's bird.)

In conclusion, we may say that as a referring expression, *I*'s sole way of being used is to be used improperly. Apes and academies will use *I* at the price of a repression of inappropriateness and under the ever present threat that this essential inappropriateness may resurge and thwart all claims to referential "propriety" and truth. Words may well aim at things, but their success is by no means guaranteed (nor is their failure): on the one hand, the rhetoricity of language (of which *Vorstellung* is exemplary) blurs the distinction between things and, consequently, risks scrambling words; on the other hand, things (and bodies) oppose their opacity to the transparency of communication, their thingness to the selective abstraction required for naming. The use of language is a wound-inflicting enterprise bearing traces of the violence that naming inflicts on words and things alike. As "theories" attempt to mask the scars, reference activates a disturbing principle: the risk of missing the target (the proper thing) or hitting the wrong one haunts the "theoretical" project (in "A Report," for example, we may say that ultimately, after several swerves and ricochets, the *I* uttered by the ape hits—the academy). Between the reassuring rational generalizations of theories and the risk of otherness hidden in and enacted by language, the literary text acts as an impossible shuttle, exposing the precariousness of each as well as its dependence on its unacceptable counterpart.

5 Speech Acts

We have got on to slippery ice where there is no friction and so in a certain sense the conditions are ideal, but also just because of that, we are unable to walk. We want to walk so we need friction. Back to the rough ground.

WITTGENSTEIN

Speech Acts and the First Person

Of the various aspects of language that analytical philosophy has explored, speech acts have proved the most readily adopted and adapted by literature. While the average critic or student of literature still considers theories of reference rather exotic, he or she is probably familiar with at least the rudiments of theories of speech acts. Many have limited their interest to Derrida's acerbic discussion with Austin and Searle. Others have tried to tap the theories and explore or exploit their usefulness for literary studies. I find it significant that the two areas of enquiry literary critics, linguists, and philosophers have shared extensively in the last twenty years—whether by choice or by accident—are the first person and speech acts, that is to say, two instances of language that deviate in some ways from common theories of reference and truth.[1] In order to include them in a comprehensive theory of language, the theoreticians have to address new problems, delineate new areas of investigation, and stretch or at least revise their general theories—hence the number of special chapters on the first person or on speech acts in works that purport to offer a general theory of language. (Frege, for one, lumps them together and warns that some aspects of the first person [the perception that I and I alone may have of myself] and some aspects of what has come to be called speech acts [e.g., the "force" of an expression] elude his enquiry into truth.[2])

I do not think that the only feature shared by speech acts and *I* is their irregularity with regard to general theories, however. I am therefore not offering them as two randomly selected examinations of marginal cases or annoying exceptions. The endless literary and philosophical bibliographies on the first person alone would suffice to indicate that the relationship between subjectivity and language is at the heart of the study of both. Even though speech act theories are a relatively recent development in the philosophy of language, the general interest Austin's work has aroused (after all, he published only a handful of papers in his lifetime—hardly enough to explain his fame other than by attributing it to the centrality of his investigation and the exceptional sharpness of his insights and teaching) both in literature and philosophy testifies to the relevance of the problems raised by speech acts for a comprehensive theory of language.

Furthermore, the theoretical problems underscored by *I* and speech acts do not belong to two different sets of epistemological or hermeneutical problems: the major tenets of speech act theories or *I* are in fact identical. They fall roughly into three categories:

1. the centrality of the speaking subject
2. the importance of the present tense (*now*)
3. the importance of presence (*here*)

In chapter 4 the ape's odd speech situation underscored the difficulties experienced by "theoreticians" in attempting to relate these three points to the historical context provided by the story: elaborating a subject that would account for the continuity of consciousness (accounting for the past, memory, etc.) and for the discontinuity of loci (the Gold Coast vs. the space of the academy, for example). These categories are not to be confused with formal markers (either lexical or grammatical). Austin, for example, cites a series of performative utterances that do not formally conform to these three criteria. The sign *dog* may be understood to mean "*I* am warning you that there is here a dangerous (or potentially dangerous) dog"; the expression "you are guilty" to mean "*I* hereby find you guilty"; or "you will . . ." to mean "*I* order you to . . ."; and so on. He is quick to point out, however, that although their formal syntax does not seem to conform to those three criteria, all these utterances do in fact include a subject (an "I"), an implied present tense (now), and an indispensable presence (here) in their deep structure:

> We said that the idea of a performative utterance was to be (or to be included as a part of) the performance of an action. Actions can only be performed by persons, and obviously in our cases *the utterer must be the performer:* hence our justifiable feeling—which we wrongly case into purely a grammatical mould—in favour of the "first person," who must come in, being mentioned or referred to; moreover, if in uttering one is acting, one must be doing something—hence our perhaps ill-expressed favouring of the grammatical present and grammatical active of the verb. There is some-

thing which is *at the moment of uttering being done by the person uttering* (Austin's emphasis on the last sentence).

. . .

The "I" who is doing the action does thus come essentially into the picture.

. . .

Thus what we should feel tempted to say is that any utterance which is in fact a performative should be reducible, or analysable into a form, or reproducible in a form, *with a verb in the first person singular present indicative active* (grammatical). . . . Unless the performative utterance is reduced to such an explicit form, it will regularly be possible to take it in a non-performative way.[3]

Indexicals—and *I* in particular—are at work in performative utterances, whether or not these utterances happen to be felicitous. This chapter therefore pursues the line of questioning I broached in my examination of the first person but focuses primarily on the network of circumstances and contexts created by and within the stories and the theories we read, rather than on the codes they elaborate and the messages they communicate. Were we to borrow Jakobson's analysis of the six components of verbal communication (addressor, message, addressee, context, contact, and code) we would say that we tend to focus primarily on the addressor (the ultimate addressor being "I"), the addressee (the reverse image of the former, e.g., "you" vs. "I," the academy in "A Report"), and the context (the sum of this chapter and chapter 6).

One final note about this chapter before we proceed with our stories. While literary critics have often tried to adopt and adapt speech act theories, philosophers have not shown the same enthusiasm for literature and literary theory.[4] When they try to relate the two fields, it is not so much to explore their possible interaction as to impose philosophical standards on literary texts. For instance, in Searle's essay "The Logical Status of Fictional Discourse," the subject and focus are not fictional discourse but logical status (note that even so, Searle addresses the "fictionality" of the literary text, i.e., its truth-value and not its literarity or its rhetoricity). The same can be said of Richard Gale's "Fictive Use of Language," and Joseph Margolis' "Literature and Speech Acts" (which concludes with what is in fact its premise: "in the first place, the very conception of literature, poetry, fiction, metaphor, the styles and genres of literature cannot be explicated directly in terms of speech acts").[5] Furthermore, despite literary critics' interest in speech acts, they, too, generally concern themselves with the applicability of speech acts to literature.⁶ In this chapter (and more generally speaking, in this book), I examine the possibility of a two-way relationship: the expectation that philosophy will provide us with new insights into the workings of the literary text and, conversely, the examination and reevaluation of these theories by literature.

Mérimée's "Venus of Ille"

The Story

"The Venus of Ille" is the story of a wedding;⁷ we cannot go any further in our account of the story since to do so would compel us to speak about this wedding. What wedding? There seem to be two weddings in this story; yet there can be in reality only one wedding since, as Austin rightly points out, a wedding ceremony is a legally regulated conventional act: if the law states that bigamy is illegal, M. Alphonse cannot legally wed twice in the same day. Surely, "lots of things will have been done—we shall most interestingly have committed the act of bigamy—but we shall not have done the purported act, viz. marrying. Because despite the name, you do not when bigamous marry twice" (*How to,* 17). Which event is then the real wedding and which is the simulacrum, the false ceremony "without effect"? Which of the two wedding-events is "The Venus of Ille" about? This question is probably the closest we shall come to articulating what the story is "about." Unfortunately, it is also precisely the question the story itself asks but leaves unresolved. "Which wedding?" immediately becomes "Which story?"

Let us try again. Since the uncertain narrative content of the story has thwarted our attempt to recount the plot, this time we shall begin our reading with the presentation of its characters. Our set of characters includes the narrator (an ironic Parisian archaeologist), M. de Peyrehorade (an amateur archaeologist), his son M. Alphonse (a good-looking young man about to wed, who seems to care much more about his title of village champion at the *jeu de paume* (a ball game similar to tennis) than about his future bride, Mlle de Puygarrig (the young woman in question, who has just inherited a fortune), and—here again we stumble. Shall we list among the characters the bronze statue of Venus uncovered by M. de Peyrehorade? But can a statue be a character? Certainly, if the story ascribes human features to it and makes it behave like a character. Back to the story then (but which story?). Does it really invite us to view the statue as a human being? If it does, then within the framework of the suspension of disbelief, M. Alphonse's wedding to the

Venus is legal. We shall then know which wedding is the "real" one and shall be able to tell the story. But as we noted earlier, the story does not dispense the information necessary for us to decide whether the statue is intended as a character or as a mere object; or rather, as a truly fantastic story, it dispenses information of both kinds—which does little to abate our uncertainty. Our attempt, then, to introduce the reader to "The Venus of Ille" by listing its characters has gotten us off to a second false start.

Perhaps we should simply examine the facts: In the middle of a tennis game,

> M. Alphonse threw his racket on the ground in a furious rage. "It is this cursed ring!" he cried, "which pressed into my finger and made me miss a sure thing."
> With some difficulty he took off his diamond ring, and I went nearer to take it, but he forestalled me, ran to the Venus, slipped the ring on its fourth finger [*lui passa la bague au doigt annulaire*] and retook his position at the head of his townsmen.[8]

When a man puts a ring (especially when it is a family ring dating "from the days of chivalry" and used for generations as a wedding band ["Venus," 251]) on a woman's finger on his wedding day, we may assume that the two are exchanging vows in a wedding ceremony. (For the sake of argument, we shall ignore for the moment the fact that the Venus is an inanimate object and therefore not a suitable candidate for a bride.) One may still object that the young man did not intend to wed the Venus; he only entrusted her momentarily with the ring he intended for Mlle Puygarrig, a gesture he could have accompanied with "Hold this for me, a minute, will you?" This objection ushers in the vexed problem of intentionality within the study of language and truth.

Intentions (part 1)

Austin's view of this problem within the framework of speech acts is clear: intentions (or the lack thereof) may be responsible for the infelicity of a speech act.[9] It entails "abuses" only and not "misfires," though. The distinction between the two is important: in the case of a misfire, our speech act will be null and void, as if it never took place; while in the case of an abuse, the speech act takes effect, but it is afflicted with a condition Austin calls insincerity. "I didn't mean to marry/bet/ promise, when I performed the speech act by which I married/bet/promised" does not automatically void my marriage/bet/promise. Intentionality may well alter the way I subsequently conduct myself, but it does not affect the operation of the linguistic or social conventions that will eventually determine whether my marriage/bet/promise holds or not. If I have pronounced, in the appropriate conventional circumstances, the appropriate performative utterance normally recognized as marrying, betting, or promising, then I have married, bet, and promised. In this regard, Austin differs radically from other philosophers who wrote about speech acts; citing as an example Hippolytus' line "my tongue swore to, but my heart did not," he comments:

> It is gratifying to observe in this very example how excess of profundity, or rather solemnity, at once paves the way for immorality. For one who says "promising is not merely a matter of uttering words! It is an inward and spiritual act"! is apt to appear as a solid moralist standing out against a generation of superficial theorizers: we see him as he sees himself, survey-ing the invisible depths of ethical space, with all the distinction of a special-ist in the *sui generis*. Yet he provides Hippolytus with a let-out, the biga-mist with an excuse for his "I do" and the welsher with a defence for his "I bet." Accuracy and morality alike are on the side of the plain saying that *our word is our bond*. (*How to,* 10, Austin's emphasis)

The discussion of intentionality thus raises nonlinguistic problems. Even if a man's consciousness were perfectly transparent to his interlo-cutors; even if we could all agree on this person's real intentions; even if Frege's problem were solved and we could communicate our intention without fearing the indeterminacies of our linguistic expression; even if, as Mary Louise Pratt so judiciously notes, the Oxford philosophers had their way and could extend the language spoken by a "Boy Scout, an honorable guy who always says the right thing and really means it" to all cases in which language is spoken; even if all these conditions are realized, can we be sure that our interlocutor's intentions are all present to his consciousness?[10] Can *he* be expected to know what he really in-tended? Could he not have intended more than one thing at a time? Even in its most simplified, unproblematic, and uncontroverted form, psychoanalysis has taught us that we may have motives and intentions that escape our consciousness at the time we act them out (slips of tongue and parapraxis are the most obvious).

An examination of Alphonse's intentions brings to the fore what is at stake here. He has just missed a couple of balls, and now all he wants is to get rid of the ring in order to improve his tennis game. It is 9:30 in the morning. He is all dressed up for his wedding. The family is sup-posed to get together for a drink of chocolate at 10:00, after which they will leave for the wedding. For the last half hour Alphonse, the village champion and pride, "well groomed, in a new suit, white gloves, patent-leather shoes, chased buttons and a rose in his button-hole" ("Venus," 225) has been sitting the game out and watching his team lose. Finally he decides to save the day, throws off his coat, and joins the game. In the next half hour he has to win the game for his team, wash up, and change back into his groom's attire. Time is then a major consideration, an overriding priority. Alphonse has certainly no intention of marrying anyone before winning the game, let alone a statue (the narrator notes ironically Alphonse's commitment to the game and indifference to his bride: "I really believe that, if necessary, he would have adjourned the wedding" [256]). At precisely this point, Alphonse's behavior no longer makes sense: why does he unnecessarily waste his precious time? The narrator, who is standing next to him, offers to hold on to the ring, but no, Alphonse refuses, running all the way to the statue to slip the ring on her finger. Why does he take the long way? The urgency of this question is compounded by the crucial position of the Venus' fingers: "her right hand, raised up to her breast, was bent, with the palm inward, the thumb and two fingers extended, while the other two were slightly curved" (240). Three fingers are conveniently stretched out more or less vertically, like hooks, and two are bent, facing away from Alphonse and blocked by the palm of the statue's hand. If he absolutely must use the statue as a hook for his personal belongings, why does he not slip the ring on one of the three extended and easily accessible fingers? Why does he bother to put it on the finger that is bent and hidden away from him, behind the hand? Oh, but the bent finger is the *fourth* finger, the *ring* finger (*l'annulaire*, contains the word *anneau*, "ring"), the one on which a groom slips a ring to wed his bride; and indeed the most appropriate finger for the ring carrying the *sempr'ab ti* (ever thine) inscription, traditionally offered by the male Peyrehorades to their brides on their wedding day.

Yet we must not oversimplify and assume that Alphonse intended to wed the statue. Then again, we must also admit that there is enough evidence to suggest that such an intention entered into his odd choice. The fact is that causality cannot exhaust the relation between one's known intentions and one's actions, all the more so, since one may have more than one intention and that, together, these intentions may not amount to a neatly bundled conceptual whole. In an extremely telling and much neglected footnote, Austin interrupts his theoretical discourse of speech acts to wonder about the transparence of consciousness and messages. "A new language is naturally necessary *if* we are to admit unconscious feeling, and feelings which express themselves in

paradoxical manners, such as the psycho-analysts describe." [11] *If* we
have feelings or intentions unknown to us, and *if* these unconscious feel-
ings and intentions manifest themselves in paradoxical linguistic forms,
a new language is indeed needed, one in which the law of the excluded
middle will no longer rule communication. That from a purely logical
viewpoint such a language is impossible is undeniable, since each
expression would then have in addition to its accepted meaning all the
other unknown and unconscious meanings intended by unknown and
unconscious feelings and thoughts, whether or not these meanings can
logically coexist.

This last point raises two questions (which are really two sides of
the same question): *if* I cannot know what I really want and intend, and
if some interference (we may call it the unconscious) disturbs the truth-
value of my *cogito,* can I still discuss my linguistic performance in terms
of intentions? And *if* my interlocutor experiences the same difficulties,
who will respond to the illocutionary force of my utterance, her *cogito,*
consciousness—or parasites? How, in my turn, am I to read her re-
sponse? And what *if* I am given several responses at a time? Although
there may be answers to these questions, it is clear that *if* any factor
affecting discourse escapes the grasp of consciousness, the theoretician
of language who hinged a theory on the mastery and transparency of
consciousness will have to go back to the drawing board. Austin does
not pursue the question further but lets the threat of a radical overthrow
of language *as he knows it* hang on a foreboding "if." Note that it is not
so much language that the unconscious threatens (on the contrary,
Freud has amply demonstrated that language serves the unconscious
quite well), but rather a certain conception of language, one in which
there is no room for ambivalence, misunderstanding, displacements,
substitutions, and wordplay.

Psychoanalysis aside, we should not overlook the obvious: Al-
phonse is not made of flesh and blood; he is a paper character. He has
no intentions except for his textual intentions. Whether or not such in-
tentions make sense in our pedestrian world in which we neither fall in
love with nor marry statues is irrelevant. The text ascribes to him just
enough oddities that can be construed as possible intentions to fog our
discussion of his "real" intentions. In fact, the more general framework
of the text's intentions goes far beyond Alphonse's. Numerous mirror
effects take place, alerting the reader to the crucial role the statue is
meant to play in the chronicles of Ille and, more specifically, in the
chronicles of the Peyrehorade family. The young bride is constantly

compared to the Venus by the narrator ("Venus," 252), Alphonse (255), and especially the old Peyrehorade, who sings a much acclaimed song at the wedding party, in which he tells of two Venuses, one white and heavenly (Mlle de Puygarrig), the other subterranean and black (the statue). If we add that despite his wife's superstitious concern, the old Peyrehorade fixed the wedding day for Friday—Venus' day—we may indeed wonder what the text's "intentions" are and whose wedding the story really intends to recount.[12] The doubling effects are intensified as we notice the strange resemblances between Alphonse and the statue. The young man is strikingly stiff and statuesque: "M. Alphonse de Peyrehorade stirred no more than a statue [*pas plus qu'un Terme*] in the midst of his parents' comings and goings. He was a tall young man of twenty-six, with beautiful and regular features but they were wanting in expression. . . . He was as stiff as a post in his velvet collar, and could not turn round unless with his whole body" ("Venus," 231–32). Even the differences between the two remain symmetrical: his facial features are regular and beautiful but totally expressionless, while the expression of the Venus' face is exactly what strikes and haunts all who gaze at her.[13] Whether the Venus and Alphonse are twins or each other's negative, they seem destined for a clash—or a union.

We may look for intentions even further. Studded with quotations (Molière, Racine, Lucian, Virgil), our story is a matrix of literary texts parasitizing each other. In writing "C'est Venus toute entière à sa proie attachée," the old Peyrehorade is quoting Racine. We recognize here the formula for illocution, in saying X, I am doing Y, in which the second verb is the explicit performative. Inevitably, a citation summons the text from which it is taken and superimposes it on the main story, thereby creating multiple narrative and semantic planes, and generating meanings. In quoting Racine's *Phèdre*, for example, he is also bringing it to bear on "The Venus of Ille." Since *Phèdre* is the story of a married woman in love with her stepson, it shares with "The Venus" a concern for the exclusiveness entailed by the marriage convention and the transgression built into a second love. It also addresses the referential confusions and mirroring effects of which the most obvious is the constant comparison between Hippolytus and Theseus, culminating in the scene where Phèdre confesses her love to Hippolytus as if he were a young and chaste Theseus (act 2, sc. 5). This effect highlights the various doubles in Mérimée's story. The theme of the monster (and the monstrous love) constitutes another motif shared by the two works: not only because of Hippolytus' murder at the hand of a monster but also because Phèdre's lineage (her mother's love for a bull results in the birth of the Minotaur who, incidentally, is also mentioned in "The Venus"), and the lexical insistence on the term *monster* throughout the play. *Phèdre* reminds us that, irregular as it may be, interaction between monsters and humans can take effect—with ominous *results*.

Within the framework of speech acts, the intertextual juxtaposition of *Phèdre* and "The Venus" cuts even farther, as it does not stop at thematic and narrative details but encompasses the overall structure of the play: *Phèdre*'s plot consists primarily in various characters' deferring and timing of a series of speech acts (confessions, accusations, inuendos, promises), that is to say, in varying the speech situations crucial to the felicity of a speech act. Accrued by the acute ambiguity of the characters' intentions (did Thésée really want his son dead; did Phèdre really want to accuse Hippolyte; did Hippolyte and Aricie really not want to inform Thésée of Phèdre's treachery, etc.). the "play" introduced by these deferments results in spectacular infelicities.

Another quotation from Molière's *Amphitryon,* where an amorous Jupiter takes Amphitryon's shape in order to seduce the latter's wife (while Mercury borrows Sosie's), underscores the possibility of an *unintentional* infidelity in "The Venus." More importantly perhaps, although tampering with the proper reference for "Jupiter" and "Mercury" leads to a breakdown in communication (Amphitryon can no longer understand Sosie), again, it is not "without effect": Sosie gets beaten up and Amphitryon's wife bears Jupiter's son.

Other quotations are worth mentioning: in Virgil's *Aeneid,* one occurs at the precise moment when Dido's love for Aeneas outweighs her moral obligation to her deceased husband; she decides to remarry. In Lucian's *Lover of Lies or the Doubter,* in which to illustrate what a lie is, a person tells the story of an animated statue who took revenge on the man who had wronged her. These various intertexts overdetermine "The Venus," assigning to it a textual "unconscious": they motivate textual details that would remain odd if left to considerations of verisimilitude or characters' motivation and, by highlighting some of the details of the story that would not otherwise be as decisive, displace the focus from a simple whodunit to an examination of the complexity of the relationship between language and multiple reference. Like the mirroring effects within the story (the doubles), the intertextual reading points to the fraying of the thread that we intuitively follow from intentions to effects, replacing it with a web of textual allusions and linguistic considerations.

Can we tell, then, what are the intentions of the story? In the final analysis, we do not know what story (either fantastic infidelity or sordid crime and madness) the text intends to communicate, but we know that it simultaneously enforces *and* overrules the suspension of disbelief; points to the implications and consequences of *either one;* examines the conditions for belief *and* disbelief, felicity *and* infelicity, sense *and* nonsense. In short, the story invites a reading that examines and reevaluates the very conditions for telling stories and communicating meanings.

Although we do not know for sure what really happened, we can still recount, of course, *some* of the majors turns of the plot. Here is just such an account of this story that I have published elsewhere:

> A young man playfully puts the wedding band destined for his bride on the finger of a statue of Venus recently discovered by his archaeologically inclined father. When he tries to retrieve his ring, it is stuck, as if the statue had bent its finger to hold onto it. On his wedding night he is found dead in bed, where, according to his terrified young wife, a huge body had joined them. The police disqualify her testimony because the horror of that night has left her "insane." The ensuing criminal investigation uncovers a rivalry between the bridegroom and another man, thus pointing at a likely suspect with a motive, but the man's footprints do not match those left in the garden by the killer. Was the young man murdered by a resentful rival? Did the statue come to claim her groom? Although the first hypothesis is dismissed for lack of conclusive evidence, no one explicitly advances the second. Even the narrator, a blasé archaeologist from Paris, does not offer any comments, despite the irony and marked condescension he expresses toward the villagers. The death of the young man remains unsolved, notwithstanding the strong indications that the statue must be the culprit.[14]

The first part of my story flows normally enough, not exhibiting any of the difficulties on which I have been dwelling. Halfway through my summary, however, at the crucial "whodunit" moment, my narrative breaks into a series of questions. From then on, I do not so much tell the story as reflect on my own difficulties in telling (or reading) the story. My account of "The Venus" clearly lacks the synthetic quality associated with a story. Children, for example, by far the experts when it comes to demanding a story would reject it. "So what next? What happened? Did the statue kill him or not?" are only a few of the questions with which they would voice their impatience with my stalling. This difficulty arises undoubtedly from the genre itself. Uncertainty and hermeneutic hesitations are the most obvious characteristics of fantastic tales.[15] In "The Venus," however, the narrative's uncertainty goes beyond the requisites of the genre: it results also from a series of questions pertaining to the felicity of a central speech act.

Effect or Effects?

By and large, the central incident does not conform to what Austin calls appropriate circumstances. The utterance should be a cut-and-dried case of "misfire" resulting in the worst infelicity: "the procedure which we purport to invoke is *disallowed* or is *botched:* and our (marrying, etc.) is *void* or *without effect*" (*How to,* 16). Can we then presume that Alphonse's unfortunate gesture was "without effect"? Is the marriage really void? The story certainly allows for the possibility of a felicitous speech act. Between felicity and infelicity stands the fatal embrace of the abominable yet exquisite body of the statue. Austin does not hesitate: when the participants are not "appropriate for the invocation of the particular procedure invoked" (rule A.2), "there is no accepted conventional procedure; it is a mockery, like a marriage with a monkey" (*How to,* 24). Yet Alphonse's horrible death suggests at least the possibility that nothing be farther away from a mockery than a marriage with an inappropriate partner: his "clenched teeth and black face denoted the most frightful agony" ("Venus," 268–69). Austin—even as he notes that " 'without effect' does not here mean 'without consequences, results, effects' "—shows no interest for the consequences, results, effects of a marriage with a monkey—or a statue. The reader knows, however, that if Alphonse's act had ominous results, consequences, and effects, it is precisely because the story does not rule out the possibility that his conventional speech act *took effect.* Effect and effects may not be as far apart as Austin would have us believe.

I find it difficult, for example, to agree with Stanley Fish's suggestion that one way of cleaning up the muddle of speech act theories and restoring their usefulness is to distinguish between a speech act itself and its consequences and effects. Indeed, his is a familiar line of argument: perlocutionary effects are contingent, unpredictable, difficult to regulate; in short, a theoretical nuisance. The solution, then, is obvious: they must be excluded from the theory.

> Speech act theory can point to these matters—they are perlocutionary effects—but it cannot explicate them because *they lie outside the area of its declared competence.* . . . Obviously this does not mean that perlocutionary effects don't occur or that we shouldn't be interested in them when doing literary criticism, but that speech act theory can offer us no special help in dealing with them, *apart from telling us that they are what it cannot*

handle. And if we insist on asking the theory to do what it cannot, we will end up by taking from it the ability to do what it can.[16]

Fish's line of demarcation between the theory and its outside rides on conventions. A conventional effect is illocutionary and therefore *in*. A nonconventional effect is perlocutionary and therefore *out* (Fish ignores the string of philosophical essays that convincingly question the distinction between conventional and unconventional[17]). He thus lumps together different kinds of effects, with different degrees of immediacy to their causes, some being long-range effects that cannot be pinned immediately to the speech act itself. If, *because* of John and Mary's marriage, Peter (Mary's rejected suitor), engages in a life of crime, is incarcerated, kills his cell mate in a fight, and ultimately commits suicide, I doubt that any philosopher in his right mind would want to count Peter's unfortunate life story as an effect of Mary's illocutionary "I do." Although it may be a consequence of Mary's choice, Peter's sad life cannot be attributed directly to the speech act and therefore cannot be considered as a string of perlocutionary effects. (Besides, a social worker may evoke his unhappy childhood, a psychiatrist may tell us that Peter had a pronounced Oedipal complex and spent his life expiating his desire for Mary-Mommy, a neurologist may find some neurological imbalance that led to his aggressiveness, Peter's father may think that this is what happens when a son refuses to go into the family business, etc.) I therefore agree with Fish that not every effect is a speech act effect. His discussion of Ohmann's reading of *King Lear* or *Major Barbara* has my full support (Fish 226–31). But I can no longer agree when he generalizes his quarrel with Ohmann and brings it to bear on all perlocutionary speech acts and on all results, consequences, and effects. Just because a single speech act cannot be made responsible for an endless string of events (this is another problem altogether, as my love triangle shows: it raises the much discussed problem of causal chains and their possible proliferation and indeterminacies), this is not to say that the same speech act cannot have any effect that is not conventional (that is not dictated by a convention).

For instance, if I suavely remind you that your aging parents are living in the Third Reich (Austin's example, *How to*, 119), I am most certainly threatening you (illocution). My threat is a felicitous illocutionary act, even if you do not take heed. If, however, my threat intimidates you or deters you from doing something, then my illocutionary utterance also has a perlocutionary force (intimidate, deter); that is, *it affects you*. Note that the perlocutionary effect did not just happen to follow my utterance (if I had complimented you on your new tie, feeling intimidated would have been totally out of place) it is inseparable from the rest of my message. I could not logically say, for example, "I threatened you, but I did not intend to intimidate you," or "I threatened you, but I hoped it would not deter you from doing something." My utterance was certainly not a benign reminder of your parents' address. When I threatened you, I aimed for a specific perlocutionary effect, otherwise, I might as well have complimented you about your tie. A threat is meant to intimidate, deter, etcetera. It does not owe its force to some accidental later consequences, added to the original effect. Nor is it an accident that in response to my threat you felt intimidated: the perlocutionary force of my threatening utterance is contemporaneous with the perception of the threat. If you understand the illocutionary force of my reminder, my illocutionary speech act is felicitous (Austin speaks of ensuring the uptake of an illocutionary act). If, however, you and your parents are committed to the idea of resisting threats, I may not deter you from your course of action. Your political convictions and your force of character would nullify the perlocutionary force of my threat. Even if ruined and orphaned, you live to regret your decision, we shall still not speak of the "delayed felicity" of my perlocutionary utterance, for your change of mind results not from my utterance but rather from the unhappy consequences that your refusal to be intimidated has brought upon you.

We then have to admit the possibility of a curious situation, in which an utterance can be at the same time a felicitous illocution (you know that in reminding you of your parents' address I am threatening you) and an infelicitous perlocution (you won't allow my bullying to intimidate you). The former is a component of communication; the latter involves a new factor, uncontrollable by the speaker (and indeed, this is what makes it so difficult to theorize). But it remains a speech act nonetheless—at least, if we maintain that to perform a speech act is also and *at the same time* (not just later) to do something in or by saying something. As long as we are not rejecting the notion of speech acts *in toto*, we have to accept that a theory may neither master nor control totally either "the area of its declared competence" or the consequences of its felicity. I am not contesting that effects and consequences are problematic or that perlocution is a can of worms ("It is the distinction between illocutions and perlocutions which seems likeliest to give trouble," writes Austin [*How to, 110*]).[18] But excessive categorization—especially when followed by the exclusion of elements that may interfere with those categorizations—is not the solution. If a person's intellectual temperament is such that he or she feels compelled to solve problems, then let him or her first address the problem (as Austin did [110–20]), not push it aside.

Fish's definition is in fact an attempt to distinguish between Austin's effect and effects; unfortunately, perlocution, which Austin decidedly—and rightly—considered among speech acts, gets lost in the shuffle. It is therefore not enough to mention effects, as do Ohmann and Fish. As Austin points out, all effects are not alike. Some (as in Ohmann's ill-chosen examples) are contingent and therefore not perlocutionary at all, but others are built into the original speech act and constitute its raison d'être. These are definitely perlocutionary effects, and the general problem of causality should not be confused—as is the case in Fish's analysis—with the questions raised by perlocution within the frame-work of speech acts.[19] The line separating the two is not always clear; we may encounter uncomfortable gray areas, but this is hardly a reason to drop the question altogether.

Austin, for instance, acknowledges that all illocutionary acts are conventional. Like Fish, he also suggests that the consequences of a speech act may not stretch indefinitely and that we "have then to draw the line between an action we do (here an illocution) and its conse-quences" (*How to,* 111). At the same time, acutely aware that the thorny problem of consequences is intricately built into the very tenets of the theory, he wonders for a moment, "Ought we not, in seeking to detach 'all' consequences, to go right back beyond the illocution to the locution—and indeed to the act (A.a), the uttering of noises, which is a physical movement?" (113–14).[20] If answered affirmatively, this ques-tion could put an end to all speech act theories. Rigorously pushing to its logical extreme a line of reasoning similar to Fish's, Austin shows how it would end up negating force altogether. For instance, Austin imagines a scenario in which one would say about illocution: first a speaker states something (simple locution); second, and only as a con-sequence of having been first stated, this utterance projects an illocu-tionary force. Austin vehemently rejects this simplistically causal per-ception of speech acts, emphasizing instead that the illocutionary and perlocutionary forces are *built into* the utterance and constitute its most fundamental semantic charge. They are inseparable from the original semantics of the utterance: "And further, much more important, we must avoid the idea, suggested above though not stated, that the illocu-tionary act is a *consequence* of the locutionary act, and even the idea that what is imported by the nomenclature of illocutions is an *addi-tional* reference to *some* of the consequences of the locutions, i.e., that to say 'he urged me to' is to say that he said certain words and *in addition* that his saying them had or perhaps was intended to have certain consequences" (114–15, Austin's emphasis). That the question of causality remains nonetheless troublesome does not escape his attention. In his various papers, when discussing the distinction between illocution and perlocution, he invariably admits that any formal criterion making it possible to tell them apart is, at best, slippery. And yet, although many categories and distinctions drawn in the first lectures of *How to* function mostly as heuristic devices, only to collapse later under his scrutinizing eye (the all-important one between constative and performative, among others), perlocution remains throughout, as does the plea to avoid the temptation of a naïvely temporal causality.

One may feel tempted to raise yet another argument. "Our word is our bond," says Austin, but the young man did not utter a word. Can there be a speech act without speech? Austin hesitates but eventually recognizes that "infelicity is an ill to which all acts are heir which have the general character of ritual or ceremonial, all conventional acts. . . . This is clear if only from the mere fact that many conventional acts, such as betting or conveyance of property, can be performed in non-verbal ways. . . . This much is obvious" (*How to,* 19). Indeed, if I wave a finger, it can be for no specific purpose, but if I am at an auction and wave a finger, I may find myself the proud owner of an indescribable relic. The difference between the two lies in the conventional aspect of auctions, which recognize finger waving as the equivalent of an explicit (verbal) bid. Finger waving then *means* bidding. Even if the locution itself is missing, its force can still be expressed by an explicit performative verb. In a still different situation, finger waving can express my discontent and be taken as a warning or a threat. Since the speech act hinges upon the explicit performative understood in the gesture, we may say that from the viewpoint of speech act theory, there is no difference between a verbal and a nonverbal speech act. In other words, a "nonverbal convention" is a contradiction in terms. Even if no word is uttered, to be recognized as meaningful an act depends on the verbal utterance into which we transcribe it. In raising my hand at an auction, I signify my intention to bid. In waving my finger at you, I admonish you. *In doing x, I am doing y* is, of course, Austin's formula for illocutionary acts. The conventional aspect of a meaningful act is therefore no more than the performative verb that makes explicit its force(s) and, of course, the general code that allows for the substitution of the actual act (waving) for the explicit performative(s) (admonish, bid, etc.).[21]

Conventions

Austin's rule A states that:

A.1. There must exist an accepted conventional procedure having a certain conventional effect, that procedure to include the uttering of certain words by certain persons in certain circumstances, and further,

A.2. the particular persons and circumstances in a given case must be appropriate for the invocation of the particular procedure invoked. (*How to,* 14–15)

The rule is so simple and obvious that it hardly seems to deserve comment. And yet Austin's next two lectures constitute just such a commentary. They do not, however, paraphrase, explain, or illustrate the rules as much as they present a myriad of cases that we may consider either as exceptions or as indeterminable borderline cases. Austin also explores and questions the exact meaning and extension of some of the key concepts he used in the formulation of the rules ("exist," "accepted," "procedure," etc.). Most of the time, he leaves open the questions he raises. After citing infelicitous speech acts that do not follow rule A.1 properly, for example, he notes that "Much more common, however, will be cases where it is uncertain how far a procedure extends—which cases it covers or which varieties it could be made to cover. It is inherent in the nature of any procedure that the limits of its applicability, and therefore, of course, the 'precise' definition of the procedure, will remain vague. There will always occur difficult or marginal cases where nothing in the previous history of a conventional procedure will decide conclusively whether such a procedure is or is not correctly applied to such a case" (*How to,* 31). What is left of a procedure if we know neither "which cases it covers [n]or which varieties it could be made to cover"? if we cannot determine "the limits of its applicability"? if " 'the precise' definition of the procedure will remain vague"? Austin's numerous illustrations of such uncertain cases clearly show that, although "difficult or marginal" for the theory, these irregularities are plentiful and cannot be dismissed as mere exceptions. And what of conventions themselves if, as he wistfully notes, "it is difficult to say where conventions begin and end" (119)?

The second set of conditions adds insult to injury:

B.1. The procedure must be executed by all participants both correctly

B.2. and completely. (*How to,* 15)

But then we are told that for B.1 "examples are more easily seen in the law; they are naturally not so definite in ordinary life, where allowances are made" (*How to,* 36); and for B.2 "here again in ordinary life, a certain laxness in procedure is permitted—otherwise no university business would ever get done" (37)! How can a procedure be at once executed correctly and completely *and* admit allowances and laxness? Must it be executed correctly and completely or not? How much laxness can it bear?

The students of speech act theories are quick (and wrong) to point out that the distinction between performative and constative eventually collapses, to be replaced with the triple distinction *locution/illocution/perlocution*—which in turn half-collapses by the end of the book (see pp. 226–29) This does not mean, however, that rules A and B should simply be discarded (or maintained). Austin warns us against such simplistic dogmatism: "It may appear in all this that we have merely been taking back our rules. But this is not the case. Clearly there are these six possibilities of infelicities even if it is sometimes uncertain which is involved in a particular case: and we *might* define them, at least for given cases, if we wished. And we must at all costs avoid over-simplification, which one might be tempted to call the occupational disease of philosophers if it were not their occupation" (*How to,* 38, Austin's emphasis). The unnarratability of "The Venus of Ille" hinges upon this warning. We cannot simply contend that, since the procedure is both incorrect and incomplete and since the participant is inappropriate, Alphonse's gesture remains without effects or even without effect. Clearly, if we indulge in some 'laxness" and make some "allowances" (rules B), if we stretch just a little the "limits of applicability" of the convention (rules A), then perhaps we have a felicitous speech act.

Such a possibility is mentioned in our story, and, not so surprisingly, it is envisioned by none other than Alphonse himself: "Besides, what would the people here think of my absent-mindedness? They would make fun of me. They would call me *the husband of the statue*" ("Venus" 259). The narrator, too, muses over conventions and their power to regulate felicitous speech acts: " 'What a detestable thing,' I said to myself, 'is a marriage of convenience! A mayor puts on a tricoloured sash, and a priest a stole, and behold, the noblest of girls may be dedicated [*livrée*] to the Minotaur!' " (266). Had the mayor forgotten to bring his sash or the priest his stole, would the noblest of girls have been any less dedicated to the Minotaur? Just because the statue is an unconventional bride, can we be absolutely sure that this convention has reached the limits of its applicability? Haven't we already been duly informed that there is no knowing where conventions begin and end? Couldn't we think that in certain attenuating circumstances this convention could be stretched just enough to include Alphonse's marriage to the Venus? The suspension of disbelief, for example, can constitute just such a circumstance: since it cancels out the distinction animate/inanimate and human/nonhuman, it protects Alphonse's action from its most obvious cause of infelicity.

Furthermore, once a speech act evokes conventions, procedures, effects, and consequences, can it cancel them out, can it neutralize them on the pretense that because of a procedural technicality, it is null and void, without effect? Is effect really as far removed from effects as Austin claims? Once summoned into this narrative, can the otherness of the statue simply be dismissed on a technicality ("he did not mean it," "the mayor did not have his tricolor sash on," "the priest forgot his stole," etc.). The statue, for one, may think differently. After Alphonse, realizing that he has forgotten to retrieve his ring after the tennis game, goes back to the tennis court, he returns to the wedding party livid and informs the narrator that he was unable to remove the ring because "the Venus . . . has clenched her finger. . . . The finger of Venus has contracted and bent up; she closed her hand, do you hear? . . . She is my wife apparently, because I gave her my ring . . . She will not give it back." The narrator's reaction takes place in two stages: "I shivered suddenly, and for a moment my blood ran cold. Then the deep sigh he gave sent a breath of wine into my face and all my emotion disappeared. 'The wretched man is completely drunk,' I thought" ("Venus," 264–65). The "enlightened" narrator is only too happy to explain away one unacceptable situation (the resistance of the statue) by another that is relatively more acceptable (drunkenness). As is often the case, causality is elicited to rationalize and dismiss unpleasantness. And yet the two events may well not be related: even though Alphonse is drunk, the statue could have bent its finger, holding fast to the ring. Venus (known for her bad taste) may not share the narrator's repugnance for Alphonse's coarseness; she may even have her own idea of what constitutes acceptable "laxness in procedure."

The effect of this episode does not rest so much on the questionable legitimacy of the "wedding ceremony" as on the narrative's insistence on the part played by the statue in the illocutionary transaction (her uptake) and on her subsequent entwining in Alphonse's wedding plans. Minotaur or statue, Beauty may just have been dedicated to the Beast (or at least, the Beast may think so). To the contortions Austin inflicts on language and its illocutionary rules, the statue opposes its stiffness, its coldness, its mute thingness. In the wedding bed the Venus appropriates and contains Alphonse within this thingness in a deadly embrace that leaves a circular mark on his body (a livid ring around his chest that mirrors the wedding ring she leaves on the floor of the bedroom). Alphonse is a victim of the absolute otherness that he casually challenged believing that since the participant was not "appropriate for the invocation of the particular procedure," his action would not have effect. At the limit of language, its lax conventions, and its ambiguities stands thingness. Reference may well try to bring this thingness into language, calling upon causality to explain its otherness—not only does the statue's materiality remain irreducible, but, given the murder weapon (her bronze body), the effect of Alphonse's silent speech act is an instance of the same irreducibility of things that language purports to deny. Felicitous or not, Alphonse's speech act has achieved an awesome effect: it has exposed the hubris and power of repression inherent in language and has brought into the open its other, the "thing-effect." As he catches a glimpse of *Unheimlichkeit,* the narrator "shivers": things are impenetrable, irreducibly alien. At the same time, however, they are perfectly tamed, designated by the words with which we replace them in our daily transactions, and subject to linguistic causality. Alphonse's wedding with the statue may be with or without effect, but another, much more ominous, effect has taken place: the *thing*.

And yet we must remember that the story is not construed as a fairy tale in which anything is possible as long it does not disrupt the story's internal semantic and narrative coherence. The narrator, at least, seems to uphold a realist view of the world, one in which statues are harmless, inanimate objects, and wedding ceremonies rely on conventions, sashes, and stoles; one in which disbelief (his own) is never suspended (except for the momentary shiver). The fantastic aspect of the story (as opposed to the marvelous—I am borrowing Todorov's distinction) results largely from the narrator's enlightened realism and his rejection of superstitions and supernatural phenomena. Since, after all, the story is told exclusively from this narrator's viewpoint, the reader has no angle on it other than this enlightened realism; the reader cannot therefore readily accept the supernatural reading that the facts seem to dictate, nor make allowances for statues in marriage procedures. We are then left with the possibility of an unconventional convention, the possibility of a felicitous speech act uniting a man and a statue, the possibility of bigamy, the possibility of effect and effects. Or again, we are left with the possibility of clear lines of demarcation, the possibility of excluding a statue from the convention as an inappropriate participant, the possibility of a perfectly normal marriage with Mlle de Puygarrig, the possibility of an unresolved murder (police archives are full of such cases), the possibility of a speech act without effect or perhaps even without effects. But either way something has happened. The *thing* has happened.

To sum up this discussion we may once more contrast Austin with Fish and Searle. Stanley Fish adopted convention as the ultimate test for speech acts. Searle introduced the distinction between brute and institutionalized facts. At first glance these definitions and distinctions appeal to our intuitive perception of conventions and seem perfectly valid. Austin, however, did not stop at that first glance and, true to his philosophical spirit, deliberately proceeded to question conventions themselves (see, for example: "Many of you will be getting impatient at this approach—and to some extent, quite justifiably. You will say, 'Why not cut the cackle? Why go on about lists available in ordinary talk of names for things we do that have relations to saying, . . . why not get down to discussing the thing bang off in terms of linguistics and psychology in a straightforward fashion? Why be so devious?' Well, of course, I agree that this will have to be done—only I say *after*, not before, seeing what we can screw out of ordinary language even if in what comes out there is a strong element of the undeniable. Otherwise, we shall overlook things and go too fast" [*How to*, 123, Austin's emphasis]). The result of his inquiry into conventions is an extensive questioning of his own theory (a questioning is neither a refutation nor a retraction).

Searle and Fish, on the other hand, present "theories." They posit that *convention* (or in Searle's case, *institution*) is an intuitive term that needs neither examining nor questioning. Hence they proceed to elaborate a theory that rests entirely on the intuitive perception of the term by readers who, *being part of these conventions*, cannot criticize or even problematize them without considerable and deliberate scrutiny (which neither Fish nor Searle invites them to exercise). Conventions and institutions are human constructs, however, and as such, imperfect. Just like language—another convention—they lend themselves to abuses, errors, and agrammaticalities and have problematic margins and boundaries; and, just like language, they harbor innumerable difficulties for "theories."

Language versus Languages

The last comparison with language is not accidental. But it does not merely reflect my own interest in language. Nor does it constitute the reduction of a story to its linguistic elements in the manner of formalism or early structuralism. The story itself thematizes, *en abyme,* language as such: narrative sequences raise explicit questions about the variety of languages, the hermeneutics of communication, and the unreliability of semantics. These sequences make up a long narrative segment, representing roughly one-tenth of the story (five out of fifty pages in my edition), about the translation and interpretation of Latin inscriptions. They bring into sharp focus the abundant scattered remarks and discussions in "The Venus" about the limits of applicability of conventions and institutions and the effect of these limits on hermeneutics and meaning.

There are two inscriptions on the statue. The first is on the pedestal: "CAVE AMANTEM." Challenged by the old Peyrehorade to translate the Latin phrase, the narrator is somewhat embarrassed.

> "But," I answered, "it has two meanings. It can be translated: 'Beware of him who loves thee; mistrust thy lovers.' But in that sense I do not know whether CAVE AMANTEM would be good Latin. Looking at the lady's diabolic expression, I would rather believe that the artist intended to put the spectator on his guard against her terrible beauty; I would therefore translate it: 'Beware if she loves thee'" ("Venus," 243).

Even a phrase as concise as this one "has two meanings." We should note that one of these meanings does not conform to the linguistic convention "completely and correctly" (rule B). It is a "lax" Latin, one that makes "allowances" for irregularities, one that stretches the rule a little—but that, nonetheless, constitutes a meaning. Neither character appeals to grammaticality (conformance to linguistic conventions) to buttress his reading, however. The narrator could simply have said that the first sense is not grammatical and that, from a purist's viewpoint, the second is therefore the only felicitous meaning. This would indeed have been an oversimplification, one of the many oversimplifications in which Austin saw at once the occupational disease of philosophers and their occupation. Implicitly admitting that *some* deviation from the convention has no effect on the felicity of a translation, the narrator opts instead for a referential contextualization of the inscription. He compares it to another "inscription" on the statue: her expression, which he interprets as diabolic. One interpretation then corroborates the other, and this in turn allows him to select one of the two meanings (we may even wish to simplify a little, as I did in a previous reading of this story, and contend that he looks at the object itself, the referent).[22]

The problem with contextualization is that contexts are legion (in fact, with a little perseverance, they are inexhaustible).

The old antiquarian brings in even more extensive contexts to shore up his preference for the first translation. Referring to Venus' notorious love affair with Vulcan, he interprets the inscription as " 'In spite of all thy beauty and thy scornful manner, thou shalt have for thy lover a blacksmith, a hideous cripple' " ("Venus," 244). Indeed, "the words used are to some extent to be 'explained' by the context in which they are designed to be or have actually been spoken in a linguistic exchange" (*How to,* 100), but how far are we to contextualize? When is a context far-fetched enough to be smiled at, as the narrator does with the mythological allusion the old man proudly presents for his approval? *Cave* is a warning, a clear illocutionary utterance. And yet whom is it warning? To which of its possible contexts shall we resort in order to interpret the warning? For example, shouldn't we extend our notion of context to the two men engaged in translating? Shouldn't they consider themselves warned against attempting to reduce a sibylline inscription to the transparency of a message? In short, into what context(s), what situation(s), and what convention(s) shall we contextualize our utterance? What shall we do with the *(s),* with the *discarded* context(s), situation(s), and convention(s)—with the remainders (more on remainders in chapter 6)?

The second inscription, on the arm of the Venus, is even more problematic. It is no longer so much a question of deciding what is there as of filling in what is not there:

> VENERI TVRBVL . . .
> EVTYCHES MYRO
> IMPERIO FECIT.

The unfinished *turbul . . .* poses a problem. The narrator hesitates between two approaches: first he looks for some "epithet applied to Venus which might assist [him]." When intertextuality fails him, he turns once more to a referential contextualization of her expression and suggests *turbulenta,* "Venus who troubles and disturbs" ("Venus," 245). The old Peyrehorade contributes still a third approach consisting of two pages of fantastic etymologies in French, Greek, and Phoenician and concluding in *turbulnerae* because, says he, "a league from here, at the base of the mountain, is a village called Boulternère. It is a corruption of the Latin word TVRBVLNERA" (246). Ultimately, Turbulnera does not "mean" anything; it *refers* to what *is there.* It is, first of all, a pure indexical. *Turbulnera* thus extends the contextualizations to the interpreter's *hic* and *nunc* and, bursting the illusion of aesthetic and scholarly distances with which translators and interpreters usually surround themselves, asserts the centrality of the subject in reading and interpreting: the Venus is "local," "from around the corner," "our very own." [23]

The ellipsis after *turbul* . . . thus triggers three different hermeneutic effects: intertextuality, referential contextuality, and self-reference. As if to underscore this contextual slippage, Mérimée encodes his own name in the inscription: *Eutyches* is the Greek translation of *Prosper*. The artist has signed his work. But what work? the statue? the story? the gift (reading another ellipsis, a little hole in the arm of the statue, the narrator suggests that Eutyches Myro may be, not Myro the known sculptor, but an unlucky lover of the same last name, who hung a bracelet on Venus' arm as an expiatory offering, in the hope of appeasing the goddess and regaining his lady's love)? The highlighted self-referential contextualization thus exceeds the boundaries of the story proper and extends to the author himself or at least his name. (Note that this process works both ways: the estranged author's name becomes *literally* part of his work, no longer autonomous. Whether it is a name engraved in a statue or written in a literary text, it no longer "belongs" to the artist; it is consubstantial with the work itself.)

But contextualization does not limit itself to the contexts explicitly mentioned in the story. Anne Hiller, for one, replaces the old Peyrehorade's mythological context with a Freudian one: "Venus libitina. . . . The Venus seems to personify the ambiguous unity of the libido, at once a hedonistic movement and a death wish [*désir de mort*] projected on the loved object and wishing its annihilation" (Hiller, 212, trans. mine).[24] In this her approach is not unlike the antiquarian's: she brings her own context to bear on her interpretation of the inscription's ellipsis. To some extent any reading, any understanding, of a text widens contextualization to include the reader and the culture he or she represents. Contexts thus may spread indefinitely, not only, as Derrida notes, because any utterance can be quoted—taken out of its own context and transferred to a new one—but because even when it is left in its own context, its perception by an unlimited number of readers (each immersed in and part of a more or less idiosyncratic set of referential and cultural contexts) activates the possibility of a dizzying proliferation of contexts.[25]

Context and conventions go hand in hand. We perceive an utterance within its immediate narrative context as well as within the context of a convention. (To some extent, an utterance also *creates* undeniably a context and a convention, as Fish reminds us, but this is mostly a chicken-and-egg discussion.) For example, just as the old antiquarian resorts to mythology (a conventional context), the reader, too, may appeal to mythology and folklore and thereby discover that an ominous marriage with a statue is a widespread topos (the folkloric and literary sources of "The Venus" have been hotly debated, mostly because the theme is so frequent that critics easily discovered—and defended—new ones.) A topos, too, constitutes a convention. That this convention may be at odds with the constructs through which we account for our daily experience, or even with our marital law, only points to the possibility of multiple and divergent conventions and procedures simultaneously evoked or perhaps created by a single speech act. Since we may not be able to add them up neatly and subsume them under one coherently comprehensive convention into which the speech act will be contextualized and by virtue of which it will acquire its illocutionary force, these multiple contextual conventions risk preventing us from ever determining the *exact* conventions, contexts, and circumstances essential to the examination of a speech act's felicity (and by extension, essential to an exact theory of language—more on this problem in chapter 6).

Futhermore, language itself is but a convention, subject to all the procedural ills that can befall conventions. Understanding even a two-word utterance such as *cave amantem* may require diverse syntactical procedures, equally meaningful though incompatible with one another. "The Venus of Ille" reminds us that the notions of convention and institution extend far beyond our intuitive understanding. Not only is it difficult to delineate a convention, as Austin notes, but, since our world is teeming with conventions, it is also difficult to isolate one convention and even more difficult to isolate one conventional procedure that would not somehow be entangled in yet other conventions.

The pragmatic insistence on delineating and exhausting the inventory of relevant speech circumstances is not without analogy to structuralism. On either side of the Channel or the Ocean, "theoreticians" proceed in a similar manner: they single out sets of "relevant data" (and leave out "irrelevant" ones), which, by virtue of being grouped together, acquire their own syntax and semantics. Therefore I am not questioning so much specific aspects of a theory as the very action by which any theory gathers its relevant data and infers from them a set of rules that it then applies to new situational data—a gesture that necessarily presupposes its own feasibility. It is this very presupposition of feasibility that literary texts such as "The Venus" question: not because literature enjoys special privileges or plays the language game by different rules; not because it is not "serious" and therefore not bound to respect the rules (or vice versa); not because the "area of declared competence" (Fish's expression) of literature or literary criticism is different from philosophy's (as Fish himself illustrates, they can follow the same presuppositions); but because the literary text, not intending to construe such theories, does not limit itself to "relevant data." Rather, it posits that any linguistic (semantic, syntactical, or semiotic) manifestation is relevant to language. It also acknowledges that the effects of language exceed communication. Thus it reminds us that the interferences of those aspects of language that "theoreticians" find irrelevant are perhaps the most relevant of all: unlike "relevant" data, they illuminate the whole area of competence of a theory, including its limitations, its failures, and, mostly, the line of demarcation between its competence and its incompetence.

The literary text is therefore not a case of nonserious language, as has been argued by philosophers and linguists alike: on the contrary, it is perhaps the only one that really takes language seriously—that takes language more seriously than it does the "theory" of language; the only one that exploits the felicity *and* infelicity of speech acts, thereby acknowledging that infelicity is not a "not doing" but an "other doing"—theories notwithstanding. It is precisely because of this inherent feature of the literary text that Austin, while setting aside literature, nonetheless had recourse to literary examples. I have already cited his use of Hippolytus' bad faith (p. 180). We should also add his scattered remarks, when, for instance, in the course of the discussion of possible misfires of rule A.1, he pointedly remarks that "the general position is *exploited* in the unhappy story of *Don Quixote*" (*How to,* 27). *Don Quixote* could be seen as a meditation on linguistic and cultural infelicities. Literature exploits infelicities. This is a far cry from a single-minded exclusion of literature from the philosophy of language. Indeed, we can easily construe *How to Do Things with Words* itself as a meditation on language's infelicities: with the exception of a few pages, the bulk of Austin's lectures consists of the creation of mininarratives illustrating infelicities. I, for one, see very little difference between Cervantes' and Austin's treatments of infelicities (there are differences between the two, but they lie elsewhere).

Furthermore, almost invariably, when discarding literature, Austin adds a restrictive clause, such as, for instance, "a performative utterance will, for example, be *in a peculiar way* hollow or void if said by an actor on the stage, or if introduced in a poem, or spoken in soliloquy" (*How to,* 22, Austin's emphasis). Indeed no literary critic will claim that the actor on stage is committed to marrying the leading lady. Art voids some of the referential aspect of truth-value. Austin's exclusion of language is therefore no more than a reminder of the renowned suspension of disbelief. *In a peculiar way,* the language of poetry works differently, not because it presents something inherently different but because it presupposes a predetermined attitude shared by its readers toward some aspects of its truth-value. This attitude constitutes but one more convention: the literary (or artistic) convention. As such it has no problem fitting in a theory that poses conventions, contexts, and circumstances as its cornerstone.

It is also worth noting that Austin's restriction comes to bear not on literature, poetry, or theater but on their use of language, which he finds "parasitic upon its *normal* use" (*How to,* 22). We may argue with the notion of the use of language. It implies a mastery of language by the speaker, which, as Austin's note on psychoanalysis shows, is far from obvious (see pp. 181–82). We may need not "a new language," as he thought, but a new *theory* of language, one that recognizes that the subject's use of language is far from exhausting what an utterance does (and as his meditation on infelicities goes on, Austin eventually comes very close to elaborating such a theory). We may also question the notion of normal use. Literary criticism has extensively examined the notions of linguistic norm and theories of *écart.* In Austin's texts, what is a norm? As we proceed through the twelve steps of *How to Do Things with Words,* we soon find out that Austin's relentless insistence on contexts and puzzles shows normal use to present as many "aberrations" as its literary parasite. If anything collapses during these twelve lectures, it is indeed the notion of norm. This, in turn, entails a collapse of the distinction between a normal use and one that would be parasitic upon it.

In the tenth lecture, Austin admits that the use of language in fiction "may be, and intuitively seem[s] to be, entirely different" (*How to,* 122). "May be" and "intuitively seems" (rather than a simple *is*) are very cautious reservations indeed, especially when followed by "further matters which we are not trenching upon." They echo the ominous "if" on which he hinges his admission that the philosophy of language relies on the intimate knowledge of our consciousness and intentions and that the Freudian unconscious would wreak havoc with this branch of philosophy. I therefore suggest that we take Austin's reservations and hesitations literally: in fiction, language *may* be used differently, but then, again, it may not.

In a literary text, language may misbehave—at least from the viewpoint of a theory of language. But it is important to remember that far from reflecting an etiolation, as Austin's ill-chosen expression states, it is a manifestation of language's enormous vigor—including the vigor needed to exceed the boundaries and obstructions that "theories" attempt to impose on it.

Nerval's "King of Bicêtre"

Unlike "The Venus," "The King of Bicêtre" presents a clear storyline:[26] a young attorney, Raoul Spifame, looks like the king of France. Eventually, he believes that he is Henry II, king of France. He is sent to Bicêtre, a mental institution, where he befriends another man subject to delusions, Vignet, a poet who claims that Du Bellay, Mellin de Saint-Gelais, Ronsard, (all bona fide Renaissance poets) intercept, steal, and plagiarize his poetry. The two men soon become inseparable. They manage to escape from Bicêtre and in the marketplace confront the real king of France. The king, troubled by the resemblance, sends them to a remote palace and orders that Spifame be treated there like a king.

While these few sentences probably suffice to give the reader a general sense of the story's major turns of events, they do little to justify our interest in "The King of Bicêtre" within the present framework. Before delving into the details of the story, I shall therefore highlight some cross references with speech act theories.

Appropriateness and Political Law

We are dealing here with an infelicity of the worst kind. Spifame's delusion harbors problems exceeding by far a simple case of mistaken identity: he does not think he is the man next door; he thinks he is the king of France, that is to say, a man who owes his authority and his unique position in French society to his origin and proper lineage. The king of France is at once the effect of the social convention we call monarchy and the center that holds the convention together (in a sense, its cause). He is also at the same time an individual and an institution (one may recall Louis XIV's notorious "*L'Etat, c'est moi*"). Should his proper lineage and rightful authority be tampered with, and should an impostor prove equally appropriate to fulfill kingly functions, monarchy, as an institution and social order, would collapse. Spifame's mistaken identity thus puts into question the social, political, and legal foundations of his society, all the more so when, as we shall see later, he exercises functions that are indeed royal privileges.

Fish

In this context we are reminded once more of Fish's insistence that speech acts do not reflect but create conventions (pp. 186–89). I am indeed prepared to concede to Fish that in the case of a conventional speech act, the convention itself is to some extent validated by the act, but I find it surprising that he does not note that the same speech act would have no illocutionary force (that is, would not be a speech act to begin with) were it not for a convention. As I noted earlier, we are clearly caught in a variation of the proverbial chicken-and-egg discussion. I find Fish's examples particularly telling: "It might be objected," he writes, "that to reason in this way is to imply that one can constitute a state simply by declaring it to exist. That of course is exactly what happens: a single man plants a flag on a barren shore and claims everything his eye can see in the name of a distant monarch or for himself; another man, hunted by police and soldiers, seeks refuge in a cave, where alone or in the company of one or two fellows, he proclaims the birth of a revolutionary government" (Fish 216). These two examples are strangely cut out of any sociohistorical context, as if proclaiming a government and annexing territories have never happened in the history of humankind before occurring in Fish's argument. What Fish does not consider is that a single man can claim a territory by planting a flag on a barren shore only 1) because there exists a convention by which a particular piece of colored cloth represents a nation and its government, and 2) because there is a second convention (already confirmed by numerous political speech acts) by which planting such a piece of cloth in any territory is generally recognized as laying claim to that territory. Paradoxically then, the illocutionary act owes its inaugural force to the fact that in a certain sense it is not inaugural: its significance ("I claim this territory") is recognized as such precisely because this act is a sign of sorts, likely to occur (and to have occurred) in a variety of contexts.

This is what Derrida calls the principle of iterability inherent in signs, that is, the reliance of a single phenomenon (a sign) on a convention by which it acquires a significance every time it occurs or recurs.[27] Without this convention, planting a piece of colored cloth anywhere would be just that, planting a piece of colored cloth, with no political consequences whatsoever. Similarly, monarchy requires the existence and authority of kings, as Fish's well-taken example shows, but kings are kings (as opposed to dictators, on the one hand, and politically non-consequential individuals, on the other) only in compliance with the monarchic convention: only the proper lineage ensures the proper identity of the person holding the position, and this lineage is proper only inasmuch as it is in accordance with an *established convention*. There is no denying that, as Fish points out, each time a king exercises his authority, he confirms and grounds anew the monarchic convention to which he owes his power, but this is a far cry from creating the convention. When the existence of monarchy and of a king corroborate each other, as is normally the case, the discussion is indeed circular; but when either the chicken or the egg slips away, the chain is irremediably broken. Similarly, if I can hide in a cave and proclaim a new government, it is because there is already a convention by which new governments are proclaimed—not to mention that, proclaimed or not, new or old, a government is in itself already grounded in a convention (or, as Rousseau says, a contract). We can imagine a different convention by which every time thunder roars, for example, a new government is proclaimed (not unlike a game of political musical chairs) and in which I could not proclaim a new government hiding in a cave—at least not unless there were a thunderstorm. (We can compare this aspect of conventions with the insights gained from another system of interlocking verbal units, Saussure's *langue*. As Saussure rightly recognized, any act of *parole* presupposes the existence of a system of linguistic conventions, *langue;* at the same time, however, there is nothing in *langue* that did not get there through *parole*. This is one more manifestation of the vexed question of the starting point.)

The Declaration of Independence

In a short, tongue-in-cheek essay, Derrida explores the relation between a founding political speech act (such as the one in Fish's example) and the authority or appropriateness (Austin's rule A.2) of a person to perform this founding speech within a given convention. Tongue-in-cheek because Derrida questions the right of the Founding Fathers, in particular of Thomas Jefferson, to proclaim the independence of the United States of America. He opens his reading with an apparently innocuous reference to Austin's rule A.2 and a question that seems to stem from his unreserved acceptance of this rule. If, as Austin claims—and Derrida agrees—"the particular persons and circumstances in a given case must be appropriate for the invocation of the particular procedure invoked" (*How to,* 15), if I must be the appropriate person to name a ship or a baby, and if a marriage with a monkey is condemned to infelicity (all Austin's examples), then the identity of the person who utters a speech act, or in our case who declares (and consequently signs) the

Declaration of Independence, becomes urgently relevant. Therefore, inquires Derrida, "*Who signs, and with what so-called proper name, the declarative act which founds an institution?*" ("Declarations," 8, Derrida's emphasis[28]). This question eventually leads him to a sterner and more clearly fundamental set of questions: "How is a State made or founded, how does a State make or found itself? And an independence? And the autonomy of one which both gives itself, and signs, its own law? Who signs all these authorizations to sign?" ("Declarations," 13).

Any American schoolboy will hasten to answer that Jefferson drafted the Declaration of Independence and the members of Congress signed it. We must then note that, unlike Fish's refugee in a cave, Jefferson did not write of his own initiative but was delegated to write. His authority originated not in his own whim, but in the group of people whom he represented. Instead of being "in the company of one or two fellows," Jefferson must therefore be in the company of at least fifty-five fellows, the cosignatories of the Declaration of Independence. The problem does not stop here, however, since, as Derrida points out, even these fifty-six did not arbitrarily and capriciously decide to declare an independent state, as is the case in Fish's example. They did so, again, not in their own name, but in the name of the good people of the United States of America: "We therefore the representatives of the United states [*sic*] of America in General Congress assembled do in the name, and by the authority of the good people of these states reject and renounce all allegiance & subjection to the kings of Great Britain." [29] Jefferson's draft thus suggests three levels of representation and delegation of authority: Jefferson represents the members of Congress; they in turn represent the United States of America. Ultimately, then, any political action taken by the Congress via its "sort of advance-pen" ("Declarations," 19), Jefferson, is "in the name and by the authority of the good people of these states."

Now, since the Declaration of Independence is supposed to be the very act by which the colonies free themselves from all allegiance to the British crown and declare their political independence, it would make little sense to think that they were independent and free before the signature of the Declaration. For example, if the force of the Declaration were mostly constative, if it only *informed* the world of a coup that had already taken place, it would have been written in the past tense as a constative document, just as "I swear" is a performative utterance whereas "I swore" is constative.[30] This observation brings us to Derrida's original question, and in fact, to a catch-22. The system of relays of representation that ultimately brings the good people of the United

States to sign (*signer* and *contre-signer*) Jefferson's document draws its appropriateness from a democratic principle grounded in an existential proposition: there is an entity such as the people of the United States, which, by means of political processes ranked here under "representation," channels and converts its collective will into political authority and entrusts it to a well-defined and limited political body (in this case, fifty-six "representatives"), which, in turn, can delegate this authority to a single individual, Jefferson. But, says Derrida, this entity on which the system of relays rests, the "people of the United States of America," is nonexistent.

> But this people does not exist. They do *not* exist as an entity, it does not exist, *before* this declaration, not *as such*. If it gives birth to itself, as free and independent subject, as possible signer, this can hold only in the act of the signature. The signature invents the signer. This signer can only authorize him or herself to sign once he or she has come to the end [*parvenu au bout*], if one can say this, of his or her own signature, in a sort of fabulous retroactivity. That first signature authorizes him or her to sign.
>
> . . .
>
> There was no signer, by right, before the text of the Declaration which remains the producer and guarantor of its own signature. ("Declarations," 10)[31]

There is therefore no standard or convention by which an appropriate person can be found who would sign the Declaration of Independence, since such an appropriateness relies on the *outcome* of the Declaration: the Declaration ought to have been already declared for any political body (or its representative) to claim the right to declare it. We may easily extend this analysis to all inaugural acts since, logically, there is no criterion of appropriateness for the performer of an inaugural act that would not be essentially tautological: such an act owes its felicity to the preexistence of the very same convention it purports to inaugurate.[32]

Note that Derrida's point differs from Fish's in that Derrida's relies on Austin's rule A.2 while Fish's relies on rule A.1. In other words, Fish contends that the convention does not so much precede the speech act as it is created by it. If this be the case, then rule A.2 (and with it, Derrida's reading of the Declaration) becomes irrelevant: if there is no convention before the act, there can be no conventional standard by which we can decide whether or not a person performing a speech act is appropriate for the procedure.

A quick excursion into the Declaration disproves Fish's views of political declarations (and subsequently, his conception of speech acts) and displaces Derrida's reading of the Declaration of Independence. The major part of the Declaration is the list of grievances against the king of Britain. This list presupposes a known convention or even a contract by which the king of Britain may expect obedience (and taxes) from his subjects in return for certain obligations. Unlike the French tradition in which monarchy was absolute (which explains the extreme subversiveness of Rousseau's *Social Contract*), the British tradition had been grounded in the clear recognition of *mutual* duties and obligations ever since the Magna Carta. The king of Britain to whom Jefferson refuses allegiance is a constitutional king (indeed, the colonies' various petitions illustrate their firm belief in their constitutional rights, within British law). He does not rule by right (of birth) only, but also by law, that is to say, according to a law by which he, too, must abide. Jefferson takes great pains to remain within the same law and to present the independence of the colonies not as a coup but as a lawful action within the British constitutional tradition: since the king of Britain did not keep his part of the deal, he is found in breach of contract, as is stated and demonstrated in the long list of grievances, some of which are breaches of clauses already found in the Magna Carta. Therefore the contract is, both by fact and by law, dissolved. It is only within this legal convention and framework that the Declaration becomes a felicitous performative.

Its rhetorical strategy is exemplary: first it states the law, and, in the spirit of eighteenth-century enlightenment, converts its historical premises into timeless universals ("We hold these truths to be self-evident. . . ." We should note in passing that since this law is in fact historically grounded, it does not contradict the tenets of Britain's major charters, as it contradicted the principle of, say, French monarchy). Second, it draws the sociopolitical consequences of these axioms in accordance with both the major British charters and eighteenth-century political philosophy (but, again, in terms that are unacceptable in an absolute monarchy: "That to secure these rights, governments are instituted among men, deriving their just powers from the consent of the governed"). Third, it shows the king to have broken most aspects of the law and therefore to have usurped the power he should no longer have by law. Only then does it conclude that since the king's actions have in fact annulled his mutual agreement with the colonies, these colonies are free *by law* to seek and declare another form of government. An impeccable legal logic grounds the proclamation of the new government in a convention (rule A.1) and derives from this very convention the new colonies' right (their appropriateness) to sever all ties with Britain (rule A.2). The meticulous attention the Founding Fathers paid to these steps shows a remarkable understanding of speech acts and constitutes an uncanny illustration of Austin's theory point for point;[33] in so doing, it also exposes the political naïveté of views of inaugural speech acts that, like Fish's, ignore historical contextualization.

The British political tradition of charters and law breaks through the vicious circle of authority in which Derrida entraps Jefferson's declarative speech act. Derrida's argument could have held for most inaugural speech acts, but not for this particular one. Even as he drafts the Declaration as a representative of the representatives of a yet unborn nation, Jefferson does not so much assume authority as enforce an authority grounded in a law to which the British constitutional tradition submits the king as well as his subjects.[34] He is therefore exercising a right that has been his ever since 1215. The only way in which Jefferson is subject to Derrida's critique involves the use of the expression "United *states* of America" before the act. Even so, the edited final version circumvents the threat of circularity in three ways: first, it removes all but one use of "United *states* of America" and replaces it with "us" or "these colonies" (see above, n. 29); second, by taking God as a witness of the speakers' purity of intention, the last paragraph of the Declaration (in which the performative force is the strongest) ensures its immunity to Austin's "abuses" (group Γ);[35] third, as Derrida readily acknowledges, invoking God adds yet another to the succession of delegated powers, and this time, one that is *causa sui* and therefore needs no further justification. This last insertion of Congress ("appealing to the supreme judge of the world for the rectitude of our intentions") echoes the beginning of the Declaration ("the laws of nature and of nature's God"). Together they frame the legal aspect of the Declaration, institute God as the ultimate law or legislator, and in so doing, jam the slippage on which (political) authority and, consequently, speech acts rests.[36]

Seen against the backdrop of the politico-philosophical problems raised by self-assigned power and authority, the political and theoretical risks illustrated by Spifame's delusion become clearer. His odd illness raises several questions, the most important of which is the relation between authority and the Law. This question is not contained within the remote framework of monarchy. It also permeates our daily and professional lives. We may wonder about the logical tension built into the relation between the authority of the self-ruled academic institution, for instance, and the inaugural (or subversive) intellectual and professional speech act, that is, between the recognized authority of an institutional tradition and an individual or a minority's attempt to advocate a new and perhaps disruptive alternative method, theory, field of study, or the like; in short, between the university and academic freedom (the current debate over "great books" and the canon is a perfect example of this tension). We may also wonder about the confining and conservative tendencies of any "theory," "system," "doxa," or "knowledge"; about the politics of "theories" and "theoreticians"; about any law that does not include among its fundamental tenets the legal possibility of its own displacement. These questions will remain unanswered at present. But they loom at the ideological and political horizons of our project (some of the responses to parts of this book's manuscript version have indeed illustrated the very play of power that I denounce throughout). Although we shall remain within the narrow boundaries of "The King of Bicêtre" and limit ourselves to an examination of law and authority in the context of speech acts, the inescapable larger ideological and political issues delineate our general framework.

The main prong of the political argument raised by the story is therefore as follows: if a person who is not appropriate for the procedure nonetheless usurps the authority to perform it, and if, as is the case in our story, no major infelicitous consequences follow this misfire, what becomes of the convention (government or monarchy) without which this procedure would no longer be one? Could Spifame seriously be politically subversive, a "precursor of socialism," as the subtitle of the collection *Les Illuminés ou les précurseurs du socialisme* indicates? Can the story be read as a political commentary or program?

Parasitic Discourse

This point is so obvious that I shall only state it without belaboring it further. From the viewpoint of a strict theory of speech acts, the discourse of a madman can only be parasitic. Spifame should therefore be "out." To add insult to injury, Vignet should be doubly excluded from the field of applicability of the theory since not only is he mad, but he is also a poet. Thus his discourse is subject to two kinds of etiolation. And yet, the very nature of their madness is rooted in speech acts (see pp. 218–23) and cannot be discussed outside the problematics of illocutionary and perlocutionary forces. Since the two men use mostly the kind of nonserious discourse normally excluded from a theory of serious language, our story's insistence on its relevance for the performative discourse of law and power will, at worst, pose a problem for the theories and, at best, illuminate further their intricacies, as well as their boundaries and margins.

Three Titles, One Story

The title of the story points to the same difficulty. In September 1839 the story appeared in *La Presse* under the title "A Singular Biography of Raoul Spifame, Lord of Granges." In 1845 it was reprinted in the "Revue Pittoresque" under the title "The Best King of France." The present title, "The King of Bicêtre" dates from 1852 and figures as the introductory piece in a collection of stories assembled by Nerval, *The Illuminés or the Precursors of Socialism.*[37] Since each change of title alters the focus of the story, the juxtaposition of the three identities (Spifame, Lord of Granges; the king of France; and the king of Bicêtre) is highly disconcerting. Is the story about the "singular" biography of some nobleman named Spifame (singular: at once individual and odd)? Is it about some—perhaps even the best—king of France (in which case, it cannot be Spifame's story since we know there was no king of France by this name)? Or is it about the king of Bicêtre, the king of a madhouse, the maddest of them all (and of course, one cannot be king of Bicêtre *and* of France)? The three titles thus provide three logically incompatible descriptions. Bewildered, we progress into the story only to discover that the narrative itself divides into three parts, each part reflecting one of the suggested titles. In the first part (corresponding to the first title, "The Singular Biography") we hear of Spifame's difficulties with the Law and its magistrates; in the second ("The King of Bicêtre"), Spifame is committed to Bicêtre, where he meets Vignet and is allowed to indulge in his delusions and "rule" over France; and in the last part ("The Best King of France"), he is first in Paris and later in a palace, treated like a king and busying himself with decreeing social reforms that are eventually implemented and find their way into the royal archives.

In the framework of speech act theory, we find the same three foci: 1) the theory proper (the elaboration of a set of rules, corresponding to the legislative system) and Spifame's marginal position in the judiciary system (Nerval says *ex-centrique*); 2) the parasitic discourse (madness and poetry, the two men at Bicêtre); and 3) the peculiar problems posed by perlocution (the political effect of Spifame's social reforms).

These parallels are too striking to be mere coincidences. They point to some underlying system of cross reference among the related triads contained in the title, the narrative, and the theory. A close examination of these triads will therefore bring forth what is at stake in their interaction for speech act theories, the actual story, and the relationship between authority and law.

Law

The Law is the domain par excellence of the reduction of ambiguity, since it admits neither the *slightly* guilty nor the *almost* innocent. As Austin puts it, "there is the overriding requirement that a decision be reached, and a relatively black or white decision—guilty or not guilty for the plaintiff or for the defendant." [38] The Law is therefore the ideal domain of the pertinence of a contract, that is, a transaction at once verbal and actual, binding by virtue of its being grounded in a larger convention that guarantees the hold of each individual transaction. Such contracts are speech acts of sorts. And indeed, examples from the judicial sphere consistently pop up in the language of the theoreticians who attempt to weigh or judge the contractual grip of an illocutionary force by distinguishing unequivocally between the felicity or infelicity of an illocutionary utterance ("slightly infelicitous" or "almost felicitous" are no more acceptable than "slightly guilty" or "almost innocent").

Law is the general thematic context of "Bicêtre." Our story distinguishes two major branches: legislative and judiciary. One writes the laws; the other reads and practices them. One elaborates the rules; the other interprets them. One is general (or even generic); the other deals in the singular, individual, idiosyncratic, and irregular. Spifame, we are told, "studied law and became a lawyer" ("Bicêtre," 937). He begins his career, then, not in legislation but in the judiciary; not among those who write the rules but among those who read and practice them. In court, not only does a lawyer try to apply her or his interpretation of the law (her or his understanding of the *illocutionary* force of the law) to a specific case (a specific speech situation); the lawyer also has to convince the judge or jury that this interpretation is valid, that is to say, has to ensure the felicity of the *perlocutionary* force of this interpretation, its uptake. Of course, the opposite lawyer holds a different view of the facts or the interpretation and tries to convince the jury and the judge of the rightness of *that* view. How can the same event, based on the same evidence, and judged by the same law, mean one thing for one lawyer and another for the other? How can one end up with one effect (the verdict) and the other with another, if they are supposed to be part of the same convention, the same logic, the same law? These questions pierce farther when we remember that ours is not an isolated case of borderline felicity. It is inherent in the very structure of the Law that it can, and indeed should, be debated each time it is applied to a particular case. One of the most fundamental tenets of the judiciary system is that each party has the right to argue for his or her interpretation and be represented by an interpreter (an attorney). It is a *constitutive* rule of the Law as we understand it today (and as "Bicêtre" illustrates) that a ruling can take place only after an open debate between interpreters, to be refereed by a judge or a jury.

There are a few ways to account for the discrepancies between such interpretations. For instance, we may say that the object of the discussion is none too sure: the court is hard put to reconstruct the incident since its details are essentially inexhaustible (theoretically, there can always be one more surprise witness who will tip the balance). Since these details are themselves mostly verbal and subjective accounts of past incidents, and since memory is at best selective, their details are subject to interpretation, too (e.g., Kurosawa's movie *Rashomon*). What really happened escapes us, which necessarily results in some free play in the lawyer's reconstruction of events (this objection is raised only in passing since, although this aspect of the judiciary raises important questions, 1] our story does not address them directly, and 2] they belong to the general problem of the viability of any constative proposition). We could also invoke attenuating circumstances, that is, a variety of contexts carefully selected so as to displace the tenor of the debate. (Since we have already dwelled at length on the relativity and the unsaturability of contexts, I shall simply refer the reader to the previous discussion, pp. 197–99.)

Intentions (part 2): Searle

And yet there is a new element in "Bicêtre," no longer the interpretation of facts and contexts but the interpretation of the Law itself; of the series of speech acts that constitute the legislative corpus; of the convention by which random utterances acquire their normative force. This task normally befalls the courts. At the risk of stating the obvious, I must underscore that normally an interpretation can take place only if something—in our case the Law—is ambiguous; or at least, if its categorization of social phenomena is in some sense unstable, shifting. To practice law is to construct an interpretation out of the parts of the legal machine that are unstable, that leave some play. By institutionalizing a judiciary system grounded in the individual's right to plead his or her case (i.e., to present the facts—both actual and legal—that can be interpreted in his or her favor), jurisprudence acts on the presupposition that the Law is inherently and by definition equivocal; that the legislator's intentions (to the extent that they are unambiguous—which is in itself highly problematic, as "The Venus" shows), once actualized in language, can no longer dictate the illocutionary force of the utterance; that the meaning of a law (the sentence meaning or propositional content for Searle) and its illocutionary force may be at odds. In short, the inalienability of the risk of infelicity comes to constitute the cornerstone of modern jurisprudence (at least as it is practiced in the Western world).

A short Hasidic story will further illustrate this last point. Two rabbis dispute a delicate point of the Law in public. At a critical moment in the debate, the voice of God echoes from the sky and pronounces, "Rabbi Elizer is right." Indignant, the rabbis rise up on their old legs and cry: "Why does Heaven and its miracles meddle when we, wise men, are conversing? The Law is not up to Heaven; it is up to men whose right it is to interpret it as they see fit." For these rabbis, as for the lawyers, the illocutionary force of the Law does not consist in reconstructing the illocutionary force intended by the legislator, but in adapting the propositional content to the context and speech situation of the interpreter (the addressee). God may have intended certain effects, claim the rabbis, but the moment He chose to manifest this intention in language, He lost control over the illocutionary force of His Law. The illocutionary force of a speech act (or of the law) is not reducible to the intentions of the speaker.

It is precisely to this contention that Searle addresses himself with a growing determination: "In speaking I attempt to communicate certain things to my hearer by getting him to *recognize my intention* to communicate just those things. I achieve *the intended effect* on the hearer by getting him to *recognize my intention* to achieve that effect, and as soon as the hearer recognizes what it is *my intention* to achieve, it is generally achieved. He understands what I am saying as soon as he recognizes *my intention* in uttering what I utter as an *intention* to say that thing" (*Speech Acts,* 43). Searle's theory of speech acts, and, by extension, of language, hinges upon the idea that an utterance is the expression of an intention. It subordinates expression to intention and preexisting meaning. Such a view is logically viable mostly if, as Derrida rightly pointed out, one envisions language only as communication: I think up a meaning, I decide to communicate it to another person, I use language for this exact purpose, and my hearer understands properly what I meant (properly: the way I intended it). End of the circuit of communication.[39]

Within the limited framework of communication, Searle narrows further the focus of the discussion by considering only the viewpoint of the addressor. The addressee (let's assume she is a woman) would then have two alternatives: either she understands the intention of the addressor, or she is flatly wrong. Searle's one-sided view of communication summarizes his rift with contemporary literary theory, which takes a strong interest in problems of reception that he, given his analysis of language, cannot acknowledge, let alone address.

His analysis of metaphor, for example, a figure based on some twisting of the kind of straightforward communication he normally advocates, is particularly revealing. It extends the precedence of intentions over reception to linguistic areas other than speech acts proper and into a general theory of rhetoric. Searle distinguishes between "speaker's utterance meaning" ("what a speaker means by uttering words, sentences, and expressions") and "utterance's meaning" ("what the words, sentences and expressions mean" [*E&M*, 77]), a distinction that corresponds roughly to Richards' classic tenor and vehicle, the crucial difference being that the speaker's utterance meaning is the meaning *intended* by the speaker and will therefore correspond not to tenor but to *intended* tenor. And what of the listener? Again, either she figures out the speaker's meaning, or she misses the point altogether. In no case does Searle consider that she may inject the utterance with additional meaning(s), which the speaker may not have consciously intended, or even that a metaphor may acquire new meaning(s) by dint of its perception in a different context (e.g., a poem read two centuries after it was written). While Searle's discussion of metaphor proceeds with exemplary consistency, it is flawed by this initial *parti pris*. Language is eventually envisioned only as a vehicle for intentions, as the listener, having moved through a series of steps ingeniously and rigorously mapped by Searle, recovers the original intention of the speaker. To put it simply, "metaphorical meaning is always speaker's utterance meaning" (77). Searle's theory of metaphor is strictly tropological: in proffering a metaphorical utterance, a speaker says "S is P" when he really means (to say) "S is R." It befalls the hearer to understand that S is really P and not R. She will first notice some incongruity in the sentence "S is P," alerting her to the fact that S cannot possibly be P (e.g., "Achilles is a lion," when she knows that he is in fact a man). At this point, Searle advises her to look into P (lion), list its salient predicates, and try to apply them to S (Achilles). Once a predicate that fits what she already knows to be true of S is found among the salient predicates of P (e.g., "is brave" rather that "has a long tail"), it can be considered to be the value of R, the term intended by the speaker (in terms of traditional rhetoric, she has adopted the *tertium comparationis* as the value of R).

Very schematically, since metaphor is not our present purpose, I shall offer two brief critiques of this view. First, Searle's formulation of metaphor is essentially *predicative* (it hinges on the predicates shared by both expressions). This, in itself, is not the object of my critique, however. Since Aristotle, theoreticians of metaphor have been divided between those who hold that metaphor is predicative and those who hold that it is *substantive* (Aristotle's definition mentions "the transfer of *the name* of one thing to another thing," which places him among the advocates of a substantive view of metaphor). Very important and enlightening insights into metaphor were advanced by each party. I therefore find Searle's glossing over the substantive view less than informative and even quite reductive, all the more so since he says nothing that the holders of the predicative view have not said before him in greater detail and with greater awareness of the complexity of the question.[40]

Second, Searle is categorical: only the value of R intended by the speaker constitutes the "speaker's utterance meaning." But we should note that there may be more than one predicate that fits both P and R. It is not a problem if, in Achilles' case, we wind up with "is brave" *and* "is strong" *and* "is generous," all belonging to the paradigm of positive values; but it can be a problem if we wind up with "has piercing eyes," "has straw-color hair," "likes meat," or even "is bloodthirsty" (since Searle recommends choosing salient and well-known features, we can rule out "has a bunion"). Since they all fit or could fit Achilles, how is our hearer to select "is brave" or "is brave and strong and generous" over "has piercing eyes" or "is bloodthirsty"? Following Searle's directive, she could have perfectly good reason to interpret the metaphor differently from the way it was intended and pin its decoding on the "wrong" predicate. Or again, we may think of a different kind of metaphor, one in which the shared predicate is not necessarily a well-known and salient predicate of P: such were the metaphors advocated by surrealist poets who intended to shock and surprise the readers rather than confirm their commonplace knowledge. I am not saying that these objections cannot be answered (indeed, other theories, including my own, have offered answers[41]), but, since Searle's theory does not grant the addressee any function other than recovering the addressor's intention, there is nothing in his analysis that addresses my elementary objections and takes into account the legitimate ways in which the hearer could reason differently from the speaker. Above all, there is nothing in his theory that even hints at the implications of the legitimacy of a reader-oriented line of reasoning for a theory of meaning based on intentionality. This critique pierces farther when we consider again the surrealistic school's vehement resistance to the grip of the S value. When André Breton, for instance, read that a commentator (who shared with Searle the belief that to understand a metaphor is to find what the poet meant) had reconstructed the S value of Saint-Pol Roux's metaphors "caterpillar's future" (*lendemain de chenille*) and "crystal mammals" (*mammelles de cristal*) as "butterfly" and "glass pitcher" respectively, he reacted indignantly to the reduction of the literary metaphors to "speaker's utterance meanings": "No, Sir, does not mean to say [*ne veut pas dire*]. Stuff your butterfly into your pitcher. What Saint-Pol Roux meant to say, be sure he said it ["Ce que Saint-Pol Roux a voulu dire, soyez certain qu'il l'a dit]." [42]

The same bias in favor of the speaker's intentions is manifest again in Searle's theory of fiction. In "The Logical Status of Fictional Discourse," the line of demarcation between fiction and nonfiction rests predictably with the speaker's intentionality: "The identifying criterion for whether or not a text is a work of fiction must of necessity lie in the illocutionary intentions of the author. . . . What makes it a work of fiction is, so to speak, the illocutionary stance that the author takes toward it, and that stance is a matter of *the complex illocutionary intentions* that the author has when he writes or otherwise composes it" (*E&M*, 65–66). As Searle unfolds what he means by an "illocutionary intention," we come to realize that it is a far cry from complexity. It is in fact quite simple: when writing fiction, the writer is not committed to the truth of his or her statement; nor is he or she committed to being able to provide evidence for its truth. Instead, the writer is only *pretending* to make an assertion.[43] This rather simplistic analysis just about sums up the difference between fiction and nonfiction. Again, not once does Searle address the problem of reception, let alone of skewed reception (I am reminded of an experiment run by Fish, who asked his literature class to read as a "poem" the random names left on the blackboard from the previous class—and they sure did[44]). Eventually, Searle's emphasis on intentions leads him to reevaluate not only language itself but also the philosophy of language: "I now think it was a mistake to take this [reference] as the central problem in the philosophy of language, because we will not get an adequate theory of linguistic reference until we show how such a theory is part of a general theory of intentionality" (xi)—a program that, incidentally, he followed with the publication of his next book, *Intentionality*, in 1984.

Madness

Searle is clearly at the opposite extreme of the conception of interpretation favored by the rabbis and illustrated by our judicial system. Since Spifame is an attorney, one would expect him to side with the rabbis against Searle. His profession demands that he perceive and exploit assertorial (constative) ambiguities. Lawyers spend their time converting illocutionary felicity into infelicity and vice versa. *Interpreting* the law is their livelihood. Surprisingly, however, Spifame sides with Searle and the principle of semantic unicity. Ambiguity, duplicity, anything fragmented, anything not unique, unified, and univocal (such as his own appearance) is unbearable for him.

It is therefore worth noting that his illness did not ensue from his actual resemblance to the king (factual doubling) but from his colleagues' teasing (doubling of linguistic references). The text insists heavily and almost awkwardly on the causes of his eccentricity in two separate sections: first, when we are informed that "as for Raoul, from this day on, he was called only Sire and Your Majesty by his fellow lawyers," and that "this joke went on in so many guises . . . that this obsession has since been seen as one of the primary causes of the mental derangement which led Raoul Spifame to such bizarre actions";[45] and second, when, as Spifame, summoned to appear before the court, crosses the vestibule of the courthouse, "he heard a hundred voices murmur: 'It's the king! Here is the king! Make way for the king!' This nickname, whose mocking effect he should have appreciated, produced on his rattled intelligence the effect of a jolt which sets off a fragile spring: his reason flew far off, humming along" ("Bicêtre," 941). Spifame's main problem is that he cannot appreciate the rhetorical status ("mocking effect") of his nickname. In other words, he cannot conceive that there may be a split between "speaker's utterance meaning" and "propositional content." He does not recognize rhetorical twists, double entendre, discourse split between two meanings, or implicit illocutionary forces. He does not understand that it behooves him, as the hearer, to suspect discourse of duplicity and rhetoricity. Instead, he believes in the absolute transparency of messages; in names that latch on tightly to subjects and adhere to them permanently (e.g., "Sire," and "Your Majesty"); in the unfailing deictic aim of language ("Here is the king"); in the irreproachable constative force of discourse; in short, in the boy scout attitude toward language. After the first scene, we are told that one of the primary causes of the mental derangement afflicting Spifame is the wisecracks, that is, the linguistic acts, to which his fellow lawyers subject him, rather than his factual resemblance with the king. In the second scene, the text insists even more heavily on the discursive causes of his illness: the man who entered the court was only slightly visionary, but the one who left it was "a real madman" (see "his madness was but a kind of common sense and logic up to this point; imprudence was his only aberration. But if there was cited before the court merely a visionary called Raoul Spifame, the Spifame who left the hearing was a real madman, one of the most distorted minds ever to be certified for the hospital" [940–1]). Note that when he entered the court, Spifame was already aware of his resemblance to the king; he had even already expressed various critiques of the legal system and government. But so far, we are told, "imprudence was his only aberration." Had it not been for his later madness, our idealistic lawyer might have been simply a visionary social reformer who got carried away, perhaps even a true "precursor of socialism." But after people mockingly *pointed* at him, *saying,* "It's the king! Here is the king! Make way for the king," he became "a true madman" (*un véritable fou*). Madness resulted not from his odd resemblance to the king but from his belief in the show and tell function of discourse, in the unquestioned grip of the deictic aim of language and the ostensive speech act. "The King of Bicêtre" is therefore not simply another story about doubles or madmen. It is a story about subjectivity and language; about the relationship between identity (as personal identity *and* as unicity or oneness) and the linguistic expression that purports to signify and designate that identity; about singular reference; above all, it is a story about absolute faith in the power of language.

Illocutionary Intentions and Madness

What, then, does Spifame's madness consist of? How does he manifest his professed royalty? He writes. Endlessly, relentlessly, he writes edicts, decrees, charters, ordinances; he creates offices; he accords privileges; he pronounces judgments. In short, Spifame's madness manifests itself in an uninterrupted series of speech acts, in the most rigorous and explicitly performative sense of the term. Not once does he utter an identity proposition ("I am the king of France," for example). Paradoxically, his "eccentricity" consists in adhering to the unquestioned centrality of intentionality in his practice of the illocutionary force of language.[46] Indeed the story carefully stages this centrality. Spifame usually occupies center stage: either he stands in the center of a circle of curious onlookers (in the marketplace) or Nerval shines the spotlight on him even when he is off-center (the theme of light plays on the various meanings of *illuminé*). Spifame's first appearance in the story is particularly revealing: "Absent-mindedly the prince's eyes, weary of counting the bent foreheads of the assembly and the sculpted joists on the ceiling, finally stopped for a long while on a single spectator at the extreme end of the hall, whose original face was completely illuminated by the sunlight; little by little all glances were directed as well toward the point which seemed to arouse the attention of the Prince. Raoul Spifame was the one being examined in this manner" ("Bicêtre," 939). Although he is positioned all the way at the end of the hall, totally *ex*-centric, he soon restructures the human topology of the hall and becomes the *center* of attention. This process is an exact visual rendition of the position he wishes to occupy in language (a position that the story equates with madness). Spifame is pure performative legislation in its most absolute, normative, and (self-)center-oriented sense.

This insistence on the centrality of the mad speaking subject echoes the two scenes in which the text explains the causes of his illness. Spifame does to his neighbor what he wants done unto him. Just as he identifies the propositional content of his performative utterances with his own intentionality without envisioning the possibility of differences between the meaning of these utterances and the state of affairs to which they supposedly correspond, he concedes to others that their utterances must correspond to the state of affairs (reference) and reflect their intentions: since they point at him and say, "Here is the king," first, he must be the king, and second, they must mean (intend) nothing other than to state that he (the king) is here. On both ends of the communication process, rhetoricity, linguistic duplicity, and the possibility of interpretation are equally excluded.

Plagiarism and Madness

Vignet's mania confirms further the notion that madness is an effect not of physical doubling but of language. If there is a functional doubling in "The King of Bicêtre," it is not so much between Spifame and Henry II as between the former and Vignet. Vignet's self-glorification as "the king of poets" is furthermore overdetermined by the parallel with Spifame's claim to kingship (otherwise, his rivalry with the poets of the Pléiade should have led him to adopt Ronsard's title, "the *prince* of poets"). And what does Vignet's madness consist of? Not surprisingly, he, too, writes. But while Spifame lives language as the doxa of a performing consciousness, Vignet's element is—at least in Austin's terms—pure parasitic and etiolated language, neither used nor meant seriously.

Or again, in Searle's terms, Vignet only pretends to refer: he is not com-
mitted to the truth-value of the propositional content of his discourse
and thus can bypass correspondence with any state of affairs. In short,
Vignet is a poet. For both madmen, madness comes from writing (the
frequent juxtaposition of the words *poems* and *ordinances* within the
same syntagm underscores this parallel).

But there is more to Vignet's problem. His madness is not, as we
might have expected, a variation of *furor poeticus*. Nor is he another
poète maudit: he could have written poetry and even complained bit-
terly of the lack of discrimination of his contemporaries who fail to
recognize his exceptional genius; he could have lived in utmost poverty,
or been afflicted with a fashionable romantic disease (such as tubercu-
losis or syphilis). But he did not. Instead, he fell victim to a peculiar
obsession: a deep conviction that his poems were, in fact, getting the
credit they deserved but that they were attributed to others. His mad-
ness consists in believing that the court poets (in particular, Saint-Gelais
and Ronsard) have stolen, plagiarized, or intercepted his work. Under-
lying his madness is the belief that the right of ownership of a work
extends beyond the actual moment of writing, to its distribution and
reception; that there is a true and original instance of discourse (him-
self) that should be recognizable at all times. Vignet is not mad because
he is a poet, as it would seem from a first reading inspired by romantic
commonplaces. Writing poetry becomes madness only when one be-
lieves that it can be owned; when one believes that there is a proper way
to own discourse (original authorship) and an improper way (plagia-
rism); when one believes in an original—and therefore true—instance,
whose claim to regulate linguistic exchanges extends beyond the tem-
poral constraints of enunciation (*énonciation*) and remains intact
throughout subsequent transactions or readings; in short, when one be-
lieves that the centrality of the subject is crucial to the legitimacy of his
discourse and that any offense against this centrality is or should be
punishable by law. This vision of language is not an exclusively poetic
vision. It is found among some poets and among some legislators alike
(in our story, Vignet the poet and Spifame the legislator share it); it is
also found among some literary critics and some philosophers.

Law and Madness

That Vignet's madness echoes Spifame's is, I hope, obvious. What I
am trying to stress is not so much this elementary parallel, however, as
the structural identity with the Law, or, more precisely, with the pur-
ported illocutionary force of the Law. The Law, Spifame, Vignet (and,

we may add, Searle, Fish, and "theoreticians" in general) all try to hold on to the mastery of an original instance and to ensure the predictability and permanence of the illocutionary force's effects in a causal manner, to ensure that the same force will *invariably* produce the same effects. At the same time, not only do they all incur the risk that circumstances beyond their control might thwart their legislative effort, but—and here lies the gist of my critique—they also fail to acknowledge that this risk is intrinsically built into the very condition of their authority. In other words, not only is there no law that cannot be subverted, no poem that cannot be intercepted or plagiarized, no authority that cannot be questioned or overthrown, but these very risks are what constitutes the raison d'être of the Law, the reason without which it would cease to exist. We may assume that in a society free of crime and criminals, there would be no need for laws, police, or courts. In a world replete like ours with criminals, however, legislative logic is necessarily circular: if we define a criminal as a person who breaks the law, we are, in fact, presupposing the existence of a law that is or is not broken. One might then think that the Law takes precedence over the criminal (this is Russell's solution to the puzzle "The king of France is bald"); but we know that there would be no need for laws if it were not for the existence of criminals. Crime—and more precisely the risk of crime—thus becomes the logical foundation of its intended negator (which is the paradox inherent in any negation). Even if we step out of criminal law, our argument stands: we may still safely presume that if the articles of the Law corresponded to innate human properties, they would not be needed; people would have an intuitive knowledge of and desire to conform to the Law. But, if we conclude, as we should, that the articles of the Law do not simply mirror innate properties, we must accept that they *purport* to supplement those properties, to remedy human shortcomings (with all the Rousseau-Derrida complexity evoked by *supplement*). The Law thus remains intentional and, as such, subject to the risk of infelicity.

In "The King of Bicêtre" the line of demarcation between madness and reason does not ride on the simple or even simplistic distinction between serious and parasitic discourse, literal and metaphorical, or fictional and nonfictional; nor does it hinge upon the difference between the felicity or infelicity of an illocution. Rather, it depends on the distinction between normative discourse grounded on the intentions, mastery, and immutability of the speaking subject, without remainders, excesses, and misses, and a different kind of discourse, one in which the same intentions, mastery, and immutability are displaced, questioned, intercepted, detoured, duplicated, or appropriated by others (as our reading of *The Three Musketeers* in chapter 6 will further illustrate). Moreover, madness is not where we would expect to find it: it is at Bicêtre, a mental institution, that *serious* "theoretical" discourse takes place; it is at Bicêtre that one believes in the authority of the origin of discourse and the centrality of the subject, in the right of ownership of discourse and in the legislative power of utterances. And it is on the outside, in the "sane" world, that the lawyer Spifame is called "Your Majesty," is honored with curtsies, is treated like a king; that the rhetoricity of discourse confirms, flatters, and encourages Spifame's madness. The narrative suggests a world in which the claims to truth, authenticity, order, originality (firstness), Law—all the highest Western values guaranteed by God's firstness and wisdom and represented on earth by an anointed king—are confined to a madhouse, while in the sane world loom duplicity, inauthenticity, artifice, doubling of reference, and the endless skidding effect of rhetoricity; in the sane world the true, unique and irreplaceable king of France, representative of law and order, is an element of doubling and confusion (Henri II is the one who eventually orders Spifame out of Bicêtre and sends him to a palace in which servants "were ordered to treat him like a king and to call him *sire* and Majesty ["Bicêtre," 953]).[47] In other words, parasitic discourse rules the sane and real world, whereas madness consists of the belief in the discourse of consciousness, intentionality, authenticity, literalism, and transparence. Socialist or other, Nerval sketches a linguistic utopia: in his new Republic the legislator is condemned to marginality or even exclusion while the polis is ruled by users of rhetoric, by poets. Or is it a utopia?

This kind of literary reductio ad absurdum is more frequent in the English tradition than in the French. One thinks of John Donne, Jonathan Swift, or Lewis Carroll. In France the more obvious are Voltaire's *Candide,* Sade's *Français encore un effort pour devenir Républicains,* and perhaps Jarry's *Ubu.* Nerval himself summons that tradition by opening *Les Illuminés* with "Not everyone is given to write *In Praise of Folly;* but without being Erasmus—or Saint Evremond, one can take pleasure in pulling out from the muddle of the centuries some singular figure which one will try to dress up once again cleverly" (*Oeuvres de Gérard de Nerval,* 937). In the first version of his preface, the narrator adds Fontenelle and Voltaire to the list of modern muses who preside over his inspiration. What all these writer-philosophers have in common is not so much their philosophy or political views as their discursive strategy, their tongue-in-cheek *rhetoric:* with unflinching false naïveté and false candor, they say one thing and mean another. The conspiratorial wink the author thus exchanges with the reader allows him to pursue logically and analytically a commonsensical truth beyond its empirical field of application, to push it to its extreme in order to bring forth its inherent absurdity, thus implicating and exposing the assumptions underlying a culture: its ideology. To the series Erasmus, Fontenelle, Voltaire, and Saint Evremond, we may add Derrida's reading of the Declaration of Independence, as well as Nerval himself, who explores legislative folly with the same good-humored innocence and finds it simultaneously absolutely logical, totally nonsensical, and remarkably effective within its politico-ideological framework.

In this perspective the contrast between Russell and Searle is telling. Russell advocates that "a logical theory may be tested by its capacity for dealing with puzzles, and it is a wholesome plan, in thinking about logic, to stock the mind with as many puzzles as possible since they serve much the same purpose as is served by experiments in physical science." [48] Searle, on the other hand, refuses to put his theory to the test of experience, refuses to subject it to the rigors of a perhaps "aberrant" or "irregular" reality. Instead, he would rather remain within the purely logical range of theory, with little concern for its applicability beyond the few examples he himself fabricates to suit his purpose. Referring to Russell's famous puzzle, "The king of France is bald," and to the string of counterpuzzles that it has inspired, Searle writes that "the illusion that the controversy is really about this point engenders an eristic search for trick examples, at the expense of any *serious* examination of the way the theory of descriptions fails to conform to any *coherent general theory* of illocutionary acts" (*Speech Acts*, 158). The discussion would then be between general theories, between coherent and totalizing— and therefore normative or legislative—systems. The principle of reality is not fully admitted into such authoritarian systems: excluded are the reality of subjects in error or in doubt about their own intentions, as well as that of the slants and changes that reception can inflict on the speaking subject's original grasp on the force and ultimate meaning(s) of his utterance. Also excluded are utterances truly contextualized (rather than invented in order to illustrate a rule), that is, fully subjected to many, perhaps incompatible, contexts and conventions. If Russell's rather simple six-word puzzle is too "eristic" for Searle's "serious examination" of a "coherent general theory," one is left wondering what exactly such an examination will examine, what data will be allowed to sift through the sieve to which Searle's coherent general theory submits linguistic facts.

Perlocution

Among the changes Searle introduces into Austin's theory of speech acts, the most significant is the elimination of perlocution. Searle's reasons are very similar to Fish's (see pp. 186–95). Since perlocution is not necessarily conventional, the speaker cannot secure the uptake of an utterance's perlocutionary force in accordance with either a rule or the speaker's intended meaning. How will the theory then account for the fact that one person is intimidated by a threat while another is not? Can it regulate and theorize personal reactions that depend on the mental and psychological makeup of the interlocutor and the infinite variations of speech situations? That the theorist cannot hope for an exhaustive inventory of these variables, neither Searle, nor Austin, nor Fish, nor I will deny. At this point, Searle joins hands with Fish to recommend that the illocutionary force be considered distinct from the perlocutionary effect: "Illocutionary acts such as stating are often directed at or done for the purpose of achieving perlocutionary effects such as convincing or persuading but it seems crucial to the theorist of speech, unlike earlier behavioristic theorists of language, to distinguish the illocutionary act, which is a speech act proper, from the achievement of the perlocutionary effect which may or may not be achieved by specially linguistic means" (*E&M,* xii). Searle draws a hard line between causes and effects and, by eliminating all effects, relegates his theory to the domain of causes only. The theory of speech acts according to Searle (and Fish) is purely a causal theory and, when translated into the context of language and speaking subjects, becomes purely intentional. And yet, a person upholding such a theory risks being in the position of the man in Freud's joke who, upon meeting his friend on a train at a station in Galicia, is indignant when the latter tells him he is going to Krakov. "What a liar you are," cries the first man, "you say you are going to Krakov so that I'll think you're going to Lemberg. But I know you're going to Krakov. So why lie?" If the force of the utterance is indeed realized when the listener recognizes the speaker's intention, as Searle claims, one also risks attributing false intentions to one's interlocutor and finding forces where there are none (and, of course, vice versa).

Distinctions and boundaries

"The King of Bicêtre" does indeed yield to the temptation to draw lines and delineate clear boundaries. The two madmen are at Bicêtre, an enclosed space. Their "theoretical" madness is contained. There are thus two worlds that do not communicate: one at Bicêtre, for the Law and the discourse of propriety and origin, and the other on the outside, for the puzzles and irregularities of rhetoric. Searle's wishes are answered: the theory no more concerns itself with the puzzle than the puzzle concerns itself with the theory. And yet it is in the nature of "theoretical" madness to be, as Searle says, general, that is to say, to extend its rule as far as possible. An expansionist principle is inherent in any *general* theory: history has amply shown that the holders of such theories try either to proselytize or to rule the nonbelievers. And sure enough, no sooner are the two men settled at Bicêtre and in their delusion than they try to communicate with the outside, to spread their message and proselytize the people of Paris, or in terms of speech act theory, to secure the uptake of their utterances' perlocutionary force. They fabricate a primitive press on which they print their charters and poetry and throw them from their cell windows, firmly believing that as soon as the people of Paris read their message, they will surrender to its truth and logic. When this attempt fails too, they do not for a moment entertain the thought that they may be wrong or that the outside world may care little about the "truths" they so cherish. Instead they explain their failure within their general frame of reference: "After a number of edicts and appeals to the faithfulness of the good city of Paris, the two prisoners were finally surprised to see no sign of mass upheaval and to awaken still in the same situation. Spifame attributed this lack of success to the surveillance of the ministers and Vignet to the unrelenting hatred of Mellin and du Bellay" ("Bicêtre," 948). Attributing their failure to the hatred and surveillance of their imaginary enemies only confirms Spifame's and Vignet's original madness. Despite the consistent misfiring of their perlocutionary acts, they never question or doubt themselves; nor are they troubled by the fact that their theories do not seem to be relevant to any speech situation except the one in which they are engaged with each other.[49] Lyotard's "philosophical" self-questioning mode never tinges their conceptual and political horizon.

Eventually, Spifame and Vignet escape from Bicêtre, not to be free but to address the people of Paris and convince them of the same truths for which they were committed to Bicêtre in the first place. The two distinct worlds meet in the marketplace. When the king and Spifame stand face to face, Spifame's centrality is finally displaced, and he comes to realize that there may be more than one viewpoint, more than one authoritative system, each negating the other's claim to supremacy. At this moment, the narrative voice loses its verve and irony and turns strangely sober and succinct: it only informs us that Spifame, unable to handle this duplicity, escapes into a furious fever. It is as if this moment had exhausted the narrative possibilities of Spifame's case study. The story concludes with two endings: a dry description of the rest of Spifame's life and an equally dry erudite note concerning the whereabouts of the law book he wrote. Thus, instead of ending with a denouement that would resolve the duality logically and satisfactorily, the narrative leaves open the paradoxical aspect of its multicentrality, as well as the rhetorical, logical, and political questions raised by Spifame's and Vignet's illnesses.

This narratological open-endedness calls attention to the narrative voice's ambivalence toward its characters. Ambiguous, tongue-in-cheek authorial judgments stud the narrative. Vignet's verses, for example, "were well turned and perhaps deserved the place he assigned to them in his thought" ("Bicêtre," 945). If his poetry indeed ranks as high as he claims, he may not be as mad as he is said to be! Besides, literary history is full of stories about plagiarism, hoaxes, and mistaken authorship, and nothing in the story as the narrative voice tells it contradicts Vignet's claim that Mellin and du Bellay have plagiarized his work. The same goes for Spifame: not only does the king give him a palace and order that he be treated like a king, but he leaves him free to spend the rest of his life writing laws, decrees, ordinances, and charters, which, incidentally, end up in the Royal Library (where they still are, collected in a volume entitled *Dicoearchiae Henrici Regis Progymnasmata;* on the verso of the title page we fine: "*Le contenu en ce présent volume six vingtz arrestz donnez l'an mil cinq cent cinquante six, par le Roy très chrestien Henry Deuxiesme, en sa Justice Royale Imperiale et Pontificale, ou executoriale des saincts decrestz, conciliaires et apostoliques, rendue par luy en persone; en son consistoire privé, sa souveraineté très excellente, temporelle ou spirituelle.*" [50]) When we realize that many of the 308 laws of this book have since been implemented, can we still be very sure that Spifame alias Henri II was not in some way the "king of France?" The boundaries between sane and sick, true and false, law and rhetoric no longer hold.

Austin's Final Word on Performative versus Constative

These questions uncannily echo the trick the narrative voice plays on the listener-reader in *How to Do Things with Words.* The much talked-about collapse of the distinction between performative and constative in the eleventh lecture in that book maintains a similar duality. Having failed to find a single expression devoid of illocutionary force,

Austin does not, as it has been said, abandon the distinction. There is therefore no need to save Austin from Austin (as Katz did[51]), no grounds to accuse him of philosophically embarrassing aporias, or, worse, to label him confused and confusing. Austin does indeed offer a way out of the corner into which his rigorous examination of linguistic facts and his refusal of easy and unproven generalizations and "theorizations" seem to have gotten him. That his solution was not judged to be one by some philosophers and by literary critics such as Fish does not constitute a commentary on Austin's work so much as on the work of these philosophers and critics: it reflects their standards and criteria for satisfactory theorizing and, in so doing, exposes their conceptual dogmatism.

The following is the conclusion of Austin's eleven-lecture argument:

> What then finally is left of the distinction of the performative and constative utterance? Really we may say that what we had in mind here was this:
>
> (a) With the constative utterance, *we abstract* from the illocutionary (let alone the perlocutionary) aspects of the speech, and *we concentrate* on the locutionary: moreover, we use an *over-simplified notion of correspondence with the facts*—over-simplified because essentially, it brings in the illocutionary aspect. This is the ideal of what would be right to say *in all circumstances, for any purpose, to any audience, &c.* Perhaps it is sometimes realized.
>
> (b) With the performative utterance, *we attend as much as possible* to the illocutionary force of the utterance, and *abstract* from the dimension of correspondence with facts. (*How to*, 145–46)

Austin invites us to perform two major mental acts: focusing (or concentrating) and abstracting. In the final analysis, the logical grounds of a speech act are not in the *intentions of the speaker,* as Searle and most speech act philosophers would have it and as Austin's original but temporary rules held, but mostly in the *reception of the listener,* in the mental acts the listener has to perform in order to perceive an utterance as either performative or constative. Mostly, because the same activities are required of the speaker as well. But the speaker alone cannot secure the felicity of an utterance: unless the listener performs the necessary abstracting and focusing, she or he will miss the expression's force, and the utterance will be condemned to infelicity. In the normal practice of language, utterances are not purely performative or constative.[52] They *become* performative or constative when the listener, guided by (perhaps lax) conventions, (infinite) contexts, and (intersubjective and ambiguous) speech situations, abstracts one aspect and focuses on another.

This solution sounds a familiar tone. It echoes Saussure's anguished insistence that "it is false to admit within linguistics any fact as defined in itself," that "there is nothing, that is to say nothing that would be determined in advance outside of the point of view," and eventually that "the point of view MAKES the object." [53] Indeed, the general and hasty contention that the distinction collapses and that Austin almost ruined a good idea by hopelessly entangling it in a mesh of counterexamples also echoes Ogden and Richards' stubborn refusal to acknowledge the paragraph in which *The Course* addresses the precedence of the viewpoint over the object. When intellectual history repeats itself, it is usually because, despite the time gap, thinkers still answer to the same ideology. What collapses in *How to Do Things with Words* is not the distinction between performative and constative utterances but the very notion of permanent distinctions dear to theorizers. Whereas the former is a minor nuisance easily remedied by "theoreticians" such as Katz, Searle, or Fish, the latter mirrors a methodological concern invalidating the "theoretical" method of investigation and, with it, the sum of the theories this kind of method may produce. What Austin does in *How to Do Things with Words* is, in fact, a *deconstruction* of the "theoretical" mode of investigation. I therefore find it highly ironic that Derrida's critique of Austin in "Signature Event Context" is so un-Derridean: that is to say, that his critique addresses mostly the propositional content of Austin's text while ignoring the power of his rhetorical strategies. [54] And yet Austin's most subversive message lies not in the discovery of performative utterance (Frege, for example, mentions them in "The Thought," see above, p. 125) but in the slow, patient, playful, and constant reversal of his propositions into their opposite, until the very notion of an "objective" or "constative" proposition collapses (which is also exactly what he says in the conclusion I quote above). That this last sentence equally describes Derrida's style and discursive strategies is, I hope, obvious to the reader familiar with both. Austin and Derrida may be a lot closer than the discussion of either "Signature Event Context" or "Limited, Inc." suggests. The numerous literary essays decrying Austin's expulsion of literature and his excessive categorization (among which I include my 1981 article on "The Venus of Ille") reflect a similar oversight.

"It was examples of this kind," Austin comments further, "like 'I apologize,' and 'The cat is on the mat,' *said for no conceivable reason,* extremely *marginal* cases, that gave rise to the idea of two *distinct* utterances" (*How to,* 145–46). Away with fabricated examples for the sole purpose of illustrating unshakable distinctions and proving a theory.

Away with utterances said for no conceivable reason. A theory may
have recourse to such examples for heuristic purposes (life is too short
to invent a full-fledged situational context for each minor example),
but, before one draws conclusions and proceeds with generalizations
based on these out-of-context expressions, one should remember that
they are "extremely marginal cases," and, in fact, a pure fiction at the
service of the "theory" to which they appear (and only appear) to lead.
Distinctions depend on contexts, abstractions, and focusing. Only with
the proper contextualization—and I take this term to include the
speaker and the listener, the situational context, and the reigning ideo-
logical contexts—can theories be addressed. This is, of course, the po-
sition of the judiciary; it is also the subject of chapter 6.

6 The Semiotic Value
Dumas' The Three Musketeers

For some years we have been realizing more and more clearly that the occasion of an utterance matters seriously, and that the words used are to some extent to be "explained" by the context in which they are designed to be or have actually been spoken in a linguistic exchange.

AUSTIN

It would seem that we have reached an impasse and that the problems posed by reference will remain unsolvable: if we can neither eliminate reference from the study of language (as do Structuralism and Poststructuralism) nor address it, as does the analytic philosophy of language, where do we go from here? The simple law of the excluded middle seems to bar us from further investigating the possibility of formulating a theory of language that accounts for reference. Shall we then advocate intellectual nihilism? Shall we take refuge in skepticism? Shall we contend that words and things do not or should not mix and that all attempts to elaborate a theory of language that takes into account its semantic *and* its semiotic aims are equally doomed to failure? Any unequivocal or unambiguous answer to the problem posed in these terms will border on an absurdity. If I were to express in a dozen words or less why this problem is indeed unsolvable, I would say, perhaps a bit abruptly (but I *am* confined to twelve words), that there is no solution because there is in fact no problem.

To make this last point clear, let us retrace our steps. In the chapters on Saussure and Frege, I have compared and opposed two brilliant thinkers largely held as the founders of two distinct and opposed schools of thought. The differences between them are obvious: Frege believes that language consists of firm units having fixed senses and permanent references; he holds that thoughts and truth are objective and independent of language or signs. Saussure, on the other hand, emphasizes the mutual dependence of thoughts and language and the reciprocal semantic influence of the terms that make up a linguistic system. One advocates the absolute, and the other, the relative. The difference between them is even sharper when we examine it exclusively from the viewpoint of reference: Frege sees reference as an essential component of language; Saussure claims that words name not objects but differences between their representations. In short, where Frege advocates a shuttle between things and words, the Saussurean tradition crosses things out and deals with the distribution of meaning among words independently of any reality.

It is easy enough to oppose the two thinkers and the traditions they inaugurated, but we must not forget that, despite their obvious differences, they share one fundamental assumption: both assume (at least at some level of their discussion) that the order of things and the order of words are radically distinct and heterogeneous. Their projects can therefore be considered as diametrically opposed solutions to the conceptual difficulties that the radical heterogeneity of words and objects imposes on "theories." And yet, although, or perhaps precisely because, each thinker adopted such extreme and uncompromising solutions, each theory eventually came to wrestle increasingly with its "other," with the very component that it set out to eliminate: *Vorstellung* for Frege, and taxonomies (and the threat of referentiality they entail) for Saussure.

Of course, cultural and historical factors left their mark on the enquiry of each thinker. Saussure, for example, was reacting to the methods of comparative philologists of the end of the nineteenth century; therefore, he strove to distinguish between synchronic and diachronic linguistics and to eliminate phonetics and taxonomies from linguistics. Frege, who was reacting at once to British and Hegelian Idealism, Psychologism, Husserlian Phenomenology, and German Philosophical Naturalism waged war on subjectivism. Conversely, it is just as important to remember that Saussure and Frege were contemporaries: Saussure wrote his *Mémoire* in 1880 and taught his *cours de linguistique générale* at Geneva from 1906 to 1911, while Frege wrote his *Begriffsschrift* in 1879, "Sense and Denotation" in 1892, and "The Thought" in 1918. We should also remember that Switzerland and Germany are not far apart geographically and culturally. (I have not been able to uncover any indication that Saussure and Frege were aware of each other's existence—neither was as widely read in his own lifetime as he is today. We do know, however, that while Frege confined his readings to anthologies, Saussure read extensively and was generally familiar with current German publications.) As they lived and wrote in the same intellectual climate, their shared assumptions about language, or, more generally, about the delineation of a subject matter and the elaboration of methods of investigation should hardly surprise us. What can and should surprise us is that these presuppositions have generally not been questioned: today, almost a century later, except for a few voices crying in the wilderness, the very same assumptions and presuppositions are still at work in the writings of most philosophers, linguists, and, to a lesser extent, literary critics.

In chapters 4 and 5 we took two instances in which the apparent simplicity of the referential function collapsed under examination, independently of whether the theories we examined integrated reference or disregarded it. These instances involved indispensable truisms and platitudes such as "When I say 'I' I cannot not be referring to myself" or "In saying 'I do,' I am not describing but performing a wedding ceremony." And yet, despite these obvious truisms, we found it generally acknowledged that "I" and speech acts present problems that could invalidate general theories. At this point, strict theoreticians usually resort to the creation of new categories in which they enclose the erratic "I" and speech acts, in order to protect the all-important norm from their indeterminacies and eccentricities. The diversity of the theories we have encountered, their radical incompatibility, and their general failure to account properly for all but the most self-serving, custom-made examples confirmed the critique of the underlying assumptions of both schools that I had suggested in the earlier chapters on Frege and Saussure.

When I wrote earlier that there is no solution because there is no problem, what I meant was that the problem had been improperly posed. As long as we insist on perceiving the orders of things and words only as two autonomous planes, the problem does indeed remain unsolvable. In theory one can conceive of separations and boundaries; language and thinking depend on such distinctions. I am therefore not recommending that we drop them; nor I am suggesting a "better" system that would put an end to the arbitrary slicing of our phenomenal and conceptual worlds. But it would be a mistake to take these distinctions in a naïvely realistic or referential way (in our case, words/things, syntax/deixis, constative/performative, consciousness/body, semiotics/semantics, etc.). Just because we mention such components, it does not mean that they exist independently of us or of our mentioning. This situation is not unlike what we find in the natural sciences. In a sense, Mendeleev's chart is a fiction: in nature, elements do not usually exist in the pure state suggested by the chart. And yet the birth of modern chemistry coincides with their identification—as theoretical or hypothetical as this identification may have been before the advent of modern technology and the artificial isolation of elements achieved in laboratories. Similarly, language allows us to account for the world surrounding us, to communicate with one another, to objectify consciousness. These are highly heterogeneous aspects involving objects, sounds, constructs, concepts, thoughts, intentions, consciousness, subjectivity, intersubjectivity, psychology, logic, conventions, law, distribution of power, etcetera—in short, a highly eclectic ragbag. The carving out of a subject matter and the delineation of a realm of application thus constitute the major theoretical and conceptual effort and test of each thinker and each school.

We must therefore pursue simultaneously two contradictory lines of thinking. On the one hand, we must not forget that interrelation between the orders of things, thoughts, and language is such that they are inextricably linked so that any attempt to isolate one of them constitutes an abstraction (none of them corresponds to a known entity outside the theoretical constructs through which it is construed). On the other hand, the heterogeneity of these orders is so radical that it resists any theoretical attempt to resorb it into *one* coherent paraphrastic system. The more a "theory" insists on reconciling these different orders, the closer it comes to stumbling on an irreducible otherness hidden at the very heart of its project.

In this last chapter, I shall not offer yet another theory of language. Nor shall I attempt to determine a new relation between literature and everyday language, or literature and philosophy (or linguistics). The sheer excess of "theories" has largely contributed to the clouding of what is at issue in their controversies. Rather than exposing or criticizing these positions, as I have previously done, I shall attempt to illustrate how *heterogeneity itself* can be made to produce semiotic networks and meanings. This final chapter will thus suggest a method consisting in the acknowledgment of boundaries, differences, and heterogeneity; resisting the temptation to homogenize them; accounting both for the interaction of words and things and for the limits of this interaction; and avoiding the reduction of semantics and hermeneutics to normative systems of exclusions. In so doing, it will constitute the true conclusion of this study.

Objects and Narratives

The episode of *The Three Musketeers* we shall read is of particular interest in that personal motivations do not propel the narrative forward, a practice our Western tradition has conditioned us to expect.[1] Instead of affecting characters, the narrative affects objects. In this episode characters are psychologically stationary: they induce neither changes nor surprises, and although a lot happens, it does not happen directly to them. It happens first to objects. Each time an object changes hands, the characters rearrange their plans and courses so as to hide, expose, or get hold of these objects. Throughout these chases, the psychological motivation of the characters remains minimal. Unlike what happens in a typical realistic novel, in this episode events do not affect the characters of the heroes so much as their belongings. The narrative itself is the trace left by the displacement and circulation of signifying objects in a series of carefully overdetermined chain reactions.

The Western reader knows intuitively that when objects unduly change place, the wheels of narrative begin to turn. Counterfeited, stolen, lost, or diverted objects mark major plot reversals. How shall we read—that is to say, attach meaning to—such displacements? Can we speak of the place of an object *in a work of fiction* other than metaphorically? As the organization of any space inescapably creates a center (and therefore a "subject"), in relation to what and mostly to whom would this place be a "place" (this question, for example, was at the heart of my critique of the analytic theories of indexicals)? Is this to say that topography engages meaning or even generates it? The stakes of the question are high: if we attempt to turn a shifting topography (the recording of places) into a topology (the comprehensive theory of the allocation of these places), it would seem that we must anchor our discourse in something other than the traces of a purely arbitrary circulation. Shall we attempt to regulate the motion of a monkey's tail on a canvas, for example? Even if we mistake the end product for a work of art, or, better yet, even if we genuinely find the monkey's work to be a masterpiece, can we generalize this particular work in such a way that our "theory" will bear equally on all the paintings created by our monkey's tail? by all monkeys' tails? by any tail belonging to any animal? And if we cannot, if our "theory" applies only to one specific occurrence that can neither be generalized nor reproduced, can we still claim that it engages meaning (and what of a theory that would not engage meaning?)? Furthermore, and in a different spirit, what is the status of the subject of language when the world of things itself begins to take on meaning and organize space? What then of this subject's place? And most especially, how does the poetics of the displaced object affect the representation of the subject of and in language?

These questions bear on the indiscernible moment when the *thing* becomes a *sign*, when thingness disappears before its representation—and in doing so, mirrors its indefinitely deferred reader. In a universe made familiar by the intentionality of language, rarely can we distinguish between things and signs. When everything is bound together, *everything means.* The least attempt to evoke an autonomous thing backfires: even as we proclaim, "The thing *is*," the copula, unable to resist the crowding of contextuality, yields to the verb *to mean:* "The thing is no more; it means." Such is the case of the chestnut tree's root that Sartre attempted to draw out of all relational systems and into an irreducible excess. Once summoned, this same root came to signify an entire ideology.

Even then, this meaning conceded, what remains of the thing? If we follow the Continental approach in its Saussurean guise, we may ask what remains of circumstances and things in a system where signifieds and values are effects of differences. What is to become of the principle of reality, of all that the system relegates to the outside? For a modernity or even a postmodernity in the wake of structuralism, Saussurean linguistics, or even American New Criticism, the stakes are high: can we really suspend diachrony and, in synchronic bliss, construct systems and eliminate contingency? Will the formalist, structuralist, or exegetical successes eliminate the raw force of reference? In other words, will the system govern the circulation of objects? Will it regulate the effects of meaning that result from that circulation? Or, on the contrary, do these effects from the outside challenge the theories, expose their fictional character, and remind us that the outside does not obligingly comply with the power of theories and systems? Lurking in exile, the outside threatens to usurp the power that alienated it and decenter the once mighty system. This first string of questions reflects a *semiotic* point of view. While a semantic reading works only horizontally, relating the signifying object to the elements of its own system in such a way that each eventually (and tautologically) confirms the other's meaning, the semiotic perspective that my line of questioning suggests works both horizontally and vertically, elaborating semantic constructs within the general framework of the *referential circumstances* in which the thing takes on an *index sui* value and, in so doing, becomes a sign.

On the other hand, what of reference, if the same object-sign, instead of remaining the symbol that it is, shifts its meaning? What of communication (and of truth), if the same proposition is to bear one day on one object, and another day on yet a different object? (In a more subversive mode, we may address the same question to signifieds—as indeed we did in the chapter on Saussure.) If, one day, *two* means "two," and the next day it means "three," what of Frege's two and two? Similarly, what will happen to Russell's object-language, if an object-word is at risk of changing its object without a warning? if the atom of Russell's atomistic construction slips?

The semantic shifts that accompany the circulation of objects risk wreaking havoc with both structures and reference; with the former because it remains closed to the circumstances in which the circulation takes place and to the given nature of these objects; and with the latter because it does not acknowledge the possibility of semantic contamination among these objects once they have become signs.

In this perspective, *The Gift* by Mauss and the "Seminar on the 'Purloined Letter'" by Lacan are particularly illuminating: both examine objects that came to acquire meanings, that is to say, became signs, during and because of their circulation.[2] Both developed theories intended to explain this process and generalize it. They represent attempts not so much to understand how signs—once they are acknowledged as signs conveying meanings and bearing on referents—work, as attempts to catch the elusive moment when an object *becomes* a sign. Their theories cross the dividing line between signs (which I take here as a generic term subsuming *words*) and objects. Unlike the Saussurean and Fregean traditions, they envisage ways in which the order of things and the order of words might communicate. Like Austin, Lacan and Mauss show a world permeable to language and, conversely, a syntax permeable to the outside world, a world in which referents and meanings are acquired or even created rather than predetermined. Lacan's and Mauss' ties with Structuralism or Poststructuralism are common knowledge. And yet, insomuch as the signs that their theories address maintain an intimate relationship with the objects they once were; insomuch as they depend on nonlinguistic contexts; insomuch as they end up evoking analytically the rules that they have contributed to elaborate; and finally, insomuch as they provide their own truth criteria, we may say that these objects-become-signs enact the very same rules, criteria, and principles that form the core of the analytic philosophy of language. Last but not least, since Lacan and Mauss also integrate their findings into the semantics of the subject, they allow us to pursue the inquiry we have broached in the previous chapters, all the while displacing the nodes of resistance from the subject to the object, or at least redefining the boundaries between them.

Since our objective is not a discussion of Lacan or Mauss for discussion's sake but an examination of alternatives to the impasse into which the contrasting views of Saussure, Frege, and the thinkers who accepted their tenets have led us, I shall adopt a tangential approach: rather than discussing in depth the anthropological or psychoanalytical essays, I shall examine specific instances of the circulation of objects whose general appeal and effectiveness have been proven by generations of enthusiastic readers and moviegoers.

There stands an object, already valorized by convention: a ribbon with twelve diamond studs, twelve precious stones: the queen's diamond studs, in Alexandre Dumas' *Three Musketeers*. But what of their original value when these diamond studs are given, given again, stolen, split up, counterfeited, given back, multiplied—in short, when they pass from hand to hand? What law can we call upon to govern their circulation? How will this circulation affect the subjects who respectively hold and relay these studs?

The Gift

What, then, are the queen's diamond studs? Initially they belong to a woman who has received them from her husband as a present for her birthday. By metonymy they represent the husband, not the man or the lover, but what makes a man or a lover a husband: the Law, namely, the system of rules by virtue of which a single incident acquires a predetermined value and a meaning (see "Nerval's 'King of Bicêtre'" in chap. 5). The single incident (here, the joining of a man and a woman) and the system are mutually corollary, each confirming the other without further ado or explanation. Although the problematics of the "gift" and the "Law" converge on these studs, they do not coincide. There are no innocent gifts: the value of a gift does not end with the actual transaction without leaving traces or remainders. In this case, dictated by the pride and the ostentation of the king rather than by his generosity, the gift of the diamond studs humiliates the lady it honors. The agonistic attitude characteristic of the king during the entire affair of the studs inscribes the initial gift in the tradition of the potlatch studied by Mauss: by evoking systems, these studs set off a series of values. Indeed, seen as part of a system, no gift is an isolated, unilateral, and altruistic action; rather, it is a peculiar kind of exchange condemned to imbalance: the giver does not so much await "reimbursement" (with or without interest) as the in-between state, that between the moment of prestation and the moment of counterprestation. This is the privileged time when the giver holds the debtor in his power. Even though she knows that she is contracting a humiliating debt by accepting the gift, the recipient is not free to decline the offering, since doing so would, from the outset, be tantamount to admitting her inferiority.[3] The gift is thus an act of aggression.[4]

Ultimately, it is an exchange of a paradoxical nature, as the perfectly successful gift would be the one that the recipient could not give back: that is to say, the one that would indefinitely prolong the moment of superiority of the giver ("The ideal would be to give a potlatch which would not be re-turned" [*Gift*, 40, n. 171, modified trans.]). In *The Three Musketeers* this aspect acquires a particular relief because the giver is not just any husband, but a king. The lady, queen but subject, can never repay her king (*The Three Musketeers* insists on the queen's penury). The gift of the studs is thus an act of sovereignty as well: in accepting the studs from the hand of her royal husband, the queen reiterates her civil and conjugal vows of obedience and submission. Eventually, the king's gift destines the humbled recipient to remain in debt for the rest of her life.

The Pledge

A clandestine interview that the queen grants to the Duke of Buckingham (her suitor) sets the merry-go-round of the diamond studs in motion. He is incognito in France and therefore at the mercy of any assassin. This fear drives the proud queen to a scarcely disguised declaration, " 'Go, go, I implore you, and *return* hereafter! *Come back* as ambassador, *come back* as minister, *come back* surrounded with guards who will defend you, with servants who will watch over you, and *then* I shall no longer fear for your days, and *I shall be happy in seeing you.*' "[5] More than a declaration, it is a promise, a pledge. Buckingham does not fail to point out and to confirm its contractual value: "—Oh! is this true what you say? —Yes . . . —Oh, then, some *pledge* of your indulgence, some *object* which came from you, and *may remind* me that I have not been dreaming" (*TM*, 131). A pledge, that is to say, a reminder, sign, and guarantee of a promise. The queen has just contracted a new obligation, a new debt that she seals with a pledge: the studs offered her by her king. Just as the studs metonymically designated the king and, in the queen's hands, became a contractual pledge of marriage and submission of the woman to her lord and master, they now designate, by the same metonymy, the queen and, in Buckingham's hands, the promise that unites the tearful lady to her lover. We shall note in passing that this twist creates a delicate situation, since the original vows were essentially performative in nature, that is, unique: if a speech act is felicitous, any subsequent identical utterance simply repeating the first will be either automatically void (as in a marriage ceremony) or a new speech act (such as "I promise," where each promise is a new one). "The Venus of Ille," for example owes its effectiveness to this principle (see chap. 5). What, then, of the second time the studs are given as a pledge? In addition, by pledging what she has *already* given (her exclusive love) and therefore *should no longer have,* the queen puts into question the very possibility of legislating the *having* of goods, of controlling their circulation, or ever devising their topography—in short, of determining the value of these evasive goods and their relationship to the subject.

Law and Cuckoldry

Clearly, regulating and controlling values pertains to the Law. This role is incumbent on the king. He is the ultimate authority, at once justifying and endorsing the cohesion of the system. He incarnates the perfect coincidence of the ultimate signified with the ultimate referent (the way God functions in a theological system). Thus, as long as the king knows nothing of the circulation of the diamond studs (that is to say, as long as this circulation is *outside* the Law, which purports to govern all circulation of meaning), there is no story: a story is precisely the game played out between the Law and its mutations, transgressions, and subversions. In *The Three Musketeers* the story is well known: Richelieu advises the king to hold a ball and to invite the queen—with her diamond studs—but only the evening before the ball. This last detail is essential to the cardinal's plan, as he does not want to give the queen time to recover the studs. But the minister does not count on the suspicion he inspires in his lord. The king, struck by the insistence of the cardinal from whom he fears "one of those terrible surprises which his Eminence was so skillful in getting up" (*TM,* 169) and moved by their old rivalry, rushes immediately to the queen's chambers to invite her to the ball—with her diamond studs. Thus, he gives her the time to foil the "terrible surprise" that would have reestablished the Law. In so doing, he becomes his wife's accomplice against the minister's plotting (or zeal) without knowing exactly what game the cardinal and the queen are playing, but suspecting that the *legitimate* authority he supposedly represents is at stake. Accomplice and victim of a transgression, the king must abdicate his right to represent the Law. We could perhaps have imputed the position of the Law to Richelieu if he, too, had not had a brush with the queen: a rejected suitor, he confuses his personal insult with that of France. Certainly, Anne's infidelity affects the king and even the minister, but that is the least of her crimes. Since every gift is in fact a pledge and, as such, implicates the Law, more than it wrongs Louis or

Richelieu, Anne's infidelity encroaches upon the Law.[6] Moreover, the king and the minister, the supposed representatives of the Law, do not wrong it any less. Of more importance than a cuckolded king is this decentering of the law in relation to its rightful position. The cuckold of the story is, in the final analysis, the Law.

On Divisibility

The die is cast.[7] Only the presence of the diamond studs on the evening of the ball will save the queen. Anne of Austria sends d'Artagnan to Buckingham with the order to retrieve her jewelry. But meanwhile in England, in a moment of intimacy, Milady (Richelieu's demonic agent) has relieved Buckingham of two of the diamond studs. The studs are therefore eminently "divisible," as there are two with Milady and ten with Buckingham. But they are equally "indivisible": if but a single stud is missing, the whole strand is denuded. Thus we must be more specific: if the studs are simultaneously divisible and indivisible, it is because they are at once *thing* and *sign,* totally autonomous as things, but caught in semiotic networks of relations as signs. As things, they can be taken, given, worn, divided, stolen, or counterfeited. Their number may then vary: there will in turn be twelve, ten, twelve, and fourteen. This variation represents an undeniable "materiality." Still, the function of the studs in *The Three Musketeers* exceeds their materiality: the king's gift is also a sign. This does not mean that the diamonds signify (in the manner of the Saussurean sign), or that they simply "designate" their referent or "express" their sense (as Frege would have it ["On Sense," 61]). If the studs function as a *sign,* it is because they have acquired *semiotic values* along the way.[8] By semiotic value I mean *the manner in which the signifying object* evokes *the referential circumstances in which it has come to acquire a meaning, and which subsequently govern its circulation.* This semiotic value differs from Saussurean value in that it integrates extralinguistic referential elements into the system: not only does a linguistic unit interact with other linguistic units (or, put more broadly, with similar units), but it also interacts with units not normally belonging to the system yet which, for some contingent, circumstantial, and purely accidental reason, are made to affect the semantics of the linguistic unit, and consequently the whole system. Thus, while Saussurean value is decidedly semantic, the value that I am suggesting here is semiotic in that it also relates to extralinguistic conditions best described as *referential.*

We may follow, for instance, the hesitations of Athos, who, faced with his family ring given to Milady and recovered by d'Artagnan, does not know how to interpret its contradictory semiotic values and, as a result, how to dispose of it (and since the progress of the narrative depends on the circulation of these semiotically loaded objects, the narrative stands still until d'Artagnan finds a compromise):

> "The jewel is yours, my dear Athos! Did you not tell me it was a family jewel?"
>
> "Yes, my grandfather gave two thousand crowns for it, as he once told me. It formed part of a nuptial present he made his wife, and it was magnificent. My mother gave it to me, and I, fool as I was, instead of keeping the ring as a holy relic, gave it to this wretch."
>
> "Then, my friend, take back this ring, to which I see you attach so much value."
>
> "I, take back the ring, after it has passed through the hands of that infamous creature! Never; that ring is defiled, d'Artagnan."
>
> "Sell it, then."
>
> "Sell a jewel which came from my mother! I vow I should consider it a profanation.'" (*TM*, 383)

If the semiotic value reflects the way in which the signifying object evokes the circumstances that govern its circulation, insomuch as the circumstances are multiple and different for each interested party (no one has a God-like omniscient perception of the myriad chains of effects of a particular situation on all the other possible interested parties), the object—at every moment of its itinerary—will carry multiple and different values for each party. This multiplicity is of utmost importance for the semiotic values. Ultimately (and *The Three Musketeers* plays upon this fact), the narratological efficiency of the signifying object depends wholly on the elusive difference between its multiple semiotic values and the semantic unicity that the speaking subject imposes upon it in order to constitute a representation of the world that would satisfy his or her personal need for coherence. It is important to notice here that the division or even the destruction of the thing does not bring about the lessening or destruction of values. Signs do not know negativity: on the contrary, any time they suffer physical damage, they gain values; like Athos' ring, they carry the trace of all the successive values that they may have acquired (in contrast with the classic example of the exchange value of money). Thus at the royal ball, twelve minus two would equal not ten but twelve minus two. It would forever express a relation between twelve and two, between the pledge of the king and that of the queen—and not the neat result of an operation. Ten diamond studs "mean" nothing. They come to signify only inasmuch as they evoke the original twelve *and* the missing two. Indeed, when the materiality of the studs is split up, their values change; while becoming other, however, the new values still carry the traces of their past. It is *because* the twelve were a mark of legitimacy, love, and power, that on the evening of the ball, ten on the queen's shoulder would be incriminating evidence.

Lacan's Signifier

Let us take another object that, when displaced and then brought to the attention of the Law, might harm a lady. In "The Seminar on 'The Purloined Letter,'" Lacan called this object a signifier. Unfortunately, the Lacanian signifier's widespread success has masked the Saussurean signifier; to the detriment of each, these two distinct concepts have had to share the same name. In spite of some taxonomic hesitations, the signifier remains constant in Saussure's teaching. Saussure never lingers on the physical, sensorial aspect of signs. Instead he relegated this aspect to phonetics, which he conceives as a distinct discipline apart from linguistics. For Saussure, both the signified and the signifier are *concepts* in that they both pertain to representation (rather than to an existentialist phenomenology). The signifier cannot be the sounds composing the spoken word: it is the idea that, for a member of any given community, represents this sound; hence the well-chosen term *sound-image* as a paraphrase of *signifier. The signifier is not material.*[9] As such, it cannot be touched, taken, stolen, returned, or torn up.

This is distinctly not the case of the Lacanian signifier. On the contrary, the Lacanian signifier is in a dialogue with (but does not endorse) the Fregean *realistic* presuppositions that would have a signifier correspond invariably to the same signified, and in turn, each signified correspond to only one referent in such a way that—arbitrary or not—a solid relation would be established between the word and the designated object. It is in this sense that one must understand "But if it is first of all on the materiality of the signifier that we have insisted, that materiality is odd [*singulière*] in many ways, the first of which is not to admit partition. Cut a letter in small pieces, and it remains the letter it is—and this is a completely different sense that *Gestalttheorie* would account for which the dormant vitalism informing its notion of the whole" ("Seminar," 53). The Lacanian signifier, at once divisible and indivisible, material and ideal, most certainly does not correspond to the Saussurean signifier. But, departing from Saussure, Lacan emphasizes all the more the essence of his own conception of the signifier-phallus: "its priority in relation to the signified" (59). Ironically, one can say that the signified (and not the signifier) occupies the foreground of Lacan's teaching: as he strives to consolidate the bar that would definitively alienate the signified, he sets it up, ipso facto, as the ultimate target of his argument.

From this perspective, the discussion on the nature of the signifier loses its urgency: thing or idea, divisible or indivisible, the signifier retains its essential homogeneity and, consequently, elicits interpretation (if only approximate). Indeed, a no-nonsense approach will hold that the materiality of a letter is evident (as is that of the diamond studs): it can be torn up, soiled, lost, stolen, returned, hidden, and so on. But its interest does not lie in this elementary aspect. To propose that "material causes" affect matter is a tautological platitude of which I shall not accuse Dumas, Poe, Lacan, or Derrida. We can shelve for the moment, then, the materiality of the letter (all the more so, since—as the truism would no doubt indicate—we will never know if the letter is divisible or not, because no one in Poe's "Purloined Letter" tries to divide it up, and no one is able to determine definitely if such a division is possible). Hence, Lacan notwithstanding, I shall avoid the word *signifier,* whose Saussurean denotation does not hold for Poe's letter or the queen's diamonds, while its Lacanian variation entails considerable ambiguity between meaning and referent—the very same difficulty that opposes Frege and Saussure and that I am trying to clarify.[10]

Duplication and Value

The inalterability of the concept remains: for Lacan, despite its displacements and permutations, the letter "remains the letter it is." It does not pick up any semiotic values in the course of the transactions to which it is subjected, and thus it remains essentially identical to itself (*singulier*) in a way that transcends any mishap that might befall it. In the case of the diamond studs, we should then ask if the "singularity" of the studs that leave the queen's chamber is the same as that of the studs that end up returning there. From the outset, this question is skewed: we cannot view this singularity as singular (as a kind of *intrinsic* value), free of semiotic values, since the indispensability of the jewelry for the king (and therefore for the queen) is coextensive with its initial semiotic value (that of a potlatch). But the plot thickens when Buckingham counterfeits the missing studs. The two new studs are "so completely imitated, so perfectly alike, that Buckingham could not tell the new ones from the old ones, and experts in such matters would have been deceived as he was" (*TM,* 213). Indeed, the resemblance of the new studs to the old is such that no one in *The Three Musketeers* questions it; from a narrative point of view, they are identical. Something has been reproduced; but then, it cannot be the studs-thing since an object is by definition singular. (Sameness is not to be confused with oneness, as the reader well knows that there are now fourteen studs in circulation.) The studs-sign, however, may be reproduced infinitely: a sign is simply that which is *re*-cognized as such; it is a sign only insomuch as I know in advance that it can recur unchanged in many contexts, bearing the same meaning and referring to the same object. Only the repetition of the same (its reproducibility) can instigate the process of abstraction through which an object becomes a sign. As we have seen, however, this in no way prevents further changes in the *value* of this sign.

What are the effects of such changes? How might they affect the initial singularity of the studs? Buckingham, whose semiotic awareness is the most keen, does not fail to address this question: " 'Here,' he said, 'are the diamond studs that you came to bring; and *be my witness that I have done all that human power could do*' " (TM, 213). What d'Artagnan must witness and testify to is the new semiotic value that Buckingham has imprinted on the studs. At the king's ball, the queen will proudly wear on her shoulder not only the mark of the legitimacy conferred by her king, or even the pledge she had offered to her lover, but also the *proof* that "all that human power could do" her lover had done out of love for her. Never has revenge been sweeter: the more imperious the king is, the more complaisant the queen proves to be—and the better she betrays him for it.

Each displacement of the studs, each stage in their itinerary, will have affected their semiotic values, independently of all intrasubjective dialectic: in this my project differs from the Lacanian *politique de l'autruiche,* which concerns the subject rather than the object.[11] If this *politique* situates the subject in slots predetermined by their *relation to the letter,* then this letter—center around which the slots revolve—must indeed remain invariable throughout the circuit, identical to itself ("it remains the letter it is"). In no way can this compare to the studs, whose value changes with each transaction (I would also argue that the same holds for the letter in Poe's story—as the message left by Dupin on the "letter" destined to the minister proves). Thus, while the *politique de l'autruiche* underlines a permanent, normative structure,[12] the slippage of values that punctuates the studs' circulation brings about a confusion of the three slots, which in turn prevents the fine-tuning that Lacan suggests in the "Seminar on '*The Purloined Letter*.' "[13] This double interference brings to mind the croquet game in *Alice in Wonderland* (rather than the card game evoked by Lacan): the croquet "manual" tries in vain to define the player or the shot in relation to the ball or even in relation to the rules that govern the ball's motion. As the hedgehog-ball or the hoop-soldier take a stroll, and as the flamingo-mallet twists itself around for a friendly peek, the reader, like Alice, will come to the conclusion that "it [is] a very difficult game indeed." [14]

Unicity and Cuckoldry

The plot thickens still more when Richelieu allows himself to be taken in by arithmetic. Believing in the essential singularity and indivisibility of the diamonds, he views them at all times as twelve—as if twelve were in fact one. Since he now holds two of them, he trusts he can win against the queen and imprudently lays his cards on the table: he gives to the king the two studs Milady has brought back and refers the king to his queen for further explanations. The king, who also holds that twelve equals one, hands the two diamond studs to the queen:

> "I thank you, Madame," said he, "for the deference you have shown to my wishes, but I think you want two of the studs, and I bring them back to you."
>
> With these words he held out to the queen the two studs the cardinal had given him.
>
> "How, sire?" cried the young queen, affecting surprise, "you are giving me, then, two more; *I shall have fourteen.*"
>
> In fact the king counted them, and the twelve studs were all on her Majesty's shoulder.
>
> The king called the cardinal.
>
> "What does *this* mean, Monsieur Cardinal?" asked the king in a severe tone. (*TM*, 221)

That is indeed a severe question. If twelve is the magical number that would reduce the many to the one, what, indeed, does *this* mean? *This,* that is to say, two or fourteen, an *other* number, which breaks up the unicity of the set and exposes the divisibility concealed by the indivisible. The king's question then bears on the production of signs and the doubts that follow their proliferation. What, then, does *this* mean. [15]

Richelieu had hoped to confound the queen and to show the king that by displacing the two studs, his wife had displaced—and thus breached—the faith she owed him. However, as she displays the twelve (or, dare we say, the ONE) on her shoulder, she defuses the threat of the two purloined studs: the "two" is reduced to an estranged excess in relation to this displayed unicity. Thereafter the two studs stolen by Milady are out of bounds. Their indicting value has vanished into thin air. Nevertheless, by simply having them, Richelieu has joined the merry-go-round of values: fraught with disqualified pieces and compromised by the obvious unicity displayed on the royal shoulder, he must grapple with the new excess-value that implicates him dangerously in the sphere of conjugal-royal intimacy—where he most certainly does not belong (hence the king's severe tone). To protect what is left of his tail feathers, the cardinal renounces his plan to expose the queen's infidelity: he drops out of the game—the only move that the two studs invalidated by the king's blind realism would still allow: " 'This means, Sire,' replied the cardinal, 'that I was desirous of presenting her Majesty with these two studs, and that not daring to offer them myself, I adopted this means of inducing her to accept them' " (*TM*, 221). As he claims the two studs, Richelieu ensures their separation from the twelve others and reestablishes the law of the ONE that the queen's infidelity had threatened. But this prudent and gallant escape route puts the cardinal in an awkward position: by leaving the Law's service, Richelieu espouses the cause of cuckoldry, thereby becoming an accomplice of the unfaithful queen, an accomplice of the English foe, and above all an accomplice of the king, who, reassured by his minister, will now happily hold his head high under the horns his wife has put on him.

Excess, Interest, Remainders

Richelieu's maneuver casts the two studs into otherness: they are no longer part of the original gift-pledge or of the system that links the royal couple. The two studs, offered by the king to the queen and, in turn, by the queen to her lover, stolen by Milady, handed over to the cardinal, and returned to the queen, who wants no part of them, seem neutralized. They are in excess.

Yet, what does "in excess" mean? Irreducibly present, the studs cannot simply vanish to remedy this excess. Their materiality, their thingness proves most embarrassing. When a thing is evicted from a system, can it cease to be a thing? Moreover, having become a sign, having acquired values, can it be simply expelled and return to being just a thing? If the "place" is the system, can an object-become-sign return elsewhere? Could the studs, for one, be *elsewhere,* that is, outside the Law that claims to establish their topology? But aren't the studs by definition always elsewhere in relation to this topology? The narration leaves no doubt: it is when they are elsewhere that they are best "in their place," or rather in their nonplace: for a rightful place is assigned by the Law, but in *The Three Musketeers* the Law itself no longer occupies its rightful place; deceived, cuckolded, multiplied, thrown off center, the Law long ago renounced the principle of identity. When objects circulate and signify, *the Law becomes difference.*

There can be no place (*topic*) in the narrative. Consequently there can be no elsewhere. Once the diegetical circumstances have allocated a semiotic value to an object, nothing may neutralize that value. Can we picture Richelieu cavalierly answering the king: "Sorry, your Majesty, I made a mistake. Since the queen has her twelve studs, these diamond studs must belong to someone else"? Although in excess, these studs must inevitably be linked to the others. Richelieu may have added a gallant pirouette to the dance of the diamonds, but ultimately he must recognize sheepishly that neither power, nor the subject, nor the Law may master values: the two studs that were to clinch his victory will ironically have sealed his disgrace.

Is this to say that the excess has been neutralized? Richelieu's conciliatory gesture may have explained the two extra studs to the king, but this explanation only repeated the question: while the king asks how there can be fourteen studs, *since there should be only twelve,* the cardinal echoes that there cannot be fourteen (his are "others"), *since there should be only twelve!* Richelieu's lie purports to reestablish order—if need be, at the expense of truth—in order to divert the threat of the Law (which has no use for the irregularities of excesses); to this end he tries to falsify the semiotic value of the studs (by claiming them) and, in so doing, admits his failure. Thus he adds "failure" and "lie" to the values that the studs have acquired on their track. Richelieu's last turn of the screw has brought back harmony to the royal household. It has not, however, resorbed fourteen into one. For the queen and for the cardinal, the studs make but an odd set: ten are a token of the queen's love for Buckingham (and, as if crossed out but still visible, of her submission to the king), two counterfeit studs bear witness to Buckingham's love for the queen, and two stray studs to Richelieu's discomfiture. We should add to these values the queen's unexpected victory. Above all, we should add the irony and the pleasure with which the queen, the reader, and even the cardinal view the blind contentment of the king and the thwarting of the Law. There lies the *quotient* of an operation prevented by its scattered remainders (twelve, two, ten, or fourteen—we can no longer count them) from ever being resorbed into unity.

I must emphasize that this operation does not end in a neat "restitution" that would save the queen's honor. Indeed, it is scarcely a question of her fidelity, and the interested parties (except, of course, the king) have no illusions about her "honor." Rather, the affair of the diamond studs concerns the Law represented (and betrayed) by the king. The Law, caught up in *presence,* has neither taken note of the disappearance of the studs nor come to grips with their "restitution." The Law—that is, unicity—has remained outside the story. The studs, although under the scrutiny of the Law, have nonetheless kept their atopic character. Ultimately, because of their proliferation, their values remain unsayable. Hence the pleasure of six generations of readers who have contributed to making *The Three Musketeers* (and in particular the affair of the diamond studs) one of the most widely read texts in French literature; hence also the reluctance of critics to admit *The Three Musketeers* into the canon of great works.[16] We shall then say with Barthes that "it is obvious that the pleasure of the text is scandalous: not because it is immoral, but because it is '*atopic.*' "[17]

On Third Parties: Marcel Mauss

I have deferred until now the discussion of d'Artagnan. *The Three Musketeers* undeniably follows the pattern of a *Bildungsroman:* a young provincial lands in Paris, where, more or less educated in the ways of the world by his adventures, he succeeds in making his mark in the adult world (the capital), which recognizes him as one of its own (the lieutenancy in the musketeers). Although absent from the title, d'Artagnan is no less the major character of the novel and the primary link for many disparate elements of the narrative. Who is d'Artagnan? Surprisingly, we know very little about him: he has no past, no secrets, no distinct features (he is but an impetuous and caddish swashbuckler). How can a character so poorly defined take over the story? Among his exploits, this is surely not the least remarkable (all the more noticeable since each of the musketeers is characterized from the outset by his secret—of which d'Artagnan immediately becomes the depository).[18] To confine ourselves to this one episode, what role does he play in the affair of the queen's diamonds? He is obviously an outsider to the world of court intrigue. Could he be nothing more than a diegetical device, a vehicle transporting diamonds from one place to another following a model at once realistic (mimetic) and literary? Is such a function within the logic of signifying objects in circulation? This last question is particularly urgent for those who would attempt to track down (if not to normalize) the effects of the circulation of signs.

Force and Origin

This was precisely Mauss' goal. His essay opens with a question fraught with semiotic implications for all circulations of signs: "*In primitive or archaic types of society what is the rule of law and interest [la règle de droit et d'intérêt] whereby the gift received has to be repaid [est obligatoirement rendu]? What force is there in the thing given that compels the recipient to make a return?* We hope, by presenting enough data, to be able to answer this question precisely, and also to indicate the direction in which answers to cognate questions might be sought" (*Gift*, 1–2, modified trans., Mauss' emphasis).

This question is decidedly "theoretical" in that it masks the presuppositions on which it rests. Although it appears on the first page of the "Program" of *The Gift*, the cited question relies on previous choices, which taint its subsequent findings. Mauss writes that the thing received is necessarily (*obligatoirement*) returned. But in the section entitled "The Method Followed," Mauss candidly informs us that he has limited his study to cases chosen according to specific criteria: only those societies that exemplify the legal point of law of interest to him enter into *The Gift*.[19] Thus Mauss' theory owes its "obligatory" effect mostly to the circular principle of selection from which it stems: we are witnessing one more gesture of exclusion, which indicates that other primitive societies have been omitted, expressly because their prestations (or the documentation we have about their prestations) do not necessarily (*obligatoirement*) follow the pattern set out by the theory. This "method" of carving the "problem" out of the mass of social phenomena in order to institute it as a rule ("what is the *rule* of law?") appears debatable at best (all the more so since, like the peasant in the *fabliau,* Mauss "knows" from the outset that there is a system governing the apparently random details, which is to be inferred from the very same phenomena whose selection it determines). Moreover, the same law that governs the phenomenon also governs the difference ("What is the rule of law and of *interest* . . . ?"): it situates the principle of accumulation *within the homogeneity of a unique value, a unique system, and a unique law*—all of which is far from obvious.

Similarly, from the outset, Mauss attributes to the object a *force* that, in order to be generalized, and thus made into a law, must remain unique and invariable ("What force does the thing possess . . . ?"). This attribution illustrates the naïve metaleptic belief that repeated identical effects (the itinerary of the gift) must at all times correspond to the same cause (the so-called force), thus installing, at the heart of the system described by *The Gift*, a metaphysical construct—in contradiction with the empirical (inferring) method that Mauss claims to have adopted. In fact, since the "Conclusions" of *The Gift* will say little more, the logical and methodological foundations of *The Gift* come dangerously close to simply begging the question.

Moreover, this monolithic conception (*one* invariable force, *one* identical point of origin and of destination) rapidly reaches its limits in *The Gift*—notably when it has to account for subsequent displacements and substitutions of relays, that is, for the proliferation of places, values, and terms. In a system that purports specifically to examine the circulation of objects, such fluttering poses real problems. From this perspective, it is particularly illuminating to note the instances in which Mauss admits to experiencing difficulties and the manner in which he resolves them. For example, in commenting upon a document he finds of "capital" importance and where he sees the "key to the problem," Mauss emphasizes that although "surprisingly clear in most instances, [the document] *is obscure in one area: the intervention of a third party*,"[20] of a person stationed between the points of origin and of destination, not merely "accidentally" but "necessarily." Indeed, if the intervention of a third party is necessary, we must acknowledge another term (neither *giver* nor *recipient*), with which Mauss' system would have to reckon, as well as a series of exchange values that would permit the substitution of one object for another, of one *taonga* for another (but, Mauss cites the "gift" precisely as the moral alternative to the "exchange value" that regulates the circulation of commodities in modern society). Therefore Mauss must admit to an "obscurity," a clouding of the initial clarity of the terms of the monolithic system that his line of questioning has raised as both a problem and its solution.

If, as Mauss wishes, the gift, while able to pass through innumerable hands, owes its force to its original giver only (i.e., to his *hau*), what of the various other parties involved? If only the person offering and the person receiving the gift (or the clans they represent) are *in* the circuit, all others are necessarily "in excess" with regard to the original pledge, hence Mauss' perplexity when faced with his documents' insistence on these intermediaries and his haste to explain away the "obscurity," that is to say, once again to brush it aside:

> But to be able to understand this Maori lawyer we need only say: "The *tonga* and all strictly personal possessions have a *hau*, a spiritual power. You give me *taonga*, I give it to another, the latter gives me *taonga* back, since he is forced to do so by the *hau* of my gift; and I am obliged to give

this one to you since I must return to you what is in fact the product of the *hau* of your *taonga.*"

Interpreted thus not only does the meaning become clear, but it is found to emerge as one of the *leitmotifs* of Maori custom. The obligation attached to a gift itself is not inert. Even when abandoned by the giver, it still forms a part of him. (*Gift,* 9)

By making *all* the values reside in the initial transaction, to the exclusion of subsequent ones, Mauss neutralizes (excludes) all intermediaries. From then on, only the first gift counts, or, more precisely, only the first giver (since Mauss' semiotics, like Lacan's, insists on the centrality of the subject: "it still forms a part of *him*"). With this interpretative twist, Mauss sweeps aside the third parties, and with them, the "obscurity."

This explanation creates more problems then it resolves. If, as Mauss claims, we are dealing with a "system of total prestations" that includes "rituals, marriages, succession to wealth, community of right and interest, military and religious ranks and even games," where "all form part of *one* system" (*Gift,* 4), and if this system is at once synchronic and diachronic (children must answer to the debts of their parents), then it becomes impossible to isolate parts of series of exchanges and to determine the original gift. If each primitive is born into a universe where his tribe and his parents are *already* engaged in a "system of total prestations," any "initial" act that *he* does may well be, in fact, the repayment of a debt, the restitution of someone else's *hau*, thus a counterprestation rather than a prestation.[21] A giver may never know if he is a giver, receiver, or third party, if he is weaving his own story or vaguely participating in another's. Ultimately, in a system of total prestation that is at once socioeconomical and religious (thus governing all aspects of the life of an individual), everyone is simultaneously giver, receiver, and third party. Consequently, the thing in circulation will carry (or risks carrying) the mark of everyone's *hau*. On the other hand, lacking an assured point of origin, it must also lack an assured point of destination. Thus the series cannot be neatly closed; it will remain open-ended. Paradoxically, the elucidation of the obscurity has brought to light the contradiction between the system of total prestations and the guarantee or even the possibility that the gift may ever return to its "place of birth" (*foyer d'origine* [10]).

In fact, there exists a quadruple wager spread out over 1) the force of the object; 2) the homogeneity of interest and remainders; 3) the itinerary of the object; and 4) the third parties through whose hands it passes. (One finds here most of the stakes in the debate opposing Lacan and Derrida as well of those we have located in *The Three Musketeers*.) From a methodological viewpoint, it is significant that the symptom of the theory's discomfort proves an excess. The excess—the remainders, what the theory pushes aside points to the limits and to the weaknesses of the generalization. The third parties of Mauss and the remainders of Lacan (the letter left by the minister in the royal boudoir and the one Dupin leaves the minister) are the many entrenchments were alterity resists a homogeneous system. Similarly, in *The Three Musketeers* the third parties (d'Artagnan) or the remainders (the two studs—but which two?) will severely test the theories—hence our interest in them.

And what of d'Artagnan? Is he himself in excess, as a strictly Maussian reading would have it? Or, on the contrary, should we say with the "other Mauss" that d'Artagnan is at once a third party, giver, and receiver? Will he escape the fate of those who hold the diamonds and who become party to the *politique de l'autruiche* (in a Lacanian reading)? Will he then be able to neutralize his own position, as does Dupin, as does the psychoanalyst, "by equating it with the signifier most destructive of all signification, namely: money"? (*"Seminar,"* 68) And what of the diamond studs once they have passed through d'Artagnan's hands? What about their force (their semiotic value), their singularity, their identity? If so far each transaction has affected them, can they not bear the mark of d'Artagnan as they do those of the others, even if the young man remains outside the narrative necessity that motivates the diamonds' circulation?

Let us return to the moment when the cards are played. The queen believes that she is doomed. Madame Bonacieux offers to send her husband to Buckingham in order to bring back the studs. But as soon as she begins to discuss this with her husband, Madame Bonacieux realizes that in the meantime he has joined the service of the cardinal, so that she no longer dares tell him of the queen's secret and of her mission. At this point, d'Artagnan intervenes, all too pleased to offer his services to the woman of his desires. With old Bonacieux disqualified, d'Artagnan proposes to play a double role: messenger to the queen *and* substitute husband to the lovely Constance Bonacieux. Thus forks the line of displacement: from the point of view of the queen's misfortunes—the first signifying chain—d'Artagnan remains a "diamond vehicle," but in so doing, he imprints on the studs' value a second direction (that of his desire) and inscribes Madame Bonacieux in the chain of debtors.

From here on, d'Artagnan, no longer a simple emissary, turns out to be an element of doubling and interference. Like Dupin, he certainly "acts as a partisan of the lady concerned,"[22] but of which one? "Remember that you belong to the queen," Madame Bonacieux tells him as she says her good-byes, " '*To her and to you!*' cried d'Artagnan. 'Be satisfied beautiful Constance, I shall become worthy of her gratitude; but shall I likewise return worthy of your love?' " (*TM*, 188, modified trans.). "*To her*": the studs, returned to the queen, will be proof of the skills, the courage, and the devotion of the young man to his sovereign. "*And to you*": the same studs, still returned to the queen but, in fact, destined for the "beautiful Constance," will prove to her that all that human power could do he, too, would have done—at the risk of his life—in order to please his lady. Thus, as he accomplishes his mission, d'Artagnan will prove to be not a third party but rather a creditor of the two ladies.

On Creditors

It appears indeed that all involved in this affair consider themselves to be in debt to the young man. The queen, for example, summons d'Artagnan, offers him her hand to kiss, and places a ring in his hand. As for Constance, she finally grants a first rendezvous to d'Artagnan. (We should note that these repayments are not interchangeable: one can scarcely imagine d'Artagnan overjoyed at respectfully and furtively kissing Constance's hand, nor can we imagine a rendezvous in a secluded house with the queen. In each case, the semiotic values attached to the object at given moments of its itinerary in its own chain offer the measure of the repayment.)

The case of Buckingham deserves special attention. The year is 1627, and France is more or less at war with England, so any commerce with the enemy is an act of high treason. We also remember that a gift (a gift of a thing or of a service) is at once an agonistic *and* a unifying operation, a declaration of war *and* an alliance.[23] Such is the case, for example, in the following passage:

> "And now," resumed Buckingham, looking earnestly at the young man, "how shall I ever acquit myself of the debt I owe you?"
> D'Artagnan blushed up to the whites of his eyes. He saw that the duke was searching for a means of making him accept something, and the idea that the blood of his friends and himself was about to be paid for with English gold was strangely repugnant to him.
> "Let us understand each other, my Lord," replied d'Artagnan, "and let

us make things clear beforehand in order that there may be no mistake. I
am in the services of the king and queen of France, and form part of the
company of M. des Essart, who, as well as his brother-in-law, M. de Tré-
ville, is particularly attached to their Majesties. What I have done, then,
has been for the queen, and *not at all for your Grace*. And still further, it is
very probable I should not have done anything of this, had it not been to
make myself agreeable to someone who is my lady, as the queen is yours."
(*TM*, 213–14)

D'Artagnan's embarrassed response is full of contradictions: I am in
the service of the king and queen (but, in this case, to serve one is not to
serve the other); I have done all I can for the queen (and the king?); I
would have done nothing for the queen if I had not done everything for
Constance (and the queen?). Embarrassment of d'Artagnan, of Dumas,
of the narrative? Let us remark that, contradictions notwithstanding,
one element persists: behind each new reason one must read the "other
reason," that which all of d'Artagnan's efforts tend to neutralize: I have
done all for the king/not at all for your Grace; all for the queen/not at
all for your Grace; all for des Essarts and Tréville/not at all for your
Grace; all for my lady/not at all for your Grace. However, lifting a debt
is more easily said than done. D'Artagnan's confused protest calls our
attention to the facts that the studs have passed through Buckingham's
hands (and that he, too, like all good ostriches, has had his tail feathers
plucked); more importantly, it calls our attention to the fact that
d'Artagnan cannot accomplish his mission without compromising him-
self and contracting a sort of alliance with the ennemy. All his Gascon
casuistry will not erase the effects of such a compromise, just as no theo-
retical contortions could erase the effects of a speech act (see Merimée's
"Venus of Ille" in chap. 5).[24] In the end, d'Artagnan will accept a pres-
ent from the Englishman, but, with his casuistry at the ready, he will
still try to wriggle out of the logic of the gift: as Buckingham offers him
four horses equipped for the upcoming campaign, and as he intends to
use them with his musketeer friends in the struggle against the English,
he counts on blood to rinse away every stain. The story comes back at
him to prove his error: all of his friends lose their horses in more or less
absurd circumstances, even before using them, as if each felt pressed to
get rid of a horse that had become a pledge of what is nearly treason.

It is as if the narrative, unable to allow the implications of a chain of
obligations with England for its supposedly blameless heroes, were
doing all in its power to scramble the value of "horse." Each horse ends
up having a price, but the narrative seems to dare the reader to deter-
mine its value. Porthos, for one, gave his horse away: " 'Gave him?'

cried d'Artagnan. 'My God, yes, gave, that is the word,' said Porthos; 'for the animal was worth at least one hundred and fifty louis, and the stingy fellow only gave me eighty' " (*TM*, 306). Aramis made an even worse deal: " 'That means I have just been duped—sixty louis for a horse which by the manner of his gait can do at least five leagues an hour' " (*TM*, 304). Sixty louis? Eighty? One hundred twenty? What on earth is the value (not the price) of these horses? The question is still harder to answer if one considers Athos' manner of disposing of d'Artagnan's horse: he lost it in a game. In fact, he won it back and lost it again so many times and bet it against so many values (the queen's diamond, one harness, then two harnesses, Grimaud split into ten parts, Planchet, etc.[25]) that he wound up nullifying all values. Ultimately, a horse is worth—a roll of the dice.

Thus, if there were neutralization, it would in no way be a function of money: in *The Three Musketeers* money proves a rather capricious value, subject to the changing semiotic values that punctuate its circulation. It would be tempting to see chance as a neutralizing factor, if it were not that even chance cannot stop the slipping and sliding of the retributions. At the end of the episode, d'Artagnan places his bets: "the two harnesses either against one horse or a hundred pistoles at your choice" (*TM*, 301).[26] A lucky roll of the dice. And what does d'Artagnan choose, d'Artagnan who was so attached to the horse? The one hundred pistoles. Why? Because Athos convinces him that the "good golden louis" (303) will be more useful than the horse in the quest for Constance Bonacieux. In the final analysis, he exchanges the horse for the young lady.

But in the *autruiche* game or in that of the prestations, he who wins, loses. The series cannot close as Mauss and Lacan would have it. The exchanges do not neutralize one another: success conceals a failure. D'Artagnan will leave behind his most cherished feather; he will not see Constance until she is on her deathbed, poisoned by Milady, who has not forgiven the young man for the defeat he inflicted upon her in the affair of the diamonds. Ultimately, his victory in the affair of the diamond studs would have caused Constance's death. And the game goes on.

Itineraries and Third Parties

D'Artagnan, an outsider at the start of the affair of the diamonds, would have doubled its logic and made it play on two levels. Creditor of the queen, creditor of Buckingham despite himself, creditor of Richelieu despite all common sense,[27] and especially, creditor of Madame

Bonacieux, the winner on the evening of the royal ball is indeed d'Artagnan. In a first chain (already second in terms of the queen's love affair) the young man has diverted to his advantage the diffuse and deferred values of the studs. The queen's victory is his deed: it is the pledge he offers Madame Bonacieux. As the queen displays her diamonds, Madame Bonacieux remains no less their primary recipient. Thus, to these displacements and divisions, we should add those of destination, or rather, those of recipients or addresses. *The itinerary leading to a destination opens up at the same time another path, which in turn negates the uniqueness of the initial destination.* In so doing, a second chain takes shape in which the earlier winner finds himself the loser according to a *politique de l'autruiche* that nothing can neutralize, where no one can "read his hand and leave the table on time to avoid disgrace" ("Seminar," 72), where only the arbitrariness of the end point of a piece of fiction can stop the game.

In short, our reading has focused on the sign or, rather, on the *object-become-sign in the course of a series of transactions and displacements.* From this point on, the story is but a series of effects resulting from the circulation of the object and the changes in its values. But no extratextual rule controls or predicts the slips, bifurcations, proliferations, and expansions of values that punctuate this circulation. The narrative gives a decisive nudge at the start, and the values are flung about and scattered throughout the text, never to be recovered by the story, the subject, or the Law.

Conclusion

I would like to take the time to anticipate some possible objections to my approach to and use of this episode. The two major points I foresee are closely related; they read more or less as follows: 1) we cannot compare the episode of the diamond studs with the purloined letter (and by extension, criticize Lacan) since there is a major difference between objects, which can lack any meaning (what does a rock "mean"?), and letters, which by definition carry a message; and 2) unlike words, objects exist independently of their semantics and semiotics. We can speak of an object *and/or* of its meaning and distinguish between the two. Conversely, words *must* have a meaning, as Saussure's analogy with the two sides of a sheet of paper shows so convincingly and elegantly; therefore we cannot speak of the circumstances in which they acquire a meaning, as we did in our analysis of the studs.

These charges are serious and would seem to invalidate my reading of *The Three Musketeers,* let alone my plea to include semiotic values in any kind of semantics. In anticipating these possible objections and attempting to quell their menace, I do not so much hope to clear my reading of charges of sloppiness as to act on the conviction that these objections rely in fact on distinctions that this study disavows and that the elucidation of their irrelevance will not only further explain my conception of the relation of semiotics to semantics but also conclude my enquiry.

Letters: Content and Force

The temptation is indeed strong to distinguish between objects and letters. Theoretically, an object can have a semiotic value of zero. It can "mean nothing," fulfill no function, claim no value, and content itself with an indefinite existence. In a text this is what Barthes has called *effet de réel,* the deficiency of the signified that benefits the category of the *réel.*[28] This is clearly not the case with a letter, which rests on a convention (correspondence) and presupposes an entire system (communication): a letter not written or addressed cannot be one. We can say as much about a blank letter, which would convey no message, or one whose content would be encoded in such a way that no one could decipher the message or even know for sure if there really was one. As such, a letter escapes the zero value. As soon as a letter appears in a text, it evokes the convention "correspondence" and the system "communication" and enters into the play of specific contextual values. More importantly for our reading, a letter is by definition loaded with a content, a message. While the semiotic values of an object do not overstrike any semantics that may already exist, those of a letter must always deal with a message. In "The Purloined Letter," if the compromising letter said nothing that could designate the queen as its addressee, it would be of no interest to the minister.[29] Similarly, if the letter had been a request for assistance or charity, the minister would have cut a sorry figure. The letter must then procure, on the one hand, a referential anchor (sender and receiver) and, on the other, a content. In addition to this, both these aspects must enter into a relationship with the circulation and the "relays" of the letter (it could, for example, fall into the hands of an illiterate, in which case we would have a very different story).

"The Purloined Letter" satisfies these elementary conditions since "the disclosure of the document to a third person, who shall be nameless, would bring in question the honor of a personage of most exalted station; and this fact gives the holder of the document an ascendancy over the illustrious personage whose honor and peace are so jeopardized" (Poe 441–42). "Bring in question" and "give an ascendancy" are effects of the values. To be more specific, they are illocutionary and perlocutionary forces. Whatever we take the letter's content to be, it functions in the narrative like a speech act. Its content has interacted with the referential circumstances that govern its circulation, with the result that the letter can now "bring in question" and "give an ascendancy." These effects achieved, the content of the letter is no longer important: the queen does not so much fear what it says (she has known it all along), but what it can *do* in the right circumstances (in the hands of her husband, for instance). What matters is not the propositional content(s) of the letter but its force.

A comparison with speech acts will elucidate this last point. If, on a cold, windy day, I stare at an open window and say to my host, "Brrr. It's cold in here," upon which she rushes apologetically to close the window, I may assume that the illocutionary force of my implicit request has overstruck its constative content: I was in fact asking her to close the window (I can hardly imagine her answering flatly, "You're right, it is indeed cold in here," without further ado). I could have achieved the same result with different contents. I could have asked sarcastically, "Do you always keep the window open on cold winter days when you have company?"; or simply, "Will you please close the window?"; or, playing stupid, "Is this window broken or something?"; or humorously, "This window is begging to be closed," etcetera. I could even have embraced myself silently and shivered obviously. The variety of options makes it clear that my request cannot be reduced to its constative content. Once it is understood by my host as a request to alleviate my discomfort by closing the window, the content of the utterance of my choice has exhausted its usefulness. In other words, once the constative content gives way to its force, it loses its semantic function. Hereafter, for all purposes, it is void. What remains is the force of my request.

Similarly, once the content of the compromising letter has brought into question the honor of the lady and given an ascendancy over her to its future readers, this content becomes irrelevant: it no longer functions *diegetically* (do we really care if Poe's queen is guilty of infidelity or high treason?). It is null and void. This shifting of the semantic focus from the message to the semiotic values explains how Lacan and Derrida, while both centering their readings on the importance of the letter, held opposite positions as to its content: Lacan claimed that the content was unknown (the letter is a pure signifier), while Derrida contended that we did know all we needed to know about this content. They were simply considering the letter at different moments of its trajectory, before (Derrida) and after (Lacan) we learn of the content's illocutionary and perlocutionary forces. The message is there at all times, but *before,* its assertoric (constative) force prevails, and *after,* its illocutionary and perlocutionary. This is to say not that the content of the letter does not matter, but that it matters only inasmuch as it interacts with the other factors that we have subsumed generically under *semiotic values.*

Note that *out* of context—to the extent that we can abstract contexts—the letter remains "the letter that it is," as Lacan claims. Our perspective, however, is *in* context: we are focusing on the chain of semantic displacement that results from the juxtaposition and entwinement of meaningful units (words, letters, object-become-signs, etc.). Such a chain of displacements is what we commonly call a narrative. Even the fleeting diegetic moment at which the content becomes perlocutionary and loses it primary constative value does not enjoy a privileged status. Out of context it is null and void (if we had the letter in hand but knew nothing about its writer or its addressee, would it still compromise the queen? As the example of the incident in *La Princess de Clèves* shows, it can compromise any number of "innocent" people, depending more on its relays than its content); but in context (i.e., placed within the plot of a story and in relation to the receiver's and the sender's referential anchorage), it becomes *one* of the factors that can unleash a series of effects and give rise to values (a handkerchief can do just as much, as in the case of *Othello*). Thus in Poe's "Purloined Letter" the message is only one of the thousand and one ways to compromise a lady, one circumstance among many at work in the forming of semiotic values (which explains why we do not care if her crime is infidelity or high treason, as long as it ensures the illocutionary "put in question" and the perlocutionary "give an ascendancy").

Let us take a second example: in *The Three Musketeers* a letter signed by Richelieu circulates:

Dec. 3, 1927

It is by my order and for the good of the State that the bearer of this letter has done what he has done.

"Richelieu"
(*TM,* 443)

Since this letter is a legal document, it is not effective unless the signature designates an authority, someone who is in a position to delegate power to "the bearer of this letter" in accordance with the Law that confers this authority upon him. The bearer may be anyone, which, at least theoretically, should permit a referential slippage without harming the efficacy of the letter. Thus, if we restrict ourselves to its content, the letter quickly exhausts its use-value (this value is the equivalent to the oo code name in the James Bond series: the right to kill). However, the circumstances in which it circulates affect it greatly: if we add that Richelieu gives this letter to Milady, who has asked him for it in order to assassinate d'Artagnan with impunity, as payment for the planned killing of Buckingham; if we add further that d'Artagnan learns of this conversation and manages to take possession of the document; and if we add finally that d'Artagnan, whom Richelieu accuses of the murder of Milady, presents this same letter to the cardinal (who tears it up on the spot), we must come to the conclusion that the content of the letter has lost its efficacy, while its semiotic values have accrued with each transaction: it is doubtful, given the circumstances of its return to Richelieu, that the letter clears d'Artagnan. The safe-conduct is rather a reminder to the cardinal that, having been the first to abuse the power entrusted to him by the Law, he no longer has the right to exercise it. Ultimately, the sum of the circumstances that the letter evokes accuses Richelieu himself of assassination while pointing to his blindness (or stupidity) about his agents. This is an extreme case in which the series of semiotic values to which the letter is submitted obliterates its content. Richelieu may tear it up without any loss for the story: the content as such is no longer functional. Only the *values* to which this content has given rise matter.

In this sense, despite the semantics of the message, a letter and an object are functionally comparable. We will thus conclude that, in the context of our discussion, the distinction between letter and object ultimately collapses: both motivate the story according to the successive semiotic values to which they give rise, *no matter what paths may have led to these values*. The content of the letter is only one of the many possible paths; it does not enjoy a privileged position or function.[30]

Words versus Objects

The same argument holds for the second objection, concerning the difference between words and objects. This objection simply enlarges the one raised by the reducibility or irreducibility of objects and letters to objects and language in general. There is no denying that, when they are thrown into circulation, words, unlike objects, already have a meaning, without which they would not be words but sheer noises (just as a letter already has a content). Whether this meaning comes about in relation to a reference, as it does for Frege, or negatively, as a function of differences, as Saussurean linguistics would have it, is secondary. The two schools converge on one essential point: speakers must agree on a minimal fixed semantic charge for each expression, if communication is to ensue. That this assumption raises enormous difficulties has been, I hope, amply demonstrated (variations such as "value," "use," "context," "force," etc. have tried to rescue the theories from the straits of absurd rigidity, but none of them has ever attempted to deny that meaning distinguishes between noise and language and that to be perceived as meaningful, the noise has to have the *same* meaning for all people in a specific community). In the founding texts (and this is what makes them so admirable), the moment when the "theory" encounters resistance is marked by what Lyotard calls a philosophical move: Saussure introduces "value" and expresses doubts, and Frege delineates *Vorstellung,* the former concept to become the most revolutionary and fruitful aspect of Structuralism (despite its obvious and—except for the quickly resolved quarrel over the arbitrariness of the sign—unnoticed clash with the theory concerning the nature of signs), and the latter to be awkwardly expelled from the theory.

I am prepared to concede to Saussure that all of *langue* is present and at work with and in every single pragmatic utterance (*parole*) and that differences and oppositions work horizontally to create meaningful units; there are, however, two important distinctions to be made. First, not all of *langue* is present to the same degree or contributes equally to the production of meaning achieved by each utterance. In a sentence containing neither dogs nor wolves, the difference between dogs and wolves, essential though it may be in the animal kingdom, comes to bear only remotely on the actual utterance in which they do not occur. (Of course, this is one of the reasons that motivated Saussure to privilege *langue* over *parole*.) Second, *langue* is not the only factor in elaborating the general signification an expression may have at a given time since contexts act as subsystems and displace the value assigned to terms by *langue* alone. I am therefore not disputing the fact that each utterance (*parole*) entertains a certain rapport with *langue;* but to advance that each utterance's signification is confined to this rapport—as Structuralism, Poststructuralism, and the various doctrines and practices marked by Saussure's influence still hold—is to make a spurious generalization, one that all the stories we have examined bluntly rebut. As an alternative, I have suggested that we speak of *semantic aim* (I might have used the expression *the semantic intention of language* if it were not for the psychological overtones of *intention* and the literary discussion of the intentional fallacy). We may say instead that while in some respects language *aims* at producing meaning semantically—that is to say, horizontally within closed and homogeneous systems in a strictly structuralist manner—other factors (namely, its deictic aim and its semiotic values) hamper or at least risk hampering this tendency.

Similarly, I fully endorse Frege's assumption that expressions and language in general entertain an indexical (vertical) rapport with non-linguistic elements and that the sense of an expression is not normally subject to radical alterations. But to limit a theory of meaning to this relation and discard all other factors would be preposterous. Frege, who advocated just such a limitation for the benefit of the Pythagorean theorem, found out nonetheless that he had to delineate a different kind of semantics (*Vorstellung*) that worked horizontally (in context) and blurred the vertical rapport he so sought. That he chose to wrest *Vorstellung* from his theory of signs was largely dictated by his mathematical standpoint; even so, he was the first to recognize that despite his efforts, he would never be able to eliminate the elements he connected with *Vorstellung* from language, or even from his own metalanguage—as his numerous, woeful footnotes illustrate so clearly.

Language exceeds the usefulness it may have for a mathematician, however. Literary criticism as well as a true philosophy of language have no reason to confine their inquiry to the kind of language that mathematicians and logicians may wish to use or define. They need not dismiss *Vorstellung*. Clearly, some semiotic stability is needed (Derrida's principle of iterability): in daily parlance, sense leads to reference and language takes aim at objects. But we must keep in mind that this aiming is not immune to failure, misfires, or misses, mostly because the deictic aim is not indifferent to the pull of the semantic aim and the semiotic values.

In theory, since the deictic and the semantic aims pull meaning in different directions, they have to negotiate their hold over meanings, to find their vector—all the more reason to fear misfires and misses. This is all very hypothetical, however. In reality, since expressions occur in contexts (conventions and circumstances) and contexts spread out indefinitely in a ripple-like manner, each force must negotiate with an infinite number of semiotic values. That the signification of an utterance is the "quotient" of such operations, does not imply that they coexist in harmony. On the contrary, as a signification of sorts emerges from the conflict of aims, forces, and values, various elements escape the monolithic attempt: they remain in excess, at once irrelevant and subversive, out of bounds and yet significantly affecting the game. As these remainders scatter, they prevent signification from being resorbed into unity.

Whatever meaning a term may have had *before* it was placed in such a context, and whether it had come to that meaning horizontally or vertically, remains an academic argument. Once this meaning circulates out of the taxonomy of dictionaries and into a speech situation, like the content of the letter it enters yet another operation, this time within the specific subsystem created by its context and its inescapable semiotic values.

Semantics and Finitude

The two objections I have cited stem from the same assumption that meaning, value, content, etcetera, are finite: they can be paraphrased, summarized, encapsulated, codified, regulated, obtained, negated, undone, and so on. These assumptions rest on the subordination of semantics to teleology. Our reading of the episode of the queen's diamonds has focused on the relationship between the *telos* and the signifying object in circulation. *The Gift* and "The Seminar on 'The Purloined Letter'" have provided the teleogical perspective, while the literary texts have enacted the very same displacements that the teleologies claim to legislate. In the four texts objects circulate only to return augmented to their point of origin. Lacan and Mauss theorize and generalize upon this initial aspect: the object *must* return to its *own* place. More importantly, they insist on analyzing this circular itinerary in terms of the Law (Lacan: "If he has succeeded in returning the letter to its proper course, it remains for him to make it arrive at its address. And that address is in the place previously occupied by the King, since it is there that it would re-enter *the order of the Law*." Mauss: "We note the circulation of objects side by side with the circulation of persons and *rights*"). But it is not enough simply to note that in these two descriptions the itinerary of the object is predetermined; we could say as much for most of the components of the successive transactions. At the source of these normative predeterminations lies the perception of what constitutes an "object": both Mauss' system of total prestations and Lacan's constitution of the subject as an effect of the signifier require that the object remain self-identical in a way that transcends its materiality— the number and the nature of its relay points notwithstanding (this was also Ogden and Richards' conception of the object of a science, a presupposition that determined their criticism of Saussure). Without the transcendental stability that inhabits such an object, one could conceive neither of the system of total prestations nor of the triads of the *autruiche,* nor of "the decisive orientation which the subject receives from the itinerary of a signifier." All the other invariables derive from this perception of the object: if there is a sign with only one value (or one set of values), there may be a place where this sign *is* (or from which it is missing) and where laws or subjects take form in accordance with a tropological model. Granted the model's finite limits, there might then even be overflows (excesses) whose neutralization would fall to the legislator, or in our case to the "theorist."

This is the point at which Lacan and Mauss join hands with the other "theories" we have examined. As different as theories may be at first glance, it is in their nature to delineate a field of application and a law that the "theoretician" may exercise within the field of application. And yet our examination of philosophical and literary texts alike has shown that the measure of the success of a theory is precisely not this carefully selected and mostly self-serving field of application; it is the force and doings of the elements that the theory was not able to integrate: the remainders. Hence the important contribution and testing power of the literary text: it simultaneously denounces, enacts, exploits, and thwarts the essential, founding, indispensable, and surreptitious gesture by which a "theory" distinguishes its outside from its inside.

Afterword

None of them was making a mistake except where he was putting forth a theory.

W I T T G E N S T E I N

I do not believe I have refuted a single theory in this book. Refutation had no part in my project. A refutation is serious and global: it denies any value to the wrong proposition. A refuted theory is a ready-to-be-shelved theory; it may still present some morbid interest to the historian of theories but not to other theoreticians. It is survived by its replacement, a "better" theory, awaiting its own refutation—and the game goes on. Nor do I deny the importance of "theories." Delineating fields, objects, questions, norms, answers, and even laws is a necessary part of thinking. I do advocate two positions, however.

The first point concerns the status of theory. Theories, though indispensable, should not be conceived as normative and rigid constructs for fear of hampering thinking. The more successful a "theory," the more rigid it is—and the faster it turns into a hindrance. I grant that we need to account for the world around us, precisely because we are subject to arbitrariness and to a radical heterogeneity, a situation we find unbearable. And yet understanding often means no more than connecting the dots, relating disparate elements and integrating them in one *Gestalt* and one narrative of sorts. This process brings to mind the wonder of our forebears as they looked at the stars and found them to represent their heroes. On the one hand, like our ancient forebears, we risk writing into the world the very same story we wish it to tell us. On the other hand, contenting ourselves with connecting the dots poses that these dots are in their "proper places," forever fixed and identical to themselves; that the world we are attempting to understand is spread before our eyes, begging to be deciphered. While there is some truth in each of these assumptions, we cannot adopt either, or both, without at least some reservations. As they unfold their explanation of the world (and I take theories of language to do just that), "theories" should examine not only the stars but the very gesture by which they have come, first, to designate them, and second, to interspace these stars with narratives to masterfully merge representation and storytelling. This reflexive query encapsulates Lyotard's (and my own) philosophical approach. That it depends heavily on the theoretical project upon which it reflects is evident, but I would like it to be equally evident that, without this philosophical moment, a strict "theory" is but a heuristic fiction suffering from amnesia; a fiction taking itself seriously; an ape making a report to its mirror image.

My second point concerns the status of the literary text. Literature is not "smarter" than theory, as our romantic heritage might lead us to believe; nor does the literary text "know" more than the theoretical one. The questions of "smarts" and knowledge are irrelevant to the comparison of the two. The difference between the literary and the theoretical texts is circumstantial: they use the same language and submit to the same linguistic rules and conventions but occur in different sets of circumstances governed by different contextual conventions. The literary text benefits from a freedom unknown to the theoretical text: it may overtly make up its stories; it may overtly borrow or plagiarize stories; it may leave gaps, unresolved questions, ambiguities, double entendres; it need not correspond to any "state of affairs"; it may even contradict itself. "Literature" is what happens when the exclusively mimetic and deictic conceptions of language best represented by Plato and Kant fail; when discourse exceeds its indexical force; when the play and the playfuless of forces is fully highlighted and exploited; when the power of repression illustrated by amnesia reflects upon itself. Literature and true philosophy can even fail and take pride in their fall (all the stories we have examined, as well as the most productive among the philosophical and linguistic texts [Saussure, Frege, and Austin], exemplify unresolved failures). If we are ever to bridge the gap between philosophy and literature, we must turn not to messages or "theories" but to methods; more specifically yet, to performances. While "theories" try to reduce their language to its deictic aim and assertoric force, literature plays down the assertoric force (as does Austin by *abstracting* and *focusing*), engages other forces into its semantic aim, and, above all, revels in its failure to convert these factors into one neatly packaged set of propositions.

As students of literature we thus face a double task: we must understand both "theoretically" and theoretically *how* language—any language—works (in principle *and* in practice, as *langue* and as *parole,* out of context and in context, indexically and semantically). We must keep in mind that it is only when the first paraphrasing and "theorizing" task brings us to despair (and I suggest yielding to this despair rather than papering it over with yet more "theories") that we cross the threshold to literature and true (reflexive) philosophy. Perhaps paradoxically, only then can we truly appreciate how language *works,* only then can we glimpse at the dazzling performance of language and broach anew the first, forever incomplete task.

Appendix

"The Little Mouse in the Rag Basket"

Next I will tell you about a silly peasant who took a wife, and knew nothing of the pleasure that came with holding a woman in his arms, because he had never tried it. But his wife already knew everything that men know how to do, because, to tell the truth, the priest did with her as he wished whenever he wished and as it pleased him.

When the day came that she married her lord, the priest said to her: "Sweet friend, take no offense, I want to do it with you, if you please, before the peasant gets to you."

And she said, "Gladly, sir. I dare not refuse you. But come quickly and without delay when you know that the time has come before my husband does the man with me, for I do not want to lose your grace."

Thus the plan was undertaken.

After this it was not long before the peasant went to bed. But she esteemed him little as a giver of pleasure and joy. He took her in his arms and embraced her roughly for he did not know how to do otherwise, and flattened her out completely under him. She who had put up a good defense said: "What do you want to do?"

"I want," he replies, "to get up my prick. Afterwards I'll fuck you if ever I can and if I can find your cunt."

"My cunt," she is quick to answer, "my cunt you won't find."

"Where is it then? Don't hide it from me!"

"Sir, since you want to know, I'll tell you where it is, on my soul. It is hidden at the foot of my mother's bed where I left it this morning."

"By Saint Martin," says he, "I'll go get it."

Without further delay, he goes to look for the cunt. But the city where the neighborhood was in which his wife had been born was farther than a league away.

While the peasant was going to get the cunt, the chaplain got into his bed with joy and delight and did whatever it pleased him to do. But I have not finished telling how the peasant was tricked. A more foolish fellow was never seen.

When he arrived at his mother-in-law's home, he said, "My dear lady, your daughter sends me here for her cunt that she hid, she said, at the foot of your bed."

The woman reflected a little, and in thinking about it realized that her daughter was deceiving him in order to play a dirty trick on him. Thereupon she goes into the bedroom, and finds a basket full of rags. Whatever she would have wanted to do with them, she cuts them up.

"I will give this basket to him."

Then he took the basket. But into the rags had gone, so deeply that it was completely covered up by them, a mouse, without a doubt.

Thus she gives the basket to him, and he immediately thrust it under his coat. He leaves her as quickly as possible to go back home.

Upon arriving on the heath, he makes an astonishing declaration: "By Saint Paul, I don't know," he says, "if my wife's cunt is awake or asleep, but by Saint Vol I would like to fuck it before arriving home if I weren't afraid it would get away from me on the way. I'll fuck it anyway, to know if what is said about it is true or not, that in cunt is a sweet and pleasant animal."

Now his prick raised its head and stands up straight as a lance. It springs into the rags and begins to ferret about. The mouse jumps out of the basket and runs away through the meadows. The peasant goes after it with great strides and at great speed. Thinking it will do something stupid he says:

"God! What a beautiful animal! In truth I think it has not yet been weaned, because it was born hardly any time ago. I clearly see that it is very small. I commend it to God the Father, the Son, and the Holy Spirit. I truly believe it is afraid of my prick. Yes, it was certainly afraid of it, by the eyes of God, when it was confronted with its black and red snout. Alas, I am convinced that it really was frightened by it. It will be a great loss if it dies! Holy Mary! It will be dead and drowned in the ditch, if it goes in. It has gotten its whole belly, back and sides wet. Stop, good Lord God, stop! What will I do if it dies?"

The peasant wrings his hands because of the mouse which is shrilling and squealing. Whoever saw it twist its lips and cheeks at the peasant would be reminded of a monkey's grin.

The peasant vainly cries: "Pretty cunt, sweet cunt, come back soon. I promise not to touch you again before returning home and turning you over to my wife, so you can get yourself out of the dew. People will get a good laugh out of this if it is known that you escaped from me. Ah! you will soon be drowned, pretty cunt, in such a dew. Come and get into my glove, I will carry you in my shirt."

All his efforts are in vain. He can call it as much as he wants, it still does not desire to return. Instead it disappears in the low grass. When he sees he has lost it, he becomes sad and thoughtful. Then he goes on his way and does not stop until he returns home.

Without a word of explanation, he sat down on a bench and started taking off his shoes. You know he was not at all happy.

His wife says to him: "Good sir, what is the matter? I don't hear you say a word. Aren't you well?"

"Me, no, lady," replies the peasant, who continues to take off his shoes and undress.

She lifts up the blankets and lets him get in bed. The peasant gets in beside her and lies down on his back. He does not say more than a monk to whom conversation is forbidden, but rather just lies beside her.

Seeing him mute and silent, she now says to him: "Sir, so you don't have my cunt?"

"Me, no, lady, no, no. It's too bad I ever even tried to get it because in trying I let it fall to the ground and now it is drowned in the meadows."

"Ah," she says, "you are making fun of me."

"Truly, lady," he replies, "I am not."

Then she takes him in her arms: "Sir," says she, "don't let it bother you. Undoubtedly it was afraid of you because it didn't know you. I believe you must have done something which displeased it. If you were holding it now, what would you do with it. Tell me."

"I would fuck it, by my faith! I would truly send it one which would knock its eye out, for it really made me angry."

She quickly replies to him: "Sir, it is now there between my legs. But I wouldn't want it to be uncomfortable even were I to receive (the city of) Etampes, since it has come back into your hands so sweetly and nicely."

The peasant stretches out his hand, takes it and says:

"I have it in my hands."

"Caress it well with your hands," she says, "so that it doesn't get away from you. Don't be afraid it will bite you. Keep a good hold on it so that it doesn't escape from you."

"I truly believe," he says, "that our cat, God keep him, would eat it if he met it."

Then he begins to fondle it until he feels that it is wet: "Alas! it is still soaked from the dew into which it fell!" the peasant says. "Ah, ah! How angry you made me today! But you will never be yelled at by me for being wet. Go rest and sleep now, I don't want to tire you further. You are fatigued from running about."

By means of this fable I want to teach that woman knows more than the devil, which you certainly know (already). You can gouge out both my eyes if I knowingly tell a lie. When she wants to trick a man, she deceives and confuses him more through her words alone than a man would do through outright trickery. Such is the conclusion I make for my fable: Let each man take care that his wife not make him a cuckold.

Translated by Lori Walters

Notes

1 Introduction

1. Since I shall refer to this *fabliau* throughout the book, I have appended its English translation by Lori Walters at the end.

2. In the French original, the wording and the rhyme ironically put into question this reduction: "*Après vos cont d'un vilain sot/Qui fame prist, et rien ne sot.*" Both verses end with "*sot*," but the first time it means "silly" and the second "knows," thus equating knowledge (or at least the kind of knowledge represented by the narrative voice) with stupidity.

3. See also: "Before my husband *does* the man with me" (*Ainz que mes sire l'ome face*), "What do you want to *do?*" (*Qu'est ce que volez faire?*), "The chaplain got into his bed with joy and *did* with her whatever it pleased him to do" (... *Et fit qanque li plot à faire*) "I believe you must have *done* something which displeased it" (*Et chose qui lo desplaisoit, Au mien cuidier, li faisiez*), "If you were holding it now, what would you *do* with it?" (*Et vos or lo tenoiez, Qu'an feroiez?*). Every time the verb *to do* appears, it is in the differential sexual context defining a man in relation to a woman.

4. Ferdinand de Saussure, *Course in General Linguistics*, edited by Charles Bally and Albert Sechehaye in collaboration with Albert Riedlinger. Wade Baskin trans. (New York: The Philosophical Library, 1959), 110.

5. My use of the term "semantic" is inspired by the French rather than the Anglo-American tradition. It evokes the ways in which expressions combine to compose complex thoughts, as well as any possible contaminations of meaning resulting from the juxtaposition of expressions in a sentence (or any length of combined sentences). It is therefore mostly syntagmatic.

6. This is not to say that every word must aim at an object. Philosophers are quick to point out that words such as *but, and,* and *not* do not designate objects; others designate either abstract entities or entities that are only partly "objective."

7. I am grateful to Frederick Tibbetts, who has called my attention to a passage in which Descartes makes a similar claim: "When I say that a body tends toward one direction, I do not wish the reader to imagine that it has, in itself, a thought or a will that makes it do so, but only that it is apt [*disposé*] to move in this direction; it may either really move that way or be prevented by some other body. It is truly in this last sense that I am using the word *to tend*, because it seems to signify [*il semble signifier*] some effort and that any effort presupposes some resistance." *The World or Treatise on Light*, chap. 12, translation mine.

8. The *fabliaux* often exploit the guaranteed comic effect of this tautological play. See, for example, *The King of England and the Jongleur of Ely*, in which, asked who he is, the poet replies "—Sire, I am the man of my lord.—Who is your lord?" asked the king.—My lady's baron, by faith.—Who is your lady please?—Sire, the wife of

my lord.—What is your name?—Sire, the same as the one who raised me.—And that one, what name did he have?—The same as mine, sire, by right" (quoted and translated by Howard Bloch, *The Scandal of the Fabliaux* (Chicago: University of Chicago Press, 1986), 14–15. See also Saussure's rationalization of this tautological procedure: "In a general way, 'to explain' [*expliquer*] is to bring back [*ramener*] to terms already known. And in linguistic conditions, to bring back to terms already known is necessarily to bring back to words; this follows from the fundamental law that there is no relation between the sound and the sense [*sens*]: every word being arbitrary, it follows that no explanation can be given; all that remains, then, is to bring the word back to others, which are themselves arbitrary." Quoted by Robert Godel, *Les Sources manuscrites du Cours de linguistique générale* (Geneva: Droz; Paris: Minard, 1957), 230. All translations from Saussure's writings are by Jon Delogu unless otherwise noted.

9. A similar effect can be found in *Alice in Wonderland,* as the mouse tells its story:

> Edwin and Morcar, the earls of Mercia and Northumbria, declared for him; and even Stigand, the patriotic archbishop of Canterbury, found it advisable—"
> "Found *what?*" said the Duck.
> "Found *it,*" the Mouse replied rather crossly: "of course you know what 'it' means."
> "I know what 'it' means well enough, when *I* find a thing," said the Duck: "it's generally a frog or a worm. The question is, what did the archbishop find?" (Lewis Carroll, *Alice's Adventures in Wonderland* [New York: Avenel Books, n.d.], 31, Carroll's emphasis).

10. Howard Bloch sees in this detachability a dismemberment which leads him to mention this *fabliau* as a variation on the theme of castration. See Bloch 74–75.

11. Jean-François Lyotard, *Le Différend* (Paris: Minuit, 1983), 12.

12. Since I intended to discuss Saussure's general philosophy of language rather than the more technical points of his linguistics, I have not mentioned or presented the very important work done in Western Europe, in particular the fine-tuning that the Prague Linguistics Circle and the school of Copenhagen contributed to the theory. Among the many excellent works on the history of modern linguistics, the reader may consult Gulio C. Lepschy, *A Survey of Structural Linguistics* (London: Faber & Faber, 1970); R. H. Robins, *A Short History of Linguistics* (London: Longmans, 1967); Georges Mounin, *La Linguistique du XXᵉ siècle* (Paris: Presses Universitaires de France, 1972).

13. I had intended to add two more chapters about Peirce and Wittgenstein that would have offered other ways out of the same impasse, but I came to realize that, in view of their complexity and their decisive contribution to the question of language and reference, these texts are best left for a separate study.

2   Saussure

1. Claude Lévi-Strauss, "L'Analyse structurale en linguistique et en anthropologie," *Word: Journal of the Linguistic Circle of New York* 1, no. 1 (April 1945): 33–53.

2. See François Wahl, ed., *Qu'est-ce que le structuralisme?* (Paris: Seuil, 1968), in which Ducrot, Todorov, Sperber, Safouan, and Wahl assess the new turn that Saussure's discoveries imprinted on linguistics, literature, anthropology, psychoanalysis, and philosophy. These essays were later published as separate books in the popular collection Points: Dan Sperber, *Le Structuralisme en anthropologie* (Paris: Seuil, 1973); Moustafa Safouan, *Le Structuralisme en psychanalyse* (Paris: Seuil, 1973); François Wahl, *Le Structuralisme: Philosophie* (Paris: Seuil, 1973); Tzvetan Todorov, *Poétique* (Paris: Seuil, 1973); Oswald Ducrot, *Le Structuralisme en linguistique* (Paris: Seuil, 1973).

3. Mostly in Maurice Merleau-Ponty, *Signes* (Paris: Gallimard, 1960), but already in his *Sens et Non-Sens* (Paris: Nagel, 1948).

4. Ferdinand de Saussure, *Course in General Linguistics*, ed. Charles Bally and Albert Sechehaye, in collaboration with Albert Riedlinger, trans. Wade Baskin (New York: Philosophical Library, 1959), xiv, hereafter cited as *Course*.

5. See "I found myself placed before a dilemma: either show [*exposer*] the subject in all its complexity and admit all my doubts, a procedure unfitting for an academic course that must be of testable material [*matière à examen*]. Or do something simplified, better adapted to an audience of students who are not linguists. But at each step I find myself stopped by these scruples." Notes of an interview by Gautier with Saussure, 6 May 1911, Robert Godel, *Les Sources manuscrites du Cours de linguistique générale de F. de Saussure* (Geneva: Droz; Paris: Minard, 1957), 13; hereafter cited as *SM*. Here and throughout this chapter, unless otherwise noted, all translations from the French are by Jon Delogu.

6. All emphasis is mine unless otherwise indicated.

7. Only F. Joseph's notes showed distinct variations from the others'. However, these differences seem to stem mostly from a lack of in-depth understanding of Saussure. Moreover, the notes written by Bally and Sechehaye in the margins of the manuscripts of Sechehaye's collation of the third course (Bibliothèque publique et universitaire de Genève, Mss. Cours univ. 432–33) indicate clearly that they disregarded Joseph's text whenever they found it in conflict with those taken by Dégallier and Mrs. Sechehaye.

8. Compare with the editors' account: "First, the task of criticism. For each course and for each detail of the course, we had to compare all versions and reconstruct F. de Saussure's thought from faint, sometimes conflicting hints" (*Course*, xiv).

9. Ferdinand de Saussure, *Cours de linguistique générale*, critical ed., ed. Rudolf Engler (Wiesbaden: Otto Harrassowitz, 1967), hereafter cited as E. For each quotation from Engler's edition, I use Roman numerals to indicate the course from which it comes (I, II, III) and an initial for the student whose notebook I am using (D for Dégallier, B for Boucharely, R for Riedlinger, G for Gautier, and C for Constantin). Arabic numerals indicate the notebook number, followed by a period and the page number; if the student filled only one notebook, the Arabic numeral indicates the page number. In this case (I R 1.47, E 317), the quotation comes from the first course, Riedlinger's first notebook, p. 47; the passage can be found in Engler's edition, p. 317. Angle brackets follow the practice adopted by Engler; they indicated either manuscript corrections or notes in the margins of the manuscripts.

10. See also in the same note "1° ⟨language is nothing more than⟩ a particular

case of the theory of Signs. But precisely on account of this fact alone it is already within the absolute impossibility of being a simple thing (nor a thing directly graspable by our intuition as to its manner of being [*dans sa façon d'être*]" [E 169). To refer to Saussure's manuscript notes kept at the Bibliothéque publique et universitaire de Genève in a file entitled "Notes de F. de Saussure," I use N followed by an arabic numeral and a page number. (The arabic numerals are used by the Saussurean archives to inventory Saussure's random notes written probably from 1897 to 1910.) When the Note is quoted in Engler's edition, I give its page number following E.

Saussure repeated this argument and alluded again to Whitney in the second course. A summary of these views can be found in the *Course*, 9–11; see in particular: "We can say that what is natural to mankind is not oral speech [*le langage parlé*], but the faculty of constructing a language [*langue*], i.e., a system of distinct signs corresponding to distinct ideas" (10).

11. See also Mrs. Sechehaye's version: "*Langue* [*la langue*] is a set of general facts, common to all languages [*les langues*]. *Langue* is that which one can observe in different languages [*dans les différentes langues*]" (III S 1.7, E 65, Sechehaye's emphasis).

12. This section does not attempt to present a panoramic view of the *Cours*'s reception. It only sketches out the reaction of a few critics who, for historical reasons, have been particularly influential among nonlinguists and whose readings of Saussure illustrate the difficulties encountered by the editors (and, indeed, by Saussure himself). See also below, "The Quarrel over the Arbitrariness of the Sign."

13. See: "A student who has himself heard a considerable portion of the lectures of F. de Saussure on general linguistics and has become acquainted with many of the documents on which the publication rests feels necessarily a disillusionment at no longer being able to find again the exquisite and captivating charm of the lectures of the master. At the price of some repetition, would not the publication of the notes from the courses have conserved more faithfully the thought of F. de S., with its power, with its originality? And the variations themselves which the editors appear to have feared bringing to the light of day, would they not have offered a unique interest?" (P. Regard, quoted by Tullio de Mauro in his Notes to the *Cours*, 406.

14. See also the chapter "Le Travail des éditeurs," *SM*, 99–129.

15. We should distinguish between nonlinguists and linguists and, among the latter, between Britain and the United States. In Britain some presence of Saussurean linguistics was ensured by the work of Gardiner, Firth, St. Ullman, R. H. Robins, R. M. W. Dixon, and J. Lyons. See also De Mauro's Notes, *Cours*, 371–73. In the United States, I shall note a major exception: Bloomfield read Saussure very attentively. Although in his early writings he expressed views very similar to Saussure's (especially on *langue*), in his late work he centered his inquiry on *parole*, in the pragmatic vein. On this subject see Samuel R. Levine, "*Langue* and *Parole* in American Linguistics," *Foundation of Language* 1, no. 2 (1965): 83–94; and Roy Harris, *The Language-Makers* (London: Duckworth, 1980), 158–67. See also Georges Mounin, *La Linguistique du XXe siècle*.

16. C. K. Ogden and I. A. Richards, *The Meaning of Meaning. A Study of the Influence of Language upon Thought and of the Science of Symbolism*, with supplementary essays by B. Malinowski and F. G. Crookshank (New York: Harcourt,

Brace & Co.; London: Routledge & Kegan Paul, 1948), hereafter cited as *MM*. Saussure is not the only target of the authors' criticism: Bréal—who had been a major influence on Saussure—is accused of indulging in "loose verbiage" (*MM*, 4), "loose metaphor" (3), "hypostatization of leading terms" (3), and, all in all, "an unsuitable attitude in which to approach the question" (3).

17. Unfortunately, the *Cours* does not fully do justice to Saussure's reflections on the priority of point of view over object. The editors erred in two ways: 1) they did not emphasize enough the importance of viewpoint as constitutive of the "object" for modern scientific investigation (one may even wonder whether they grasped its full range of implications) and 2) they edited into a single paragraph various sections in which Saussure grappled with viewpoint.

18. Gaston Bachelard, *La Philosophie du non* (Paris: Presses Universitaires de France, 1940), 104–27.

19. At least, this is what the criticism of Saussure entails. Fortunately, Richards himself practised a method of literary investigation that owes its richness mostly to the fact that it did not conform to the method he advocates here.

20. For an excellent account of Ogden and Richards' reading of Saussure, see Frederic Jameson, *The Prison-House of Language: A Critical Account of Structuralism and Russian Formalism* (Princeton, N.J.: Princeton University Press, 1972), 3–39.

21. Jonathan Culler, *Saussure* (Hassocks, England. Harvester Press, 1976). A revised edition of the chapter on Saussure appeared in Culler, *Ferdinand de Saussure* (Ithaca, N.Y.: Cornell University Press, 1986). All quotations are from the 1976 edition.

22. We should notice, however, that Bally and Sechehaye had proceeded with more caution and shown more respect for the ambiguities in Saussure's thinking: they *never* linked *langue* and the linguistic sign causally or subordinated one to the other in any explicit manner.

23. Although Chomsky played a leading role in the downplaying of Saussurean linguistics, he devotes a total of only about two to three pages, scattered among various works, to Saussure. It is therefore difficult to address the detail of his critique (otherwise, I would have included him among the critics of Saussure whom I discuss). He did, however, accuse Saussure of having elaborated a nomenclature, an accusation that, because of Chomsky's overwhelming influence on linguistics in the United States, has since been readily accepted. See Noam Chomsky, *Current Issues in Linguistics* (London: Mouton & Co., 1964), 23–24. See also Chomsky, *Aspects of the Theory of Syntax* (Cambridge, Mass.: MIT Press, 1965), 4, 8, 47. On Chomsky's reading of Saussure see the excellent remarks and bibliographical Notes of De Mauro, *Cours*, 400–404.

24. A familiar tangle: we have been warned that "there exists really no starting point more valid than another upon which to ground the demonstration." Since, nonetheless, I do have not only to start but also to find a proper sequence or "narrative" for my demonstration, a starting point and a coherent sequence are clearly indispensable. I shall therefore start with *langue*, but my election of a starting point rests on purely pragmatic considerations extrinsic to Saussure's linguistics. These considerations reflect my own project (and its presentation) and not Saussure's. I

may have to resort to yet unexplained concepts when presenting early terms, but the details should fall into place when the picture is complete.

25. There is some confusion in Saussure's text, because the French word *langue* also designates a national language (French, English, German, etc.). Saussure would have avoided the confusion if he had made a lexical distinction between a national language (*une langue*) and the general system of signs (*la langue*). Any attempt to settle whether there was indeed some confusion in *his* mind remains sheer conjecture. In our translation, we usually use *language* for *une langue*.

26. De Mauro stipulates that Saussure must have been attentive to the debate between Durkheim and Tarde. He also relies on Saussure's private testimony that he was interested in the quarrel between the "theoretical" and "historical" schools of political economics (*Cours,* 451–52).

27. "Note that I have defined things rather than words. These definitions are not endangered by certain ambiguous words that do not have identical meanings in different languages. For instance, German *Sprache* means both 'language' [*langue*] and 'speech' [*langage*]; *Rede* almost corresponds to 'speaking' [*parole*], but adds the special connotation of 'discourse' [*discours*]. Latin *sermo* designates both 'speech' [*langage*] and 'speaking' [*parole*], while *lingua* means 'language' [*langue*], etc. No word corresponds exactly to any of the notions specified above; that is why all definitions of words are made in vain; starting from words in defining things is a bad procedure." (*Course,* 14)

28. For a baffled linguist's reaction to abuses of Saussure's terminology, of which the signifier is exemplary, see Georges Mounin, *Linguistique et philosophie* (Paris: Presses Universitaires de France, 1975), 143–56.

29. On the quarrel about "difference" and "opposition" see Eric Buyssens' criticism of Saussure in "Mise au point de quelques notions fondamentales de la phonologie," *Cahiers Ferdinand de Saussure* 4 (1949): 37–60 (in particular the section "Saussure contre Saussure"), as well as Henri Frei's response, "Saussure contre Saussure?" ibid. 9 (1950): 7–28. (See also Buyssens' rebuttal, "Dogme ou libre examen," ibid. 19 (1952): 47–50.)

30. Godel emphatically reminds us that Saussure was very consistent in the use of the terms *difference* and *opposition.* See *SM,* 196–98.

31. In his "Translation and Meaning," Quine imagines a scenario of what he calls radical translation (radical because it is the "translation of the language of a hitherto untouched people"). His example is as follows: an anthropologist-linguist is engaged in field work among natives about whose language he knows nothing. A native points at a rabbit scurrying by and says, "Gavagai." The anthropologist wonders whether *gavagai* means "animal," "white," or "rabbit." In order to find out, he points at objects that are either animals, white, or rabbits, and asks, "Gavagai?" noting the reaction of the native until the elicited responses consistently indicate one of the three possibilities.

What I find interesting in this example is that the three options ("animal," "white," and "rabbit") reflect age-old discussions on the nature of names (genus vs. specific, subject vs. property), and that they correspond to existing English words. Quine does not so much as consider the possibility that the native's categories of knowledge may not overlap with the Westerner's: *gavagai* could have meant "that from which I can have a meal and a pelt" (thus including sheep but not chicken); it could have meant "anything that can endanger my vegetable garden" (thus including other rodents, goats, etc., and even hail); or "raw material for a two-portion meal" (including a Cornish hen or a large bowl of cereal), and so forth. Quine's "radical" translation is anything but radical: it amounts to an appropriation of differences by one cognitive system with the result that these differences are resorbed into sameness (English and the cognitive categories it commands). Under any other name, a rabbit remains a rabbit.

Putnam, who muddles a little the cognitive space either by imagining that *gavagai* may refer to "undetached parts of rabbit" (as opposed to a rabbit ready to be eaten whose parts are detached) or by evoking "rabbithood," remains nonetheless within the generic boundaries of "rabbits." Even as Martians, whose world is supposedly totally different from ours, pop up in the example, a rabbit remains a rabbit— whether its parts are detached or not. Not once does Putnam suggest that *gavagai* could be extended to a pheasant's undetached parts, for example, or to the detachable fruit of a banana tree. Putnam's basic criterion for carving the world into discrete cognitive categories seems at first about to rock the philosophical boat but eventually joins a familiar and innocuous atomism. See Hillary Putnam, *Meaning and the Moral Science* (London: Routledge & Kegan Paul, 1978), 42–55; and Williard Van Ornam Quine, *Word and Object* (Cambridge, Mass.: MIT Press, 1960), esp. chap. 2, "Translation and Meaning," 26–79.

32. In this excerpt "language" is consistently the translation of *langage*.

33. See Benjamin L. Whorf, *Language, Thought, and Reality* (Cambridge: Cambridge University Press, 1956); and Bronislaw Malinowski, "The Problem of Meaning in Primitive Languages," "Supplement I," in *MM*, 297–336.

34. Saussure's attempted distinction between "a definite object for the senses like a horse, fire, the sun," etcetera and an "idea" such as "he placed" does little to alleviate the difficulty: he objects to the former as a taxonomy but seems quite content with the latter. One may wonder if this distinction is valid: unless we think of naming in the very narrow sense that extends to "definite objects for the senses" only (i.e., as a noun—but this would beg the question), *he placed* is some kind of name for a specific action performed by a definite subject. In Saussure's own words, *he placed* names an "idea." However, if, as he suggests, *he placed* corresponds to an indivisible idea (just as do *tree* and *fire*), it must be perceived as a distinct *entity* that constitutes a linguistic *unit*. As Godel rightly emphasizes, the true question is therefore not the delineation of the sign but that of linguistic entities that will remain recognizable as such, that is, perceived as identical each time they occur in *parole*, or in Derrida's terms, that will remain iterable. From this perspective I see no difference between *a horse* and *he placed* (see also: "And I will add that I make no fundamental difference between a *value*, an *identity*, a *reality* [in a linguistic sense], a concrete element of linguistics" (II B 31, E 248, Bouchardy's emphasis). For example, in the case of the word *Messieurs* repeated a few times in the course of a speech, Saussure asked in what sense we may say that it is or is not identical each time; or, similarly, he wonders what allows us to perceive homonyms as different beyond confusion and, therefore, as different entities (*Course*, 107–11); see also, for example, the following passage not reproduced in the *Cours:* "But next, if we consider this other

point that in the same sentence I may say for example: SON *violon a le même* SON [his violin has the same sound]—if just now I were to concentrate on the identity of the sound, I would see here that the auditory piece [tranche acoustique] *son* repeated twice does not represent an identity. By the same token if one comes upon the same auditory progression in '*cet animal* PORTE PLUME *et bec*' ['this animal has feathers and a beak'] and '*prête-moi ton* PORTE-PLUME' ['loan me your pen'] we do not recognize that there is there an identity. There must be an identity in the idea evoked. It carries, this identity, an undefinable subjective element. The exact point where there is an identity is always delicate to fix" (III C 294, E 243, Constantin's emphasis).

35. Emile Benveniste, *Problems in General Linguistics,* trans. Mary Elizabeth Meek (Coral Gables, Fla.: University of Miami Press, 1971), 44.

36. See Hans Aarslef, *From Locke to Saussure* (Minneapolis: University of Minnesota Press, 1982), esp. the chaps. "Taine and Saussure," 356–71, and "Bréal and Saussure," 382–97.

37. See also Godel's remarkable treatment of the problem of entities and units, *SM*, 189–251.

38. See also: "Let us return to the figure of the signified with respect to the signifier:

One sees that it [the figure] has its raison d'être but that it is only a byproduct of the value. A signified alone is nothing; [it is] absorbed in an amorphous mass; the same goes for a signifier. But the signifier and the signified establish a relation by virtue of the determined values, which are born from the combination of so many acoustic signs [*tant de signes acoustiques*] with so many cutouts [*tant de découpures*] that one can make from the mass" (III D 277, E 255–56).

39. Tullio de Mauro, *Une Introduction à la sémantique* (Paris: Payot, 1969), 130.

40. Charles Bally, "L'Arbitraire du signe, valeur et signification," *Le Français moderne,* June–July 1940, 193–206. All references to this essay are to pp. 194–95.

41. Albert Sechehaye, Charles Bally, and Henri Frei, "Pour l'arbitraire du signe," *Acta Linguistica* 2, fasc. 3 (1940–41): 169.

3   Frege

1. We could make an exception for Leibniz, who dreamed of a *mathesis universalis,* in which atomic elements of thought would be shown to be irreducible and complete and would serve as the basis of a *lingua sive characteristica univesalis.* (We could also mention Comenius and Trendelenburg in this context.) However, Leibniz himself never came close to elaborating and formulating his system of signs, and his theory remained largely utopian. On this subject see Christian Thiel, *Sense and Reference in Frege's Logic* (Dordrecht, Holland: D. Reidel Publishing Co., 1968), particularly the chapter entitled "The Notion of the *Begriffsschrift,*" 5–21; see also

Hans D. Sluga, *Gottlob Frege* (London: Routledge & Kegan Paul, 1980), 1–80.

2. See, for example, "It would be strange if the most exact of all sciences [here: arithmetic] had to seek support from psychology, which is still feeling its way none too surely." Gottlob Frege, *The Foundations of Arithmetic*, trans. J. Austin (Oxford: Basil Blackwell, 1953), 38ᵉ; hereafter cited as *Foundations*.

3. Gottlob Frege, *Posthumous Writings*, ed. Hans Hermes, Friedrich Kambartel, and Friedrich Kaulbach (Oxford: Basil Blackwell, 1979), 255.

4. Toward the end of his life, Frege himself characterized his initial motivations in these words: "I started out from mathematics. The more pressing need, it seemed to me, was to provide this science with a better foundation. . . . The logical imperfection of language stood in the way of such investigations. I tried to overcome these obstacles with my concept-script [*Begriffsschrift*]. In this way I was led from mathematics to logic" (ibid., 253).

5. Gottlob Frege, "The Thought: A Logical Inquiry," in *Logic and Philosophy for Linguists* ed. J. M. E. Moravcsik (The Hague: Mouton, 1974), 287; hereafter cited as "The Thought."

6. For a clear introduction to Frege, geared to the needs of literary critics who may be newcomers to analytical philosophy, see David Gorman, "Discovery and Recovery in the Philosophy of Language: Dummett and Frege," *Diacritics*, Winter 1983, 43–62.

7. Among the numerous comments on this choice, see Reinhardt Grossmann, *Reflections on Frege's Philosophy* (Evanston, Ill.: Northwestern University Press, 1969), 154–81; and Ignacio Angelelli, *Studies on Gottlob Frege and Traditional Philosophy* (Dordrecht, Holland: D. Reidel Publishing Co., 1967), 43–47.

8. See Frege's *Begriffsschrift;* see also the opening paragraph of "On Sense and Reference," in *Translations from the Philosophical Writings of Gottlob Frege*, ed. Peter Geach and Max Black (Oxford: Basil Blackwell, 1970), 56; hereafter cited as "On Sense."

9. Frege wrote extensively about the definition of *object* (see *Foundations of Arithmetic;* and his "On Concept and Object" [hereafter cited as "On Concept"], "On Function and Concept," and "On Sense and Reference," in *Translations from the Philosophical Writings;* for our purposes, I shall present only that which is relevant to the discussion of *Sinn, Bedeutung*, and *Vorstellung*.

10. Michael Dummet, one of the deans of Fregean studies, notes the ambiguous status of "object" but fails to underscore the extent to which his own reading undermines the distinctions that he is painstakingly drawing (see further pp. 138–140): "For Frege, the relation of a proper name of a concrete object to that object is the prototype of the relation of reference. Even in this case, the objects which serve as referents cannot be recognized quite independently of language: it is only because we employ a language for the understanding of which we need to grasp various criteria of identity, both for objects identified by means of names and for those identified ostensively by means of demonstratives, that we learn to slice the world up conceptually, into discrete objects" (Michael Dummett, *Frege: Philosophy of Language* (New York: Harper & Row, 1972), 406–7).

11. All emphasis is mine unless otherwise indicated.

12. See Dummett 93–94. Dummett notices this imprecision but fails to realize the extent to which it is symptomatic of an important source of confusion ("Confusion never arises in Frege's own writing" [94]).

13. The parenthetical "(an object)" is Frege's.

14. See: "A proper name (name, sign, sign combination, expression) *expresses* its sense, *stands for* or *designates* its reference. By means of a sign we express its sense and designate its reference" ("On Sense," 61, Frege's emphasis).

15. See Frege on this subject: "In hearing an epic poem, for instance, apart from the euphony of the language we are interested only in the sense of the sentences and the images and feelings [*Vorstellungen und Gefühle*] thereby aroused. The question of truth would cause us to abandon aesthetic delight for an attitude of scientific investigation. Hence it is a matter of no concern to us whether the name 'Odysseus,' for instance, has reference, so long as we accept the poem as a work of art. *It is the striving for truth that drives us always to advance from the sense to the reference*" ("On Sense," 63).

16. In *Posthumous Writings,* Frege cites a similar example in which he categorically denies that literature may have any truth-value: "The sense of the sentence 'William Tell shot an apple off his son's head' is no more true than is that of the sentence 'William Tell did not shoot an apple off his son's head.' I do not say, however, that this sense is false either, but I characterize it as fictitious" (130). Frege suggests the terms *mock sense* and *mock thought* for literature, theater, and painting.

17. Searle solves this difficulty by taking into account the speaker's intention (for a critique of "intentionality" see my chapter on speech acts). In his essay "The Logical Status of Fictional Discourse," he presents fiction as a "pretended reference," that is, a discourse by an author who knows that he or she is only pretending to refer to characters or events but, in so doing, manages to create these very characters or events ("By *pretending* to refer to people and to recount events about them, the author *creates* fictional characters or events" [73]). Once these characters or events are "created," a second distinction takes care of truth-value: even though the characters and events remain fictional, once they are created *as fiction,* one can speak *about* them; thus once the fictional identity of, say, Odysseus, King Arthur, or Sherlock Holmes is established, one can make "serious" statements *about* them. This secondary discourse differs from the first in that it is subject to truth-value. Hence I can say that, although in a primary way King Arthur "does not exist," in a secondary way he does exist, because "it is the pretended reference which created the fictional character and the shared pretense which enables us to talk about the character" (71). "King Arthur was a perfect knight" would then be true, while "King Arthur was a coward" would simply be false. John R. Searle, *Expression and Meaning: Studies in the Theory of Speech Acts* (Cambridge: Cambridge University Press, 1979). On Searle's essay, see also pp. 340–45.

18. See "Frege's distinction between sense and reference could not correctly be called a 'distinction between two ingredients in the intuitive notion of meaning.' *Reference, as Frege understands it, is not an ingredient in meaning at all.* . . . Reference, for Frege, is a notion *required* in the theory of meaning—in the general account of how language functions—just as the notion of truth is so required: but the reference

of a term is no more part of what is ordinarily understood as its meaning than the truth-value of a sentence is" (Dummett 84).

19. See, for example, the opening pages of "The Thought," in which Frege painstakingly distinguishes between the task of psychology and that of logic, within the context of the quest for the meaning of the word *truth* ("In order to avoid this misunderstanding and to prevent the blurring of the boundary between psychology and logic, I assign to logic the task of discovering the laws of truth, not of assertion or thought" [280].)

20. Although he generally seems to avoid *Bedeutung* at that time (but not the verb *bedeuten*), we still find some confusion. In "Notes for Ludwig Darmstaedter," dated July 1919—that is, one year after "The Thought"—he again uses *Bedeutung* for the object itself: "If an astronomer makes a statement about the moon, the moon itself is not part of the thought expressed. The moon itself is the reference of the expression 'the moon'" (*Posthumous Writings*, 255, modified trans.).

21. For an interesting discussion of this problem of the confusion between reference and the referent, and its substantial implications, see Dummett, 401–29.

22. Incidentally, in "The Thought," Frege envisages a similar distinction regarding "sense" but, forever consistent in his antipsychologism, waves it aside: "The apprehension of a thought presupposes someone who apprehends it, who thinks. He is the bearer of the thinking but not of the thought. *Although the thought does not belong to the content of the thinker's consciousness yet something in his consciousness must be aimed at the thought.* But this should not be confused with the thought itself" ("The Thought," 296. As "thought" is to sentence as "sense" is to expression, I rely here on "The Thought," in which Frege is more explicit).

23. It is significant that Soviet logicians informed by Marxism and Russian Formalism (which offers numerous points of contact with Saussure and was considerably influenced by the *Cours*) would criticize the realist *parti pris* of Frege's theory of sense and would call it a metaphysical bias. See, for example: "The scientific creation of this very prominent German logician and mathematician offers itself as a good illustration of the above-quoted words of Engels about men who, making their contribution to human knowledge of the world, nevertheless start from frequently unfounded and one-sided premises and commit theoretical blunders. The unfounded and one-sided premises from which Frege started—the prejudice about the unchangeability of the objects of the world, the idea of the possibility of the diversification and identification of any object with which we have a cognitive concern, the conviction about the full universality and unchangeable character of the laws of thought considered by formal logic, the notion of the completely extensional character of the logic of contentful thinking, etc.—were *metaphysical* presuppositions. Frege did not see either the dialectical character or the process of knowledge as a whole, or how the dialectic appears in the evolution of mathematical logic itself" (B. V. Birjukov, in *Two Soviet Studies on Frege,* trans. Ignacio Angelelli [Dordrecht-Holland: D. Reidel Publishing Co., 1964], 88, Birjukov's emphasis).

24. Ferdinand de Saussure, *Course in General Linguistics,* ed. Charles Bally and Albert Sechehaye, in collaboration with Albert Riedlinger, trans. Wade Baskin (New York: Philosophical Library, 1959).

25. On *objectivity* and *existence* in Frege's theory, see Jeremy D. B. Walker, *A Study of Frege* (Ithaca, N.Y.: Cornell University Press, 1965), 28–31; and Sluga 117–21.

26. Frege was labeled by some a realist (see Walker 22–31; and Dummet 408, 412), and by others an uninhibited Platonist (G. P. Baker and P. M. Hacker, *Frege: Logical Excavations* [New York: Oxford University Press; Oxford: Basil Blackwell, 1984], 314–15). Despite their differences, both address the same feature of his theory. A special case is the thesis advanced by Sluga: he disagrees with Dummett's view that Frege was opposed to German Idealism; according to him, by the 1850s, German Idealism had been superseded by philosophical and scientific Naturalism. Frege's foil would then be German philosophical Naturalism and not Idealism. What is more, writes Sluga, Frege contributed regularly to the *Deutsche Philosophische Gesellschaft,* whose explicit goal was the "cultivation, deepening, and preservation of German individuality in philosophy in the spirit of German Idealism" (cited in Sluga 59). Even so, the historical quarrel does not affect the formal understanding of Frege's theory, as Sluga adds that Frege "shared the idealists' antipsychologism, their belief in an objectivist epistemology, and their apriorism and rationalism" (60).

A final note on this question: In "On Sense," Frege explicitly argues with "idealists or skeptics" (61), and in "The Thought" he imagines and refutes objections that could have been raised either by naturalists or by idealists (291–93).

27. Richard Rorty, *Consequences of Pragmatism* (Minneapolis: University of Minnesota Press, 1982), 96.

28. Frege was well aware of the repressed demons of Western epistemology denounced by Derrida. Derrida and Frege differ mostly in the attitude they adopted with regard to the problem: whereas Derrida launched an immense revisionist project, Frege consolidated what he could save of knowledge, namely, mathematics and logic.

29. See also Frege: "Thoughts are independent of our thinking. A thought [*Gedanke*] does not belong specially to the person who thinks it, as an idea [*Vorstellung*] does to the person who has it: whoever thinks it encounters it in the same way, as the same thought. *Otherwise* two people would never attach the same thought to the same sentence. A contradiction between assertions of different people would be impossible. A dispute about the truth of something would be futile. There would be no common ground to fight on" (*Posthumous Writings,* 127; dated 1897).

30. We must note Frege's dissatisfaction with the term *apprehend;* in a footnote (Frege's footnotes are particularly revealing) he adds: "The expression 'apprehend' [*fassen*] is as metaphorical [*bildlich*] as 'content of consciousness' [*Bewusstseinsinhalt*]. The nature of language does not permit anything else" (ibid.).

31. See Frege: "As I do not create a tree by looking at it or cause a pencil to come into existence by taking hold of it, neither do I generate a thought by thinking. And still less does the brain secrete thoughts, as the liver does gall." See also: "Psychological treatment of logic arises from the mistaken belief that a thought [*Gedanke*] (a judgement as it is usually called) is something psychological like an idea [*Vorstellung*]. This view leads necessarily to an idealist theory of knowledge" (Frege, *Posthumous Writings,* 137, 143).

32. On the value of excess see pp. 390–93.

33. In this respect, *Vorstellung* resembles connotation: it is the association that an expression brings to a person's mind. As such, it is hardly a novel distinction. Baker and Hacker (47, n. 34), for instance, quote similar distinctions in Descartes, Boole, Lotze, and *Port-Royal's Logic.*

34. For a good discussion of these criteria, see ibid., 41–49.

35. Wittgenstein, *Philosophical Grammar,* trans. A. J. P. Kenny (Oxford: Blackwell, 1974), 155.

36. The full sentence is clearer: "A painter, a horseman, and a zoologist will probably connect different ideas with the name 'Bucephalus.' *This constitutes an essential distinction between the idea and the sign's sense,* which may be the common property of many and therefore is not a part or a mode of the individual mind. *For one can hardly deny that mankind has a common store of thoughts which is transmitted from one generation to another*" ("On Sense," 63).

37. Gottlob Frege, *Ecrits logiques et philosophiques,* trans. Claude Imbert (Paris: Seuil, 1971).

38. See also the Translators' Preface to Frege's *Posthumous Writings* (trans. Peter Long and Roger White): "'Vorstellung' is a notorious crux for translators and we have *by and large* rendered it by 'idea,' preferring this *in general* to the quasi-technical 'representation' with its Kantian overtones and the too narrow 'image.' Admittedly our rendering reads awkwardly in some contexts and may mislead the unwary. But Frege, again in the second piece entitled 'Logic,' helps the reader by explaining how he is there using 'Vorstellung' and we have occasionally singled out the word for special mention where we thought there was a danger of misunderstanding" (vii).

39. See Frege: "In the inquiry that follows, I have kept to three fundamental principles: Always to separate sharply the psychological from the logical, the subjective from the objective. . . . In compliance with the first principle, I have used the word 'idea' [*Vorstellung*] always in the psychological sense, and have distinguished ideas from concepts and objects" (*Foundations,* X^e).

40. According to Sluga, for example, by Frege's time, Idealism had long since subsided, to be replaced by Scientific Naturalism. Frege's quarrel would then be not so much with German Idealism as with philosophical and scientific Naturalism, which, in Germany, carried strong psychological overtones. If this is the case, the translation of *Vorstellung* by "idea" is an unfortunate anachronism (see also, n. 26).

41. See "A logically perfect language [*Begriffsschrift*] should satisfy the conditions, that every expression grammatically well constructed as a proper name out of signs already introduced shall in fact designate an object, and that no new sign shall be introduced as a proper name without being secured a reference" ("On Sense," 70).

42. Dummett's use of *tone* is identical with what "On Sense and Reference" calls idea. See Dummett: Frege "accounts for tone as a matter of association with a word or expression of certain 'ideas' (*Vorstellungen*), by which he means mental images" (85).

43. See Frege: "Language is a human creation; and so man had, it would appear, the capacity to shape it in conformity with the logical disposition alive in him. Certainly the logical disposition of man *was* at work in the formation of language but

equally alongside this many other dispositions—such as the poetic disposition. And so language is not constructed from a logical blueprint" (*Posthumous Writings,* 269).

4   The First Person

1. The third fragment is extremely short. It consists in the opening lines of a letter to the ape written by someone as a reaction to the ape's "report," which he has just read. The fragment is too short for us to derive much from it. What matters is that here, too, "I" is not the ape but a well-read human.

2. Franz Kafka, "A Report to an Academy: Two Fragments," trans. Tania and James Stern, in Kafka, *The Complete Stories,* ed. Nahum N. Glatzer (New York: Schocken Books, 1971), 260; hereafter cited as *Stories*.

There are traces of this first attempt in the final version: "My ape nature fled out of me, head over heels and away, so that my first teacher was almost himself turned into an ape by it, had soon to give up teaching and was taken away to a mental hospital. Fortunately he was soon let out again" ("A Report to an Academy," trans. Willa and Edwin Muir [*Stories,* 258]).

3. Very little has been written about "A Report to an Academy." To my knowledge, none of the readings focuses on the contribution of *I* to the story. Most critics read it as a commentary on ethical problems (nature/culture, man's lower and higher instincts, violence/reason). The readings that I deplore the most for their possible anti-Semitic implications are those in which the bottom line is that the ape stands for those assimilated Jews who, despite their effort to become what they are not by aping their betters, remain Jews. The analogy between the ape and assimilated Jews is normally attributed to Kafka's problematic relationship with Judaism: at once love and hatred, mixed feelings toward both assimilated Prague Jews like his father and those fresh from the *shtetel,* his half-hearted Zionism, and so on, all of which I shall not dispute. See, for instance, William Rubinstein, "A Report to an Academy," in *Franz Kafka Today,* ed. Angel Flores and Homer Swanders (Madison: University of Wisconsin Press, 1958), 55–60; or Robert Kauf, "Once Again: Kafka's 'A Report to an Academy,'" *Modern Language Quarterly* 15 (1959): 359–66.

The best work in this perspective is Marthe Robert's *As Lonely as Kafka,* trans. Ralph Manheim (New York: Harcourt Brace Jovanovich, 1982). Robert's enquiry is essentially biographical. She uses letters, testimonies, and the literary corpus to understand the man. To the extent that one can infer anything about a man from his work, she uses the work judiciously. Her analysis does little to cast light on the works themselves, however (for a critique of the approach of which she is the most interesting representative, see Gilles Deleuze and Felix Guattari, *Kafka: Toward a Minor Literature,* trans. Dana Polan (Minneapolis: University of Minnesota Press, 1986).

4. Walter Benjamin, *Illuminations,* ed. Hannah Arendt, trans. Harry Zohn (New York: Schocken Books, 1968), 122.

5. Leo Hamalian, Introduction, in *Franz Kafka: A Collection of Criticism,* ed. Leo Hamalian (New York: McGraw-Hill Book Co., n.d.), 8.

6. At the back of my mind is a very useful critique made by a colleague who read an early version of this chapter and objected to my approach, arguing that "A Re-

port" was not about "I" but about nature/culture, violence/reason, animal/human, audiences/sadists, etcetera. Maybe so; but whatever it is "about," "A Report" conveys it by means of a very effective use of the first person. In this study, I examine the "how" rather than the "what" of "A Report," on the assumption that they will prove closely related.

7. Franz Kafka, "Wedding Preparation in the Country," trans. Ernst Kaiser and Eithne Wilkins, *Stories*, 53. Unless otherwise indicated, all emphasis is mine.

8. Reported by Maurice Blanchot, *L'Espace littéraire* (Paris: Gallimard, 1955), 17. See also Dorrit Cohn's meticulous account of the change of person in "The Trial," from *I* in an early draft to the third person in the final version. Dorrit Cohn, "K. Enters the Castle. On the Change of Person in Kafka's Manuscript," *Euphorion* 62 (1968): 28–45.

9. Even if it is a speech, so that we are dealing with a "serious" situation, can such a speech be devoid of "performing" elements? It is, after all, about "the life I formerly led as an ape," that is to say, closely related to the identity and public persona of the speaker. If an academy today were to invite Bob Hope or Joan Rivers to speak about their lives, would they not expect bits of performance? Would they not expect to be *entertained,* at least as much as *instructed?* Would *they* be "serious"?

10. The move from *it* to *he* when referring to the ape is not accidental. There are no rules for speaking apes in our grammar books. Even though he/it is not a man, upon seizing power our ape is no longer just an ape. For lack of an appropriate pronoun for halfway creatures, I am in the odd position of having to choose between man and beast (i.e., to impose on the story the very same "solution" that it so elegantly resists). I then choose *he,* since it is more in line with our linguistic conventions ("it" does not speak in those conventions). I am well aware, however, of the irony with which this choice tints my own discourse.

11. Gottlob Frege, "The Thought: A Logical Inquiry," in *Logic and Philosophy for Linguists*, ed. J. M. E. Moravcsik (The Hague: Mouton, 1974), 285–86; hereafter cited as "The Thought."

12. See, for example: "Scratch yourself raw between your toes, but you won't find the answer" (*Stories,* 253); or "One stands over oneself with a whip; one flays oneself at the slightest opposition" (258); as well as the long metaphor of the gate, which I cite pp. 217–18). This colorful language is all the more noticeable if we remember that Kafka normally shuns metaphors and images.

13. See, for example, the difficulty that a philosopher encounters, when he tries to explain this section of "The Thought" without associating the subjective aspect of "I" with *Vorstellung.* In "Frege on Demonstratives," John Perry opens his essay with the recognition that the examination of indexicals led Frege "to say that when one thinks about oneself, one grasps thoughts that others cannot grasp, that cannot be communicated" (474). Since the whole purpose of Frege's enterprise is to ensure that thoughts would be communicated in an absolutely unambiguous way, Perry is quite right in adding immediately that "nothing could be more out of the spirit of Frege's account of sense and thought than an uncommunicable, private thought" (474). The major part of his paper then attempts to rescue Frege from the straits of this untenable contradiction.

Perry's difficulty stems from the fact that he takes the "primitive way"—in which, according to Frege, one is presented to oneself—to be a "thought" in the strict sense of the term, thus pertaining to *Sinn,* which, as we know, must be objective. If such were the case, then there would indeed be an inconsistency in Frege's thinking. Perry's interpretation of this "primitive way" in which one is presented to himself and to nobody else therefore bars him from saving Frege on purely Fregean terms. His solution then consists in adding distinctions and subdivisions: *role/sense* (where "role" relates the "sense" to its context); *sense completers* (that give spatiotemporal or syntactical specifications to a "thought"); *sense had/sense expressed* (where "sense expressed" takes on the added semantic charge the sentence owes to its context); *entertaining/apprehending* ("Let us speak of entertaining a sense and apprehending a thought" [493]). As subtle and insightful as these observations and distinctions are, despite the obvious overlapping of the terms added, they do not do much for Frege. In fact, they make his presentation of "thought" appear less developed and suggestive than I take it to be. See John Perry, "Frege on Demonstratives," *Philosophical Review* 86, 4 (1977): 474–97.

14. Yehoshua Bar-Hillel, "Indexical Expression," *Mind* 63, no. 251 (1954): 359–79. In this essay, Bar-Hillel disputes Russell's contention that purely descriptive and scientific discourse can and should dispense with indexical expression.

15. See Frege: "A proper name (word, sign, sign combination, expression) *expresses* its sense, *stands for* or *designates* its reference. By means of a sign we express its sense and designate its reference" ("On Sense," 61, Frege's emphasis).

16. "On Sense and Reference," "On Function and Concept," and "On Concept and Object." The three essays were written more or less simultaneously and were published between 1891 and 1892.

17. For a discussion of "associated conditions" and "circumstances," see chaps. 5 and 6.

18. See Russell's discussion of the position best identified with Frege: "But, I shall be asked, what do you know about what is happening in the brain? Surely nothing. Not so, I reply. I know about what is happening in the brain exactly what naïve realism thinks it knows about what is happening in the outside world" (Bertrand Russell, *An Outline of Philosophy* (London: George Allen & Unwin, 1927), 138; hereafter cited as *Outline.* See also the Introduction to Bertrand Russell, *An Inquiry into Meaning and Truth* (New York: W. W. Norton & Co., 1940), in particular the amusing refutation of behaviorism's claim to scientific observation, 14–15; hereafter cited as *Inquiry.*

19. See Russell: "The hierarchy must extend upward indefinitely, but not downwards, since, if it did, language could never get started. There must, therefore, be a language of lowest type. I shall define one such language, not the only possible one. I shall call this sometimes the 'object-language,' sometimes the 'primary language'" (*Inquiry,* 76).

20. Rousseau, *Discourse on the Origins and the Foundations of Inequality among Men.* (One may wish to contrast this view with the one Rousseau expresses in the *Essay on the Origin of Language.* On this contrast see Jacques Derrida, *Of Grammatology,* trans. Gayatry C. Spivak (Baltimore: Johns Hopkins University Press, 1977); and Paul de Man "Metaphor (the Second Discourse)" in *Allegories of Reading* (New Haven, Conn.: Yale University Press, 1979), 135–59.

A different view, equally opposed to Russell's "object-language," can be found in Nietzsche's notes: "Knowledge, strictly speaking, has only the form of tautology and *is empty*. All the knowledge which is of assistance to us involves the identification of things which are not the same, of things which are only similar. . . . Only in this way do we obtain a concept. Then afterwards we behave as if the concept, e.g., the concept 'man,' were something factual, whereas it is surely only something which we have constructed through a process of ignoring all individual features. We presuppose that nature behaves in accordance with such a concept. But in this case first nature and then the concept are anthropomorphic. The *omitting* of what is individual provides us with the concept, and with this our knowledge begins: in *categorizing*, in the establishment of *classes*" (Friedrich Nietzsche, *Philosophy and Truth: Selections from Nietzsche's Notebooks of the Early 1870s*, ed. and trans. Daniel Breazeale [Atlantic Highlands, N.J.: Humanities Press, 1979], 51 (sec. 150).

21. Russell's critique of Descartes is in line with his analysis of particulars; what he objects to is the sense of *I* as a person (which he finds substantialist): "I think we ought to admit that Descartes was justified in feeling sure that there was a certain occurrence, concerning which doubt was impossible; but he was not justified in bringing in the word 'I' in describing the occurrence, and it remains to be considered whether he was justified in using the word 'think' " (*Outline*, 170).

22. See Russell: "In the learning of an object-word, there are four things to be considered: the understanding of the heard word *in the presence* of the object, the understanding of it *in the absence* of the object, the speaking of the word *in the presence* of the object, and the speaking of it *in the absence* of the object" (*Inquiry*, 80–81). With indexical expressions, only two of these four aspects apply: I can hardly hear or speak of "this dog" in the absence of the said dog.

23. It has been objected that there is a another kind of "here." You may ask me, for example, where the car keys are. In my answer, pointing to the table a few feet away from me, I may say either "Here!" or "There!" No matter what I say, however, it is in relation to *my* location that I shall indicate where the keys are. Consequently this secondary discussion, as important as it has been for philosophers, is irrelevant to our argument. See G. N. A. Vesey, "Self-Acquaintance and the Meaning of 'I,' " in *Bertrand Russell Memorial Volume*, ed. George W. Roberts (London: George Allen & Unwin; New York: Humanities Press Inc., 1979), 339–47. For an interesting discussion of this indeterminacy and the ways it affects the relationship between *I* and *here*, see Roderick Chisholm, *The First Person* (Minneapolis: University of Minnesota Press, 1981), 41–52.

24. Russell suggests that we understand "here" as "the place of this," and "now" as "the time of this," thus hoping to eliminate the problems that "I" poses. Unless "I" is included in "this," however, this definition is incomprehensible: how shall I know what "the time of this" is, unless it is *my* time at the moment in which I am asking the question? In the same manner, how shall I know what "the place of this" is, unless I can establish it in relation to *my* place at that moment?

25. At this place in Russell's text, a footnote informs us, "Or, if we take 'I-now' as fundamental, exactly the same problems will arise concerning it as those that otherwise arise concerning 'this.' "

26. Gareth Evans, whose book *The Varieties of Reference* is Russellian in essence,

offers an interesting variation on the derivation of "I" from other indexicals. He chooses *here* as the most fundamental word, while emphasizing that "here" is not "where I am," but rather a network of thoughts: "The suggestion is wrong, anyway, in giving a primacy to 'I' over 'here.' . . . To understand how 'here'-thoughts work, we must realize that they belong to a system of thoughts about places that also includes such thoughts as 'It's F *over here*,' 'It's F *up there to the left*,' 'It's F *a bit behind me.*' Here'-thoughts are merely the least specific of this series. We may regard this as an *egocentric* mode of thought.

The subject conceives himself to be in the centre of a space (at its point of origin), with its co-ordinates given by the concepts 'up' and 'down,' 'left' and 'right,' and 'in front' and 'behind.' . . . A subject's 'here-thoughts' belong to this system: 'here' will denote a more or less extensive area which centres on the subject" (Gareth Evans, *The Varieties of Reference* [Oxford: Clarendon Press, 1982], 153–54, Evans' emphasis).

Despite Evans' emphatic tone and repetetive argument, I find his demonstration unconvincing. How shall I know what is "up," "down," "to the left," or "behind *me*," unless I have a sense that: 1) I am; 2) I am somewhere in space; and 3) I know exactly where in that space I am—so that I can know where "up," "down," "to the left" or "behind *me*" are? What is at stake here is precisely the "subject," his or her relationship to perceptions, and his or her language (his or her "I"); Evans' demonstration begs the question, in that it presupposes the very same factor (the subject) that it sets out to derive from "here." Evans' blindness to this presupposition leads him directly into the trap around which Russell was tiptoeing so carefully.

On the priority of "here" over "I," see also Vesey.

27. See Russell: "If you excite a dog by saying 'rats!' when there are no rats, your speech belongs to a language of higher order, since it is not caused by rats, but the dog's understanding of it belongs to the object-language" (*Inquiry,* 84). Or again, "The man, therefore, who understands only object-words, will be able to tell you everything that *is* in the larder, but will be unable to infer that there is no cheese" (90, Russell's emphasis).

28. This example warrants a distinction: for Russell, recalling what I had for breakfast would not apply here, since habit informs me that I usually have breakfast and that, therefore, there is something here to be recalled. On the different mechanisms of memory, see ibid., esp. 192–202.

29. Borges' "Funes the Memorious" presents an enlightening variation on this theme: Funes suffers from a "perfect memory." In Russell's terms, the "afferent current" keeps running in the brain and keeps producing efferent impulses, without ever being stored away. Any "additional stimulus" is then a "new" stimulus. Funes' mental universe knows only *presence,* as his memories are never stored *away* but at all times crowd his brain. (We could also say that he never goes beyond the object-language, but that would be a new and, in fact, impossible version of Russell's object-language.) The result of this peculiar abnormality is that Funes' memory is so accurate that it retains the specificity of each percept, to the extent that a dog seen from a garden *is not* the same dog seen from the house, and a dog seen at 3:00 *is not* the same dog seen at 3:01. Therefore he wishes to coin new names for each percept in

each fraction of his present, even though these names would be given to what we normally consider the "same" objects. Eventually, his brain's linguistic space is so cluttered that he can no longer effect the necessary abstraction leading to "concepts": he can no longer "think." Jorge Luis Borges, *Labyrinths: Selected Stories and Other Writings*, ed. Donald A. Yates and James E. Irby (New York: New Direction, 1962), 59–68; the story is translated by James E. Irby).

30. Published in 1927 (thirteen years before *Inquiry*), *An Outline of Philosophy* is less radical in its elimination of the past. Russell's critique of the notion of substance brings him to elaborate on the traditionally timeless *substratum:* "And it must be understood that the same reasons which lead to the rejection of substance lead also to the rejection of 'things,' and 'persons' as ultimately valid concepts. I say 'I sit at the table,' but I ought to say: 'One of a certain string of events causally connected in the sort of way that makes the whole series that is called a 'person' has a certain spatial relation to one of another string of events causally connected with each other in a different way and having a spatial configuration of the sort denoted by the word 'table.' I do not say so, because life is too short; but that is what I should say if I were a true philosopher" (*Outline*, 254–55).

31. The opening lines of Russell's own autobiography are revealing: "*My first vivid recollection* is my arrival at Pembroke Lodge in February 1876. To be accurate, *I do not remember* the actual arrival at the house, though I remember the big glass roof of the London Terminus, presumably Paddington, at which I arrived on my way, and which I thought inconceivably beautiful" (*The Autobiography of Bertrand Russell* [Boston: Little Brown & Co., 1967], 7). The grounding of the subject *as a subject* conforms to the theory: one can speak of a biography, that is, of a consciousness engaged in representing itself over time as such, once one has established the string of events that constitute one's "I." I-now does not make a "subject": inasmuch as consciousness exists in time only, memory must precede consciousness. We can wonder, however, whether "the big glass roof of the London Terminus" is the starting "prominent incident," or a memory to which Russell was gradually led by association. We may of course imagine that Russell often found himself in the London Terminus, so that the sight of the glass roof, having many "associative links with the present" constitutes the "prominent incident from which all further memories proceed"; or again, that he often found objects and places "inconceivably beautiful," so that the predicate acted as his link with the present. If this be the case, we have to imagine that Russell's memories were stored away in perfect order, thus enabling him to reel off his life story by means of an orderly summoning of the neatly preserved series of I-now's that made up his life. This possibility seems highly unlikely (besides, even then we would notice that Russell "cheats" a little, since he starts his narrative not with the London Terminus but with Pembroke Lodge, which he claims as a "first recollection"—only to disclaim it in the next sentence). It would be more likely that, whatever the prominent recollection was, in whatever order subsequent recollections were brought to his consciousness, Russell then made an editorial choice: he decided to tell his biography in chronological order—independently of the order in which the recollections came to his mind. This apparently simple explanation raises a thorny problem, however: since his autobiographical narration re-

spects linear time, we must presume that when he sat down to write his autobiography, Russell had in his "brain" the whole set of his recollections; as he came to relating a period of his life, he carefully picked the recollections pertaining to that period, thus creating the chronological order of his narrative in a mimetic way, notwithstanding the "mess" of his associations. The problem is that this method requires all his life's events to be simultaneously present to his consciousness, all his I-then's to be encapsulated in his I-now; this, of course, is incompatible with the theory he presents in *Outline* and in *Inquiry*. The question remains open.

32. Marcel Proust, *Remembrance of Things Past: Swann's Way*, trans. C. K. Scott Moncrieff (New York: Modern Library, 1958), 58.

33. A "uniquely referring use" of an expression occurs in the case of indexicals and expressions beginning with the definite article "the" followed by a noun in the singular ("the table," "the old man," "the king of France"). Peter F. Strawson, "On Referring," in his *Logico-Linguistic Papers* (London: Methuen & Co., 1971), 1–2; hereafter cited as "On Referring."

Strawson distinguishes between *expression* and *sentence;* since the two classes function identically with respect to truth, I shall avoid cluttering my terminology with this distinction and adopt the normal use of *sentence.*

34. At this point, Russell introduces an existential condition: a person uttering "The king of France is bald" is asserting two things about the king of France: 1) that there is today one and only one king of France (the existential proposition); and 2) that this king of France is indeed bald.

35. Russell would probably recommend that I say, "You are right in asserting that there is one and only one king of France and that he is bald," or "You are wrong in asserting that there is one and only one king of France and he is bald." I do not wish to dwell too long on the Strawson-Russell debate. The reader may, however, consult Russell, "Mr. Strawson on Referring," in *Essays in Analysis,* ed. Douglas Lackey (London: George Allen & Unwin, 1973), 120–26. Among the numerous essays on this debate, I shall mention C. E. Caton, "Strawson on Referring," Arthur Jacobson, "Russell and Strawson on Referring," and Herbert Hochberg, "Strawson, Russell, and the King of France," all in *Essays on Bertrand Russell,* ed. E. D. Klemke (Chicago: University of Chicago Press, 1970), 213–19, 285–308, 309–40 respectively.

36. Strawson, "Reply to Mackie and Hidé Ishiguro," in *Philosophical Subjects. Essays Presented to P. F. Strawson,* ed. Zak Van Straaten (Oxford: Clarendon Press, 1980), 267; hereafter *Phil. Subjects.*

37. See also Strawson: "If as a result of mistaking a part of someone else's body for a part of his own, he thinks, 'And I'm bleeding profusely,' when in fact he is not bleeding at all, then what he thinks is false but—and because—the reference to himself is unshaken" (*Phil. Subjects,* 267).

38. That Kafka never wrote this sentence is a tribute to the economy and the irony of his story. The closest he comes to a clear statement to this effect is "Yet, as far as Hagenbek was concerned, the place for apes was in front of a locker—well then, I had to stop being an ape" (*Stories,* 253), followed at the end of the story with "On the whole, at any rate, I have achieved what I set out to achieve" (259). We

should therefore resist the temptation to bridge over the two extremes, or to plug a neat expression (such as evolution for example) in the gap carefully constructed by Kafka. For such "plugs" see, for instance, "'A Report to an Academy' is the story of a mutation" (Marthe Robert, *Kafka* [Paris: Gallimard, 1960], 85, trans. mine); see also her mention of the ape as one of Kafkas's many "hybrids" (esp. *As Lonely as Franz Kafka,* 189–93). I find the words *mutation* and *hybrid* highly objectionable, in that they name brutally the silence on which the story hinges and present an interpretation as if it were a textual fact.

39. See Strawson, *Individuals: An Essay in Descriptive Metaphysics* (Garden City, N.Y.: Anchor Books, 1963), esp. the chapter "Persons," 81–113; hereafter cited as *Individuals.*

40. Toward the end of his chapter on "persons," Strawson introduces a second definition: instead of "corporeal" and "states of consciousness" characteristics, he suggests "M-predicates," where *M* stands for material (Strawson's example is "weighs 10 tons"), and "P-predicates," where *P* stands for person. For P-predicates he offers a series of examples, as well as some generalizations. The examples are: "is smiling," "is going for a walk," "is in pain," "is thinking hard," "believes in God," "feels tired," "is depressed," "is coiling a rope, playing ball, writing a letter." What these activities share, says Strawson, is some level of intention and consciousness—which makes P-predicates a variant of what he previously termed states of consciousness

This new definition raises important questions for our reading of "A Report." Shall we say that predicates such as "is flying" or "scratches his fur" are P-predicates? At first, Strawson seems to accept as P-predicates only those ascribable to human beings, so that P-predicates would preclude those contingent on the anatomy of apes. Nothing in his *logical* line of arguing indicates by what criteria one can determine the extension of P-predicates, however (unless we hold tautologically that P-predicates are for persons, and persons are those to which P- and M-predicates apply). But then, we would have said, *eo ipso,* that *person* and *human being* are synonymous. Such a conclusion would beg the question: we set out to determine the concept of the person and found it to be the type of entity to which we can ascribe both M- and P-predicates; now, if we need to know *already* what "person" is to find such types (i.e., human beings), then our argument is indeed circular.

I think that some hesitations presented as afterthoughts at the end of the essay attest to Strawson's awareness of this difficulty: rigorously pursuing his line of reasoning, he analyzes the case of some hypothetical creatures unlike human beings. Not once, however, does he say that these creatures are indeed persons (although he does say that they share some characteristics with persons). When he comes close to having to pronounce on the question, he uses such restrictions as "sometimes," "not, happily, a very large part" (*Individuals,* 111); or, again, after having stated that "the fact that we find it natural to individuate as persons the members of a certain class of moving natural objects does not mean that such a conceptual scheme is inevitable for any class of beings not utterly unlike ourselves" (110), one page later, he nonetheless refers to the very same example that brought him to this far-reaching conclusion as "fantasy" and "hypothesis."

The case of his "Reply to Mackie and Hidé Hishiguro" is even more confusing: after having emphatically insisted that the definitions of *I* and *persons* rest on "human beings" ("the immunity of 'I' from reference-failure (of either kind) in the thought or speech *of any human user of it,* whatever his condition, is guaranteed by the role of the expression in the ordinary practice, well established *among human beings,* of reference to themselves and each other" [*Phil. Subjects,* 267]), he proceeds to praise Hidé Ishiguro for having suggested that "whatever the facts of the matter may be, the concept of a person is such as not to exclude the possibility of persons of a quite different constitution from that of a standard human being" (272). In fact, this last citation is Strawson's own rendition of Hishiguro's point. In the essay to which Strawson is replying, Hishiguro stops short of making this statement and announces rather abruptly that "a fetishist's worship of an inanimate object, and his talking to it or engaging in various ritualized acts with it, does not turn an inanimate object into a person. Nor does the mere fact that certain people talk to and believe they communicate with dogs, goldfish or even plants, establish that dogs, goldfish or plants are persons" ("The Primitiveness of the Concept of a Person," in *Phil. Subjects,* 74). Indeed, there is no *logical* reason to stop at dogs, fish, or even plants, and Strawson's rendition of her thinking is in fact a critique of her *unmotivated* refusal to accept her own conclusions, as well as praise for those inevitable conclusions. And yet it contradicts his own analysis of *I.*

In summary, if this discussion is not very clear, it is simply because neither Strawson nor Hishiguro dares accept the conclusions that their arguments invite. Indeed, the choice is uneasy: either Strawson admits the circular aspect of his argument, or he suggests criteria to distinguish between the extension of P-predicates and that of "person" (in which case he may very well legitimize the claim of the ape to "personhood"). These hesitations and retractions point out that *I* cannot be explained *logically* by means of "person," since logic has proved unable to account for the heterogeneity and not so excluded middles. In Strawson's case the unsatisfactory result of this ragbag is a refusal of the logical conclusions to which his argument leads. Instead, he alternates between pure logic (according to which hypothetical organisms, goldfish, or plants can be seen as "persons") and empiricism (in which case "person" is eventually coextensive with "human beings"—at the expense of pure logic). Since the latter tendency prevails in Strawson's writings, I confine my argument to its framework.

41. Emile Benveniste, *Problems in General Linguistics,* trans. Mary Elizabeth Meek (Coral Gables, Fla.: University of Miami Press, 1971), hereafter cited as *Problems.*

42. See, for example, the opening paragraph of his essay on the colloquium held in Royaumont at which French linguists and philosophers from the Oxford School tried to exchange ideas: "Philosophical interpretations of language generally arouse a certain apprehension in the linguist. Since he is little informed about the movement of ideas, the linguist is prone to think that the problems belonging to language, which are primarily formal problems, cannot attract the philosopher and conversely, that the philosopher is especially interested within language in notions that he, the linguist, cannot make use of. A certain timidity in the face of general ideas probably enters into this attitude. But the aversion of the linguist for everything that he sum-

marily qualifies as 'metaphysical' proceeds above all from a more and more vivid awareness of the formal specificity of linguistic facts, to which philosophers are not sensitive enough" (*Problems,* 231).

43. Gertrude E. M. Anscombe, "The First Person," in *Mind and Language,* ed. Samuel Guttenplan (Oxford: Clarendon Press, 1975), 59, Anscombe's emphasis. See also: "The suggestion of getting the object right collapses into absurdity when we work it out and try to describe how getting hold of the wrong object may be excluded" (58).

44. Zeno Vendler's "transcendental 'I'" addresses the same problem. Vendler, "Note on Parasyllogisms," in *Contemporary Aspects of Philosophy,* ed. Gilbert Ryle (Stockfield, England: Oriel Press, 1976).

45. We could resolve this confusion with a clever twist, by relating Anscombe's use of the word *idea* not to Frege but to Wittgenstein (Anscombe translated Wittgenstein's *Tractatus* into English with an introduction that by now is considered canonical). She is by and large considered a disciple of Wittgenstein and has written extensively about his work. I do not think that it would be adequate to rely on Wittgenstein here; it would indeed be nothing more than a clever twist, since the context of "The First Person" is clearly Fregean (she mentions him three times), and since the evocation of Wittgenstein would cast no light on the specific questions raised by her essay: instead, it would rely on outside information to bypass the problem.

46. For more on Anscombe and the first person see pp. 161–63.

47. Among the philosophical texts that I would have liked to examine more closely, I shall mention Chisholm, *The First Person.* His theory rests on what he terms direct attribution. Since the ape is a textbook case of such direct attributions, it would again validate the theory without accounting for the irony of the story.

Among the linguists, I could have cited Jakobson's theory of shifters (Roman Jakobson, *Shifters, Verbal Categories, and the Russian Verbs* [Russian Language Project, Department of Slavic Languages and Literatures, Harvard University, 1957]). I have omitted Jakobson's theory since with respect to our (and the ape's) viewpoint, it does not differ enough from Benveniste's views to justify a separate treatment.

48. There is indeed a third mode of reading, normally called allegorical, although I prefer to call it analogical: according to an analogical reading, "A Report" is not a story about an ape, nor is it about the development of language and consciousness; it is about *another* "story" similar enough to "A Report" to allow for a complete analogy, a sort of tropological reading according to which "A Report" is the vehicle of the trope while the other story carries the true semantic charge and functions as its tenor. At this point critics all too often abandon the text altogether and eagerly discuss the hidden message they have "uncovered." I have already mentioned the interpretations that reduce "A Report" to an allegory of the conflict between nature and culture, libidinal forces and sublimation, or to a commentary on the delicate situation of Prague Jews (see above, n. 3).

49. "Ape" here relies not on some essentialist view of apes or ape-ness but on the simple fact that he looks like an ape. Had he looked like a man, he might still have interested learned academies, but he would have had no place in a circus. Throughout his speech, his appearance undermines the referential function of his discourse.

In fact, he is neither an ape nor a man, if by these terms we mean a creature (ape or man) with which we are familiar. I should call him an "ape-who-has-acquired-some-human-traits-among-which-the-ability-to-speak-is-the-most-certain," but, to quote Russell, life is too short. Calling him an ape is therefore as much of a pragmatic *parti pris* as deciding to use *he* rather than *it* when referring to him. (I might have opted for Red Peter, had he not rejected this name so violently.) For lack of a proper generic term, I shall therefore keep calling him an ape.

50. For a remarkable reading of a scar that strongly recalls the case of the ape, see Erich Auerbach, "Odysseus' Scar," in his *Mimesis: The Representation of Reality in Western Literature*, trans. William R. Trask (Princeton, N.J.: Princeton University Press, 1953).

51. Franz Kafka, "In the Penal Colony," trans. Willa and Edwin Muir, *Stories*, 145.

52. This fact and the word *artist* have directed the readers of Kafka toward series of analogical readings. For a reading of the story as the lonely fate of artists, see Robert Stallman, *The Art of Modern Fiction* (New York: Reinhard & Co., 1949), 360–73; Steinhauer calls Stallman's reading into question but replaces it with yet another analogical interpretation: "Kafka is not writing about an artist but about an ascetic saint" (Harry Steinhauer, "Hungering Artist or Artist in Hungering: Kafka's 'A Hunger Artist,'" *Criticism* 4, no. 1 (1962): 33.

53. Even so, I would shun an analogical reading in which the formula is $A = B$. Although such interpretations are often plausible and even ingenious, they tend to be equally reductive. See, for example: "the 'wound' is the basic stigma of the ape who has become a human being." (Has he?) "The wound is the metaphor for the condition of man who, though he lives, lives only in a disabled state in a hybrid world that represents neither complete freedom nor complete bondage." Wilhelm Emrich, *Franz Kafka: A Critical Study of His Writings*, trans. Sheema Z. Buehne (New York: Frederick Ungar Publishing Co., 1968), 149.

54. The ape's second syllogism is incorrect. To make this point clearer, let us use the paradigmatic syllogism proving Socrates' mortality, albeit with a slight change, analogous to the one the ape introduces: All men are mortal; Fido *is not* a man; therefore Fido *is not* mortal. The absurdity of the negative premise in the example of Fido is, I hope, obvious. In order to circumvent this kind of abuse, modern logic introduces a restriction in the major premise: all apes *and only* apes are in front of lockers. This correction creates more problems, however, as it requires another bit of information that may not be available or correct, as in, for example: all men *and only* men are mortal (while we know that mortality is not an exclusively human property). For more on syllogism and literature, see my *Tics, tics, et tics: Figures, syllogismes, récit dans Les Chants de Maldoror* (Lexington, Ky.: French Forum Publishers, 1984).

55. I am grateful to Stephen Harrigan, who called my attention to the frequency of the expression "I cannot" in this story, especially since most occurrences have to do with language and consciousness. To name just a few: "I cannot comply with your request" (*Stories*, 250), "I cannot communicate" (251), "I cannot deny" (252), "I cannot reach back to the truth" (253), "I cannot tell now" (254), "I cannot distinguish" (256), "I cannot bear it" (259).

5   Speech Acts

1. To my knowledge, there are only two studies that articulate in some detail the connection between studies of the first person and theories of speech acts: Elisabeth Bruce, *Autobiographical Acts: The Changing Situation of a Literary Genre* (Baltimore: Johns Hopkins University Press, 1976); and Leah Hewitt, "Getting into the (Speech) Act: Autobiography as Theory of Performance," *SubStance* 16, no. 1 (1987): 32–44.

2. See Gottlob Frege, "The Thought: A Logical Enquiry" in *Logic and Philosophy for Linguists*, ed. J. M. E. Moravcsik (The Hague: Mouton, 1974), 282–84; and Gottlob Frege, "On Sense and Reference," in *Translations from the Philosophical Writings of Gottlob Frege*, ed. Peter Geach and Max Black (Oxford: Basil Blackwell, 1970), 67–68; see also the section on Frege in chap. 4.

3. John L. Austin, *How to Do Things with Words*, ed. J. O. Urmson and Marina Sbisà (Cambridge, Mass.: Harvard University Press 1981), 60–62; hereafter cited as *How to*. Searle makes a similar claim in his discussion of "the principle of identification." See John R. Searle, *Speech Acts: An Essay in the Philosophy of Language* (Cambridge: Cambridge University Press, 1969), 78–94; hereafter cited as *Speech Acts*. Unless otherwise indicated, emphasis is mine.

4. The most notable works in the literary perspective are Bruce, *Autobiographical Acts;* Hewitt, "Getting into the (Speech) Act"; Shoshana Felman, *The Literary Speech Act: Don Juan with Austin, or Seduction in Two Languages* (Ithaca, N.Y.: Cornell University Press, 1984); and Mary Louise Pratt, *Toward a Speech Act Theory of Literary Discourse* (Bloomington: Indiana University Press, 1977).

5. John R. Searle, "The Logical Status of Fictional Discourse," in his *Expression and Meaning: Studies in the Theory of Speech Acts* (Cambridge: Cambridge University Press, 1979), hereafter cited as *E&M;* Richard Gale, "The Fictive Use of Language," *Philosophy. The Journal of the Royal Institute of Philosophy* 46, no. 178 (October 1971): 324–39; Joseph Margolis, "Literature and Speech Acts," *Philosophy and Literature* 3, no. 1 (Spring 1979): 39–52. One notable exception to this trend is an insightful essay written by a linguist, George L. Huttar, "Metaphorical Speech Acts," *Poetics* 9, no. 4 (August 1980): 383–401.

6. Felman is the notable exception, as well as Mary Louise Pratt, "The Ideology of Speech Act Theory," *Centrum*, n.s., 1, no. 1 (1981): 5–18, in which she reevaluates the general theory as well as her own earlier work.

7. This section borrows from my "Et la Chose fut: 'La Vénus d'Ille' de Mérimée," *Poétique*, no. 41 (1981): 156–70.

8. "The Venus of Ille," in *The Writings of Prosper Mérimée Comprising His Novels, Tales, and Letters to an Unknown, with an Essay on the Genius and Achievement of the Author by George Saintsbury,* trans. William M. Arnold, Olive Edwards Palmer, and Emily Mary Waller (New York: Frank S. Holby, 1905), 4: 257; hereafter cited as "Venus."

9. For the second part of our discussion of intentions, see pp. 212–16.

10. Pratt, "Ideology of Speech Act Theory," 5. This short essay goes much farther in its analysis of the relevance of the theories for literary studies than does her book. For a good reading and critique of the two, see Hewitt.

11. John Austin, "Other Minds," in *Philosophical Papers,* ed. J. O. Urmson and G. J. Warnock (Oxford: Oxford University Press, 1977), 109.

12. For a detailed analysis of the doubling effect between the statue and Mlle de Puygarrig, see Anne Hiller, "*La Vénus d'Ille* de Mérimée: Figuration d'un dualisme," *Australian Journal of French Studies* 12, no. 2 (1975): 209–19.

13. *Terme,* simply rendered by "statue" in English, is the Roman God of boundaries. His statue was commonly erected to delineate property lines. Both Venus and Terme belong to the general context of Roman mythology in which they stand for opposite values: she is the goddess of transgression, and he is the god of property/propriety.

14. Ora Avni, "1837. Prosper Mérimée Publishes *La Vénus d'Ille.* Fantastic Tales," in *A New History of French Literature,* ed. Denis Hollier (Cambridge, Mass.: Harvard University Press, 1989), 679.

15. In a recent enlightening study of "The Venus of Ille," Ross Chambers has considerably sharpened the definition of the fantastic, in stressing the consequences of narrative indeterminacies. Forced to choose a story in order to progress as a narrative (even though this story may be contradicted later by others), the narrative singles out one of the confused narrative threads, to the exclusion of the others. This exclusion constitutes an act of violence toward the other possible stories crowding the narrative space. Violence, then, rather than indeterminacies, is the telltale sign of the fantastic, and, as Chambers convincingly shows in this reading of the story, it functions both thematically and narratologically. Ross Chambers, "Violence du récit, Boccace, Mérimée, Cortàzar," *Canadian Review of Comparative Literature* 14, no. 2 (1986): 159–86.

16. Stanley Fish, "How to Do Things with Austin and Searle," in his *Is There a Text in This Class? The Authority of Interpretative Communities* (Cambridge, Mass.: Harvard University Press, 1980), 226–27.

17. See especially P. F. Strawson, "Intention and Convention in Speech Acts," *Philosophical Review,* October 1964, 439–60. Of course, it all depends on what we mean by *convention* (see further pp. 302–12).

18. See also Austin's awareness of "the dubiety about what constitutes a subsequent action and what is merely the completion or consummation of the one, single, total action" (*How to,* 43).

19. Cf. Fish: "Here is another instance where the abuse of speech-act theory is also a comment on its limitations: just as it stops short of claiming knowledge of what happens after the performance of an illocutionary act, so is it silent on the question of what (if anything, the whole world may be conventional) preceded it. No one would deny that these are matters for a literary critic to inquire into, but they are the province of rhetoric (the art of persuasion, a perlocutionary art) and psychology. Speech-act theory can tell us nothing about them" (227).

This quotation sums up my disagreement with Fish. Although I generally agree with his critique of various attempts to use speech acts in literary criticism, I take exception to his clean-up method. The question is not one of "after" or "before," as Fish puts it. We are not discussing a haphazard contiguity. In the case of a speech act, what Fish calls "after" is in fact inseparable from the utterance itself: it is its force at the moment it is issued. What may (but does not have to) come "after" is its validation (or infelicity). We should also note that the reduction of speech acts to convention anchors Fish's views in the second (out of twelve) of Austin's lectures and makes no use of the subsequent insights found in *How to Do Things with Words* (including the critique of convention). Furthermore, a typical "theory," it fails to question its own cornerstone (that is, the parameters and limitations of *convention*—a problem that Austin does address, see below, pp. 306–8). Instead, it eliminates from the purported scope of the theory anything liable to interfere with its neatness. Again, I much prefer Austin's "messy" approach.

20. Austin refers here to a rule established in his previous lecture: "We may agree, without insisting on formulations or refinements, that to say anything is (A.a) always to perform the act of uttering certain noises (a 'phonetic' act), and the utterance is a phone" (*How to*, 92).

21. Searle makes a similar distinction between brute and institutional facts. "I am brandishing a club" is a brute fact, while "I am threatening you" is an institutional one of sorts. Or again, to cite Searle's example, "a man has five dollars given the institution of money. Take away the institution and all he has is a rectangular bit of paper with green ink on it. A man hits a home run only given the institution of baseball; without the institution he only hits a sphere with a stick" (John Searle, "How to Derive 'Ought' from 'Is,'" *Philosophical Review* 73 (1964): 54. See also Paul Ricoeur, "The Model of the Text: Meaningful Action Considered as Text," *New Literary History* 5, no. 1 (1973): 91–117.

22. Avni, "Et là chose fut."

23. We may wish to engage in wordplays with *boule ternaire* (the tripartite circle) for Boulternère, which, like the squaring of the circle, polarizes between sense and reference. But the crucial indexical effect of "a league from here" gets lost in the pun.

24. Elaborating on the notion of context to include the reader was Roland Barthes' major point of disagreement with traditional criticism, in his *Critique et Vérité* (Paris: Seuil, 1966). The concept is also operative in most of the reader-response-oriented theories.

25. Jacques Derrida, "Signature Event Context," *Glyph*, no. 1 (1977): 172–97; reprinted in his *Margins of Discourse*, trans. Alan Bass (Chicago: University of Chicago Press, 1982).

26. The following reading of "The King of Bicêtre" uses as its starting point my "A Bicêtre: Austin, Searle, Nerval," *MLN*, May 1983, 624–38.

27. We are clearly treading on treacherous ground: on the one hand, if a sign is to be recognized as such, and if the principle of iterability is to be maintained, this sign must retain roughly the same signification from one occurence to the other. On the other hand, because of contextual and referential semantic and semiotic contaminations, part of a sign's semantic charge may be altered with each occurrence. The reader has surely recognized the tension previously underscored between Saussure's *signified* and *value* or between Frege's *Sinn* and *Vorstellung*. Chapter 6 suggests a way out of this predicament.

28. Jacques Derrida, "Declarations of Independence," trans. Tom Keenan and Tom Pepper, *New Political Science*, no. 15 (Summer 1986): 7–15; hereafter cited as "Declarations."

29. Derrida quotes Jefferson's draft, which was later edited by Congress. The

final and copiously edited version shows that the Founding Fathers were very much aware of the problems raised by Derrida: their correction in fact defuses or at least displaces most of Derrida's criticism. The final version of the Declaration of Independence says (my emphasis on the changed expressions): "We therefore the representatives of the United states of America in General Congress assembled, *appealing to the Supreme Judge of the world for the rectitude of our intentions,* do in the name, & by the authority of the good people *of these colonies, solemnly publish & declare, that these* United *colonies* are & of right ought to be free & independent states." This version changes Jefferson's text considerably in that it refers to the "people of the colonies" and not "the people of the United states of America," thus ensuring that the moment at which the declaration is signed constitutes the turning point from colonies to States, and avoiding Derrida's catch-22. (And indeed, the word *state* is systematically expunged from Jefferson's draft: once it is simply eliminated, once replaced with *us,* and twice with *colonies.*

30. Whether the Declaration of Independence was in fact, historically, a performative or constative document remains in question. A case may be made for the claim that since the vote on Lee's resolution that the colonies "are [expunged: at that very moment], and of right ought to be, free and independent states" took place on 2 July (this phrase is reproduced in the Declaration of 4 July), that resolution was actually the performative document while the Declaration of 4 July was a constative attempt to explain to the world what had happened on 2 July (of course, this would only displace our discussion from the document of 4 July to the one of 2 July). For this discussion see, for example, Garry Wills, *Inventing America: Jefferson's Declaration of Independence* (Garden City, N.Y.: Doubleday & Co., 1978), 334–45, and appendix, which contains Jefferson's draft and the final version. Wills, who makes this point forcefully and convincingly, nonetheless acknowledges that because of historical misreadings, forgetfulness, and sheer confusion, the events of 2 July were wrongly condensed into those of 4 July (Jefferson's own forgetfulness largely contributed to this historical error), and the Declaration of Independence, although intended as a constative document, has come generally to be accepted as a performative proclamation. Since this discussion is clearly not fully conclusive (though fascinating), I think it best to assume, with Derrida, that "one cannot decide—and that's the interesting thing, the force and the coup of force [*coup de force*] of such a declarative act—whether independence is *stated* or *produced* by this utterance" ("Declarations," 9, Derrida's emphasis).

31. The ambiguity of the word *people* in English is cleverly exploited by Derrida. In the Declaration, does it mean "nation" or "persons"? Derrida clearly takes it as "nation" ("Or ce peuple n'existe pas. Il n'existe pas avant cette déclaration, pas comme tel.") Back to English: the translators added a clause using the plural, implying "persons"; then they returned to the singular, as in the French, implying "nation" ("But *this* people *does* not exist. *They do* not exist *as an entity, it does* not exist, before this declaration, not as such.") Clearly, no one is disputing that there were people in those territories—but was there a people?

32. On this question see an interesting attempt to define political authority in terms of speech act theory: Patrick H. Nowell-Smith, "What Is Authority?" *Philosophic Exchange* 2, no. 2 (1976): 3–15. See also its attempted refutation in R. R.

McGuire, "Speech Acts, Communicative Competence, and the Paradox of Authority," *Philosophy and Rhetoric* 10, no. 1 (1977): 30–45.

33. We cannot discuss here the signing of the declaration, but we should note the long time it took for all the signatures to be collected, as well as the fact that, as the Declaration was almost immediately perceived as an performative document, the question of its signing became increasingly important. For the riveting details see Wills, 340–44, and compare with Austin's rules B.1 and B.2 ("[B.1] The procedure must be executed by all participants both correctly and [B.2] completely" [*How to*, 15]).

34. Indeed, unlike logicians, historians—whose task it is to explore contexts as much as events—are sensitive to the political continuity illustrated by the Founding Fathers. S. E. Morison, for example, notes that "many ideas of the germinal Americans can be traced back to the mother country. In England these ideas persisted through the centuries, despite a certain twisting and thwarting at the hands of Tudor monarchs and Whig aristocrats; in America they found opportunity for free development. Thus we . . . find stout old English prejudices embalmed in the American Bills of Rights, and institutions long obsolete in England . . . lasting with little change in the American States until the middle of the nineteenth century. It was an unconscious mission of the United States to make explicit what had long been implicit in the British constitution, and to prove the value of principles that had largely been forgotten in the England of George III" (*The Oxford History of the United States* [Oxford: Clarendon Press, 1927], 1:39f.; cited by Ernst Cassirer in *An Essay on Man: An Introduction to a Philosophy of Human Culture* [New Haven, Conn.: Yale University Press, 1966), 181).

35. "Γ.1 Where, as often, the procedure is designed for use by persons having certain thoughts or feelings, or for the inauguration of certain consequential conduct on the part of any participant, then a person participating in and so invoking the procedure must in fact have those thoughts or feelings, and the participants must intend so to conduct themselves" (*How to*, 15).

36. Derrida's critique remains pertinent for other political speech acts. Using the same argument borrowed from speech act theories, Sandy Petrey questions the legitimacy of the revolutionary oath taken by the French National Assembly on 20 June 1789 and concludes with the tautological situation underscored by Derrida that "by the authority vested in it, the National Assembly declared that authority was vested in it." Sandy Petrey, *Realism and Revolution: Balzac, Stendhal, Zola, and the Performances of History* (Ithaca, N.Y.: Cornell University Press, 1988), 23.

37. *Illuminé* means at once "enlightened" and "crazy," so that even the title of the collection conveys the same ambiguity.

38. John L. Austin, "A Plea for Excuses," in *Philosophical Papers*, 188.

39. Searle envisions the possiblity that some of these steps may, in effect, be condensed into one, but this factual telescoping does not alter the *logical* sequence. See John R. Searle, "Reiterating the Differences: A Reply to Derrida," *Glyph* 1, no. 1 (1977): 198–208.

40. For a thorough survey of this quarrel, see Paul Ricoeur, *The Rule of Metaphor: Multidisciplinary Studies of the Creation of Meaning in Language*, trans. Robert Lzerny (Toronto: University of Toronto Press, 1977).

41. See, see my *Tics, tics, et tics: Figures, syllogismes, récit dans les Chants de Maldoror* (Lexington, Ky.: French Forum Publishers, 1984), pt. 2.

42. André Breton, *Point du jour* (Paris: Gallimard, 1970), 23, trans. mine.

43. Note that Searle is aware of what has been called after Wimsatt the intentional fallacy, but he remains firmly entrenched in his convictions. "There used to be a school of literary critics who thought one should not consider the intentions of the author when examining a work of fiction. Perhaps there is some level of intention at which this extraordinary view is plausible; perhaps one should not consider an author's ulterior motives when analyzing his work, but at the most basic level it is absurd to suppose a critic can completely ignore the intentions of the author, since even so much as to identify a text as a novel, a poem, or even as a text is already to make a claim about the author's intentions" (*E&M*, 66).

44. Stanley Fish, "How to Recognize a Poem When You See One" in his *Is There a Text in This Class?*

45. Gérard de Nerval, "The King of Bicêtre," in *Oeuvres de Gérard de Nerval* (Paris: Gallimard/Pléiade, 1956), 1: 940, trans. here by Mark Gross and Ora Avni; hereafter cited as "Bicêtre."

46. See Nerval's preface to the collection *Les Illuminés*, "My Uncle's Library": "In these times, when literary portraits are fashionable, I wanted to depict some of philosophy's *eccentrics* (*certains excentriques de la philosophie*). . . . These reflexions have led me to develop mostly the amusing and perhaps instructive aspect that the lives and the characters of my *eccentrics* might present" *Oeuvres de Gérard de Nerval*, 937–38, trans. mine, Nerval's emphasis.

47. For the social and legal function of the king, see also chapter 6, esp. "Law and Cuckoldry."

48. Bertrand Russell, "On Denoting," in his *Logic and Knowledge* (New York: G. P. Putnam's Sons, Capricorn Book, 1971): 158.

48. See: "It must be said the two companions, seeing hardly anyone but themselves in the world, without respite spent their time, the one asking for favors, and the other granting them" ("Bicêtre," 948).

50. "Contained in this present volume six and twenty decrees pronounced in the year one thousand five hundred and fifty six by the very Christian King Henry II, in his Imperial and Pontifical Justice, or executorial of sacred decrees, conciliar and apostolic, rendered by him in person; in his private consistory, his very excellent sovereignty, temporal or spiritual."

51. J. Katz, "How to Save Austin from Austin," in his *Propositional Structure and Illocutionary Force* (Hassocks, England: Harvester Press, 1977).

52. I use the word *normal* here because in the next paragraph, Austin mentions the possibility that purely constative utterances may be found in mathematical formulae in physics books. Since I do not take a mathematical formula to be normal language, as Frege's *Begriffschrift* illustrates so well, we can safely assume that Austin answers negatively the question of whether a philosopher can theorize the logical status of an expression independently of its reception.

53. For the full quotation see p. 31.

54. Derrida, "Signature Event Context."

6   The Semiotic Value: *The Three Musketeers*

1. The following reading of *The Three Musketeers* borrows extensively from my "Ils Courent, ils courent les ferrets: Mauss, Lacan et *Les Trois Mousquetaires*," *Poétique*, May 1985, 215–35; trans. Jonathan Rosenthal as "The Semiotics of Transactions: Mauss, Lacan and *The Three Musketeers*," *MLN*, September 1985, 728–57.

2. Marcel Mauss, *The Gift: Forms and Functions of Exchange in Archaic Societies*, trans. Ian Cunnison (Glencoe, Ill.: Free Press, 1954), hereafter cited as *Gift;* and Jacques Lacan, "The Seminar on 'The Purloined Letter,'" trans. Jeffrey Mehlman, *Yale French Studies*, no. 48 (1972): 38–72; hereafter cited as "Seminar." I shall also keep in mind Derrida, "The Purveyor of Truth," trans. Barbara Johnson, *Yale French Studies*, no. 52 (1975). These essays are constant points of reference for this chapter, as is Barbara Johnson's commentary, "The Frame of Reference: Poe, Lacan, Derrida," *Yale French Studies*, no. 55/56 (1977): 457–505; reprinted in Johnson, *The Critical Difference: Essays in the Contemporary Rhetoric of Reading* (Baltimore: Johns Hopkins University Press, 1982). I shall discuss some of the issues opposing the powerful texts about Poe's story: the "materiality" and "divisibility" of the letter, the questions raised by the "proper course," the "point of origin," the "content of the letter," the "quotient" and the "remainders." Since these texts are widely known, I shall only allude to the issues.

3. Cf. Mauss: "One does not have the right to refuse a gift or a potlatch. To do so would show fear of having to repay, and of being abased in default. One would 'lose the weight' of one's name by admitting defeat in advance" (*Gift*, 39).

4. Cf. Mauss: "But the remarkable thing about these tribes is the spirit of rivalry and antagonism which dominates all their activities. . . . But the agonistic character of the prestation is pronounced. Essentially usurious and extravagant, it is above all a struggle among nobles to determine their position in the hierarchy to the ultimate benefit, if they are successful, of their own clans" (*Gift*, 4–5).

5. Alexandre Dumas, *The Three Musketeers* (London: J. M. Dent & Sons, 1966), 131; hereafter cited as *TM*.

6. In this regard one could cite the argument that separates ethnographers or sociologists into two camps: the partisans of the "altruistic gift" and those of the "nonaltruistic gift." While the altruistic gift takes place in a system that has no other goal than itself (Malinowski, Mauss, Lévi-Strauss, Von Neuman, Morgenstern, and even, in a different way, Bataille), the nonaltruistic gift is conceived of as the means that lead to power in a general economy of the least effort or cost (Bailey, Barth, Blau, Kapferer, Paine, etc.). This distinction more or less covers what I have called the (altruistic) gift and the (nonaltruisitic) pledge and what the analysis of the object in circulation puts into question.

This ideological debate stems initially from the importance that pragmatics attribute to the intentionality of the subject. In this sense the parallel established by Parkin with Saussure's distinction between *langue* and *parole*, is particularly pertinent, as is his attempt to muddle the limits that separate the two domains (David Parkin, "Exchanging Words," in *Transaction and Meaning: Directions in the Anthropology of Exchange and Symbolic Behavior*, ed. Bruce Kapferer (Philadelphia: Institute for the Study of Human Issues, 1976).

7. This section is to a large extent a commentary on the controversy between Lacan and Derrida regarding the divisibility and the materiality of the letter in Poe's "Purloined Letter."

8. David Parkin establishes a distinction that resembles my notion of semiotic value; the vagueness of the word *meaning* clouds his distinction, however. "The gift may assume a variety of forms, material and non-material, and may be said to release symbolic 'meaning' in the context of the relationship. The symbol itself may be regarded as de Saussure's 'sign,' which can be broken down into two components: the 'signifying,' in other words the locus or gift itself, and the 'signified,' or the social relationship. The general 'meaning' of the symbol is then the social implications and consequences of the perpetuation of this particular culturally recognized relationship of gift exchange as distinct from other form relationships" (Parkin 170–71).

9. Cf. Saussure: "The linguistic sign unites not a thing and a name, but a concept and a sound-image. *The latter is not the material sound,* a purely physical thing, but the *psychological imprint* of the sound, the impression that it makes on our senses. The sound-image is sensory, and if I happen to call it 'material,' it is only in that sense, and by way of opposing it to the other term of the association, the concept, which is generally more abstract" (Ferdinand de Saussure, *Course in General Linguistics,* ed. Charles Bally and Albert Sechehaye, in collaboration with Albert Riedlinger, trans. Wade Baskin [New York: Philosophical Library, 1959], 66).

10. For a critique of Lacan's appropriation of the Saussurean terminology, see Vincent Descombes, *Objects of All Sorts: A Philosophical Grammar,* trans. Lorna Scott-Fox and Jeremy Harding (Baltimore: Johns Hopkins University Press, 1986), esp. chap. 5.

11. See Lacan's claim: "Which is why we have decided to illustrate for you today the truth which may be drawn from that moment in Freud's thought under study— namely, that it is the symbolic order which is constitutive *for the subject*—by demonstrating in a story *the decisive orientation which the subject receives from the itinerary of a signifier*" ("Seminar," 40).

For the definition of *la politique de l'autruiche,* see: "In order to grasp in its unity the intersubjective complex thus described, we would willingly seek a model in the technique legendarily attributed to the ostrich attempting to shield itself from danger: for that technique might ultimately be qualified as political, divided as it here is among three partners: the second believing itself invisible because the first has its head stuck in the ground, and all the while letting the third calmly pluck its rear; we need only enrich its proverbial denomination by a letter, producing *la politique de l'autruiche,* for the the ostrich itself to take on forever a new meaning" ("Seminar," 44). *La politique de l'autruiche* condenses *autruche,* "ostrich," and *autrui,* "other people."

12. See Lacan: "Sans doute, pour jouer l'atout, faut-il qu'on ait la main. Mais cette main n'est pas maîtresse. Il n'y a pas trente-six façons de jouer une partie, même s'il n'y en a pas seulement une. C'est la partie qui commande, dès que la distribution est faite selon la règle qui la soustrait au pouvoir de la main" (Jacques Lacan, *Ecrits I* [Paris: Seuil, 1966] 7).

13. This is all the more true in that the "three" is dictated by the caprice of a fiction ("The Purloined Letter") and in that, if there is any "truth" in fiction, it is

that we should avoid taking any work at face value, while avoiding also the over-generalization of one of its hermeneutic effects to the extent that it might transcend the formal specificity of the text in which it occurs. Thus there is no theoretical necessity to stop at "three": to the three moments of the *politique de l'autruiche* one could add a fourth, a glance that the third, busy plucking the feathers of the second, would not see; and so forth. Logically, the series is open and the Lacanian signifier should be able to continue its drift indefinitely.

14. Lewis Carroll, *Alice's Adventures in Wonderland* (New York: Avenel Books, n.d.), 122.

15. This insistence on the *one* was particularly emphasized by Barbara Johnson.

16. The apologetic introduction to the conservative French Garnier edition of *The Three Musketeers* (Paris: Garnier, 1968) reflects the discomfort of critics forced into the scandal of this pleasure: "*The Three Musketeers* in the *Classiques Garnier!* Alexandre Dumas *père* enshrined in the Pantheon of French literature! Why not?"

17. Roland Barthes, *The Pleasure of the Text,* trans. Richard Miller (New York: Hill & Wang, 1975), 23.

18. D'Artagnan brutally throws himself on Athos' wounded shoulder (Athos won't admit to the seriousness of his wound), gets himself all tangled up in Porthos' cape—thus discovering that his baldrick, which everybody is admiring, is richly decorated on one side only—and calls attention to the feminine handkerchief that Aramis accidentally dropped and is trying to hide from his friend. In this manner he gets hold of all the virtual stories the budding narrative may comprise.

19. "We confine the study to certain chosen areas. . . . Again, since we are concerned with words and their meanings, we have naturally chosen only areas where we have access to the minds of the societies through documentation and philological research. This further limits our field of comparison. Each particular study has a bearing on the *systems* we set out to describe and *is presented in its logical place*" (*Gift,* 2–3, modified trans.).

20. The document in question is as follows: "I shall tell you about *hau. Hau* is not the wind. Not at all. Suppose you have some particular object, *taonga,* and you give it to me; you give it to me without a price. We do not bargain over it. Now I give this thing to a third person who after a time decides to give me something in repayment for it (*utu*), and he makes me a present of something (*taonga*). Now this *taonga* I received from him is the spirit (*hau*) of the *Taonga* I received from you and which I passed on to him. The *taonga* that came from you, I must return to you. It would not be right on my part to keep these *taonga* whether they were desirable or not. I must give them to you since they are the *hau* of the *taonga* which you gave me. If I were to keep this second *taonga* for myself I might become ill or even die. Such is *hau,* the *hau* of personal property, the *hau* of the *taonga,* the *hau* of the forest. Enough on that subject" (*Gift,* 8–9).

21. See Rodolphe Gasché, "L'Echange héliocentrique," *L'Arc,* no. 48 (1972): 70–84, whose reading of Mauss intersects my own.

22. Edgar Allan Poe, *The Portable Poe,* selected and edited by Philip Van Doren Stern (New York: Penguin Books, 1977), 461.

23. "The gift is thus something that must be given, that must be received and that

is, at the same time, dangerous to accept. *The gift itself constitutes an irrevocable link*" (*Gift*, 58).

24. Thus, despite his loyalty to the king and to France, despite Athos' reminder that they are at war with England and that the queen's lover is the enemy, d'Artagnan will attempt to foil Richelieu's plans and to prevent Buckingham's assassination.

25. Grimaud and Planchet are the footmen of Athos and d'Artagnan.

26. There again, there is a muddling of values: "the Englishman calculated fast: the two harnesses were worth *three hundred pistoles*. He consented" (*TM*, 301).

27. If we limit ourselves to the realistic motivation of psychological plausibility, the gratitude and admiration that Richelieu pledges to d'Artagnan are illogical. One can scarcely understand why Richelieu, who, because of d'Artagnan, has lost the game he wanted so much to win, is in such a hurry to summon the young man and to assure him that he "wished him well," that "His Eminence is very well disposed towards him, and that his fortune perhaps depends upon this interview" (*TM*, 247). The same goes for the promotion to lieutenant after d'Artagnan admits to the assassination of Milady. This magnanimity is absurd unless we attribute it to the role that Richelieu plays in the logic of gifts and debts: undoubtedly caught in a chain in which he emulates successively the king, the queen, the lover, and the third party.

28. Roland Barthes, "L'Effet de réel," *Communication*, no. 11 (1968): 84–89.

29. One can compare this letter to the one that circulates in *La Princesse de Clèves*. After it has fallen out of the Vidame de Chartres' pocket, the letter is erroneously attributed to the Duc de Nemours. This referential misunderstanding is due to the pronouns: since the letter bears no name and evokes no identifiable referential circumstances, each of its readers interprets the letter's *I/you* dialectic in his or her own way according to his or her concerns of the moment. Each one can, as he or she wishes, either claim the letter or refuse to admit any relation to it. Moreover, each one is free to believe or not to believe the affirmations of the others. Eventually the letter winds up compromising all those who either held it or heard of it.

30. As a negative example, we may quote the episode in which the jealous king learns from a spy that his queen has received a secret missive. Suspecting that it might come from Buckingham, he has the letter brutally seized (the queen hides it on her person), only to discover that his foreign wife (Anne of Austria) is plotting against the life of Richelieu with her brother, the king of Spain and sworn enemy of France (whose motives are purely political: Richelieu is the strong man in France, and without him the king is as good as defeated). Now this would seem like a very serious affair and should irremediably confound the queen and neutralize her influence at court, if not lead her to prison, or worse. Surprisingly, the king expresses his relief, and the letter has no consequences. This highly improbable incident makes sense only if we understand it not so much by means of psychological or political motivation or any other aspect of verisimilitude, but as an extraneous element in the narrative chain governed by the semiotic values of the studs: if it is not related to the shuttle of objects between the Englishman and the queen, *it does not count*—even though, to all intents and purposes, the content of the letter from the king of Spain is far more incriminating than any evidence the king might find on his queen's shoulder on the evening of the royal ball, had d'Artagnan failed in his mission.

Index

Abuse. *See* Agrammaticality

Agrammaticality: communication of, xiii, 46, 119, 143, 171; and conventions, 195

Aim: *See* Deictic aim; Semantic aim

Anscombe, Gertrude E.: and Descartes's cogito, 155, 157; on equality, 156; on first person, 154–58; and Frege, 155, 156–57; on immunity of *I* to reference-failure, 154–55; and "A Report to an Academy," 157–58, 162–63; vs. Russell, 155; on self-consciousness, 162–63; vs. Strawson, 155; and *Vorstellung*, 156–57. See also *I*; "Report to an Academy, A"

Aporia, xii; and Austin, 227, 230

Austin, John: on conventions, 189–90; 191–92, 195; and Derrida, 228; on effects, 186, 193; and Frege, 228; on intentionality, 179–80; on law, 211; on literature, 200–202; on oversimplification, 192, 196; on performative vs. constantive, 192, 226–27; on perlocution, 187–88, 189; on psychoanalysis and philosophy, 181–82; on reception, 227–28; and Saussure, 228; on translating Frege, 108; on use of examples, 228–29. *See also* Fish, Stanley; Searle, John; "King of Bicêtre, The"; Speech acts theories; "Venus of Ille, The"

Baker and Hacker, 111–12, 284nn.32, 33

Bally, Charles, 62, 73–76; and Frege, 73–74, 99. See also *Cours de linguistique générale, Le,* editors of; Saussure, Ferdinand de, and editors of *Le Cours de linguistique générale*

Bedeutung. See Frege, Gottlob, on reference

Benveniste, Emile, 146–54; and Descarte's cogito, 151; on first person, 146–54; on first person's immunity to reference-failure, 148, 150, 152; and Frege, 121–22, 126–27, 149; on nonperson, 148; on philosophy, 146–47; and "A Report to an Academy," 153–54; on Saussure, 55–61, and Strawson, 148–49, 151; on subjectivity, 151–53; on taxonomies, 56–59. *See also* "Report to an Academy, A"

Borges, Jorge Luis, 290n.29

Bréal, Michel, 34, 60, 276n.16

Carroll, Lewis: *Alice in Wonderland,* 66, 245, 274n.9; *Through the Looking Glass,* 65

Chomsky, Noam: Culler on, 38; and Frege, 109; on Saussure, 277n.23

Conventions: Austin on, 191–92; 195; Fish on, 187, 195; grey areas of, 191–92; Searle on, 195; and speech acts, 191–95; translation as limit of applicability of, 196–99; in "The Venus of Ille," 191–99

Cours de linguistique générale, Le: editors of, 15, 18–21, 275n.8; structure of, 26. *See also* Saussure, Ferdinand de

Circular arguments: and Anscombe, 157; and Evans, 289n.26; and Fish, 203; and Frege, 105–6 (*see also* Frege, Gottlob, and use of "otherwise"); and Russell, 131–32; 289n.24; and Strawson, 142–43; and systems, 10–11, 273n.8; Culler, Jonathan, 35–40; and Chomsky, 38; and Ogden and Richards, 38–39; on starting point, 36–39

Deictic aim, 8–9, 11; and experience, 9, 10, 12–13; and knowledge, 8–9, 12–13; and madness, 217–18; vs. semantic aim, 262–63; and "theories," 266; vanishing of, 53; and *Vorstellung*, 262;

Deictic aim (*cont'd*)
  weakness of, 7–8. *See also* "De la sori-
  sete de estopes"; Semantic aim
De Mauro, Tullio, 46, 72, 100, 278n.26
Denotation vs. connotation: and Bally's
  distinction between value and significa-
  tion, 73–74; as sense vs. *Vorstellung*,
  285n.33; as value vs. signified, 53–54
Derrida, Jacques: on Austin, 228; on Dec-
  laration of Independence, 204–6, 208;
  on divisibility of signifier, 243; on itera-
  bility, 55, 203, 262; on Poe's "Purloined
  Letter," 243, 258–59; on Rousseau,
  288n.20
Descartes's cogito, 115; Anscombe on,
  157; and Russell, 130, 289n.21; and
  Strawson, 143, 151
"De la sorisete des estopes," 2–13, 269–
  72; agrammaticalities in, 46; and Bally,
  74–75; difference vs. opposition in, 49–
  50; entities in, 67; and Frege, 83, 85;
  273n.3; *parole* vs. *langue* in, 44–45;
  performance in, 4–5, 12–13; Saussure's
  predicament and, 73
Dumas, Alexander. See *Three Musketeers,
  The*
Dummett, Michael: on Frege's object,
  281n.10; on Frege's reference, 89–91,
  282n.12; and "theory," 90; on *Vorstel-
  lung*, 110–11

Excess, 246–53; D'Artagnan and, 252–
  53; Frege's sense and, 98
Exclusion: of irrelevant data, 199–200; of
  perlocution, by Fish, 187–89, 224; of
  perlocution, by Searle, 224; of puzzles,
  by Searle, 223; of temporality, by Rus-
  sell, 134–35; and "theories," 199–200;
  of third parties, 249–52; of *Vorstel-
  lung*, 105–6, 109–12, 124, 126,
  285n.39

Fabliau. *See* "De la sorisete des estopes"
First person. See *I*
Fish, Stanley: on conventions, 195, 203–
  9; on conventions and effects, 186–89;
  on perlocution, 224; on poetry, 216;

and "theory," 195, 200. *See also* Speech
  acts theories; "Theory"
Frege, Gottlob, 78–112; on apprehending
  (*fassen*), 97, 98, 103–4, 125–26,
  284n.30; Baker and Hacker on *Vorstel-
  lung* of, 111–12, 284nn.33, 34; and
  Bally, 99; *Begriffsschrift*, 79–80,
  280n.1, 281n.4; and Benveniste, 121–
  22, 126–27, 149; on concept (*Begriff*),
  85; and "De la sorisete des estopes,"
  83; Dummett, on, 89–91, 110–12,
  281n.10, 282nn.12, 18; and effects of
  transactions on sense, 235; on equality,
  82–84, 119; and exclusion of *Vorstel-
  lung*, 105–6, 109–12, 125, 126,
  285n.39; on fiction and art, 87–8,
  102–3, 106–7, 282nn.15, 16, 285n.43;
  on first person, 115, 122–27, 141–42;
  on his own expression, 80, 81, 104–6,
  284n.30; and idealism, 96–97, 98,
  101–2, 108–9, 284n.29, 285n.40; on
  intentionality, 86; on knowledge, 83–
  84, 95, 97–98; and Mauss, 236; on
  natural languages, 79–81, 83–84,
  281n.4, 285n.43; on object (*Gege-
  stand*), 84–85, 92, 281n.9; on objectiv-
  ity, 95–98; and Ogden and Richards,
  92–93; project of, 78–82, 231; and
  psychologism, 78–79, 91–92, 108–9,
  281n.2, 283nn.19, 22, 284n.31,
  285n.39; realism in theory of, 123,
  284n.26; on reference (*Bedeutung*), 85–
  93, 102; and Russell, 128–29, 288n.18;
  and Saussure, 43, 66, 72, 83, 93–95,
  230–32, 236; on sense (*Sinn*), 93–98,
  102; on subjectivism, 126, 231; and
  "theory," 81; on thought, 97–98,
  284n.29, 285n.36; and translation of
  Vorstellung, 107–9, 285nn.38, 40; on
  truth, 86–88, 124, 282nn.14, 15,
  283n.18; and use of "otherwise," 94–
  95, 98, 284n.28; on *Vorstellung*, 99–
  112, 262

Gifts. *See* Transactions
Godel, Robert: on entities, 29; on *langue*
  vs. *parole*, 45; on semiology, 24; on
  starting point, 28–29; on value, 58–59

Hacker, P. M. *See* Baker and Hacker
"Hunger Artist, A," 167–68. See also *I*

I, 113–59; Anscombe on, 154–58, 162–63; Austin on, 176–77; Benveniste on, 146–54; Evans on, 289n.26; Frege on, 119–20, 122–27, 141–42; Kafka on, 8–19, 118–19, 287n.8; and language theories, 113–16, 150; and memory, 124, 135–39, 290n.9; Russell on, 130–39; and self-consciousness, 162–65; and speech acts, 175–78, 297n.1; Strawson on, 139–46; and *Vorstellung*, 125, 287n.13. *See also* "Hunger Artist, A"; "In the Penal Colony"; "Report to an Academy, A"; "Wedding Preparations in the Country"
Idea. See *Vorstellung*
Ignorance. *See* Knowledge
Intentionality, 179–86, 212–216; Austin on, 179–80, 181–82; consciousness and, 180–82; contexts and, 182–85; Frege on, 86; in "The King of Bicêtre," 212–19; law as, 218–19, 221; madness of, 218–22; in Russell's treatment of indexical expressions, 131–32; Searle on, 213–17, 302n.43; in "The Venus of Ille," 179–86
"In the Penal Colony," 163–65; readings of, 296nn.52, 53. See also *I*, Kafka on

Jakobson, Roman, 10, 38, 295n.47

Kafka, Franz. *See* "Hunger Artist, A"; *I*; "In the Penal Colony"; "Report to an Academy, A"; "Wedding Preparations in the Country"
"King of Bicêtre, The," 202–29; and academia, 208–9; and Declaration of Independence, 204–9; Derrida and, 203, 205–7, 208; and Fish, 203–4, 206; and Hasidic tradition, 213; intentionality in, 212–16, 218–22; legislation vs. jurisprudence in, 211–13; madness in, 217–24; parasitic discourse in, 209–10, 222; perlocution in, 224–26; plagiarism in, 219–20; political law in, 202–9;

tongue-in-cheek in, 222–23, 226. *See also* Austin, John; Fish, Stanley; Searle, John; Speech acts theories
Knowledge: and deixis, 7–8, 9; and experience, 2–3, 8–9, 12; and ignorance, 3–5; Nietzsche on, 289n.20; Odgen and Richards on, 32–34; scientific, Frege on, 83–84; and self-consciousness, 161–71; and structuralism, 5; "theoretical," 14, 32–33

Lacan, Jacques: and analytic philosophy, 236; and Mauss, 236; and object of science, 163–64; on Poe's "Purloined Letter," 258–59; and quotient, 247, 262; and Saussure, 47, 236, 304n.10; on signifier's divisibility, 240–42; and "theory," 264
Langue, 42–46; Gödel, 45; vs. *langage*, 42; vs. *parole*, 45; as starting point, 28–40
Law: centrality of, 219; and cuckoldry, 239–40; as intention, 221; interpretation of, 211, 213; in "The King of Bicêtre," 202–9, 211–17; and madness, 219, 220–23; place of, 246–47; political, 202–9; and presence, 248; and risk of infelicity, 211–17; and "theory," 221; in *The Three Musketeers*, 237–38; and transactions, 237, 239
Lucian, 184
Lyotard, Jean-François, 14, 30, 261, 266

Man, Paul de, vii, 159, 288n.20
Mauss, Marcel: and analytic philosophy, 236; on force and origin, 249–51; and Frege, 236; and Lacan, 236; and Saussure, 236; and "theory," 264; on third parties, 249–52. See also *Three Musketeers, The*, and Mauss
Meaning of Meaning, The. See Ogden and Richards
Mérimée, Prosper. *See* "Venus of Ille, The"
Moby Dick, 6
Molière, *Amphitryon*, 184; *Le bourgeois gentilhomme*, 114

Nerval, Gérard de. *See* "King of Bicêtre, The"

Object: become-sign, 234–35, 236, 240–42; divisibility of, 240–42; vs. letter, 257–60; and narratives, 233–39; of science, 22, 30–33, 263–64
Ogden and Richards, 29–35, 30; and Frege, 92–93; and knowledge, 32–34; on *langue*, 30–34, 42; on starting point, 33–34; on viewpoint, 30–32, 228

Performance, and knowledge, 4–5, 12, 273n.3; in "A Report to an Academy," 159, 167
Perry, John, 287n.13
Pledge. *See* Gifts
Potlach. *See Three Musketeers, The;* Transactions, Mauss on
Princesse de Cleves, La, 259, 306n.29
Proust, Marcel, 66, 137–38
"Purloined Letter, The": Derrida on, 258–59; and Dumas, 253; Lacan on, 258–59; and semiotic value, 257
Putnam, Hillary, 278n.31

Quine, Williard Von Ornam, 278n.31

Racine, *Phèdre,* 183–84
Reception: Austin on, 227–28; Barthes on, 299n.24; denial of, by Searle, 213–16; dogmatic, 217–18; in Hasidic tradition, 213; vs. intentions, 221–22; and jurisprudence, 211–13; as uptake, 224
Remainders, xii, 221, 247–48, 252, 262
"Report to an Academy, A," 116–21, 159–74; and Anscombe, 157–58, 162–63; and Benveniste, 153–54; as first person narrative, 116–17, 160, 159–60; fragments of, 116–17, 124, 146, 172, 286nn.1, 2; logical status of ape's speech in, 120–21; memory in, 121–22, 124, 136–39, 172–73; as parable, 117–18; performance in, 159, 167; readings of, 154, 160, 170, 286nn.3, 6, 293n.38, 295n.48, 296nn.52, 53; and

Russell, 135–39; self-consciousness in, 160–71; and Strawson, 142, 144–46, 293n.40; wounds in, 161–62; 165–66, 169–71; 173. *See also* "Hunger Artist, A"; *I,* Kafka on; "In the Penal Colony"; "Wedding Preparations in the Country"
Resistance: of bodies, 173; of difference, 170–71, of reference, 145; of referent, 168; to "theory," 261; of the thing, 193–95
Richard III, 7
Richards, I. A., 277n.7. *See also* Ogden and Richards
Risk: idealism as, 96–97; inherent in circulation of objects, 235–36; inherent in use of language, 173–74; and philosophy, 83; and "theory," 169; in translating, 197; *Vorstellung* as, 97, 100–102
Rorty, Richard, 96
Russell, Bertrand, 128–39; vs. Anscombe, 155; on anthropocentrism, 128–29; and atomism, in philosophy of language, 129–31, 133; on autobiography, 137–38, 291n.31; on Descartes, 130, 289n.21; on first person, 115, 130–39; and Frege, 128–29, 288n.18; on *hic* and *nunc,* 129–30, 134–35, 289n.22, 290n.27; on memory, 132–59; object-words in theory of, 11, 129–30, 235–36, 288n.20; and psychologism, 128–29; on puzzles, 223; and "A Report to an Academy," 135–39; vs. Strawson, 140–41, 292n.35; and transactions, 235–36. See also *I*; "Report to an Academy, A"

Sartre, Jean-Paul, 85, 235
Saussure, Ferdinand de, 17–77; on arbitrariness of sign, 54–60; and Austin, 228; Bally on, 19, 73–76; Benveniste on, 56–58; Chomsky on, 38, 277n.23; Culler on, 35–40; and "De la sorisete des estopes," 44–46, 53, 49–50, 67, 73, 74; on difference vs. opposition, 48–50, 64, 278n.29; and editors of *Le Cours de linguistique générale,* 15, 19–20, 27–28, 35–36, 61–62, 67–68, 71,

275n.8; on entities, 29, 66–67; first course of, 21–22, 27; and Frege, 43, 66, 72, 83, 93–95, 230–32, 235–36; and game of chess, 5–6, 44, 65–66; Godel on, 24, 28–29, 45, 58–60; hesitations of, 15, 20, 59, 61, 66–67, 69–73, 275n.5; and Lacan, 47, 236, 304n.10; on *langue*, 21–22, 25, 27, 30, 33–34, 42–46, 52–53, 261 (*see also* "De la sorisete des estopes": *parole* vs. *langue in*); legacy of, 17–18, 40, 47, 76–77, 276n.15; de Mauro on, 46, 72; and Mauss, 236; and *Le Mémoire sur le système primitif des voyelles dans les langues indo-européennes*, 64–65; on naming, 50–52; Ogden and Richards on, 29–35, 42; on *parole*, 40–41, 44; and pedagogy, 19, 21–27, 58–59; on phonetics, 231; on point of view, 31–32, 45–46, 228, 277n.17; project of, 18–21; second course of, 21, 23–25, 60–61, 68–69; and semiology, 23, 24; on signified vs. signifier, 46–48, 61–62, 236, 280n.38, 304n.9; on speech (*langage*), 24, 41–43, 277–78n.10; on starting point, 20–26, 27, 28–40, 277n.24; on systems, 26, 36–37; and taxonomies, 38, 50–55, 231, 232, 279n.34; terminology of, 20, 35, 60–62, 278n.28; third course of, 25–26, 69–71; on translation, 50, 54, 278n.31; on value, 49, 60–76. See also *Le Cours de linguistique générale*; Semiotic value; Value

Searle, John: on contexts, 223; on conventions, 195, 298n.17, 299n.21; on fiction, 177, 216, 220, 282n.16; on intentionality, 213–17, 227, 302n.43; on metaphor, 213–14; on perlocution, 224; on puzzles, 223, 225; and "theory," 195, 223; on Wimsatt's intentional fallacy, 302n.43. *See also* Speech act theories; "Theory"

Sechehaye, Albert, 19. *See also* Saussure, Ferdinand de, and editors of *Le Cours de linguistique générale*

Semantic: definition of, 273n.5; reading, 235; unicity, 241

Semantic aim, 9–10, 11; vs. deictic aim, 11, 13–14, 50, 262–63; and Saussurean linguistics, 7–8, 261–62. *See also* Deictic aim; "De la sorisete des estopes"

Semantics: definition of, 273, n.5; limits of, 196 (*see also* "De la sorisete des estopes"); as system, 6, 11, 13; tautological, 10–11, 273n.8. *See also* Semantic aim

Semiology: Godel on, 24; Saussure on, 23

Semiotic, reading, 235

Semiotics, object of, 1–2. *See also* Deictic aim; Object; Semiotic value

Semiotic value, 230–64; definition of, 240–42; and duplication, 243–45; and force, 257–60; and speech acts, 257–59; and unicity, 239–40. See also *Three Musketeers, The*

Signifier: Derrida on, 243; divisibility of, 240–42; Lacan on, 242–43, 304n.10; in *Le Cours de linguistique générale*, 61–62; Saussure on, 46–48, 242

Speech acts theories, 171–229; content vs. force in, 258–59; contexts in, 191–95, 197–99, 212; conventions in, 189–90, 191–95, 198–200; and Declaration of Independence, 204–9, 299n.29, 300nn.30, 31, 301nn.33, 34, 36; Derrida on, 203, 205–7, 208, 209n.29, 301n.36; effects of, 186–90; 193; first person in, 175–78; Fish on, 187–89; 203, 206, 298n.19; and Frege, 175; and intentionality, 179–86, 212–16; and law, 211–13; and literary criticism, 177–78, 297nn.4, 6; and literary text, 200–202; and Lucian's *Lover of Lies or the Double*, 184; and madness, 217–24; and Mérimées's "Venus of Ille," 178–202; and Molière's *Amphitryon*, 184; and Nerval's "King of Bicêtre," 202–26; parasitic discourse in, 209–23; performative vs. constative in, 192, 226–27; perlocution in, 187–88, 189, 211, 224–26; and plagiarism, 219–20; and political law, 202–9; and psychoanalysis, 181–82; and Racine's *Phèdre*, 183–84; Searle on, 213–17; and semiotic value, 257–59; and thingness, 194–

Speech acts theories (*cont'd*)
95; and transactions, 238–39; and
translation, 196–98; and Virgil's
Aeneid, 184. *See also* Austin, John;
Derrida, Jacques; Fish, Stanley; Searle,
John; "King of Bicêtre, The"; "Venus of
Ille, The"

Starting point: Culler on, 36–39; *langue*
as, 28–40; Ogden and Richards on,
33–34; Saussure on, 26, 31

Strawson, Peter F., 44–45, 139–46; vs.
Anscombe, 155; and Benveniste, 151;
on Descartes, 143; on first person,
139–46; and Frege, 141–42; on immu-
nity of *I* to reference-failure, 141–42,
144, 292n.37; on "meaning" vs. "use,"
139; on person concept, 143–45,
293n.40; and "A Report to an Acad-
emy," 142, 144–46, 293n.40; vs. Rus-
sell, 140–41, 292n.35. *See also* "Report
to an Academy, A"

Structuralism, 5–7, 230, 235, 261; and
analytic philosophy, 199

System: and knowledge, 6; limitations of,
52–55; Saussurean (or semantic), 5–8,
23, 26, 36–37, 42, 52–53, 235; in
Saussure's *Mémoire,* 64–65; social, 4–
5; and taxonomy, 49–50; and value,
62–68. *See also* Saussure, on *langue*;
Semantic

Taxonomies: Benveniste on, 56–59;
Chomsky on Saussure's, 38; Culler on,
38–39; Godel on, 58–59; Saussure on,
50–55, 231, 279n.34; and systems, 49–
50

"Theory": and amnesia, 266; and Culler,
38–39; definition of, 14, 173–74, 199–
200; and deictic aim, 266; and Dum-
met, 90; and Fish, 195, 200; and Frege,
81, 228–29; and heterogeneity, 176,
233; intuitive, 14; and Lacan, 264; and
law, 220–21; and literature, 199–201;
as madness, 221–22, 225; and Mauss,
264; object of, 30, 263–64; and Ogden
and Richards, 30; resistance to, 261;
and Saussure, 21; and scars, 172–73;

and Searle, 195, 223; use of examples
in, 228–29, 232

Thing: at limit of language, 193–95, 235;
resistance of, 15; and speech acts, 194–
95; and systems, 246

Three Musketeers, The, 233–63; compro-
mising gifts in, 253–55; content and
force in, 257–60, 306n.30; cuckoldry
in, 239–40, 246; excess in, 246–48,
252–53; identity and duplication in,
243–46, 253; itineraries in, 252–53,
255–56, 263; Lacan's signifier in, 242–
43; law in, 237–38, 239–40, 246–48;
materiality and divisibility in, 240–42,
244; and Mauss, 237–39, 249–53; ob-
jects and narrative in, 233–36; objects-
become-signs in, 234–36, 240–42, 246;
politique de l'autruiche in, 244–45,
255, 256, 304n.11; remainders in, 247–
48, 252, 262; semiotic value in, 240–
42, 244–45, 247, 260, 263; and speech
acts, 238–39, 258; thingness in, 246;
third parties in, 248–253, 255–57; to-
pology and narrative in, 234; topology
and structuralism in, 235; unicity in,
238–39, 241–42, 245–48, 252. *See also*
Derrida, Jacques; Lacan, Jacques;
Mauss, Marcel; Semiotic value; Topol-
ogy

Topology: definition of, 234; and narra-
tive, 234; and structuralism, 235; and
"theories," 265–66

Transactions: and Frege, 235; and law,
237, 239; Mauss on, 237–38; as
pledge, 238; and Russell, 235–36; and
speech acts, 238–39

Translation: Quine and Putnam on,
278n.31; Saussure on, 50, 54, 278n.31;
in "The Venus of Ille," 195–99; of *Vor-
stellung,* 107–9

Unicity: and cuckoldry, 245–46; and divi-
sibility, 240–42

Value, 60–76; Bally on, 73–76; and du-
plication, 243–45; editors of *Cours de
linguistique générale* on, 61–62; excess

of, 253–55; Godel on, 58–59 (*see also* taxonomies); Saussure on, 60–76; vs. signified, 68–76; and system, 62–68; and unicity, 240–42; 243–46. *See also* Semiotic value

"Venus of Ille, The," 178–202; citations in, 183–85; conventions in, 192–99; effect vs. effects in, 186; as fantastic story, 179, 182, 185, 194, 298n.15; intentionality in, 179–86; telling story of, 178–79, 185; thing in, 193–95; translation in, 195–99; as whodonit, 185

Virgil, 184

Vorstellung, 99–112; Anscombe, 156–57; Baker and Hacker on, 111–12; Dummet on, 110–11; exclusion of, 105, 109–12; and first person, 125; translation of, 107–9

"Wedding Preparations in the Country," 118–19

Wittgenstein, 44–45, 78, 106, 175, 265, 274n.13, 285n.36, 295n.45

Designed by Martha Farlow

Composed by Graphic Composition, Inc., in Sabon

Printed by Thomson-Shore, Inc., on 50-lb. Glatfelter and
bound in Joanna Arrestox A with Rainbow Antique endsheets